MEMOIRS

OF THE

PRINCE DE TALLEYRAND

EDITED, WITH A PREFACE AND NOTES, BY

THE DUC DE BROGLIE

OF THE FRENCH ACADEMY

TRANSLATED BY

Mrs. ANGUS HALL

WITH AN INTRODUCTION BY

THE HONORABLE WHITELAW **REID**

AMERICAN MINISTER IN PARIS

VOLUME III

WITH PORTRAITS

———

G. P. PUTNAM'S SONS

NEW YORK   LONDON

27 WEST TWENTY-THIRD ST.   27 KING WILLIAM ST., STRAND

1891

The Knickerbocker Press
New York

CHARLES MAURICE DE TALLEYRAND-PÉRIGORD, PRINCE DE BENEVENTO
AFTER F. GÉRARD

CONTENTS.

PART IX.

THE SECOND RESTORATION—ADDENDUM—TALLEYRAND'S REPLY TO HIS ACCUSERS.

1815.

PART X.

THE REVOLUTION OF 1830—APPENDIX.

1830—1832.

ILLUSTRATIONS.

MEMOIRS

OF THE

PRINCE DE TALLEYRAND

PART VIII.—*Continued.*

THE CONGRESS OF VIENNA.

1815.

Talleyrand wins over Lord Castlereagh—The Emperor of Russia wishes the King of Saxony to form a kingdom on the left bank of the Rhine—Talleyrand proposes further alliances in case of war—He denies the right of Spain to demand satisfaction for the dismissal of M. Casa Florez—Prussia wishes to absorb the whole of Saxony—Lord Castlereagh favours her demands—Bavaria, Hanover and Holland join the Triple Alliance—Lord Castlereagh is brought to see the necessity of preserving a Saxon Kingdom—His utter ignorance of military topography and continental geography—Anecdote of Prince Kaunitz—Account of the expiatory ceremony of the 21st January at Vienna—All the sovereigns present attend it—The Austrian Emperor's want of confidence in Metternich—Talleyrand's reasons for disapproving of the proposed marriage between the Duc de Berry and the Archduchess Anne of Prussia—King Louis's satisfaction at the Duke of Wellington replacing Lord Castlereagh at Vienna—Prussia dissatisfied with the share of Saxony assigned her—Swedish Plenipotentiary complains of the tone of the French Press as regards Bernadotte—Conversation between Wellington and the Emperor Alexander respecting France—Arrangements for Saxony completed—The question of the Slave Trade settled—Anecdote of Prussian

arrogance—Question as to the retention of the Legion of
Honour—Lord Castlereagh quits Vienna—Stops in Paris on
his way home—Progress of Italian affairs—Archduchess Marie
Louise objects to receiving Lucca in place of Parma—Metternich unwillingly admits the necessity of abandoning Murat—
Talleyrand expatiates on the principles of legitimacy—Considers that the English by their rule in India have lost all ideas
of right and fairness—Conversation between the Emperor
Alexander and Talleyrand on European affairs—Pecuniary
compensation easier to England than any others—Her offer to
pension off Murat, if France will abandon the Slave Trade at
once—Talleyrand sees his way to utilising this "Mania"—
Summary of the treaties between the Allied Powers in 1813
against France—Metternich asks to postpone the Italian affairs
until after the King has seen Lord Castlereagh—Details of the
laws for the navigation of the Rhine—Russian duplicity with
regard to Switzerland and Poland—Anecdotes showing the
estimation in which the Emperor Alexander was held in Vienna
—Buonaparte escapes from Elba—Swiss affairs finally concluded—Reception by the King of Saxony at Presburg, of
Talleyrand, Metternich and Wellington—Orders sent to the
allied troops to hold themselves in readiness to move—Declaration of the Allies against Buonaparte—The island of Elba to
be occupied in the name of the Allies—Special Conference
summoned to consider the present position—Declaration of
Austria as to the Valtelline, Bormio, and Chiavenna—Disposition of the troops sent against Buonaparte—Emperor of
Austria orders Madame de Montesquiou to give up the charge
of his grandson—King Louis obliged to quit Paris—Goes to
Ostend—Emperor Alexander's protestations of friendship and
support—Wellington leaves Vienna to take command of the
troops—Treaty of March 25 consequent on Buonaparte's invasion—Murat invades the Papal States—Count Blacas's narrative
of the King's departure from France—Conversation between
the Emperor Alexander and Lord Clancarty respecting the
future Government of France—The former wishes the Duc
d'Orleans to replace Louis on the French throne—Talleyrand
leaves Vienna to join the King—Successfully frustrates a
design to postpone signing the final act of the Congress.

MEMOIRS

OF THE

PRINCE DE TALLEYRAND

No. 20.—THE PRINCE DE TALLEYRAND TO KING LOUIS XVIII.

VIENNA, *Jan.* 6, 1815.

SIRE,

The courier by whom I had the honour to send your Majesty the convention which was signed by M. de Metternich, Lord Castlereagh, and myself, on the 3rd January, had already been gone twenty-four hours, ere I received the letter dated Dec. 27th, with which your Majesty has deigned to honour me.

In strengthening the hope I indulged that I had on this occasion done nothing contrary to your Majesty's views and intentions, your letter was the highest reward for the efforts I had made to obtain a result so happy, though apparently so improbable, and I could only feel, with scarcely less profound emotion, how gratifying it is to serve a master whose feelings both as king and man are so generous, touching, and noble.

I had just received your Majesty's letter when Lord Castlereagh called to see me. I thought I ought to read to him those passages which referred to himself and the Prince Regent. He was extremely touched by them, and wishing to acquaint[1] his Government of the terms in which your Majesty speaks of the Prince, he begged I would allow him to make a note of them, to which I consented, induced by the twofold consideration of his assurance that it should be regarded as an inviolable secret, and that the praise given to the Prince Regent by your Majesty

---

[1] Text : "et désirant de pouvoir faire connaître " = "and wishing to be able to make known." Var. : "et *désirant faire connaître* = "and desiring to make known."

would, under present circumstances, produce the very best effect.

The Emperor of Russia is sending General Pozzo back to Paris, after having detained him here for two months and a half, without having once seen him, and there are those who maintain that he has ordered his return because he looks upon him as a *Censor* who speaks too frankly, and whom therefore he desires to remove. The Emperor of Russia would wish your Majesty to believe that it is out of regard to your Majesty, and in order to do something that will be agreeable to you, that he has conceived the idea [1] of giving to the King of Saxony, in place of his own kingdom, several hundred thousands of souls on the left bank of the Rhine. General Pozzo is to be charged with the task of obtaining your Majesty's consent to this arrangement. But your Majesty knows that the question of Saxony must not be looked at solely upon the grounds of fairness, but likewise of balance of power, that the principle of right would be violated by the forced removal of the King of Saxony to the Rhine, and that the King of Saxony would never give his consent thereto. Lastly, that putting fairness on one side, Saxony could not be given to Prussia without materially altering the relative strength of Austria and entirely destroying the whole balance of power in the Germanic confederation.

The attempts of the Emperor of Russia in Paris as well as in Vienna, will therefore completely fail, owing to the prescience of your Majesty, who has always aspired to uphold those principles, without which there can be nothing stable in Europe, nor in any single state, as they alone can guarantee security to each, and peace to all. The tone adopted by General Pozzo at Vienna was too favourable towards France to be in accord with what the Emperor of Russia desired to do here. M. Pozzo is therefore to leave on Sunday or Monday, that is on the 8th or 9th.

I still believe that the occasion for war, owing to the alliance between your Majesty, Austria and England, will not supervene ; nevertheless, as it is only prudent to foresee the worst and be prepared for all emergencies, it appears to me necessary lest such should happen, to consider the best means of strengthening the union by inducing other powers to join us. I have therefore proposed to Lord Castlereagh and M. de Metternich, to unite with us in negotiating with the Ottoman Porte, to make, if needed, an advantageous diversion. They have fallen in with my proposition, and it has been agreed that we shall give joint instructions to the ministers of the three courts at Constanti-

---

[1] Text : "qu'il a conçu l'idée" = as translated. Var. : "qu'il a *donné* l'idée" = "that he had given the idea."

nople. I think it advisable that your Majesty should hasten the departure of your ambassador.

It would perhaps be advantageous to establish similar relations with Sweden, but the method of carrying this out will have to be carefully weighed, and I shall reserve entering upon this with your Majesty in another letter.

The funeral service on the 21st Jan. will be held in the cathedral here, the Archbishop of Vienna officiating. He is an old man of eighty-three, by whom the Emperor was brought up. Nothing that can render the ceremony imposing [1] will be omitted.

I have the honour to be. . . .

No. 23.—THE AMBASSADORS OF THE KING AT THE CONGRESS, TO THE MINISTER OF FOREIGN AFFAIRS AT PARIS.

VIENNA, *January* 6, 1815.

MONSIEUR LE COMTE,

The accord between the Austrian and English legations and ourselves is increasing. There is perfect unanimity on the broad principle, that the Courts of Berlin and St. Petersburg cannot be permitted to lay down the law. The work of the Statistical Commission, which proves that Prussia does not require Saxony to obtain more than what the treaties had assured to her, is now at an end, and since yesterday there are signs that the Prussian ministry does not feel itself on quite such firm ground as it at first believed. It now, therefore, awaits fresh proposals, which are being prepared. Whether more or less territory is taken from Saxony or ceded to the Grand Duchy of Warsaw, is an Austrian question, which if carefully handled, need not provoke our direct intervention, and we have only to see that the general balance of power is preserved.

On our arrival here, every thing seemed at a standstill. Austria, or rather her minister, took but a feeble interest in this question of equilibrium. Now every one feels the importance of boundary limitation, and if it is not satisfactorily settled, it will be the fault of the Court of Vienna, and its Cabinet. As far as it rests with us, we are hastening the conclusion of matters, so as to terminate the Congress as soon as possible.

The report on the affairs of Switzerland is being prepared. News received from Berne announces a change in the home revenues of this Canton. This will facilitate the conclusion of Swiss affairs, and we have informed the deputy of the Canton

[1] Text: "imposante" = as translated. Var. : "*plus* imposant" = "more imposing."

of Berne that if he obtained the Bishopric of Bâsle and the return of the funds which are in England, it would be advantageous for his country to consent to it, and to join in the general scheme which the powers judge most expedient under present circumstances.   No further result has been achieved.

Be pleased to accept. . . . .

No. 16³.—King Louis XVIII. to the Prince de Talleyrand.

Paris, *January* 7, 1815.

Mon Cousin,

I have received your letter number 18.   I am very well satisfied with your converse with the two brothers.[1]

I confess I thought the time was passed when they would desire to exclude my plenipotentiaries from the most important of the deliberations.   Your firmness has prevented its recurrence, but we must not stay our hand on account of this success ; the germ of the evil will still continue to live, as long as the powers, whose alliance ought to have ended last April, believe in its existence.   Your letter to Lord Castlereagh is perfect, and I defy anyone to gainsay the conclusion thereon, but I confess it grieves me to see a false pity turning against the King of Saxony, the sophistry used by Robespierre, to hasten the consummation of the greatest of his misdeeds.

I am glad the Emperor of Austria has taken the law into his own hands and defends the rights of Saxony, provided he does not do the same to maintain the usurpation of Naples.

He does not perhaps know the real state of affairs there, but the discoveries lately made, and the measures recently taken, ought, however, to have enlightened him, and give you a grand opportunity of proving to him, that there will always be those who desire the unity of Italy, so long as there is fire on the hearth.

They speak of undertakings, and they pretend to wish that they had not been kept,[2] but it is not thus that wrong has been wrought.   There is another cause, and one more shameful than history has yet recorded ; for if Antony basely abandoned his fleet and his army, it was at least himself, and not his minister, whom Cleopatra had subjugated.   But despicable as is this obstruction, it is none the less real, and the only way to recall a

---

[1] Lord Castlereagh and Lord Stewart.

[2] Text : " on prétend désirer qu'ils n'ont pas été tenus " = as translated.   Var. : " on prétend désirer *des preuves* qu'ils n'ont pas été tenus " = " They pretend to wish for proofs that they have not been kept."

man to his senses, is to give him so many noble motives, that he will find in them a safeguard against his little weaknesses.[1]

I await with impatience the letter you mention respecting the marriage. This subject seems but secondary compared with those now being dealt with at Vienna ; but it is urgent, in the interests of France, that the Duc de Berry should marry, and to this end it is important that the Russian matter should be settled.

I am much gratified by and quite reciprocate your good wishes for the coming year. Wherefore I pray God may have you, my dear cousin, in His safe and holy keeping.

LOUIS.

No. 24.—THE AMBASSADORS OF THE KING AT THE CONGRESS TO THE MINISTER OF FOREIGN AFFAIRS AT PARIS.

VIENNA, *January* 10, 1815.

MONSIEUR LE COMTE,

Affairs here are much the same as we had the honour to describe to you in our last despatch.

As we therein announced, a first proposition has been made on the part of Russia. She has asked for a counterproposal and Prussia is engaged in drawing up a plan on which she bases her reconstruction.

The sacrifices demanded of Saxony, do not seem objectionable to England and still less so to Austria, although the latter is interested in not appearing to lend herself to them.

The affairs of Italy have not advanced since the delivery of the Austrian memorandum on the subject of Tuscany and Parma.

The report on the affairs of Switzerland is finished ; it will be discussed at a sitting of the commission to be held the day after to-morrow, the 12th. As soon as it is definitely adopted, we shall communicate it without delay to the ministry.

Be pleased to accept. . . .

---

[1] This passage in the king's letter refers apparently to the supposed attachment of Prince Metternich for Queen Caroline of Naples, wife of Murat, an attachment which prevented his pronouncing against Murat, and in favour of the re-establishment of the House of Bourbon in the Kingdom of Naples.

No. 21².—The Prince de Talleyrand to King Louis XVIII.

VIENNA, *December* 7, 1815.

SIRE,

I should not have had the honour of writing to your Majesty to-day, if I had not had to give a reply, asked of me, by direction of the Comte de Jaucourt.

It is with regard to the satisfaction demanded by the Court of Madrid, for the dismissal of M. Casa Florez.

My opinion, since your Majesty has deigned to ask for it, is, that no satisfaction whatever is due ; because satisfaction supposes a wrong, whereas your Majesty's Cabinet has done none ; further, if any satisfaction were due, it could not be of such a nature as the Court of Madrid demands.

I will not trouble your Majesty by recapitulating the grounds on which I form this opinion, having already fully explained them in the letter which M. de Jaucourt will have the honour to submit to you.

The extradition theory, which M. de Cevallos endeavours to establish in accordance with the privileges of the Jews and the customs of some ancient nations, is altogether absurd.

M. de Labrador, to whom I showed his letter, greatly deplored it. I am inclined to believe that the Court of Madrid has some cause of complaint which I cannot fathom, but which is quite outside the dismissal of M. de Casa Florez, which only serves them as a pretext.

This I gather, from the complaints, that Spain is not supported here by France, in the affairs of Naples and the Queen of Etruria.

It is only I believe in Spain, that it has happened, that your Majesty's Embassy has not begun by demanding the restitution of Naples to its legitimate sovereign, and also repeated this same demand on every occasion, both by word of mouth and in writing, confidentially and officially. M. de Labrador has assured me that in none of our dispatches has he found cause to think that we did not second him to the utmost of our power. The Court of Madrid therefore is raising grievances, which it must be perfectly aware, have no foundation whatever.

Affairs here have made no visible progress since my last letter. We shall I believe, have a Conference to-morrow, which has been delayed for several days by the Prussians, who were not ready. The subject for discussion will be the affairs of Poland and Saxony.

Of the two principles involved in the Saxon question, one, that of justice, will be quite secured;[1] the other, that of balance of power, will be less completely so. Lord Castlereagh has not entirely renounced his former views; his inclination is still strongly in favour of Prussia. He persuades himself that a too limited restriction of the sacrifices of the King of Saxony, will be an incalculable source of discontent to Prussia. He is naturally irresolute and weak. His memorandum of the 10th October embarrasses him. He would not like, he told me, to contradict himself like M. de Metternich, who according to him has no *character* to sustain, and never hesitates to change his opinion. On the 18th of last month, he considered it would suffice to give Prussia 400,000 souls in Saxony; to-day he would give double the number without any scruple; on the 23rd of October he wanted her total destruction.

The annihilation[2] of Saxony, as regards equilibrium, means that of Austria more than any other power.

But M. de Metternich treats the whole with a flippancy and indifference which always astonish me, accustomed as I am, to these traits in him.

As for us, Sire, in order not to contradict ourselves or change our language from one day to another, we have only to carry out your Majesty's commands. This is the advantage gained by following principles which do not change, instead of mere fancies which change perpetually.

The service on the 21st January will positively be held in the cathedral. The Archbishop, who has been unwell for the last few days, is now better, and it would require a very serious relapse to prevent his officiating.

I have the honour to be . . . .

No. 17³.—King Louis XVIII. to the Prince de Talleyrand.

PARIS, *January* 11, 1815.

Mon Cousin,

I have received your letter No. 19. This letter will be a short one. Complete satisfaction with your conduct; entire approval of the treaty of which the courier brings you the ratification—there you have the contents!—I will despatch General Ricard with all possible speed and complete secrecy, of which I see the necessity.

---

[1] Var.: "*et c'est celui qui nous importait le plus*" = "and this is what concerns us most."

[2] Text: "*La destruction*" = as translated. Var.: "*La question*" = "the question."

I am greatly touched by the service which is to take place on the 21st. You will learn with equal sentiments, that here on the same day, the precious remains of the King and Queen will be conveyed to St. Denis. I pray that God may keep you, my cousin, in His safe and holy keeping.

LOUIS.

P.S.—Whilst we are doing so well, let us endeavour to finish the Neapolitan affair.[1]

12th, Morning.

I re-open my letter to tell you that General Ricard is at present at Toulouse, where he commands a division. I have to-night despatched a courier conveying his immediate summons to Paris.

L.

No. 18³.—KING LOUIS XVIII. TO THE PRINCE DE TALLEYRAND.

PARIS, *January* 15, 1815.

MON COUSIN,

I have received your letter No. 20. In my last despatch, believing I was more pressed than I really was (not having correctly calculated the time required to draw up the ratification), I was exceedingly laconic, but pray believe, that in reading your No. 19, I experienced feelings similar to yours on the receipt of my despatch of the 27th December. I am not indifferent nor ever shall be indifferent, to such interests as those which form the subject of the Congress of Vienna. I can however be quite as secure as Alexander, and even share in that security, for I have not told you to communicate a portion of my letter to Lord Castlereagh, knowing well that you would do so of your own accord.

I earnestly wish to see realised the hope expressed in your letter to the Comte de Jaucourt, that Prussia would be satisfied without usurping Saxony. Then all would be smooth and we should have the glory of cutting the gordian knot without the aid of the sword. Nevertheless I approve of negotiating with the Porte and will hasten the departure of the Marquis de Rivière.[2] He has not quite recovered from a very severe illness, but I know his zeal.

---

[1] This postscript does not appear in the text of the archives.

[2] Charles-François de Riffardeau, Marquis, afterwards Duc de Rivière, born in 1763. Entered the French Guards at seventeen. He emigrated in 1789 and became aide-de-camp to the Comte D'Artois, who entrusted him with several missions to Brittany and Vendée. Returning to France with Pichegru in 1804, he was arrested,

I am fully prepared for General Pozzo di Borgo. Were it a question of a prince, not already a sovereign, I might with pleasure see him form a small state on my frontier; but to the King of Saxony, supposing he did consent to the exchange, I could not yet extend my hand. To be just to oneself is a sacred duty, to be so towards others is no less so; and he, who when only having alms to live on, refused to abandon his rights, will not betray those of others, equally legitimate, when he commands more than twenty-five millions of men, and when besides justice, he has the general interests of Europe to defend.

The Swedish question is a very delicate one. The last treaty placed Russia in such a position, that without much trouble, she could occupy Stockholm.[1] Is it prudent to involve a kingdom in so dangerous a war, without at the same time guaranteeing[2] to it, in case of reverses, some indemnity which it would even be difficult to find? Gustavus IV. has more than once told me, that he considered his uncle was the legitimate King of Sweden; but in abdicating for himself, was that unfortunate Prince able also to abdicate for his son?[3] In admitting this hypothesis, which would legitimize the election of Bernadotte, are there no consequences which might cause one to hesitate ere forming an alliance with him? I shall read with interest your reflections on these two[4] points.

But the existence of Bernadotte leads me back to another and much more dangerous one, that of Murat. My despatch of 27th December related to Naples and Saxony. We are in a good position as regards the latter, let us work with the same zeal and success for the former.

The Sardinian ambassador has asked me for an audience, the Comte de Jaucourt will tell you the result. Wherefore I

tried by a military commission and condemned to death. Pardoned by the intercession of the Empress and Murat, he was at first confined in the Fort of Jouy, and afterwards condemned to transportation for life. In 1815, Louis XVIII. appointed him Brigadier-General, and Ambassador at Constantinople; but the return of the Emperor prevented his departure. At the second restoration he was created a peer of France, and governor of Corsica, and subsequently again appointed Ambassador to the Ottoman Porte. He was recalled in 1820, created hereditary Duke in 1825, and became Governor to the Duc de Bordeaux in 1826. He died in 1828.

It is well known that the Venus of Milo, discovered by the Comte de Marcellus, was brought to France by the Duc de Rivière.

[1] The Treaty of Fredrichsham (Sept. 17, 1810) by which Sweden ceded Finland to Russia.

[2] Suppressed in the text of the archives.

[3] Gustavus IV., when compelled to abdicate in 1809, refused to extend this act to his son. In 1814 he addressed a protest to the Congress against the usurpation of Bernadotte, and claimed the Swedish throne for his son. He was however not listened to. His son, known as the Prince de Wasa, became a Field-Marshal in the Austrian service.

[4] Text: "deux" — as translated. Var. : "*divers*" = "different."

pray God to guard you, my cousin, in His safe and holy keeping.

LOUIS.

NO. 19³.—KING LOUIS XVIII. TO THE PRINCE DE TALLEYRAND.

PARIS, *January* 19, 1815.

MON COUSIN,

I have received your letter, No. 21. I was not in doubt as to your opinion on the Spanish matter, but I am very glad to find it is in accord with the measures I had taken. I am also pleased that M. de Labrador does not share the insane ideas of his cabinet. May he inspire it with views more in accordance with reason and its own interests.

Last week I was well satisfied, but to-day I note with dis-quietude Lord Castlereagh's tendency to return to his former weaknesses, and also Prince Metternich's fickleness. The former should bear in mind, that that which elevates a reputation, is to uphold justice or return to it loyally, if unfortunately it has been deviated from. The latter forgets that to aggrandize Prussia, is to weaken Austria.

As for me I will never lend myself, as you know, to the entire spoliation of the King of Saxony.

I believe he will be obliged to cede something, but if they exact what would reduce him to a fourth or even a third-rate power, I shall be no party to it. I await with impatience the result of your conference, and I am no less anxious to see at last the commencement of the great Neapolitan affair.

We are in the midst of mourning and grief. I would I could have been present at the ceremonies which take place on Saturday. The fear of gout however prevents me, but one suffers as much in arranging for them as in being present.

Pray thank the Archbishop on my behalf, for having himself officiated. Wherefore, my cousin, may God have you in His safe and holy keeping.

LOUIS.

NO. 25.—THE AMBASSADORS OF THE KING AT THE CONGRESS TO THE MINISTER OF FOREIGN AFFAIRS AT PARIS.

VIENNA, *March* 19, 1815.

MONSIEUR LE COMTE,

We have the honour to forward to you a copy of the protocol of the last meeting of the 14th December. At the one held on the 14th of this month and of which the protocol will not be signed until next meeting, Prince de Metternich communicated the reply of the Sardinian court, with respect to the reunion of Genoa and Piedmont, and although this document only concerns the next protocol, we transmit it to the ministry herewith.

The fate of the imperial fiefs, over which the Sardinian legation reserves the contingent rights of its sovereign, cannot be definitely settled until the other affairs of Italy are arranged. The report on Swiss affairs has been signed and been submitted to the conference of the eight powers. As soon as a final decision has been arrived at, it will be made known to the king.

If the influence of the Emperor of Russia had not opposed the best interests of Switzerland, perhaps something better could have been arranged ; but his hand, protecting as it does whatever pertains to ill-conceived or badly-exercised liberties, is sufficiently powerful to obstruct those principles which would bring about a true re-establishment.

We have nevertheless obtained all it was possible to do in this matter, and it has been agreed to grant indemnities for the acts of violence committed on certain estates in the Pays de Vaud, and the Valtelline.

The commission appointed to regulate the navigation of the large rivers has not yet assembled.

The English ministers have asked for instructions and supplementary information on this subject. The Prussian ministers would like to exclude France from all participation in the control and administration of the Rhine navigation. We find the same difficulty here that has met us everywhere and we hope equally to triumph over it ; but you will understand, M. le Comte, that this will form a fresh subject for discussion.

The Prince de Hardenberg has brought forward a scheme for the reconstruction of Prussia, and you will observe with some surprise that the whole of Saxony is therein assigned to Prussia. But as this plan shows an excess of six hundred and eighty-one thousand souls over the population of Prussia in 1805, and gives seven hundred thousand souls to form a domain for the King of Saxony, this affords some room to vindicate the question of recognition of rights and balance of power, in arranging the new Germanic Confederation.

Bavaria has formally agreed to the union formed between France, Austria and England, the object of which is, not to suffer any of the powers individually to dictate to Europe. Holland and Hanover will also agree to this.

You have been informed, M. le Comte, that the embassy of

the king deemed it becoming to hold a funeral service on the 21st January.   The Prince de Talleyrand has requested the king's minister at the court of Vienna to make known to the sovereigns in the name of the French embassy that the service will take place in the cathedral at Vienna.   The sovereigns have not only replied that they would assist at the ceremony, but all have added expressions of sympathy for the king.

The Empress of Austria told M. de la Tour du Pin, that her health would not admit of her being present, that she dare not expose her nerves to such painful emotions, and begged him therefore to present her excuses to the king, adding that she would do so herself to Madame la Duchesse d'Angoulême.   The Archduchess Beatrice, her mother, replied at once that she would be present.   There remain only the Emperor and Empress of Russia whose replies have not yet been received, but who, no doubt, will also attend.

This ceremony, solemn as it is seemly, will recall an epoch very unfortunate for France, and the century that has just passed, but it will also give rise to beneficial reflections among nations.

I have the honour to be. . . .

No. 22².—The Prince de Talleyrand to King Louis XVIII.

VIENNA, *Jan* 19, 1815.

SIRE,

I have received the letter your Majesty has deigned to honour me with, and found fresh motives for devotion and courage in the evidences of goodwill therein contained.

I have the honour of writing to your Majesty to-day, only that there may not be too long an interval between my letters, for I have no news whatever to communicate.

Matters progress but slowly ; nevertheless we are not idle. Bavaria has joined the triple alliance.   Hanover and Holland will follow later.   The Grand Duke of Darmstadt has joined Bavaria with the same object, and promises 6,000 men.

The Commissioners are at work on the affairs of Italy, Switzerland and general statistics.   My letter to the British cabinet, which will be submitted to your Majesty, will show you how matters stand in this respect, the obstacles that arise, and how it is that everything cannot be arranged as might be desired. Austria, England, Bavaria, Holland, Hanover, and nearly the whole of Germany are in accord with us, as to keeping the king and a kingdom of Saxony.   A Saxon kingdom will therefore be preserved, although the Prince de Hardenberg, in a scheme he recently submitted for the reconstruction of Prussia, dared to ask for the whole of Saxony. M. de Metternich has to reply to this scheme, and I have been waiting for his answer ere despatching my courier; but it is not yet finished. I have only seen the outlines which are all thoroughly satisfactory. Moreover a single glance at the Prussian scheme shows that what she had in 1805 would be restored to her, which is all that she has a right to expect, and that five hundred thousand subjects would be preserved to Saxony. But Prussia pretends that she ought to have six hundred thousand more than she had in 1805, under the pretext of the additions obtained by Russia and Austria. Lord Castlereagh, M. de Metternich and myself, being fully agreed upon the principle of right, it now remains for us to understand each other respecting the balance of power in order to make a unanimous proposition.

This therefore occupies us daily, and to-day again I had a conference with them on this subject. M. de Metternich, at first, seemed quite inclined to make endless concessions. I had to restrain him by making him face the consequences which such acquiescence (by placing his kingdom in danger) would bring on himself. He now hotly defends what before he would have [1] abandoned. I have advised him to bring some of the ablest Austrian officers to our conferences, to give their opinions and the reasons for those opinions; and in order to oblige him to follow this advice, I told him that if he did not bring them, I would say that I had told him to do so. He has decided to adopt my suggestion. The Prince de Schwartzenberg will have a talk with Lord Stewart, and will come with some of his officers to a conference we shall hold the day after to-morrow. Unfortunately, Lord Castlereagh, even should he in spite of his old leaning towards Prussia, and the fear he has of compromising what he calls his *character*, be willing (after having in his note of the 11th October, given up the whole of Saxony) now to allow only a very small share to Prussia, has on all questions of military topography, and even on the simplest matters of continental geography, such imperfect notions, I may say, such utter ignorance, that while it is necessary to prove the smallest details to him, it is extremely difficult to convince him of them. It is said that an Englishman who was here in Prince Kaunitz's time, retailed a number of absurdities respecting the German states, and that Prince Kaunitz, instead of amusing himself by refuting them,[2] exclaimed in a tone of the greatest surprise, "It is really marvellous how ignor-

---

[1] Text: "ce qu'il aurait" = as translated. Var.: "ce qu'il *avait*" = "that which he had."

[2] Suppressed in the text of the archives.

ant the English are!" How often have I had occasion to
mentally make the same observation during my conferences with
Lord Castlereagh!

In the arrangement that is being carried out in Italian affairs,
we have reason to hope that the Archduchess Marie Louise will
be put down for a considerable pension. I must tell your
Majesty that in this matter I am greatly interested, for as a
result, the name of Bonaparte,[1] will certainly, for the present and
also the future, be struck off the roll of sovereigns; the island of
Elba being only life-hold, and the son of the archduchess being
debarred from the possession of an independent state.

The preparations for the ceremonial of the 21st are nearly
completed. The desire to be present is so great that it will be
difficult for us to accede to all the requests. The church of St.
Stephen, the largest in Vienna, would not hold all who wish to
come.

The sovereigns have all had notice of the ceremony, and all,
except the Emperor and Empress of Russia who have not yet
replied, have intimated their intention of being present.

The Empress of Austria, whose health does not admit of her
attendance, begs to be excused by your Majesty; these are the
words she herself used. But her mother, the Archduchess
Beatrice, will be present.

The ladies will all be veiled, this being the mark of the
deepest mourning.

General Pozzo is still awaiting his instructions. He is told
to hold himself in readiness, and this he has done for more than
a week, but his orders have not yet arrived.

General Andreossy[2] passed through here on his return to
Constantinople. His language is fair. He gave me all the
assurances of good faith I could desire. He is a man of intelligence who has filled responsible positions, and much appreciates
being employed.

I have the honour to be. . . .

---

[1] Var. : "*Buonaparte.*"

[2] Antoine-François, Comte Andreossy, born 1761. Was Lieutenant of Artillery
in 1789, became General of Brigade in 1797. He accompanied Buonaparte to Egypt
and returned with him in 1799, aided him on the 18th Brumaire, and became shortly
afterwards an Inspector of Artillery. He was Ambassador to London in 1802, and
subsequently at Vienna and Constantinople in 1809. He was recalled in 1814. In
1815, Andreossy was one of the Commissioners with the foreign armies. He retired
from public life after the second restoration, and died in 1828.

No. 23².—The Prince de Talleyrand to King Louis XVIII.

VIENNA, *Jan.* 21, 1815.

SIRE,

I have the honour to-day to send to your Majesty a report of the ceremony that took place here this morning.

I have had a short but circumstantial account drawn up for insertion in the *Moniteur* if your Majesty approves [1] of it. I thought it would be only necessary to relate the facts and abstain from offering any opinions or remarks which the readers will naturally make for themselves and probably be more impressed thereby.

This account includes the address delivered by the curé of St. Anne, a Frenchman by birth. It is not a funeral oration or a sermon but an address. There were only a few days in which to compose it, to make it harmonize with the object of the ceremony as well as with present circumstances; and the position of the principal people who would assist thereat; and it was therefore less important that it should be eloquent than that it should be guarded, and those who heard it thought that in this respect it left nothing to be desired.

Nothing was wanting to the ceremonial; neither the pomp due to the object, the choice of the spectators, nor the grief that the event it recalled must ever excite. It ought, as the memorial of a great misfortune, to offer a solemn lesson. It had both a moral and a political aim; and the heads of the great embassies and people of the highest rank who dined with me to-day,[2] led me to believe that this end has been attained.

I cannot speak too strongly in praise of the kindness and attention shown by the Emperor of Austria in permitting and ordering such arrangements as would add either to the proper conduct or the grandeur of the ceremonial. He alone, among all the sovereigns, appeared in black; the others wore uniform.

I have received the greatest assistance on all sides, especially from M. le Comte Alexis de Noailles.

M. Moreau, the architect charged with all the preparations, displayed both zeal and intelligence. The music was pronounced very fine. It was by M. Neukomm,[3] who conducted the

---

[1] See the *Moniteur* of January 30th.   [2] Suppressed in the text of the archives.
[3] Sigismond Neukomm, a German composer, born at Salzburg in 1778. A pupil of Haydn's. In 1804 he went to St. Petersburg, where he was appointed musical director of the Imperial Theatre. He went afterwards to Vienna, and subsequently in 1809 to Paris, where he was presented to M. de Talleyrand who introduced him into society. He lived with the Prince till 1814, and accompanied him to Vienna, where a requiem, composed by him for the occasion, was sung on the 21st

performance jointly with M. Salieri.[1] I entreat your Majesty to have the kindness to bestow on these three artists, as well as on M. Isabey[2] who has been of the greatest use, a proof of your satisfaction by sending me, for them, the decoration of the Legion of Honour.

I also entreat your Majesty to accord me the same honour to MM. Rouen,[3] Formont,[4] Damour, Saint-Mars[5] et Sers, *attachés* to your Majesty's embassy, with whose conduct I have reason to be extremely satisfied, and who alone, amongst the *attachés* of the various embassies at the Congress, have no decoration.

On Wednesday I will despatch a courier, by whom I shall have the honour to write to your Majesty on the subject of the marriage, of the great importance of which I am fully aware, and have never lost sight.[6]

I have the honour to be. . . .

No. 26.—The Ambassadors of the King at the Congress to the Minister of Foreign Affairs at Paris.

VIENNA, *Jan.* 24, 1815.

MONSIEUR LE COMTE,

We have the honour to submit herewith the protocol of the conference of the eight powers, held Jan. 16th. The

of January in the church of St. Etienne of that city by 300 choristers. In 1816 he accompanied the Duc de Luxemburg to Rio de Janeiro, to which the latter had been accredited. Returning to Paris, he resumed his residence with the Prince de Talleyrand and followed him to London in 1830. He died in 1857.

[1] Antonio Salieri, a celebrated Italian composer, was born in 1750. He came to Vienna in 1766, with Grosman, director of the Imperial Chapel, to whose office he succeeded in 1775. Salieri went to Paris several times and there brought out some operas which had a brilliant success (*The Danaïdes*, which he composed, but which Gluck wrote, *Tarare il Pastor fido*). He returned to Vienna in 1789 and devoted himself entirely to church music. He died in 1825.

[2] Jean-Baptiste Isabey, born at Nancy in 1767, early made a name for himself as a painter. He studied under David, was presented at Court, and painted portraits of the Duc d'Angoulême and Duc de Berry. He lived in Paris during the whole of the Reign of Terror. Later on he joined Buonaparte, whom he painted standing, and who appointed him to superintend the decoration and even the ceremonial of court solemnities at the Tuileries.

He went to Vienna in 1847 and there painted a celebrated picture representing the meeting after a conference of all the personages who took part in the Congress. He lived until 1855.

[3] M. Rouen, a French diplomat, commenced his career in 1813, at Weimar, as attaché to the legation. Followed M. de Talleyrand to Vienna, was secretary at Turin in 1816. Subsequently Consul-General in Greece (1828), and Minister at Rio de Janeiro in 1836.

[4] M. de Formont was employed at the Foreign Office in 1814. He was attached to the French Embassy at Vienna. Afterwards he became Consul-General at Livorno.

[5] M. de Saint-Mars was the translator at the Foreign Office, and was attached as such to the French Embassy. He remained on at Vienna as chief secretary.

[6] Var. : "P.S.—The departure of General Pozzo appears to be fixed for Tuesday, 24th."

question of the slave-trade has been since modified by the effect of a convention, entered into between Lord Castlereagh and the Portuguese ambassador. The latter, in the name of his government, has agreed that Portugal shall give up the slave-trade north of the equator from this time forward. England in return paying an indemnity of £300,000 sterling for the damage done by English cruisers ; £500,000 sterling towards a loan which Portugal has to repay, and annulling the last treaty of commerce signed in 1810.[1] Portugal likewise covenants that at the end of eight years, the slave-trade shall no longer be carried on in any of her possessions. Spain has insisted that the date, already stipulated for in her treaties, should remain fixed definitely.

France retains the position she occupied after the treaty of Paris, ever ready to discourage the slave-trade, and fixing five years as the term for its abolition.

You will see, M. le Comte, that the great advantages offered by England to Portugal will dispose her the more readily to enter into arrangements for the immediate abolition of the slave-trade.

It will be for you to consult with the Minister of Marine on this matter ; if, as it is said, our traders do not carry arms in quest of slaves, some arrangement might perhaps be possible without any loss to France. This idea, however, can only be touched upon with great caution.

The negotiations as to the limits of Poland and Saxony are being carried on. In two days the Vienna cabinet is to submit a counter-project.

The Prussians seem disposed to answer this by an *ultimatum*, and the Emperor of Russia holds out some hopes of interposing his good offices with the court of Berlin, to induce her to relinquish her claim to annex the kingdom of Saxony.

Lord Castlereagh always appears disinclined to discuss this question thoroughly ; he often repeats that he will only insist on the preservation of conservative principles, and that he neither can nor will pledge the English nation to make sacrifices on a simple question of greater or less population. Notwithstanding this obstacle, we nevertheless hope that if Saxony agrees to give up five or six hundred thousand souls, she will be allowed to exist.

This we trust to announce definitely ere eight days have

---

[1] A friendly treaty of commerce and navigation, between England and Portugal, signed at Rio de Janeiro, on the 19th of February, 1810. This treaty, imposed by England, had stipulated for some very hard conditions, especially regarding the commerce of the Brazils, which was then a Portuguese colony.

elapsed.   Austria, who should receive back the district of
Tarnopol, lost in Poland in 1809, is willing to give it up on
condition that Russia cedes a larger territory to Prussia.   All
this tends to the solution of this first and most important
question which has blocked the progress of the congress.

Italian affairs have not progressed ; they are at a standstill
in the office of M. de Metternich.

Those of Switzerland are about to be discussed in the
conference of the eight powers.   According to the latest
accounts received from Berne, the deputy of that canton has
received authority to accept the bishopric of Bale as indemnity
for its losses, on the condition that it is to be given over to them
entirely, and that no privileges shall be claimed for its inhabitants which would not accord with those formerly enjoyed by
the old canton of Berne.   The Bernese have at the same time,
expressed their gratitude for the generous sacrifices which his
Majesty was prepared to make in order to procure the restoration of their ancient territory.   We believe that his Majesty
will find them most faithful and devoted allies.

We cannot conclude, M. le Comte, without informing you of
the effect produced here on every one by the ceremony of Jan.
21st.   We thought that one of the best and most efficacious
means of consecrating those principles which we are endeavouring to establish, was to invite all the sovereigns and plenipotentiaries to attend it.

It having been decided in the beginning of January to cele-
brate this anniversary, the ambassadors of the king hastened to
make their intention known to the Austrian court as well as to
the English, Spanish, and Portuguese legations, and sought to give
as much *éclat* as possible to the ceremony by their preparations.

Although it was in the interest of all the sovereigns to do
honour to the memories which this anniversary recalls, the
king's ambassadors are too fully cognisant of the terrible
impressions left by the Revolution, to expect that universal
homage would be accorded, unless great pains were taken in
the matter.

Even on the evening before the ceremony, the Emperor of
Russia declared that there was no object to be gained by it,
and his envoy at the Austrian court alleged various pretexts
for not being able to attend.

But you will see, M. le Comte, that we have succeeded in
triumphing over all these obstacles and that the sovereigns, the
envoys and the people of Vienna, all assisted at the ceremony
with feelings of the deepest respect.

The legation has been engaged in drawing up an address.

which, if somewhat lacking in that degree of eloquence which such grand memories should inspire, has nevertheless produced the best possible effect, in showing the position of France, her regrets and her love for her king, without accusing or assigning guilt to any one.

The king's ambassadors were not satisfied, however, merely to proclaim these views from the pulpit. The Prince de Talleyrand, inspired M. de Gentz to write an article which, in drawing the attention of Europe to this ceremonial, will prove to you that the object we had in view has been attained. The article is in the *Observatoire* of Vienna, January 23rd.[1]

You will have been able to form an opinion, M. le Comte, from our first report, already forwarded to the king, of the general feeling inspired by the ceremony, the emotion that has been manifested, and the reminiscences it will leave in this country.

On the same day, all the most distinguished among the visitors and inhabitants of Vienna hastened to express their condolences to the Prince de Talleyrand.

The Emperor of Austria ordered a *fête* (which was to have taken place on the 21st) to be put off till next day. Perhaps you will deem it advisable that in all the principal papers, the account of the *fête* of the 22nd, should be preceded by these words :—" The entertainments, interrupted by order of the Emperor on account of the 21st January, have recommenced."[2]

The catafalque has remained on view in the cathedral since the day of the ceremony. Numbers of people still go there to testify their profound respect.

Be pleased to accept. . . .

No. 24².—The Prince de Talleyrand to King Louis XVIII.

VIENNA, *January* 25, 1815.

SIRE,

I was present at a conference yesterday with Prince de Metternich and Prince Schwarzenberg, the object of which was to decide what portion of Saxony, in the opinion of the Austrian officers, could or could not be given up to Prussia, without compromising the safety of Austria.

The Emperor of Austria wished this conference to take place and also desired that I should be present.

Two plans were submitted. The one preserved Torgau to

---

[1] See the *Moniteur* of February 2nd. [2] See the *Moniteur* of February 2nd.

Saxony, provided the fortifications of Dresden were rased.   The other gave Torgau to Prussia, but unfortified ; Dresden being likewise dismantled.

In both schemes, Prussia would keep Erfurth.

It was decided to submit both plans to the Emperor of Austria, and that whichever he adopted should then form the subject [1] of a memorandum, which he would himself give to Lord Castlereagh : for it is Castlereagh who must be satisfied.

Russia has offered to give back to Austria, the district of Tarnopol, which contains four hundred thousand inhabitants. Austria will renounce this, on condition that an equal population is given to Prussia, of that part of Poland which adjoins her, in order to diminish, as much as possible, the sacrifices Saxony has to make.   This will be fully explained in the memorandum.

I am unaware which of these two plans has been adopted, but I know that Lord Castlereagh was sent for by the Emperor of Austria this evening.   I will inform your Majesty by the next [2] courier, what passed at this audience.

Your Majesty will judge of the confidence placed by the Emperor of Austria in his minister, when you hear that this morning he sent the Comte de Sickingen to me, to ask whether what had been reported to him by M. de Metternich, respecting yesterday's conference, was true.

The Emperor Alexander, with his liberal ideas, has found so little favour here, that they have been obliged to triple the details of the police in order to protect him from being insulted by the people, during his daily walks.

I have the honour to forward to your Majesty an article from the *Beobachter*, which I got M. de Gentz to draw up.   I attach the translation which he did himself and which is very good.   I thought the article might be inserted in the *Moniteur* under the head of " Vienna."   It is of such a nature, that the other papers will be able to insert it as well.

I have the honour to be . . . . .

THE PRINCE DE TALLEYRAND TO KING LOUIS XVIII.

(Private.)

VIENNA, *January* 25, 1815.

SIRE,

It appears that General Pozzo is to leave this week and to return to Paris.   He has probably received instructions from the Emperor Alexander relative to the marriage.   I think I

---

[1] Text : " le sujet " = as translated.   Var. : " *le projet*," " draft."
[2] Text : " le prochain " = as translated.   Var. : " le *premier*," " the first."

ought to-day to submit to your Majesty some views on a subject so delicate and so important[1] in its various aspects.

Your Majesty desires, and has every reason to desire, that the princess, whoever she may be, whom the Duc de Berry is to espouse, should come into France as a Catholic princess. Your Majesty makes this condition an absolute one, and cannot well refrain from doing so. As the most Christian king and eldest son of the Church, you could not on this point, carry condescension further than did Buonaparte,[2] when he asked for the hand of the Grand Duchess Anne. If this condition is accepted by the Emperor Alexander, your Majesty, on the supposition that you have given your promise, would certainly not feel at liberty to retract it. But it appears that the emperor, without desiring to oppose his sister's change of religion, does not wish it to be supposed that he has had any hand in this change, as might with reason be inferred if it had been made a stipulation. He would prefer it looked upon as the result of the princess's own decision when she becomes subject to other laws, and that the change should take place after, instead of before, the marriage. He therefore considers that his sister should enter France with her private ecclesiastical establishment, though he is willing that the pope[3] who accompanies her should wear a lay garment. The reasons which make him adhere to this, are, his personal scruples, being strongly attached to his own faith, and the fear of hurting the feelings of his people on such a tender point.

By insisting on these provisos for himself,[4] he will release your Majesty from all engagements to the contrary, and will himself furnish the excuse for such release, by deferring his consent to the conditions of the marriage.

Now I am fain to confess to your Majesty that everything that can tend towards such release, seems to me to be most desirable.

Eight months ago when, in the midst of joys excited by the present, and bright hopes which it was pleasant to cherish for the future, it was nevertheless impossible to look upon events with that feeling of security which fears no alarm, and a family alliance with Russia might then appear, and did seem to me, to offer advantages, the importance of which ought to raise it above all considerations and which in another aspect of affairs, I should have placed in the first rank and looked upon as decisive.

But to-day, when Providence has seen fit to secure the throne

---

[1] Text: "si delicate et si grave" = as translated. Var.: "*aussi* delicate et *aussi* grave" = "equally delicate and equally important."

[2] Var.: "*Buonaparte.*"   [3] Priest of the Greek Church

[4] Suppressed in the text of the archives.

she has so miraculously restored, when it is surrounded and guarded by the loyalty and love of the nation, when the coalition is dissolved and France has no longer any need to count on the help of strangers, but that on the contrary, the other powers look to her—your Majesty in coming to a decision will no longer have to make a sacrifice to the exigencies of combined strength, but only consult the expediences which are unavoidable in such alliances.

The Grand Duchess Anne, of all the five daughters of the Emperor Paul, is said to be the one endowed by nature with the greatest beauty, a gift most precious and most desirable in a princess who, in the course of events, may be called upon some day [1] to sit on the throne of France, for the French, more than any other nation, feel the need of being able to say of the princes whose subjects they are :

"Le monde en les voyant, reconnaitrait ces maitres." [2]

The Grand Duchess seems to have been brought up with the greatest care, combining, from what one hears, inward goodness with outward beauty. She is twenty-one years of age, so that we need not fear those sad consequences, that so often follow a very early marriage. She was originally destined for the reigning Duke of Saxe-Cobourg, before Buonaparte [3] demanded her hand. It only rested with him to urge his suit, for it is certain that if he had been willing and able to wait, they would have asked nothing better than to bestow her upon him. I do not know whether these two circumstances might be considered as disadvantageous to the union of this princess with the Duc de Berry ; candidly, I should have preferred that they had not occurred, if the marriage is to take place.

Again, looking at the condition of the mental faculties of the Grand Duchess's grandfather, Peter III., and her father Paul I., in conjunction with those of the late King of Denmark, the reigning Duke of Oldenburg, and the unfortunate Gustavus IV., and the fact that their deplorable infirmity may be regarded as the fatal lot of the House of Holstein,[4] I cannot help dreading, lest through

---

[1] Suppressed in the text of the archives.
[2] "The world on seeing them, would recognize its masters."
[3] Var. : "*Buonaparte.*"
[4] Holstein belonged formerly to the House of Schauenburg. This line becoming extinct in 1459, the states elected as chief Count Christian of Oldenburg, nephew to the last Count of Holstein Schauenburg, who had just died. Christian of Oldenburg had been elected King of Denmark in 1448, as descended in the female line from the ancient royal family of the Waldemars, which had also become extinct. The grandsons of Christian I. divided Holstein (1544) and thus became the founders of the two branches : the eldest or royal branch, which reigned in Denmark in a

such a marriage, this taint may be conveyed to the royal family of France, and perhaps to the heir to the throne.[1]

The necessity which obliges the Grand Duchess, not merely to change her religion, but to change it in such a manner, that it will be impossible to attribute it to any other but purely political motives, would, it seems to me, furnish a sufficiently strong objection.

For such an act would inevitably tend to foster among the people those feelings of religious indifference which are the great evil of the times in which we live.

Marriages unite not merely those who contract them, but also their respective families. Cordial relations between them are of the utmost importance, even among private individuals ; how much more so, in the case of kings, or princes who may one day become sovereigns ? That the House of Bourbon should ally itself with other Houses inferior to it, is a necessity, since Europe cannot offer one that is its equal. I will therefore raise no objection to the House of Holstein, which although occupying the three Northern thrones, is comparatively young among sovereigns.

But I should certainly say that when the House of Bourbon deigns to honour another with her alliance, it would be better that it should be one which would feel itself honoured, rather than pretend to equality on the grounds, that nobility and ancient lineage can be compensated for by extent of territory. Of the Grand Duchess Anne's four sisters, one has married an arch-duke, and the three others, small German princes.[2] Shall Russia,

---

direct line till 1863, and the younger or ducal branch, which was again sub-divided into two lines, that of Holstein-Gattorp, and that of Holstein-Gattorp-Eulin. The first of these ascended to the throne of Russia in 1762 as Peter III., son of Charles Frederic, Duke of Holstein-Gattorp, and Anne, daughter of Peter the Great. The second line gave birth in 1710 to Adolphus Frederic, Duke of Holstein-Gattorp-Eulin, who at the Peace of Abo in 1743, was placed on the throne of Sweden by Elizabeth, Empress of Russia, in place of the Prince Royal of Denmark. Thus the reigning families of Denmark, Sweden, and Russia, were descended from the same source. On the other hand the deplorably weak mind of the Czar Peter III. cannot be ignored, nor how very precarious was the mental weakness of his son the Czar Peter. As for the King of Denmark, Christian VII., he became insane in 1772. In the same way the Duke of Holstein Oldenburg became incapable of reigning, and was replaced by his cousin, the Prince of Lubeck. Nevertheless, despite what M. de Talleyrand says, it does not appear that Gustavus IV., King of Sweden, had inherited this infirmity of the House of Holstein in the same degree.

[1] The whole of this paragraph does not appear in the text of the archives.

[2] It must be remembered that the Emperor Paul had five daughters, Alexandra, born in 1788, married to Joseph Antonio, Archduke of Austria, brother to the Emperor Francis. Helena, born in 1784, married to Frederic-Louis, hereditary Prince of Mecklenburg-Schwerin. Marie, born in 1786, married in 1804 to Charles Frederic, hereditary Prince of Sax-Weimar. Catherine, born in 1788, married in 1809 to Paul Frederic Augustus, hereditary Prince of Holstein Oldenburg. Lastly, Anne, born in 1795, the one referred to.

who has not been able to place any of her princesses on a throne, now see one of them called to that of France?

Such a prospect would, I must confess, be too great a piece of luck for her, and I should be sorry that the Duc de Berry should find himself in such very close and intimate relationship, with a host of princes, all in the lowest ranks of sovereignty.

Russia, in marrying her princesses as she has done, aims, above all things, at having a pretext for interfering with the affairs of Europe, to which she has been almost a stranger for the last century. The effects of her intervention, so far, have sufficiently manifested the danger of her influence. How much greater would not this influence become, if a Russian princess was called to sit on the throne of France!

A family alliance, I know, is not a political one, neither does the one necessarily lead to the other.

The projected marriage would certainly not incline France to favour the ambitious views and revolutionary ideas possessed by the Emperor Alexander, and which he tries to veil under the specious name of liberal opinions. But how to prevent other powers from taking a different view, and conceiving such an amount of distrust as would weaken the ties they had with us, or deter them from entering into such alliances, or Russia from taking advantage of this, to gain her own ends? These, sire, seem to me the possible objections to the marriage of the Duc de Berry with the Grand Duchess Anne. I felt I ought to point them out frankly to your Majesty, but I have certainly not exaggerated them. Your Majesty will best be able to judge whether they are as weighty as they seem to me.

I would add, that it appears to me due to the greatness of the House of Bourbon, especially at this time when all her branches, blown down by the same tempest, have sprung up again simultaneously, only to consult your own heart as to the means for perpetuating your lineage. I hear great praise of the young Princess of Sicily, daughter of the Prince Royal.[1] Portugal, Tuscany and Saxony offer many others, among whom your Majesty might make a selection. I have the honour to send a list of them herewith.

Should the impossibility of coming to an understanding, on account of religion, cause the negotiations respecting the marriage

---

[1] Marie-Caroline-Thérèse de Bourbon, born in 1798, daughter of François, hereditary Prince of the two Sicilies, and of Marie Clementine, Archduchess of Austria in 1816. She married the Duc de Berry who died four years after. On September 29, 1820, she gave birth to the Duc de Bordeaux. It will be remembered how she tried to stir up revolts in 1832 in favour of her son. Arrested on November 7, 1832, she was confined in the Château de Blaye and was taken back to Sicily the following year. She died in 1870.

with the Grand-Duchess to fall through, or if your Majesty should consider it advisable to give it up, I would entreat you to arrange matters in such a way, that the affair shall not be finally decided, until after those which occupy us here are completed. For if the Emperor Alexander has shown us so little good-will notwithstanding the hopes of a brilliant settlement for his sister and the advantage to him of such a prospect, what may we not expect from him, when it is once lost ?

I have the honour to be. . . . .

No. 20[3].—KING LOUIS XVIII. TO THE PRINCE DE TALLEYRAND.

PARIS, *January* 28, 1815.

MON COUSIN,

I have received your letter, No. 22. Long before this reaches you, you will have seen the Duke of Wellington, whose appointment in place of Lord Castlereagh, was very agreeable to me.[1] I saw him before he left, and was more than satisfied with him, and I hope he has not departed dissatisfied with me. He also has a " character " to keep up, that of *King*, not *Maker*, but what is much better *Restorer*. He is besides not at all troubled by what his predecessor has done, since if he wishes to walk in his footsteps, he has as it were, merely to choose between the two extremes. I do not exactly know the amount of the population[2] of Saxony. I believe the king will have to consent to a reduction of fifteen hundred thousand inhabitants, but if more than this number is required, remember what I wrote to you last time.

Count Jules de Polignac[3] arrived here on Sunday. His reports, identical with those I have previously received from various quarters, describe Italy as in the greatest state of ferment, and the existence of Murat as most dangerous. I have reason to believe that England would enter into some agreement to assure this man pecuniary aid if he would relinquish his usurped throne. I would gladly assent to this arrangement provided

---

[1] Wellington had just been appointed ambassador to the Congress (January 24).

[2] Var. : "total."

[3] Auguste-Jules, Count, afterwards Prince de Polignac, born in 1780, was at the first restoration nominated Major-General, Commissioner Extraordinary at Toulouse, and Minister to the Holy See. On April 17, 1815, he was made a peer of France. In 1820 Count Polignac received the title of Roman Prince from the Pope. Ambassador at London in 1823, he became Minister of Foreign Affairs and President of the Council in 1829. After the departure of Charles X., from whom he had separated, Prince de Polignac was arrested at Granville on August 15, and taken to Vincennes. The Chamber of Peers condemned him to perpetual imprisonment (dead in law). He was pardoned in 1836 and withdrew to England, and returned to die in Paris in 1847.

that it is at the same time agreed, that if he is obstinate, force should do what negotiations have failed in effecting.

The sad, yet consoling ceremony of Saturday passed off very satisfactorily. I beg you will express my sentiments to the sovereigns who assisted at that at St. Etienne, and particularly to inform the Empress of Austria how greatly I was touched by her wishes and the regrets she desired to show me on this occasion.

Wherefore, my dear cousin, I pray God may have you in His safe and holy keeping.

LOUIS.

P.S. General Ricard arrived here yesterday,[1] and will be in Vienna soon after this letter.

No. 27.—THE AMBASSADORS OF THE KING AT THE CONGRESS TO THE MINISTER OF FOREIGN AFFAIRS AT PARIS.

VIENNA, January 31st, 1815.

MONSIEUR LE COMTE,

The counter-project announced in our last despatches has been sent in by the Vienna cabinet. Seven hundred and eighty-two thousand souls have been taken from Saxony. As soon as it is officially communicated to the French embassy, we shall have the honour to forward it to you.

The Prussians do not appear satisfied with it. Nevertheless, the Emperor Alexander seems to approve and we hope he will prevail upon his ally to accept it, and so put an end to a question which for so long has divided the congress. It will be decided in a few days.

Yesterday, Lord Castlereagh received his recall to England, and the arrival of the Duke of Wellington is announced.

Lord Castlereagh leaves Vienna, preserving his favourable views as regards Naples. He seems to lay great stress on keeping on good terms with France.

Neither the affairs of Switzerland nor those of Italy have occupied the conference. M. de Metternich has not considered it expedient to bring them forward since the question arose as to deciding their order of precedence.

Confidence in the king's judgment, and the consideration shown to his ambassador at the congress increase in proportion as every one is persuaded that justice and judgment prescribe all the measures of the French cabinet. From day to day

---

[1] Suppressed in the text of the archives.

we note marked indications that the coalition is dissolved, and that the union of the Southern Powers against a system of expediency, so strongly urged by the Northern Powers, will consolidate peace, and act as a guarantee against any fresh troubles that might arise.

Be pleased to accept. . . .

No. 25².—The Prince de Talleyrand to King Louis XVIII.

VIENNA, *February* 1, 1815.

SIRE,

The audience given to Lord Castlereagh by the Emperor of Austria, only resulted in the former's declaring that the emperor appeared to him full of integrity and frankness. Beyond this Lord Castlereagh was staunch in his opinion, that Prussia ought to be great and powerful, and that she should receive a large part of Saxony, and in particular Torgau. I wished to save this place; the Austrians wanted it at first, and then, as is their custom, relinquished it. The consequence is that neither one nor the other of the schemes I had the honour to mention to your Majesty has been adopted. A third has now been drawn up by which seven hundred and eighty-two thousand Saxons are given up to Prussia, and this scheme of the Austrians, in the shape of a rough draft, has been submitted to the Prussians, who have accepted it *ad referendum :* their answer has not yet been received.

We had announced from the first that we would consent to Saxony being deprived of from four to five hundred thousand souls ; Lord Castlereagh after having at first given it up, and because he had done so, obstinately insisted that they should lose a million. Though very badly supported by the Austrians, I succeeded in getting it arranged, that the mean of these two numbers should be adopted, and I am even now surprised at my success. The Saxon minister, who is here, had drawn up a plan of the different parts of the kingdom, which might be considered as not absolutely necessary to its existence. The population of these parts was about 750,000. In the scheme only 32,000 more are ceded, and of these, some portion must through exchanges, revert to the ducal houses of Saxony.

The Prussians they say are, or feign to be, but little disposed to be content with what is offered them. It is not merely a question of territory with them, but also one of self-esteem.

After having, and that only recently, demanded the whole of Saxony, after having occupied it, after all the powers, except France, had given it up to them, after having over and over again declared they would never surrender it, it must be rather painful for them now to have to renounce two-thirds of the kingdom. But they will not fight without the help of Russia, and the Emperor Alexander, who has got what he wanted in Poland and who only takes a selfish interest in Saxony,[1] will, according to all appearance, advise the Prussians to accept the proposals made to them. We have reason to believe that with some slight alteration, they will be accepted.

Nothing seemed more irrevocably settled than the fate of Saxony when we arrived here. Prussia demanded the whole of it for herself, and Russia backed her up. Lord Castlereagh had completely abandoned her, and so had Austria, except as regards some minor frontier arrangements. Your Majesty alone took up the defence of Saxony ; you alone maintained the principles of right. You had to overcome all kinds of influences ; the spirit of coalition which was very strong, and what was perhaps more difficult, the self-esteem of all the great powers, who by their pretensions, declarations and concessions had so far compromised themselves, as to make it almost impossible for them to recede without shame ; but by noble opposition to an injustice, all but accomplished, your Majesty has gained the glory of overcoming all these obstacles, and not only have you triumphed over them, but the coalition has been dissolved, and your Majesty has come to an understanding with two of the greatest powers, which may perhaps, later on, save Europe from the dangers which menace it, through the ambition of some of the states.

Saxony, which was a third-rate power, will continue to be so. Her population, joined to that of the ducal possessions, and those of the Houses of Reuss and Schwarzburg, which are incorporated in the kingdom, will still present two million inhabitants, to interpose between Prussia and Austria and between Russia and Bavaria.

The affairs of Saxony once settled, I shall give myself up to those of Naples, and for this purpose will put forth all the energy and tact I possess.

England will not oppose, but will not assist us openly or in any decided way, seeing that she has again compromised herself in that affair, as your Majesty will perceive by the document which I have the honour to send you herewith.

Lord Castlereagh had, on this point, received instructions

---

[1] Suppressed in the text of the archives.

from his government, given after the letter which I wrote to him, but which are in the sense I have indicated.

Lord Castlereagh will only remain here eight days with Lord Wellington. I have reason to believe, from what he told me of the despatches he had received from his government, that his partiality for Prussia, and his obstinacy on the Saxon question, must be imputed to Lord Liverpool [1] as much as to himself. Lord Bathurst sends instructions that Prussia is to be treated with great liberality, and that having gone so far as they had done regarding Saxony, it was a point of honour with the English government not to draw back.[2]

Nevertheless, the treaty he has just concluded is entirely approved of, and he has been informed that the ratifications will be sent to him by the next courier.

He dilated greatly on his wish to see the best possible feeling established between England and France. He did not deceive himself into believing that the result of the arrangements made here could be a peace of long duration. His desire is that war should not break out again for two years. His prayer is that France, England, and Austria should be friends,[3] and as he deems it necessary to be always prepared, and to arrange everything in advance, he proposes to keep up a direct correspondence with me. But he considers a change of the ministry would be desirable in Austria, as they are very weak, to say nothing more.

I was, on the whole, well satisfied with the views he expressed.

He proposes to ask for an audience of your Majesty on his way through Paris.

I have the honour to be . . . . .

---

[1] Robert Jenkinson, Earl of Liverpool, born in 1770, entered the House of Commons in 1790, and became Commissioner at the India Office, Master of the Mint, and Member of the Privy Council. He joined Lord Addington's Cabinet as Secretary of State for Foreign Affairs (1801), and was Home Secretary under Pitt in 1804. This he held till 1808, when he was made War Minister, and finally became First Lord of the Treasury in 1812. He remained at the head of affairs till 1827, and died the following year.

[2] Text: "retrograder" = as translated. Var.: "*trop* retrograder" = "draw back too much."

[3] Text: "soient amies" = as translated. Var. : "soient *unies*" = "be united.

No. 21[3].—King Louis XVIII. to the Prince de
Talleyrand.

Paris, *February* 4, 1815.

Mon Cousin,

I have received your letters Nos. 23 and 24. I did not
answer the first at once, as it did not treat of business, though I
was not the less satisfied or touched by its contents. Neither St.
Denis, nor any of the other churches in Paris, except St. Thomas-
d'Aquin, where the preacher only read the last will of the Martyr
King, have re-echoed a discourse which could in any way
approach that pronounced at St. Etienne. I wish you to make
my opinion known to the author.[1]

I was also greatly pleased with M. de Gentz's article, which
I sent off at once to the *Moniteur*. Further, I have given orders
to the Count de Jaucourt on the subject of the rewards you
desire of me for the artists who assisted at the ceremony of
the 21st.

The cession of Erfurth to Prussia does not trouble me much,
but I shall be sorry to see the fortifications of Dresden destroyed,
especially if the King of Prussia retains Torgau. I wish however that the Emperor Francis would at least give the first
scheme the preference, and make Lord Castlereagh adopt it, the
latter, however, is probably no longer in Vienna. You are aware
how strongly the Duke of Wellington urged the abolition of the
slave-trade when here. You will shortly receive the report on
St. Domingo, made to me at the council last Monday, by M.
Beugnot. I confess that I am beginning to see the benefit
which may accrue from the almost immediate abandonment of a
traffic, which, it appears to me, would be very difficult to continue
beyond the time fixed by the treaty.

Marshal Soult is writing to you about Bouillon.[2] The point
in question is one of protection, not of possession, and for that
reason it is important that this duchy should remain under the
Prince de Rohan, who, moreover, notwithstanding the protection

---

[1] Count Alexis de Noailles, one of the plenipotentiaries at the congress, wrote the
address read by the priest at the ceremony of Jan. 21, in the Church of St. Etienne.
[2] Charles-Alain-Gabriel, Prince de Rohan Guémené, Duc de Montluçon
and de Bouillon, born in 1754 emigrated in 1791, entered the Austrian army
and rose to the rank of Field Marshal. In 1814, he was made a peer of France.
The Congress of Vienna recognized him as sovereign of the Duchy of Bouillon, but
this was contested by the English Admiral Phillip d'Auvergne. The matter being
referred by the Congress to supreme arbitrators, decided in favour of the Prince de
Rohan. These arbitrators acknowledged the right to an indemnity on the part of the
King of the Netherlands for the cession made to him of the Duchy. But the tribunal
of Liége upset this decision. The Prince de Rohan died in   .

accorded by England to his antagonist has a hundred times as much right to it.

Wherefore, my dear cousin, I pray God may have you in His safe and holy keeping.   LOUIS.

P.S.   Your ideas with regard to the marriage, are absolutely mine.   I shall receive General Pozzo di Borgo, and not hasten anything.

No. 28.—THE AMBASSADORS OF THE KING AT THE CONGRESS TO THE MINISTER OF FOREIGN AFFAIRS AT PARIS.

VIENNA, *February* 8, 1815.

M. LE COMTE,
        The rough draft of the arrangements to be made respecting the King of Saxony and his kingdom, proposed by the Austrian cabinet, seems to have been accepted with a few slight modifications.   There is even a talk of the King of Saxony leaving Berlin, and going to Prague, or even Vienna, if the Austrian court wishes it.

If under these circumstances no more favourable results have been secured for Saxony and Poland, it can only be attributed to the prejudice of the English cabinet, and the weakness of that of Vienna.   The difficulties to be overcome were endless, but the cause of royalty, legitimacy and right is saved, and that portion of Saxony which has been preserved, joined to the territories of the ducal houses, opposes a mass of two million inhabitants between Austria and Prussia.

The details of the arrangement, as it is to be, will be delayed here a few days, but will follow closely on this despatch, which conveys the announcement that the principal difficulties to the progress of affairs at the congress, have been overcome.

Lord Castlereagh leaves here on Monday next, and in order to have the honour of seeing the king, will pass through Paris and embark at Calais.   We trust that his departure, and the manner in which Lord Wellington has spoken in reference to Neapolitan affairs, will not injure that cause to which we must now devote all our energies and zeal.

The affairs of Switzerland will be gone into this week. M. de Metternich promises an answer on those of Italy.   The conferences for the settlement of the rights of navigation on the large rivers still continue, and those respecting the affairs of Germany will be resumed.

We have, M. le Comte, again to draw your attention to the French journals, and especially to what they say of the Prince

Royal of Sweden.   They mix him up with Murat, without any regard to the difference in their positions and our engagements with them.   The present state of Europe, which has everything to fear from the encroaching nature of the Russian government and everything to hope from unanimous accord between the older cabinets, compels us to be most careful in the handling of Sweden, and seems to make it imperative on us to neglect nothing, in order to preserve friendly relations with her.

We think we ought to report some observations, of an almost official character, addressed to M. de Noailles by M. le Comte de Lowenhjelm, Swedish plenipotentiary at the congress.   We send you his actual words :—

"The ex-King of Sweden proposes to go to France.   I have reason to believe that he wishes it; the papers say so.   We have seen what he has done for the House of Bourbon ; we could not suppose that the King of France, whose generosity is so well known, would refuse him shelter.   We only ask for some sort of communication on this subject, and we shall be satisfied.

"The Prince Royal is quite settled in Sweden since the union with Norway.   He is very popular and much looked up to.   He wishes to be on good terms with France.   We do not ask much from you.   The Prince of Sweden has not forgotten his origin ; he must always be somewhat anxious ; he needs some token of friendship.   He is, when all is said, a *parvenu*, and he has all the susceptibilities of one which we cannot prevent. But he will be very sensible to the least kindness.   For instance, one word, one sign of kindness from the king to the Princess Royal, who is in Paris, will touch him deeply and have the best possible effect.

"Your papers continually speak of the prince in an unpleasant way, inserting paragraphs which must do him harm by their stinging observations.   The Foreign Office in all countries has some influence over the press.   Put a stop to these invectives, which do not proceed from your cabinet.   I reiterate this request—nay, I conjure you !"

Be pleased to accept. . . .

No. 26.—The Prince de Talleyrand to King Louis XVIII.

Vienna, *February* 8, 1815.

Sire,

The Duke of Wellington arrived on the evening of the 1st.   The next day, the Emperor of Russia went to see him at ten in the morning, and began by saying, " Everything is going wrong in France, is it not ? "

" By no means," replied the duke, " the king is greatly beloved and respected, and behaves with exemplary prudence."

" You could tell me nothing that would give me so much pleasure," replied the Emperor. " And how about the army ? "

" As far as offensive warfare goes, no matter against what power," Lord Wellington answered, " the army is as good as it ever was, but in questions of home policy, it is worth nothing."

These answers, according to what Prince Adam told me, impressed the emperor more than he cared to show. They certainly influenced the resolution he had been urged to come to, respecting the affairs of Saxony, which when Lord Wellington arrived, still presented a good many difficulties. These may now be considered as removed.

It is not to the Emperor of Russia alone that the Duke of Wellington eulogises your Majesty. Wherever he goes he sings your praises, not limiting himself to general terms, but entering into details, and citing facts, thus adding to the high esteem in which your Majesty is held here. He spoke of the affair at St. Roche [1] as a mere trifle ; the German papers had greatly exaggerated it. He admitted that everything in France was not yet quite as one could wish, but he added that all would come right in time. According to him, what is most wanted there, is a ministry. There are ministers, he says, but no ministry.

The conclusions to be drawn from his utterances are, that as in matters of interior policy, the army is not yet quite sound, it will be necessary above all things to avoid raising questions in which it may have to play a part ; and that as for the animosity, which may still linger in men's minds, it should occasion neither surprise nor uneasiness. A too sudden conversion is always suspicious. This is the view I take, and the whole world has recognized its justice.

Last Saturday I gave a state dinner in honour of Lord Wellington, and asked all the members of the congress to meet him. I was very pleased that it should be the French legation which introduced him.

The Austrian scheme, respecting which I had the honour to write to your Majesty in my last letter, did not satisfy the Prussians. They wanted more—especially Leipzig. The King of Prussia, in an audience he granted Lord Castlereagh, expressed himself very strongly on this point, pretending that, after having

---

[1] There had been some confusion and a species of riot at the church of St. Roche, on the occasion of the burial of an actress—Mademoiselle Raucourt.

given him Saxony and allowing him to occupy it, it was making him play a most humiliating part, now to assign him only a small portion ; that he had conquered Leipzig, and that all the allies, after the battle was won, considered the town belonged to him, and had congratulated him thereon.

Lord Castlereagh, ever firmly impressed with the view that Prussia ought to be powerful, and wishing above all to avoid war (Lord Wellington is himself of opinion that England is not in a position to take the field, and that France is the only power that could do so), maintained that in order to pacify the Prussians, it was necessary to give them something more.

With a view therefore to enlarge their portion, Holland has been diminished by one hundred thousand souls and Hanover by fifty thousand ; Fulda has also been given to them. The Emperor of Russia who, to do him justice, desired to contribute to this arrangement, gave them back the town of Thorn ; so that the matter may now be considered arranged, but not definitely so.

Saxony will be reduced to less than fifteen hundred thousand inhabitants, but to this number must be added the population of the Duchies of Saxony and the States of Schwarzburg and Reuss, incorporated in the kingdom, and which if the latter had belonged to Prussia would also necessarily have belonged to her. Non-consent to the reduction of Saxony to less than fifteen hundred thousand souls, would have necessitated a protest, and such a protest would have compromised the principles of legitimacy, which it is so important to preserve and which we have preserved as it were by a miracle.

Prussia would, as a matter of fact, have obtained two millions of subjects, which she could not acquire without danger to Bohemia and Bavaria ; and the imprisonment of the king, who will now be free, would probably have been prolonged indefinitely. (I have asked Prince Hardenburg to allow the king to go to Prague and that orders to that effect might be given at once ; to this he consented and gave me his promise ; to-morrow the order will be sent to Berlin and the king will be allowed to depart.)

Saxony, though we have been unable to obtain all we desired, remains a third-rate power. If it is a misfortune that she has not a few hundred thousand inhabitants more, this misfortune is comparatively slight, and perhaps not without a remedy ; whereas if Saxony had been sacrificed in the face of Europe, which either would not or could not, save her, such a misfortune would have been very great and fraught with the most dangerous consequences. It was therefore necessary, above all things, to save her, and your Majesty has the sole glory of having done so

There is not a single person who does not feel and admit this, and yet it has all been accomplished without becoming at variance with any one, while at the same time, acquiring fresh support in Neapolitan affairs.

Lord Castlereagh, whom I informed, in order to flatter him, that your Majesty has done me the honour to say that you wish to see him on his way through Paris, has decided on returning by that route; he had originally intended going *via* Holland. Lady Castlereagh has asked permission to visit the Duchess of Angoulême. They will only be in Paris for twenty-four hours. They intend leaving here on Monday the 13th, but not without Lord Castlereagh's having taken some steps relative to the Neapolitan question which I thought it advisable he should do. The Duke of Wellington is all right in this respect. I hope Russia and Prussia will also be with us. Nevertheless, I foresee more than one difficulty, but I will do my best to overcome them.

It would both complicate and damage this affair, to allow Bernadotte's matter, which is of quite a different nature, to be mixed up with it.

Bernadotte did not obtain Sweden by conquest but by adoption of the reigning king, and the consent of the nation. He is not king, but only heir presumptive. One cannot attack him without attacking the king who adopted him, a king, whose legitimacy the very man who is to succeed him acknowledges, whom all Europe recognizes, and whom your Majesty also acknowledges, having made peace with him direct. As long as the king lives Bernadotte has only contingent rights, which as regards Europe, are almost non-existent; consequently the litigation of which they would form the subject, is neither within the cognisance of Europe nor the congress.

It is no doubt a misfortune, and a great misfortune, that this man should have been called to the Swedish throne. But it is an evil for which if there is no remedy, we can only leave to time and the course of events to ameliorate.

War, which no one has any wish to bring about, and which almost every one is unable to undertake, will, in all probability not occur. There will therefore be no occasion to propose an alliance with Sweden, or for Sweden to demand a guarantee, which your Majesty might fear to give.

General Ricard has arrived; but I hope that under present circumstances his journey will have been unnecessary.

General Pozzo has not yet left, I have even persuaded him not to take any steps to hasten his departure. I find him very useful, in matters I wish brought to the Emperor of Russia's notice.

I understand that the King of Saxony is to go to Presburg till affairs are concluded.

In a conference, held to-day the negro-question was settled. Spain and Portugal will definitely cease the slave-trade in eight years. Eight years for those two countries are much less than five years were for us, taking into account the immense difference of the respective possessions and above all their enlightenment.

We have ceded nothing, nevertheless the English are quite satisfied with us. Lord Castlereagh thanked me in open congress, for the great assistance I had given him.

Another conference took place this evening, to receive the Prussian reply to the propositions made them. The gist of their answer is an acceptance. They will get neither Luxemburg nor Mayence. Your Majesty's instructions proscribed their obtaining the latter place ; they will not get the former either.

The next few days will be occupied in drawing up and signing the articles for insertion in the protocol, of the arrangements agreed on for Poland, Prussia and Saxony.

I have the honour to be. . . . .

No. 22.—King Louis XVIII. to the Prince de Talleyrand.

PARIS, *February* 11, 1815.

MON COUSIN,

I am in receipt of your letter No. 25. The praise bestowed by Lord Castlereagh on the Emperor of Austria would have been very flattering to a private individual ; but when bestowed on a sovereign who had just displayed great weakness, it almost sounded like irony. As for me, I ought certainly to be satisfied, seeing how matters have stood for the last three [1] months, respecting the fate of the King of Saxony ; but I had hoped for better things from the Emperor Francis, and I shall not be easy until I see at least his last plan adopted.

The document added to your despatch is anything but reassuring to the King of Naples, in whom I take a very different interest to what I do in the King of Saxony ; but although it unveils the most repulsive secret in diplomacy ever heard of, it does not discourage me, and I feel assured that by maintaining a resolute front, from which I will never depart, we shall end by removing the danger and scandal of Murat.

I am surprised that the Duke of Wellington did not reach

---

[1] Text : as translated. Var : "*quatre*" = "four."

Vienna on the first of the month, but I do not fancy he has made any needless delay. I suppose, therefore, that Lord Castlereagh will be here towards the end of next week. To say truth, I have not been very much impressed by his conduct at the congress ; but I am, and with reason, too much wedded to the alliance I have just formed, not to take care that he shall go home thoroughly satisfied with me. Wherefore I pray, my dear cousin, that God may have you in His safe and holy keeping.

LOUIS.

No. 29.—THE AMBASSADORS OF THE KING AT THE CONGRESS TO THE MINISTER OF FOREIGN AFFAIRS IN PARIS.

VIENNA, *February* 12, 1815.

M. LE COMTE,

We have the honour to transmit herewith the protocol of the conference of the eight powers, on the question of rank and precedence. At a second conference held since, this subject was submitted for fresh consideration, and returned for examination to the commission specially charged with it. Lord Castlereagh, who left for London this morning, announced that his government had sent instructions respecting salutes at sea, and named which of the English plenipotentiaries were prepared to discuss it. We shall therefore be able to judge as to the degree of moderation in their views on this subject.

The affairs of Saxony are definitely arranged. The different articles determining the divisions have been settled, as well as the arrangements in the North of Germany resulting from the reconstruction of Prussia.

The King of Saxony has been informed of the results obtained, and has been invited to come near Vienna. We believe that, as far as the political existence of Saxony and her sovereign are concerned, everything has been obtained that ordinary negotiations could secure.

The claim of Prussia to keep Leipsic has been energetically combated ; they at last abandoned it in exchange for Thorn, an important military post, which the Emperor of Russia consented to give back to them. We may here mention a rather remarkable fact, as showing the revolutionary and bragging spirit of a nation which has troubled the peace of Europe for the last sixty years, and whose government, more than any other, furthered the progress of the revolution for its own ends.

One of their principal officers, General Grollmann,[1] known as

---

[1] Charles-Guillaume de Grollmann, born in Berlin in 1777, enlisted in 1795, and served in the lower grades all through the campaigns of 1806 and 1807. In 1809

one of the chiefs of the League of Virtue (*Tugendbund*) and whom the Prussian cabinet had sent to Vienna, in order to take advantage of what he could learn there, wrote to Lord Wellington to tell him that the army would never consent to the separation of Leipsic (which stood as a monument of glory) from the Prussian kingdom !

East Friesland has been ceded by Prussia to Hanover ; by this arrangement England obtains a communication by the Ems, which is of some importance as regards her continental relations.

We were just about to enter upon Swiss affairs, when a fresh demand from Austria adjourned the examination of the report sent in by the commission.

After the proposals made by M. de Metternich respecting Parma and Etruria, we had hopes of carrying out this affair according to the spirit of our instructions. But the opposition which the Archduchess Marie Louise appears desirous of raising to the cession of Parma, will renew the uncertainties in this matter.

The affairs of the South of Germany next claim our attention. The interests of Austria and Bavaria will probably cause some delay. The main point of difficulty is a special treaty entered into at Paris between these two powers, and which it will now be impossible to carry out, owing to the greater part of the available territory having been much diminished by the cessions made to Russia, Prussia, Holland, and Hanover.

In addition, M. le Comte, we have to bring to your notice a matter to which it is desirable you should draw his Majesty's attention.

The Royal Almanack has added to its list of the Legion of Honour, all those foreign sovereigns, and other persons not French, who have received this decoration. Several times already we have been asked whether the king had retained this order, and under what form, and whether foreigners could and ought to continue to wear it ; and that if so, an official communication to that effect either from the Minister of Foreign Affairs in Paris, or the Chancellor of the Order, would be de-

---

he entered the Austrian service and was attached to the staff of the Archduke Charles. An implacable enemy to France, he quitted Austria after the peace, and went to Spain, where he obtained a command in the Foreign Legion, which had just been organized by the Junta of Cadiz. Included in the capitulation of Valencia, he was made prisoner and confined in Beaune. He contrived to make his escape, returned to Prussia and entered the staff of the Prussian army. After the peace he was made general and was sent to the Congress of Vienna. He again took part in the campaign of 1815. Later on he filled some important posts in the administration and obtained various commands. He died in 1843.

sirable. It could be sent to the various legations in Paris and through those of France in other countries.

We also think it would make a good impression to continue payment to those foreign officers, who have received a brevet of pension, with the decoration.

From time immemorial, England has always had a vast number of foreign military pensioners. She has thus made many friends. If France continues these pensions, however reduced, to the Poles, the Germans, and the Italians, she will attach valuable men to herself and thereby gain partisans, of whom, by the course of events, she has been deprived.

Such an example of fairness and generosity will greatly influence the success of the demands which many French military men have still to make from abroad.

We entreat you, M. le Comte, to take the king's commands on this matter, and to make them known to us, so that we may be in a position to answer the questions addressed to us.
Be pleased to accept. . . .

NO. 27.—THE PRINCE DE TALLEYRAND TO KING LOUIS XVIII.

VIENNA, *Feb.* 15, 1815.

SIRE,
Lord Castlereagh leaves to-day, the 15th, and although he will rest every night, he expects to arrive in Paris the eighth day after his departure. He will remain there the following day, so as to reach London on the 1st or 2nd of March.

The fate of the Duchy of Warsaw, that of Saxony, that which is here known as the reconstruction of the Prussian monarchy, the additions given to Hanover, the circumscription of the United Provinces, which will now bear the title of the Netherlands, are all matters completely settled. These were the most difficult points, and the only ones likely to bring about war. Lord Castlereagh therefore bears to England the news, that peace will be preserved. Saxony will retain about 1,300,000 souls. The king, to whom a courier has been despatched, will be after the end of this month, not at Presburg (I represented that the choice of that place was rather like banishment) but at Brünn, on the road to Vienna, to which place nothing will prevent his going, as soon as he has consented to the cession agreed upon by the powers.

The Duchy of Luxembourg, together with Limburg, and some adjoining territories have been given to the Prince of

Orange, as an indemnity for his ancient hereditary lands, which he has ceded to Prussia, and the latter does not approach our frontier anywhere, which I think your Majesty considers very important.[1]

The Duchy of Luxembourg in other respects remains German, and the fortress of Luxembourg will be a federal one.

The retrocessions demanded by Austria from Bavaria, and the equivalents to be given back to the latter, are the most important, and indeed the only important, matters as regards territorial arrangements still to be settled in Germany. The two courts each claim our support ; the one wants to concede nothing for which she does not get an equivalent, and will not give up those things which the other specially desires. We, from different motives, have an almost equal interest in treating both with consideration, which makes arbitration a very delicate matter. Nevertheless I trust, that whatever may be the difficulties that arise, they will not be beyond our powers. As to the territorial arrangements in Italy, the commission charged with the preparation of a scheme for them, has proposed to give back to the Queen of Etruria, Parma, Placentia, and Guastalla, with legations at the Papal court, and to give Lucca, the Precidios,[2] the sovereignty of Piombino, and the reversion of the island of Elba to the Grand Duke of Tuscany.[3] The Archduchess Marie Louise would only receive a pension from Tuscany, and some fiefs formerly held by the German Empire, and now belonging to the Grand Duke of Tuscany, to whom they were given by the Imperial Diet as part of an indemnity. These fiefs, situated in Bohemia, bring in a revenue of 400,000 florins.

This scheme was brought forward through our influence, and met with approval for two reasons ; the first, because it diminished the number of small sovereigns in Italy ; the second and most important, because it removed the son of the arch-duchess and took all prospect of a sovereignty from him.

Austria has been more than a month without coming to a decision. The emperor has at last resolved to restore the two

---

[1] See the treaty of May 31, 1815, concluded between the Netherlands on one part and Great Britain, Austria, Prussia, and Russia on the other, which definitely constituted the new kingdom according to the decision arrived at by the Congress.

[2] Under this name was designated that part of the Tuscan littoral which Philip II., King of Spain, had reserved for himself when he abandoned Sienna and its territory to the Florentines. This coast-line extended from the mouth of the Ombrone to the Roman frontier. In 1801 it was ceded to France, which gave it to the King of Etruria. In 1814 it remained with Tuscany.

[3] Ferdinand, Archduke of Austria (1769-1824) son of the Emperor Leopold, created Grand Duke of Tuscany in 1791, deposed in 1799, Elector of Salzburg in 1803, Grand Duke of Wurzburg in 1805, reinstated in his Tuscan states in 1844.

duchies to the Queen of Etruria ; he could not in fairness, he said, retain for himself and his heirs, one of the states belonging to the House of Bourbon, with whom it was both his wish and his interest to remain on good terms. But knowing that his daughter made a point of having an independent establishment, he thought of Lucca, and has charged his minister to negotiate this affair with the archduchess, giving him instructions which contained the arguments he was to use for this purpose.

M. de Metternich has therefore made a counter-project, according to the wishes of the emperor, which he has transmitted to us ; and which is almost completely acceptable to us ; as the son of the archduchess is not named therein, and the reversion of Lucca falls to Austria or Tuscany. Although we may yet have several objections to raise, I believe, from my conversation with M. de Metternich on the subject, that he will give in to them.

This counter project declares :

> That the duchies shall be restored to the Queen of Etruria, with the exception of Placentia and a district round the town, containing a population of 30,000 souls.
> That Lucca shall be given to the archduchess for her life only, with two pensions, one from Austria, the other from France ;
> That Austria shall receive absolutely :
>> 1. Placentia and the surrounding district above-named.
>> 2. That part of Mantua which lies on the bank of the Po.
>> 3. The Valtelline.
>> 4. Lucca, after the archduchess.
>> 5. Lastly, the Imperial fiefs ; as much to compensate to the State of Parma for the town and country round Placentia, as by way of exchange.

The propositions to levy a pension on France as a compensation for matters by which she will gain nothing ; to make Lucca revertible to the Austrian monarchy ; and to place at the disposition of Austria the Imperial fiefs (even those which are inclosed in the neighbouring states) were almost equally inadmissible, and this M. de Metternich was all but prepared to admit.

There would have been less objection to surrendering to Austria that part of Mantua which is on the right bank of the Po, or even to abandoning Placentia, which, according to what General Ricard told us, is, from its actual situation and the present position of Italy, of very little real importance.

The Valtelline is no longer as it was formerly, indispensable to Austria's communication with Lombardy, and therefore, unimportant to take away from her. Switzerland, to whom it formerly belonged, has reclaimed it, it has been promised to her, and the Emperor of Russia, as I shall have occasion later to tell your Majesty, seems to make it a point that it should be given up to her.

It was before he had been to see the archduchess, that M. de Metternich presented his counter-project, and discussed it with me. His great conceit and excessive levity prevented his foreseeing that it could not be a complete success. But at the very first word the Archduchess Marie Louise did not seem satisfied about Lucca, nor even to care about this principality, where, she said, she would not care to live as long as Napoleon was in the island of Elba. She wants, or rather her councillors want, rights equal with those accorded her by the treaty of April 11. She does not ask to keep Parma but she wishes for an equivalent, or something approaching to it. There would be no other way of satisfying her but to give her the legations, at the same time assuring the reversion to the Holy See. But the court of Rome, which cannot even reconcile herself to the idea that she has lost Avignon, would exclaim at this, and might even go so far as to have recourse to arms, which would compromise her greatly. M. de Metternich has asked for three days to make up his mind as to taking either one[1] side or the other, after which he will give me an answer.

These difficulties once removed, there will be nothing more of importance except the report on the Italian question, to which I shall come presently.

The arrangements respecting the free navigation of rivers are as yet, only in embryo, but the basis has been agreed upon, and this will assure all the advantages to commerce that European industry could demand, and to France especially those which the possession of Belgium would secure to her, by the navigation of the Scheldt.

Lastly, the abolition of the slave-trade, a matter regarded by the English with a passion bordering[2] on frenzy, has been agreed to by the only two nations who had not, as yet, relinquished it.

Lord Castlereagh is therefore sufficiently armed against all the attacks of the opposition, and carries with him everything needed to flatter public opinion.

But as I took pains to point out to him, the ministers of a representative government must not only satisfy the popular

---

[1] Text : as translated.   Var.: " *ce* parti " = " this side."
[2] Text : as translated.   Var.: " *portée* " = " carried."

party, but they must also satisfy the government. "This," I said, "you can only do if you work together with us and according to our [1] views, in the affairs of Naples."

I have employed the last eight days in trying to bring him to face this question, and if I have not succeeded in making him take our side, which he does not feel at liberty to do, I have at least made him desire almost as earnestly as ourselves, the expulsion of Murat, and he has gone away determined to do his utmost to get his government to consent to this. Two things perplex him : the one how to pronounce against Murat without seeming to violate the promises given him [2] (this is what Lord Castlereagh calls not compromising his character), the other, to decide on the means necessary to insure success in case of resistance, without compromising the interests or wounding the prejudices and exciting the fears of any one. He has promised that three days after his arrival in London, he will despatch a courier with the decisions of his court, and imbued as he is with my [3] reasons, he hopes this will be favourable. What I wish is, that without entering into discussions, which always weaken the point at issue, Lord Wellington should be authorized to declare that his court recognizes Ferdinand IV. as King of the Two Sicilies. I pray your Majesty to speak to Lord Castlereagh [4] in this spirit when he comes to Paris. During the latter part of his stay in Vienna he showed himself very willing to follow the line I urged upon him. He spoke against Murat to the Emperor of Russia, whom he saw with the Duke of Wellington. He told the Emperor of Austria, " Russia is your natural enemy. Prussia is devoted to Russia. You cannot count upon any power on the Continent except France ; it is your interest therefore to be friends with the House of Bourbon, and this you cannot be until Murat [5] is expelled."

The Emperor of Austria replied : " I fully admit the truth of what you say."

Finally, when he and Lord Wellington went together to M. de Metternich, he said, " You will have a very hot discussion over the affairs of Naples. Do not imagine you can escape it. This business will, I warn you, be brought before the congress. Take your measures accordingly, and, if necessary, send troops into Italy."

They each told me separately, that this declaration threw M.

---

[1] Text : as translated. Var.: "*un autre* sens' = " another view."

[2] It will be remembered that by the treaty of January 11, 1814, Austria had guaranteed the throne of Naples to Murat. England had recognized this treaty.

[3] Text : as translated. Var.: "*nos*" = " our."

[4] Text : as translated. Var.: "lui " = " him."

[5] Text : as translated. Var.: "*sans* que " = " unless."

de Metternich into *un grand abattement :* these are their words, and your Majesty will the better understand M. de Metternich's despondency when you have read the secret articles of the treaty he made with Murat, and of which I have the honour to send you herewith a copy. That, under such circumstances, he should have guaranteed him the kingdom of Naples one can easily conceive. But that he should have carried degradation to such a point, as to insert a clause in this treaty, by which Murat *generously renounces his right to the kingdom of Sicily and guarantees that kingdom to Ferdinand IV.*, is something almost beyond belief, even when it is proved.[1]

Your Majesty will no doubt learn with some little surprise that the principle of legitimacy enters but little into the calculations of Lord Castlereagh or even those of the Duke of Wellington as regards Murat. It is a principle which does not affect them greatly and which they hardly seem to understand. With Murat, it is the man, not the usurper, whom they detest. The principles pursued by the English in India have deprived them of any exact ideas of[2] fairness. Nothing made such an impression on Lord Castlereagh, who wants peace above all things, as my declaration to him that peace was impossible if Murat was not expelled, seeing that his remaining on the throne of Naples is incompatible with the existence of the House of Bourbon.

I also had an interview with the Emperor of Russia last Monday morning, the 13th instant. I only wished to see him about Naples, and remind him as to the promises he had given me in this matter. But he took the opportunity to speak about many other things of which I shall have to inform your Majesty. I pray that your Majesty will permit me to relate them in the form of a dialogue as I have often done before in other letters.

I began by telling the emperor that I had for some time forborne to intrude upon him, in order not to interfere either

---

[1] The actual treaty of alliance signed January 11, 1814, between Austria and Naples, was followed by various secret articles of which the following is an analysis :

The Emperor of Austria undertakes to obtain in favour of his Majesty King Joachim Napoleon and his descendants a formal act of renunciation from his Majesty the King of Sicily, himself and his heirs in perpetuity, of all his claims to the kingdom of Naples. This renunciation shall be recognized and guaranteed to his Majesty the King of Naples, by his Majesty the Emperor of Austria, and his Imperial . Majesty will do his utmost to obtain the same recognition and guarantee from the other allied powers.

On his part, the King of Naples promised to guarantee Sicily to King Ferdinand, and undertook to pay him an indemnity (Art. I.).

The Emperor of Austria likewise guaranteed to the King of Naples a good military frontier in the north (Art. IV.). An additional article promised him an increase of four hundred thousand souls taken from the Roman States.

[2] Text : as translated. Var.: " *sur* la " = " respecting."

with his business or his pleasures; but that as the carnival had put an end to the latter, and as the former had been settled, I was now anxious to see him. I added that even the congress had only one important matter still to decide.

"You wish to speak of the Neapolitan affairs?"

"Yes, sire," and I reminded him that he had promised me his support.

"But you must help me."

"We have done so as far as matters depended on us. Your Majesty knows that, as it was impossible to attempt the complete re-establishment of the kingdom of Poland, we have not been, on account of these special arrangements, in opposition to your views, and your Majesty has surely not forgotten that at the beginning of the congress, the English were very adverse on the question."

"How about the affairs of Switzerland?"

"I am not aware that in Swiss matters we have ever been in opposition to your Majesty. We were desired to do our very utmost to allay irritation. I do not know how far we have succeeded in this, but it is all we have aimed at. The Bernese were the most incensed, for they had lost the most, and therefore had more to reclaim. An indemnity was offered them, which they considered quite insufficient; we have induced them to be satisfied with it. I only know that they ask for the bishopric of Basle absolutely, and that they are quite determined to accept nothing less."

"And what will you do for Genoa?"

"Nothing, sire."

"Oh!" in a surprised and reproachful tone.

"It is impossible for us to do anything. The king will never give up anything French."

"Could nothing be obtained from Sardinia?"

"I cannot possibly say."

"Why did you cede the Valtelline to Austria?" [1]

"On this point, sire, nothing has yet been decided. The affairs of Austria having been so badly managed. . . . ."

"It is her own fault," said the emperor, "why does she not employ clever men?"

"Austria having been induced to make many sacrifices, which must have cost her a good deal, I thought it only fair,

[1] The Valtelline, formerly an imperial fief, had in former times been given to the bishops of Coire. These had ceded it to the Grisons in 1530, which for a long time had to defend it against Spain. Napoleon joined this district to the kingdom of Italy and formed it into the department of the Adda. In 1814 it was given to Austria, which in 1859 ceded it to Piedmont together with Lombardy.

especially in matters of small importance, to do what would be agreeable to her."

"The Valtelline formed part of Switzerland, and it had been promised to be given back to her."

"The Valtelline has been separated from Switzerland for more than eighteen years; she never knew the rule under which your Majesty would replace her. To give her back to the Grisons, to which she formerly belonged, would be to make her very unhappy. It therefore seems most suitable to me to form [1] her into a separate canton, if Austria does not obtain her."

"That can be arranged; and now what are you doing for Prince Eugene?"

"Prince Eugene is a French subject, and as such has nothing to demand. But he is the King of Bavaria's son-in-law; having become so, in consequence of the position to which France has attained, and of the influence she possesses, it is therefore only fair that France should endeavour to secure for him what, owing to this alliance, it is only reasonable and possible that he should have. We therefore are desirous of doing something for him. We wish him to become a dependent prince of the House of Bavaria, and that in consequence of this, the king's share in the distribution of the disposable territories should be a larger one."

"Why not give him a sovereignty?"

"Sire, his marriage with a Bavarian princess is not sufficient ground for so doing. Prince Radziwill is the King of Prussia's brother-in-law, but he has no sovereignty." [2]

"But why not give him Deux Ponts for instance? It would be a very trifling matter."

"I beg your Majesty's pardon. The Duchy of Deux Ponts has always been looked upon as something considerable; besides which, hardly enough disposable land remains to fulfil the engagements already entered into."

"And the marriage?"

"The king has done me the honour to inform me that he still earnestly desires it."

"And so do I," replied the emperor, "and my mother does the same. She speaks about it in her last letters to me."

"The king," I answered, "awaiting a reply from your

---

[1] Text: as translated. Var.: "*faire*" = "make."
[2] There is an error here. Prince Antoine-Henry de Radziwill, Governor of the Grand Duchy of Posen, had married in 1796 the Princess Frederica-Dorothea-Louise, daughter of Ferdinand, Prince of Prussia, and grand-daughter of King Frederic-William I. He was therefore by marriage cousin-german to King Frederic-William III.

Majesty, has refused several other proposals that have been made to him."

" I also have refused one.[1] The King of Spain asked my sister in marriage, but being informed that she would require to have her own private ecclesiastical establishment, and that this was a necessary condition, he withdrew his demand."

" The conduct of his Catholic Majesty in this matter will show you in what way his most Christian Majesty would be obliged to act. *The king thought it would be better first to finish the affairs of the congress, before treating of this matter.*"[2]

" I should, however, like to know where I am."

" Sire, the last orders I received were in conformity with what General Pozzo told your Majesty."

" Why do you not carry out the treaty of April 11th ? "

" Having been absent from Paris for five months, I do not know what has been done in this matter."

" The treaty has not been carried out and we must insist on its fulfilment. This is a point of honour with us ; we could on no account depart from it. The Emperor of Austria is as anxious as I am about it, and is very much offended that it is not carried out."

" Sire, I will not fail to report what your Majesty[3] has told me. But I must bring to your Majesty's notice[4] that owing to the agitation prevailing in the countries bordering on France, especially Italy, there might be some danger, if means for intrigue were furnished to persons who might be only too ready to make use of them."[5]

Finally we returned to Murat. I briefly recapitulated all the legitimate, moral, and beneficial reasons which ought to combine Europe against him. I pointed out the difference between his position and that of Bernadotte, which the emperor quite realized ; and in support of what I had said, I quoted the *Almanach Royal,* which I had just received. He begged me to send it to him, adding : " What you tell me has given me the greatest pleasure. I feared the contrary, and Bernadotte dreaded it even more than I."

Thereupon the emperor spoke of Murat with the greatest contempt. " He is," said he, " a scoundrel who has betrayed us ; but," he added, " whenever I take up a thing, I always like to be

---

[1] Text : as translated. Var.: " *mais j'ai été en même temps refusé,*" = " but I at the same time have been refused."

[2] Suppressed in the text of the archives.

[3] Text : " Votre Majestie me fait." Var.: " Vous me faites " = " you do me."

[4] Text : " Dois faire observer." Var.: ' dois observer."

[5] These last phrases refer to the Emperor Napoleon, to whom the French government had not paid the moneys as agreed by the treaty of April 11, 1814.

sure of bringing it to a satisfactory conclusion.   If Murat resists,
he must be driven out.   I have spoken about this [1] to the Duke
of Wellington.   He thinks it would require a very large muster
of troops, and that when it came to a question of embarkation,
great difficulties would arise."

I answered that I did not want troops (for I know they
would have been refused me) but only one line, a single line,
inserted in the future treaty, and that France and Spain would
undertake the rest ; upon which the emperor replied, "You may
count upon my support."

During the whole course of this conversation he [2] was very
distant, but on the whole I was rather satisfied than dissatisfied
with him.

Lord Castlereagh has spoken to me with great warmth
respecting the treaty of April 11th, and will, I have no doubt,
also speak of it to your Majesty.   The matter has been revived
again lately, and is now in every one's mouth.   I must inform
your Majesty that it often crops up, and in a very unpleasant
manner.   It has sensibly influenced the question of the *Mont
de Milan*,[3] which interests so many of your Majesty's subjects
and servants.

It has therefore occurred to me that your Majesty might
extricate yourself from whatever is difficult of fulfilment in the
treaty of April 11th, by coming to some understanding with
England.

During the first days of my stay here, Lord Castlereagh
expressed a wish to offer France some compensation if she
would at once renounce the slave-trade.   Pecuniary compensations are, as a rule, easier for England than any others.   I then
thought it advisable to defer this proposal without actually
refusing it, and reserve it for future consideration.

Latterly, in speaking of Murat, and the provision it would
be indispensable to make him, if (Europe having pronounced
against him), he submits to her decision, Lord Castlereagh did
not hesitate to say that England would willingly undertake
to assure an income to Murat, by assigning him a sum in the
English funds, if France consented to renounce the slave-
trade.   If such an arrangement were deemed practicable, I have
no doubt but that it would be easy to include the pensions
stipulated for by the treaty of April 11th, in the payments
provided for by England.

This arrangement, owing to the mania of the English for the

[1] Text : as translated.   Var.: "*a-t-il ajouté*" = "he added."
[2] Text : as translated.   Var.: "*l'Empereur* a été froid" = "the Emperor was very
distant."
[3] A Life Insurance Office instituted by Napoleon.

abolition of the slave-trade, would certainly have the advantage of drawing England into a closer alliance with our cause in Naples, and inducing her to second our efforts there.

It now remains to be seen whether, in the present state of her colonies, France, in renouncing the slave-trade for the four years and three months it has still to run, would make a greater or less sacrifice than the actual good to be hoped for from the arrangement which I have just mentioned. I therefore venture to entreat your Majesty to examine this question closely, so as to make your intentions on this point known to Lord Castlereagh, who will probably not fail to speak to your Majesty about it.

I could have wished that the treaty of January 3rd, (which, the congress once ended, will be void) might have been prolonged to some more or less distant date, if only by a mutual declaration. But there were some difficulties about this, as the character of M. de Metternich does not inspire much confidence. Lord Castlereagh assured me, however, that when the treaty expires, the spirit which dictated it will survive. He is, above all things, anxious not to give offence to the other continental powers, but this does not prevent his wishing to establish intimate relations between the two governments, and that they should not cease in their mutual desire for the preservation of peace. In a word, he has left Vienna with views I cannot but praise, and in which he will be confirmed by what he hears from your Majesty's own lips.

I perceive that my letter is somewhat voluminous, and I fear lest your Majesty may find it too long for all that it contains. But I would rather run the risk of being too lengthy than suppress any details which your Majesty might consider necessary.

By the next courier, I shall have the honour to forward the treaties of the coalition, which I have succeeded in obtaining. When your Majesty has examined them, I would beg you to send them to M. de Jaucourt, in order that they may be deposited in the Foreign Office.

The departure of General Pozzo has again been talked of.[1]

I have the honour to be. . . .

NO. 23.—KING LOUIS XVIII. TO THE PRINCE DE TALLEYRAND.

PARIS, *February 18th,* 1815.

MON COUSIN,

I have received your letter No. 25,[2] and have read it with much satisfaction. I should certainly have preferred that

---

[1] Text: as translated. Var.: "On a reparlé" = "They have spoken again."
[2] Var.: "No. 26."

the King of Saxony should keep his entire kingdom, but I never expected it, and I consider it quite a miracle, seeing how little support we received, that we were enabled to secure to him what is left.   On one point I have great pleasure in expressing to you my satisfaction.   That is, that Prussia has got neither Luxembourg nor Mayence.   Such near neighbourhood would have been very much opposed to the future peace of France.   Let us leave the sword in its scabbard.   General Ricard's journey will have been useless, but it will have proved to my allies my eagerness to be quite straight with them.

Lord Wellington's conduct touches [1] but does not surprise me ; he is a loyal man ; your remarks upon what he said are perfectly true.

I expect, equally with yourself, difficulties in the Neapolitan affair, but we must overcome them.   Setting aside all sentiment, Murat's existence becomes every day more dangerous.   Bernadotte's case is a peculiar one, but the principle once allowed, you must admit the consequences.

The papers are full of the admirable conduct of the governor (whose name I cannot at this moment recollect) of the fortress of Königstein.[2]   I should like to make him a Commander of the Legion of Honour ; but before doing so, I want to know, first if the facts are true ; secondly, would the King of Saxony like my giving him this decoration ; I desire you to ascertain these two points.   Whereupon I pray God may have you, my cousin, in His safe and holy keeping.

LOUIS.

No. 28.—The Prince de Talleyrand to King Louis XVIII.

VIENNA, February 20th, 1815.

SIRE,

I have the honour to send your Majesty the documents mentioned in my last despatch.   Even if they are not a complete collection of the treaties entered into by the allied powers, they are at least the most important ones : they are :—

---

[1] Text : as translated.   Var.: "à Vienne"= "at Vienna."

[2] The *Moniteurs* of the 6th and 10th February, 1815, give an account of the fortress of Königstein.   It is probable that the fact to which the king alludes is the one reported in the following terms on the 10th February : "The fortress of Königstein, situated about three leagues from the Bohemian frontier, plays just now as prominent a part as during the Seven Years' War.   The great allied powers had already recognized its neutrality at the time that Buonaparte's armies still occupied these countries. General de Zeschau gave up his command at this time to escape the proposals made to him and which compromised his honour."

A convention made in the form [1] of a memorandum, between Austria and Russia on the 29th March, 1813, and called the Convention of Kalisch. [2]

The treaty of peace and alliance between Russia and Prussia. This has often been spoken of as the treaty of Kalisch, because it was negotiated, and, as it seems, also drafted there. But it was signed at Breslau on the 26th February, 1813. [3]

The treaty of Reichenbach, in the same year, and dated June 27, between Austria, Russia, and Prussia.

The treaty of Töplitz of September 9, between the same powers, together with the secret articles of this treaty.

Lastly, that of Chaumont, which was to perpetuate the alliance against France for twenty years after the war, which it was proposed to renew before the expiration of that time, and which tended to render that coalition perpetual. This the treaty of January 3 has dissolved.

It may interest your Majesty to look over these various documents. In them you will find an explanation of some of the difficulties we have had to contend against ; also the reason of the embarrassment experienced by the allies themselves, especially Austria, from not having made, when it entirely depended on herself, such stipulations as the most ordinary common sense ought to have made her see were indispensable.

I pray your Majesty to have the kindness, after having read these documents, to send them to M. le Comte de Jaucourt, for safe custody at the Foreign Office.

I have already had the honour to announce to your Majesty that the Kings of Bavaria and Hanover had agreed to the treaty of alliance of the 3rd January. I wished to send them their deed of agreement, at the same time as that for Holland ; but as this latter is not yet finished, and the Prince de Wrède has urged on me the exchange of the ratifications with that of Bavaria, I have the honour to forward them to-day to your Majesty. I also send duplicates of the deeds of agreement which I have

---

[1] Text : as translated. Var.: "forment" = "form."

[2] There is apparently some confusion here. There never was a Convention of Kalisch on March 29, 1813, between Austria and Russia. Besides at that time Austria was still the ally of France. Perhaps M. de Talleyrand meant to speak of the Convention signed on March 19, at Breslau, between Russia and Prussia, to regulate the manner of occupying the countries of the Rhine Confederation as well as their administration.

[3] The treaty of alliance between Russia and Prussia was signed at Breslau on February 27, and not on the 26th, by M. de Hardenberg, and on February 28 at Kalisch, by Prince Koutousoff. The treaty of Rechenbach was signed between England and Prussia on June 14, and not on the 25th. Austria took no part in it then. On the contrary she adhered to the treaty of Töplitz of September 9. after the rupture of the Congress of Prague.

signed.   These two last deeds are those for ratification by your Majesty.   I pray you to have the goodness to send them to M. le Comte de Jaucourt, that he may, if your Majesty thinks fit, prepare the ratifications.

A courier just arrived, brings me the letter of the 11th of this month, with which your Majesty has honoured me.

I shall await with great impatience the next, in which your Majesty will, I hope, inform me of the result of your interviews with Lord Castlereagh.   I should like the paragraph about Naples to be of such a nature that it may be shown to M. de Metternich, it cannot be too positive.

I have the honour to be. . . . .

No. 29.—The Prince de Talleyrand to King Louis XVIII.

Vienna, *February* 24, 1815.

Sire,

Joachim's minister here,[1] has received a complete memorandum, with instructions to send it to me after having shown it to M. de Metternich, to whom he has in fact communicated it.

The object of this memorandum is to ask for an explanation of certain steps which he says I have taken against him at the congress, and to demand whether your Majesty considers that you are at peace with him or not.   Joachim's minister feeling sure that this memorandum was written and ordered to be sent to me in consequence of some statements he himself had made, on the supposition that no arrangement would be arrived at respecting Saxony, and that war would break out, thought he could not now make use of it (this supposition having fallen through) without compromising his master's interests rather than serving him.   He has therefore taken upon himself to suppress the memorandum and it is not to be sent to me.

I heard all these details from the Duke of Wellington and consulted with him as to what course should be taken with regard to the communication M. de Metternich had received respecting the note.   We both agreed that M. de Metternich must be persuaded to utilise it, in order to send a declaration to me as well as to the Duc de Campo-Chiaro, to the effect that Austria

---

[1] This was the Duc de Campo-Chiaro, who was first an officer in the Neapolitan army, then Councillor of State and Master of the King's Household, under King Joseph, and subsequently Minister of Police under Murat.   He was at various times charged with diplomatic missions.   He was sent to Vienna in 1814, but was not recognized.   After the restoration he was removed from office, became for a short time Minister of Foreign Affairs, but was obliged soon after to retire in 1820.

will not permit any foreign troops to pass through her territory, and to support this declaration by recalling the troops now on the frontiers of Poland and Saxony[1] and sending them to Italy.

The Duke of Wellington spoke in the same sense to M. de Metternich, whom I afterwards saw and to whom I expressed myself in similar terms. The result is that to-day the Emperor of Austria has ordered the despatch of 150,000 men to Italy, and that the declaration mentioned above will be sent to us to-morrow.

Austria's principal pretext for putting off Neapolitan affairs was that she was not ready and that she feared Murat might bring about a revolution in Italy. This objection was not without weight and made some impression on the English and the Russians, but it will fall to the ground the moment the Austrians have a considerable force in Italy.

For this we are indebted to Joachim's memorandum, which makes us look upon that incident as a very happy one.

The fact of the failure[2] of this memorandum seeing that it was both insulting and contrary to its author's interests, since the affairs of Saxony have been arranged, proves that we may congratulate ourselves on this having occurred; in fact, but for this, Austria would have been unable to send a large force into Italy. If I can obtain a copy of the memorandum from M. de Metternich, I will have the honour to forward it to your Majesty.

In this state of affairs, does not your Majesty consider that the assembly of troops in the south of France under any pretext except the real one, might be advantageous?

Swiss affairs will in all probability be completed in a few days, with the exception of one point, that of the Valtelline which it seems decided to leave unsettled, and always excepting the consent of the cantons to the proposals made to them. For it was decided to propose to them what was considered most expedient, before insisting on it.

Austria and Bavaria are in negotiation respecting the retrocession, demanded by Austria, of territory occupied by Bavaria, and a compensation to be given to the latter. As these two powers are far from coming to an understanding, it has been suggested to ask France and England to mediate. But it seems to me that by allowing England to have the sole honour of this mediation, France will be able to influence the arrangements without compromising herself with either of those two powers whom it is equally her interest to conciliate.

[1] Suppressed in the text of the archives.
[2] Text: as translated. Var. : "non remise" = "non-delivery."

M. de Metternich has come to ask me with an air of great mystery to let Italian affairs stand over till the 5th or 6th of March, by which time he fancies I shall have received the commands which your Majesty may be pleased to send me after having seen Lord Castlereagh.

Although unable to discern the motive for this request, I could not well refuse it.[1] But on the other hand I see inconveniences must arise, inasmuch as Austria has arranged all that concerns her interests outside of Italy, and that the affairs of that country, which really are the most important to us, will remain exposed, to chance and we ourselves to all the difficulties Austria may place in our way. I therefore do not want Bavarian matters to be concluded too quickly. Thus, though my impatience to be once again near your Majesty after such a long absence, needs not the spur of the *ennui* with which Vienna seems to be affected since the opening of the congress, I find myself obliged not to hurry matters just now; on the contrary to retard all action as much as I can, and to wait.

I attach to this letter the deed of agreement with Holland, which I have just signed. I pray your Majesty after having ratified the deed, to order its return to me by M. le Comte de Jaucourt.

I have the honour to be . . . . .

No. 4.—LE COMTE DE BLACAS D'AULPS TO PRINCE TALLEYRAND.[2]

PARIS, *February* 25, 1815.

PRINCE,

The king has received your despatch No. 27, but his Majesty having at present a rather severe attack of gout defers replying to you until he has seen Lord Castlereagh whom we expect at any moment.

[1] This is the explanation of the mysterious conduct of M. de Metternich. Towards the middle of February the Congress were all agreed on the question of Parma. That duchy was to return to the ancient dynasty. Marie-Louise was to get the duchy of Lucca, which at her death was to be re-united to Tuscany. But the empress positively refused to take Lucca, and insisted on having Parma. Metternich was forced to yield to her wishes. He therefore resolved to give Parma to the empress and to indemnify the Queen of Etruria by means of Lucca and some pensions. But foreseeing violent opposition on the part of Talleyrand whose personal views obliged him to hold very strong opinions on questions of legitimacy, he preferred addressing himself to Louis XVIII. direct. Lord Castlereagh, who was returning to London, undertook the charge of this negotiation on his way through Paris. It was for this reason that M. de Metternich asked for a few days' respite to give the English minister time for an interview. (See what the king says about his interview with Lord Castlereagh in his letter of March 3.)

[2] This letter is not to be found in M. Pallain's collection.

I do not however like the courier to leave without sending you news of the king. The attack of gout came on rather mildly, and for the last few days his Majesty has already felt better. After what you have said as to the state of the negotiations, it is very evident that you are not by any means near the end of your efforts. The consent of the King of Saxony, notwithstanding the subtraction of thirty thousand souls, will not, I hope, retard the settlement of this great question : that of Naples presents many other difficulties, which would be still more formidable, but for the resolute firmness to which you have accustomed the congress, and the useful co-operation afforded by Lord Wellington, who seems greatly disposed to second you, and to combat the prejudices or scruples of M. le Prince de Metternich. The king will leave nothing undone to convey to England through Lord Castlereagh, the most decisive expressions on a subject so closely allied to the interests of all the powers which only seek the consolidation of peace.

As to the abolition of the slave-trade, if it is found necessary to make any concessions on this point, let us at least endeavour to obtain a fair return, by formal engagements on the part of the cabinet of St. James's ; and let us make sure that it will agree to the re-establishment of Ferdinand IV. on the throne of Naples. This is the aim towards which every step must henceforth be taken to further the king's views on a matter which becomes as it were of paramount importance.

Accept Prince. . . . .

BLACAS D'AULPS.

No. 30.—THE PRINCE DE TALLEYRAND TO KING LOUIS XVIII.

VIENNA, *February* 26, 1815.

SIRE,

I have the honour to send your Majesty a copy of M. de Metternich's declaration mentioned in my last despatch, also a copy of the reply I sent him.

Your Majesty will see that this reply is absolutely in accordance with the import of the letter written by me to Lord Castlereagh, in which I said, that in the operations against Murat, we should not pass through Italy.

I could have wished that the declaration of Austria against Murat was more explicit. But it was dangerous to give him a pretext for violent action, as the Austrians are not fully prepared in Italy. Orders have been issued to hurry on the troops. They will have a hundred and fifty thousand men there, and also a reserve of fifty thousand in Carinthia, which will be sufficient to inspire Murat with respect, or stultify his attempts. But as matters move very slowly here, the Prince de Schwarzenberg has asked for a delay of seven weeks to admit of his forces reaching their destination. The memorandum which decided their departure, always seems to me a happy incident. I am going to Presburg to-morrow to visit Madame de Brionne [1] who received the sacraments yesterday and who has asked to see me. I shall be back again on Monday night or Tuesday, and as affairs are still in abeyance they will not suffer in any way from my two days' absence.

General Pozzo leaves for certain on the 1st or 2nd of March, he will be about ten days on the road.

The Emperor of Russia is very busy with the Archduchesss Marie-Louise's affairs. He has had a scheme drawn up by which the legations would be almost entirely taken away from the Pope. In so doing he places himself in opposition to the principles agreed upon between the plenipotentiaries of the great powers. At present his new scheme rests in the portfolio of M. d'Anstett.

I have the honour . . . .

No. 24.—King Louis XVIII. to the Prince de Talleyrand.

PARIS, *March* 3, 1815.

MON COUSIN,

I have received your letters numbered 27 and 28. I did not write to you last week, first because I awaited the arrival of Lord Castlereagh,[2] and afterwards, as is usual when an attack of gout comes on, I was very feverish, which does not conduce to the dictation of a letter.[3]

Lord Castlereagh arrived on Sunday evening, I saw him on Monday and Tuesday, and found him very well disposed to the basis of the Neapolitan matter, but as a minister, some-

---

[1] Louise Julie Constance de Rohan Montauban was born on March 6, 1734. Married October 3, 1748, Louis Charles of Lorraine, Prince of Lambese, Comte de Brionne, became a widow January 28, 1761, and died March 29, 1815, at Presburg. She had welcomed M. de Talleyrand on his first entrance into Parisian society, and he retained the warmest affection for her to the day of her death.

[2] Text: as translated. Var.: "J'attendais *Lord Castlereagh à tout moment* et ensuite parcequ'*ainsi que c'est mon usage*, au commencement *de la goutte, j'ai eu* la fièvre ce qui ne rend pas très apte à dicter" = "I awaited Lord Castlereagh at every moment, and then, as is my habit when gout comes on, I got feverish, which is not conducive to dictation."

[3] The king here makes a mistake, all the rough drafts of his letters written by himself are still in the archives of the Foreign Office at Paris.

what fastidious and very strongly attached to the Vienna cabinet.

After repeating all you had yourself told me he had said to Prince Metternich, he went on to various proposals on which he said he was quite agreed with the Austrian minister. The gist of these propositions is, that the court of Vienna asks nothing better than to co-operate in the expulsion of Murat, "provided" he added "that your Majesty shows as much consideration for the north of Italy, as Austria has manifested for the interest of the south, and that Parma, Placencia, and Guastalla are given to the Archduchess Marie-Louise, the three branches of the house of Bourbon undertaking to indemnify the house of Etruria."[1] I assured him that the state of Parma was an hereditary succession, which had come into my family through Queen Elizabeth Farnese,[2] that neither France, Spain, nor the kingdom of Naples had anything to do with it,[3] and that therefore, setting aside all family interest, justice alone forbids my allowing those to whom this principality belongs to be robbed of it ;[4] but that if Austria insisted on the convention of April 11th as regards the Archduchess Marie-Louise being carried out, I would consent to the Queen of Etruria or rather her son, receiving Lucca and the Presidios as an indemnity, provided that the sovereignty of Parma is recognized as belonging to him, and will revert to him on the death of the Archduchess Marie-Louise. Then Lucca, as well as the Presidios, will be reunited to Tuscany.

---

[1] Var. : "'*Mais,*' *m'a-t-il dit,* '*en cedant pour le sud de l'Italie, elle attend la même complaisance de la part de vôtre Majesté pour la partie du nord, et elle voudrait* que Parme, Plaisance et Guastalla *appartinssent* à l'archiduchesse Marie-Louise et que les *trois cours* de la maison de Bourbon se *chargeassent* d'indemniser la reine d'Etrurie*'" = "'But,' he said to me, 'in ceding thus for the south of Italy, she expects your Majesty to show the same complaisance for the northern part, and she would wish that Parma, Placenzia and Guastalla should belong to the Archduchess Marie Louise, and that the *three courts* of the House of Bourbon should *charge themselves* with indemnifying the Queen of Etruria.'"

[2] The duchy of Parma had belonged ever since 154 to the family of Farnese. The male line died out in 1731. Elizabeth, the niece of the last duke, married to Phillip V., King of Spain (the first Bourbon king), got this duchy presented to her son Don Carlos. The treaties of the quadruple alliance (1781), the treaty of Vienna, between France and Austria (1725), and the treaty of Seville, between France and England (1729), assured him the possession of it. Duke Charles having been called to the throne of Naples, the duchy of Parma passed on to Austria (treaty of Vienna, 1736). The treaty of Aix-la-Chapelle (1748) returned the duchy to Don Phillip, the second son of Phillip V. and Elizabeth Farnese. In this way the duchy of Parma returned finally to the House of Bourbon.

[3] Var. : "que cela n'avait rien de commune avec," etc = "that this had nothing in common with."

[4] Var. : "*exproprier une branche de ma famille*" = "dispossess one branch of my family."

He did not seem disinclined [1] to this arrangement, which after all is of greater interest to Austria [2] than to England.

Yesterday I saw Baron Vincent, who brought a special and secret message for me. He gave me a confidential memorandum on the principal point which related to Parma, concerning which I have just written to you, and on which head he told me his instructions were very precise and imperative. I replied by a counter-project in the same sense as my answer to Lord Castlereagh, and we parted, each maintaining his own ground.[3] Nevertheless I believe it will not be difficult to arrange this matter. M. de Vincent told me that after this preliminary overture, Prince Metternich would prefer to carry on the negotiations in Vienna,[4] but entirely between you and himself, and without the presence of any other member of the French legation. Not seeing any objection [5] to this I promised that it should be so ; and I will send you by the first courier the two documents [6] of which I speak, with a few words [7] of instruction.

Your conversation [8] with the Emperor of Russia has interested me much, although his part of it is somewhat volatile and erratic. I am however thoroughly satisfied with the way in which you spoke to him.

I must not forget [9] to tell you that Lord Castlereagh insisted strongly on two points when I saw him ; first on the article of the treaty which assures the payment of the English debt ; second on the fulfilment of the convention of April 11th respecting the Buonaparte family (a matter to which I will revert in my next letter). He did not say a word about the slave-trade.

My gout is better, I am in hopes that this attack will not last so long as usual. Whereupon I pray God may have you, my cousin, in His safe and holy keeping.

LOUIS.

---

[1] Var.: "*Il ne m'a paru du tout éloigné*" = "he did not seem at all disinclined."

[2] Var. : "*tiens plus à l'Autriche qu'à*" = "is more to Austria than to."

[3] Var. : "nous nous sommes séparés *chacun sur son* terrain, mais je crois" = "we parted, each on his own ground, but I think."

[4] Var. : "*mais il m'a dit* qu'après cette première ouverture *faite à moi personellement*, M. de Metternich désirait que la négociation *continuât* à Vienne" = "but he said to me, that after this first overture, made to me personally, M. de Metternich wished the negotiation to be continued at Vienna."

[5] Var. : "*N'y voyant pas de difficultés*" = "not seeing any difficulties in this."

[6] Var. : "*copie des deux pièces*" = "a copy of the two documents."

[7] Var. : "*Notes*" = "Memorandums."

[8] Var. : "*Je vous dirai en peu de mots que* votre conversation" = "I will tell you in a few words that your conversation."

[9] Var. : "*encore* oublier" = "also forget."

P.S.—I have just received your letter numbered 29. I think [1] with you that the incident of Murat's memorandum not having been delivered is very satisfactory. You will find in this letter and will receive further detailed in the next, the key to the mysterious request made to you by M. de Metternich.

No. 30.—THE AMBASSADORS OF THE KING AT THE CONGRESS TO THE MINISTER OF FOREIGN AFFAIRS AT PARIS.

VIENNA, *March* 3, 1815.

MONSIEUR LE COMTE,

By the fifth article of the treaty of Paris, the signatory powers were bound to proceed in future Congress to frame laws for the navigation of the Rhine, equally favourable to the commerce of all nations. The special commission charged with this part of the negotiations has adopted a basis in conformity with the treaty of Paris, and has decided among other questions of importance to French commerce, that the tariffs should not be increased, and that the powers should each separately contribute towards the revenue accruing from the dues, a sum proportionate to the distance traversed by the river through their respective territories. France, which only possesses one bank, will have to share with the opposite bank that portion of the revenue which will devolve on her.

This however was not the most difficult question to decide. The right to participate in the administration of the dues was denied to France, and she was only to send a French delegate to the central commission, which is to be charged with that administration. This was a subject of the hottest discussion, but the firmness and constancy which have won success for the king's embassy in matters of much greater importance, have again prospered on this occasion. This is the more satisfactory as the obstacles were difficult to surmount, for in addition to special interests it was necessary to overcome the unfriendly attitude assumed by more than one of the intervening powers towards France in this matter.

It was further agreed that France if she wished, might levy dues in advance, on the navigation between Bâle and Strasburg, and in this respect revert to the convention of 1804 under which dues were only payable from Strasburg to Holland. But although we deemed it best to secure this right for ourselves, it will be well to ascertain whether it would interfere with our trade, and whether it may not favour land transport on the

---

[1] Var. : "considère" = "consider."

German bank, to the detriment of water carriage. We therefore pray you, Monsieur le Comte, to ask the Financial Secretary
of State to consult the Chambers of Commerce of the departments bordering on the Rhine, on this matter. They will be
able to point out how far the measure will be advantageous or
injurious, and whether it will be better to establish the same
regulations as exist on the rest of the river or to give this
portion unlimited licence.

You will find attached hereto, Monsieur le Comte, a memorandum which we beg you will read carefully. The remarks in
it respecting the conduct of a custom-house official are of no
importance, but we thought we ought to accept the proposals
of the *bureaux* of Neubourg and Germersheim, as they put a
stop to an abuse of which the merchants of Strasburg were the
principal victims. We allude to the increase in the tariff of dues
between Strasburg and Mannheim. Formerly there was only
one *bureau*, that of Neubourg, for both towns ; the allies established another at Germersheim. France being no longer possessed
of the territory between Strasburg and Mannheim can only therefore levy dues for that portion of her former territory through
which the Rhine flows. This demand is fair, and we beg you,
M. le Comte, to consult with the Minister of Finance on this
matter as well as on the preceding ones, so as to put in operation
the arrangement between the *bureaux* of Germersheim and
Neubourg dealt with in the memorandum, and apportion the
collection in such a manner, that France and the provisional
directory of customs, shall only receive between them the sum
due by the commerce of Mannheim and Strasburg, in accordance
with the convention of 1804 and proportionate to the distance
traversed by the river through their respective territories.

Be pleased to accept. . . .

No. 31.—The Prince de Talleyrand to King Louis XVIII.

SIRE,

The Duke of Saxe-Teschen,[1] who went as far as Brünn
to meet the King of Saxony, has returned here this morning.
The king rests to-day about two stages from Vienna, and will

---

[1] Albert, Duc de Sax-Teschen, son of August II., Elector of Saxony and King
of Poland, was consequently the uncle of Louis XVIII. and of King Frederic-
Augustus. Born in 1738, he married in 1766 the Archduchess Marie-Christine,
daughter of the Emperor Francis I. He was made Governor of the Netherlands,
commanded the Austrian troops in that country in 1792 and laid siege to Lille. He
became a Field Marshal and died in 1822.

await at Presburg the departure of the two northern sovereigns, who would certainly feel embarrassed by his presence here and whom he himself probably has no wish to meet. It was thought that he would be too far away at Brünn; there was however no suitable residence to offer him between Brünn and Vienna, hence the preference for Presburg, notwithstanding the reasons I had the honour to communicate to your Majesty in one of my former letters.

The Emperor of Russia talks of leaving, and preparations for his departure have even commenced. Report fixed it for the 14th of this month, then the 17th, and now they talk of the 20th. The emperor has promised to be at home for the Russian Easter, and I believe this is the only one of all the promises he has made that he will keep, for he would find it inconvenient not to do so. When he is once gone, the other sovereigns will not remain either. The Emperor of Austria who for his part, has for some time meditated a journey into his Italian provinces, does not wish to postpone it beyond the month of April. Thus the necessity or the wish of every one to leave, will hasten the conclusion of affairs.

I have, as I promised M. de Metternich, allowed those of Italy to remain dormant until I hear of Lord Castlereagh's visit to Paris, and his arrival in London.

Austria and Bavaria are agreed on all but one point, that of Salzburg, which Austria wants entirely, while Bavaria desires to retain a part. I have strongly advised each of the two negotiators separately, to endeavour to come to some understanding, rather than incur the intervention of Russia and Prussia, which will become inevitable if they do not agree. I trust my advice will bear fruit, and I gave it in order to avoid the necessity of having to pronounce in favour of one, which I could[1] not do, without displeasing the other, while it is almost equally important to us to be friends with both.

Swiss affairs are or will shortly be laid, by the commission which has prepared them, before the Conference by which they have to be confirmed. There is no longer a question of retaining Porentruy; this together with the bishopric of Bâle is given as we desired to the canton of Berne; the fate of the Valtelline alone remains undecided until Italian matters are settled; even Russia has agreed to this.

Laharpe, the philosopher, who thinks he never can do harm enough to the Bernese, took it into his head to exclude the canton of Berne from the Supreme Executive Council of the

---

[1] Var.: "pouvait" = "would."

Federation,[1] and he succeeded in getting his illustrious pupil to support this foolish idea, in consequence of which a Russian minister went to one of the ministers of Ferdinand IV. whom he did not know and said to him, " Try and obtain the consent of France to the exclusion of the canton of Berne from the number of the executive cantons, and the Emperor Alexander, who is singularly desirous to be satisfied on this point, will be on your side." The same minister went on the same day to M. de Metternich to whom he said, " The Emperor Alexander has not yet made up his mind about Murat, he will aid you to uphold him as you wish, if you will agree that the canton of Berne shall not be one of the executive cantons." M. de Metternich replied that such a proposal was not tenable.[3] I on my part rejected it the moment he uttered the first words. The Russians have consequently withdrawn their scheme, and have by this attempt only gained the disgrace that attaches to such gross duplicity, which they apparently hold to be most admirable diplomatic finesse.

When the Emperor Alexander first asked for the greater part of the duchy of Warsaw, he said it was in order to form a kingdom to console the Poles, by giving them a semblance of their ancient political existence, and to atone as far as possible for the outrage done to morality by the division. Subsequently he abandoned this point, and announced [4] that he would give to that portion of the duchy of Warsaw which he should obtain, a special constitution, but now he wavers even as to this. Prince Adam Czartoryski, whose penetration does not nearly equal his loyalty, begins to see that he has been nursing a chimerical hope, and of this he complains.

It is probable that the Emperor Alexander will get out of the difficulty with the Poles, by stopping only a moment in Warsaw, and with Prince Czartoryski, by parting from him coldly and avoiding all explanations. Your Majesty will be able to judge how much the emperor will be regretted when he leaves here, by what happened a few days ago.

---

[1] The Act of Mediation of 1803 had decided that the Helvetian Diet should meet alternately at Friburg, Soleure, Bern, Basle, Zurich, and Lucerne. The cantons of which these towns were the capitals then became *cantons directeurs* for one year. The *avoyer* or burgomaster of the *canton directeur* then became by right *laudamann* of Switzerland for one year. He had charge of the seal of the Confederation. All foreign ministers were accredited to him. He had a right of police over the other cantons and also to call out the troops. Laharpe tried to deprive Bern of the right to become in her turn a *canton directeur*.

[2] It will be remembered that M. de Laharpe had been tutor to the Emperor Alexander.

[3] Var.: " que ce qui l'on demandait " = " that that which was asked for."

Var.: " mais annonça " = " but announced."

In the difficulty of knowing how to pass the time, now that there are no more dances, and how best to overcome the *ennui* with which every one is assailed, all sorts of games and amusements are being started. One of them which has become very much the fashion, is getting up lotteries at the different *réunions*. The night before last, a lottery of this kind took place at Princess Marie Esterhazy's.[1] She wished with much ingenuity (which has been severely criticized) to arrange matters in such a way, that the four principal prizes should fall to ladies specially taken notice of by the Emperor of Russia and the King of Prussia, both of whom were present. But this arrangement was upset by Prince Metternich's little daughter, who went up to the basket containing the tickets and drew one out of her turn. This ticket was found to entitle her to the most magnificent prize of all which the Emperor of Russia had brought. The emperor could not hide his annoyance, to the great amusement of all those present (your Majesty will remember that the emperor latterly did not attend any of M. de Metternich's balls and did not even speak to him when he met him elsewhere). Everything went wrong with the emperor that evening. A prize brought by the young Princess d'Auersperg, whom the emperor rather affected, was won by one of the King of Prussia's aides-de-camp. The emperor insisted, he even went so far as to point out that it had been intended for her, but the aide-de-camp replied that it was far too precious for him to give up. This delighted every one ; so much so, that the emperor is beginning to find the evening parties in Vienna not quite so pleasant as he did on his first arrival.

I have just seen the detail of the troops that are marching towards Italy. There are 120 battalions and 84 squadrons, making in all 120,000 infantry and 15,000 cavalry. The generals in command are Bianchi,[2] Radetzky,[3] Frimont,[4] and Jerome

---

[1] Marie-Josephine de Lichtenstein, born in 1768, married in 1783 to Nicholas, Prince Esterhazy de Galantha, Austrian Master of Ordnance.

[2] Bianchi was a Field Marshal Lieutenant in 1815. He commanded an Austrian corps at Leipsig in 1813, and in 1814 he was placed in command of the troops sent to operate against Lyons. In 1815 he directed the campaign against Murat and took Naples. He was made Governor of Galicia in 1815 (1768-1855).

[3] General Radetzky was born in 1766, entered the army in 1788, became chief of the staff of Prince de Schwartzenberg in 1814. In 1831 he took command of the Austrian troops in Lombardy, remained a long time in that country and had to put down the insurrection there during 1848-1849. He retired in 1854, and died the following year. He had been Field Marshal since 1836.

[4] Jean-Philipe, Comte de Frimont, Prince d'Antrodoco, was born in 1756 in Belgium and belonged to a French family. He served first in France, emigrated in 1791, and rejoined the army of Condé. He then entered the Austrian service and became Field Marshal Lieutenant. In 1812 he commanded an Austrian auxiliary corps of the Grand Army. He subsequently went through the campaign of 1813 and

Collorido.[1]   There is besides a reserve of 50,000 men in Carinthia, Styria, ...

General Pozzo is waiting a last despatch from the emperor before starting.

I have the honour to be . . . . .

No. 35.—The Prince de Talleyrand to King Louis XVIII.

VIENNA, *March* 7, 1815.

SIRE,

I feel sure your Majesty is already aware, or will have learnt before the receipt of this letter, that Buonaparte has quitted the island of Elba, but in any case I hasten to transmit the news [2] to your Majesty.

I first heard of it in a letter from M. de Metternich, to which I replied, that I saw from the dates that Buonaparte's escape was connected with Murat's request to Austria, to allow his troops to march through his provinces.   The Duke of Wellington shortly afterwards sent me a despatch from Lord Burghersh,[3] *the English minister at Florence*,[4] of which I have the honour to transmit herewith a translation, as well as an extract from a letter from the vice-consul at Ancona, also sent me by Lord Wellington.

Buonaparte embarked at Porto-Ferrajo, at nine o'clock on the evening of the 26th of February.   He had with him about twelve hundred men, ten pieces of artillery, six of them field-pieces, and some horses, and provisions for five or six days.   The English, who had undertaken to watch his movements, have done it so carelessly that they will find some difficulty in excusing themselves.   The direction he has taken towards the north seems to indicate that he intends proceeding to Genoa or the south of France.

1814, and commanded the army of occupation in France until 1818.   In 1821 he was sent to put down the insurrection in the kingdom of Naples.   He died in 1831.

[1] Jerome, Comte de Collorido, second son of the minister to the Emperor Leopold II., born in 1775.   He particularly distinguished himself in 1813.   He commanded an Austrian corps at Dresden and won a victory at Kulm.   After the war he was made Master of Ordnance, and Commander-in-Chief in Bohemia.

[2] The news had reached Vienna on March 6.   It was not made public till March 11.

[3] John Fane, Earl of Westmoreland (1784–1859) known till his father's death (1841) under the title of Lord Burghersh, first entered the army and served in Sicily and Portugal.   In 1813 he was attached to the staff of de Schwartzenberg.   In 1814 he was appointed Minister at Florence.   In 1822 he became Privy Councillor and was then sent as Ambassador to Naples (1825), then to Berlin (1841), where he remained till 1851, and finally to Vienna.   He retired in 1855.

[4] Suppressed in the text of the archives.

I cannot believe he would dare to make any attempt on our southern provinces. He would not risk doing so, except in consequence of such favourable intelligence as there is no reason to suppose he has received. It is however none the less necessary to take every possible precaution in that quarter, and to send picked and perfectly safe men there. As for the rest, any enterprise of his against France will be that of a bandit ; as such he will have to be dealt with, and all measures permissible against brigands ought to be employed against him.

It seems to me much more probable [1] that he intends operating in the north of Italy. The Duke of Wellington tells me that there are two thousand English and three thousand Italians in Genoa *who fought in Spain* [2] and then entered the King of Sardinia's service ; he has no doubt but that these troops who fought in Spain, and who, he says are admirable, will do their duty.

The King of Sardinia is at Genoa just now, and must have his guard there. There are also three English frigates in the harbour. If therefore Buonaparte made an attempt on Genoa with his twelve hundred men it would fail. The only fear is that he may cross the mountains towards Parma and Lombardy, where his presence would be the signal for a long planned revolution, which the shameful behaviour of the Austrians and the false policy of their cabinet has only too greatly favoured, and which, supported by the troops of Murat with whom no doubt Buonaparte is in accord, would set the whole of Italy in a blaze. The Prince of Schwartzenberg and M. de Metternich have both told me that if Buonaparte was to reach the north of Italy it would embarrass them terribly, as they are by no means yet prepared. Express messengers were sent last night to all the troops destined for Italy, to hasten their departure ; but whatever despatch these forces may use it will be quite a month or more ere they reach their destination, and many events may happen in a month.

It appears that the Prince de Schwartzenberg will himself be ordered to Italy. In any case your Majesty will assuredly consider it necessary to concentrate sufficient troops in the south, to act according to circumstances.

The results of this occurrence cannot yet be foreseen, but they may prove fortunate if they can only be turned to good account. I will do all that in me lies to prevent any delay here and to make the congress come to some resolution which will reduce Buonaparte from the rank which, through some unaccount-

[1] Var.: " vraisemblable " = " probable."
[2] Suppressed in the text of the archives.

able weakness he was allowed to retain, and thus place him beyond the possibility of preparing fresh disasters for Europe.

There has been some deliberation as to the method of making the King of Saxony acquainted with the cessions which the powers have decided he must make to Prussia and to which his consent is necessary. It has been decided to prepare an extract from the general protocol containing these and embody it in a private protocol, which, out of greater consideration, will be delivered to the King by the Duke of Wellington, the Prince de Metternich, and myself. For this purpose we shall all three go to Presburg the day after to-morrow.

Refusal on the part of the King of Saxony would not only be futile as regards himself, but very vexatious for every one, especially at present, when it is most important to unite all views and opinions against the enterprises of the man from Elba. We will do all we can to induce the King of Saxony to submit with a good grace to the exigencies of circumstances.

The affairs of Switzerland are at length concluded. The Russians, compelled to give up the idea of excluding the canton of Berne from the number of directorial cantons, demanded that it should at least be required to modify its constitution by the introduction of a representative party. All the powers agreed to this request, which is in accordance with the spirit of the times, and France could not well refuse it.

The letters of M. de Watteville [1] and M. Mülinen [2] show that this demand is not of a nature to raise serious difficulties in Berne. This also is the opinion of M. de Zerleeder.

I have the honour to be......

No. 25.—King Louis XVIII. to the Prince de Talleyrand.

PARIS, *March* 7 1815.

Mon Cousin,

I have received your letter number 30. I believe that M. de Metternich's declaration, with which under other circumstances I should not be very well satisfied, is explained by

---

[1] Nicholas-Rodolphe de Watteville, a Swiss statesman, born in 1760, member of the Grand Council of 1796, member of the Swiss deputation that went to Paris in 1802, was *landamann* in 1804, 1811, and 1815. He died in 1832.

[2] Frederic de Mülinen, born in 1760, was a member of the Grand Council before the Revolution. In 1802 he was one of the leaders of the insurrectionary movements and came to Paris as member of the deputation : again entered the Grand Council and was made *avoyer*. Later on he became President of the Confederation, and died in 1833.

what I told you the other day and by the documents sent herewith. The instructions will sufficiently acquaint you with my wishes, so that it is superfluous to add more here.

I had intended to-day to resume the subject of the convention of the 11th of April last. Buonaparte has spared me the trouble. Before receiving this despatch you will no doubt have heard of his audacious attempt. I have at once taken all the measures I considered best to make him repent it. I count with confidence on their success. I this morning received the ambassadors, and addressing them each in turn, I requested them to inform their courts that they had seen me, and that I was not at all disquieted by the news I had received, being fully persuaded that it will no more upset the tranquillity of Europe than it has my own.

My gout has improved greatly since the other day.

Whereupon, my cousin, may God have you in His safe and holy keeping.

LOUIS.

No. 26.[1]—KING LOUIS XVIII. TO THE PRINCE DE TALLEYRAND.

PARIS, *March* 11, 1815.

MON COUSIN,

I cannot write to you as to the position in which I now find myself, but I send the Duc de Rohan Montbazon,[2] who will give you all the information you desire. I hope he will be useful to you with the Emperor of Austria.

My confidence in you leaves me no room to doubt that you will under these circumstances do all that such important interests as those which the Duc de Rohan will communicate to you, require.

Whereupon I pray God may have you, my cousin, in His safe and holy keeping.

LOUIS.

No. 33.—PRINCE DE TALLEYRAND TO KING LOUIS XVIII.

VIENNA, *March* 12, 1815.

SIRE,

I have received the letter of the third of this month with which your Majesty has deigned to honour me. I await that which will contain the instructions relative to the affair

---

[1] This letter is not found in M. Pallain's collection.

[2] Charles-Alexis-Gabriel, Duc de Rohan Montbazon, born in 1764, emigrated in 1791, entered the Austrian service and became Field Marshal. He returned to France in 1814 and became a peer of France.

with M. de Metternich, who has already asked me if I was not yet in a position to deal with it. The mystery in which he wished to envelop it, the step he has taken with your Majesty unknown to me, and his wish to arrange it with me alone, all go to prove that he knows as well as any one, the many objections to which his scheme is open. In acquiescing in it your Majesty will certainly be making a great sacrifice, and in my opinion even one which cannot but be of consequence. I admit nevertheless it would not seem too great to me, if Austria in return would honestly join us against Murat, and if M. de Metternich is sincere in his offer.

On Wednesday evening, the Duke of Wellington, M. de Metternich and I, went to Presburg, where we arrived at four in the morning. At mid-day the King of Saxony received us together. He took the protocol which M. de Metternich gave him, and handed it unopened to his minister who was present, saying that he would acquaint himself with its contents, and then turning to us, addressed a few civil words but in a very cold and distant manner. At one o'clock we had the honour of dining with him and the Queen. In the evening he received us separately, M. de Metternich at four o'clock, myself at five, and the Duke of Wellington at six. Several times he expressed sentiments of gratitude to your Majesty. Next day we all three had a very long conference with his minister, Comte d'Einsiedel, who does not understand French very well and speaks it still worse. At these interviews we exhausted all the reasons which should induce the king to consent to the reductions agreed upon by the powers for the benefit of Prussia.

The king and his minister overwhelmed us with objections; they seemed to nourish the hope that all which had been settled was still open to negotiation. This hope being again expressed in a memorandum addressed to us by the king's minister on the Saturday, we deemed it necessary to crush it by a positive declaration contained in the reply which we sent him just as we were leaving Presburg. I have the honour to send herewith copies of these two documents.

The Prussians have demanded, that that part of Saxony which has been given to them, should at once pass from a military occupation to a regular administration, and that the other part should be provisionally held under military occupation. This demand, which it would be difficult to refuse, will probably determine the King of Saxony to assent.

According to the information we have received, he wishes to consent, but at the same time wants to appear to his people to have yielded only to stern and overpowering necessity.

We received intelligence at Presburg that Buonaparte, repulsed by a cannonade at Antibes, which he had summoned to surrender, had disembarked in the Bay of Juan.[1] These are the last news we have of him. It is thought that he cannot have had any correspondence either with Marseilles or Toulon, since he did not go there, nor with Antibes, where he was repulsed. This intelligence is very reassuring. But the powers have none the less thought over the best means of offering aid to your Majesty, should it be needed. An order to concentrate and hold themselves in readiness has been sent to the English, Prussian, and Austrian troops, which are in the neighbourhood of the Rhine. The Emperor of Russia has directed his army, which had returned to the Vistula, to draw near the Oder and the Elbe.

As long as we were ignorant of Buonaparte's destination, or what he intended doing, no declaration against him could be issued. We however took action as soon as we knew this.

The document has been drawn up by the French legation, and sent to the Duke of Wellington and the Prince de Metternich. It will be read to-morrow in committee of the eight powers who signed the treaty of Paris, where it will probably undergo some alterations. When it has been agreed on, I shall have the honour to transmit it to your Majesty by a courier, who will leave a copy with the prefect of Strasburg, to whom I will send orders to print and distribute it both in his own and the neighbouring departments. I will do the same to Metz and Chalons. I will also tell M. de Saint-Marsan to take the same steps to promulgate it in Nice, Savoy, and Dauphiné.

The Emperor of Russia, who on the whole proves generally staunch in present circumstances, is despatching General Pozzo with a letter to your Majesty, to whom he offers all his troops. This is aid which it would be sad if France could not dispense with, and yet it should not be positively refused. Your Majesty will surely not feel obliged to accept it, except in an extreme case, which I hope will not present itself.

Your Majesty has no doubt ordered troops into the south. If I might venture to suggest a chief to place at their head, I would mention Marshal Macdonald, a man of high honour, whom one can trust completely as possessing the confidence of

---

[1] Napoleon, who disembarked at three o'clock on the 1st of March in the Gulf of Juan, immediately sent a detachment of twenty-five men to secure the batteries on the coast. The company arrived at Antibes, the Commandant, Colonel Cuneo-d'Ornano allowed them to enter and then made prisoners of them, despite the ferment among his own soldiers. This was the sum total of the affray at Antibes. Not a single cannon was fired.

the army, and because, having signed the treaty of April 11th for Buonaparte, his example in marching against him would carry great weight.

I have seen a list of the general officers named for the command of the 30,000 men whom your Majesty has ordered to assemble between Lyons and Chambéry. Several of the names are unknown to me, but there are some in whom I could have no confidence, among others General Maurice-Matthieu,[1] who is, I believe, a devoted adherent of Joseph Buonaparte.

His presence in the Pays de Vaud cannot but be dangerous at this moment. I will work to get him removed by the aid of England and Russia, and also Austria, who has some influence in the canton.[2] The Emperor of Russia (I must do him this justice) has already, of his own accord, written to the new cantons in a manner very satisfactory to us.[3] I have informed M. Auguste de Talleyrand[4] of this, advising him to discuss it with Baron Krüdener,[5] the Russian *chargé d'affaires*.

This incident of Buonaparte's appearance in France, in other respects so disagreeable, will at least have this advantage, that it will hasten the conclusion of matters here. It has redoubled the zeal and eagerness of every one. The deed committee will begin its work in earnest. Thus the end of our sojourn here may be shortened by several weeks.

I have the honour to be..................

---

[1] Maurice Mathieu, Comte de la Redorte, was an officer of cavalry in 1789. He became General of Division in 1799, had command both in Germany and Italy and passed thence into Spain, where he was made Governor of Barcelona and Chief Commandant of Catalonia. He was made a peer of France in 1819. General Mathieu had married Mademoiselle Clary and was therefore brother-in-law to King Joseph and Bernadotte,

[2] Joseph was at Prangins when he heard of his brother's disembarkation. He quitted this château on the evening of the 19th, and passed the frontier during the night. It was fortunate that he departed so quickly, for the next morning a Commissary of the Federal Government arrived with a picket of soldiers, to take possession of his person and conduct him to Bern. In acting thus, Switzerland acceded to the pressure put on her by the foreign ministers, who were accredited to the Diet.— (*Memoirs of King Joseph*, Vol. X.)

[3] Var.: "qui nous a convenu" = "which suited us."

[4] At that time French ambassador in Switzerland.

[5] Alexis Constantine, Baron de Krüdener, born in 1774, a Russian statesman, formerly secretary to the Embassy at Madrid and Warsaw, then Minister at Curland, Ambassador at Vienna (1784), at Copenhagen (1786), and at Berlin (1800). He died in 1802. He had, in 1783, married Mademoiselle Wietinghoff, who as Baronne de Krüdener, acquired a well-known celebrity.

No. 34.—The Prince de Talleyrand to King Louis XVIII.

VIENNA, *March* 13,[1] 1815.

SIRE,

I have just come from the conference, where the declaration, which I had the honour of mentioning to your Majesty in my letter of yesterday, has been signed. It was drawn up this morning in the conference of the five powers. This evening it was submitted to that of the eight powers, who adopted it. I hasten to forward it to your Majesty. I am also sending copies to the prefects of Strasburg, Besançon, Lyons, Nancy, Metz, and Chalons-sur-Marne, asking them to print and circulate it in their respective departments and amongst the prefects of the neighbouring ones. I feel assured your Majesty will deem it advisable to order its publication in all parts of the kingdom. M. de Saint-Marsan, to whom I have sent a copy, is forwarding it to Geneva and Nice.

I think the strength of this document leaves nothing to be desired, and I hope it will not fail to produce the required effect, not only in France, but throughout Europe, where it will be widely distributed.

One of Buonaparte's sisters (Pauline Borghésé), who crossed over from the island of Elba to the continent of Italy, was stopped at Lucca,[2] and Jérôme, who was at Trieste, will be taken with Joseph to Gratz, as soon as the Canton de Vaud has complied with the demand I have desired M. de Talleyrand to make, jointly with the Austrian and Russian ministers. Austrian and Russian officers bear the request to the Pays de Vaud, and are instructed to conduct Joseph Buonaparte as far as Gratz.

Orders have been issued to occupy the island of Elba in the name of the allies.

Thus all tends towards the same end, with a unanimity and concord between all the powers such as I do not believe has ever before been witnessed.

I have made inquiries about the generals nominated to com-

---

[1] Var. : March 14.

[2] We have nowhere found this arrest of the Princess Pauline confirmed, which would only have been a useless violation of personal rights. It is affirmed on the contrary, that she passed the period of the Hundred Days at Naples and at Rome. As for King Jérôme, he certainly was at Trieste, together with the queen, when at the moment of being carried off by the Austrian police, he was enabled to embark secretly on board a Neapolitan frigate which had been sent him by Murat, and thus gain France in safety,

mand the troops between Chambéry and Lyons.   General
Sémélé,[1] Dijeon,[2] and above all General Marchand,[3] are, I am
informed, worthy of all confidence.   I have not met any one who
knows General Roussel d'Urbal.[4]

I have the honour to be.[5] . . . .

DECLARATION.

The powers who signed the treaty of Paris, assembled in
congress at Vienna, being informed of Napoleon Buonaparte's
escape and his entry by force of arms into France, feel it due to
their own dignity and to the interests of social order, to make a
solemn declaration of the sentiments with which this event has
inspired them.

In thus breaking the agreement by which he was established
in the island of Elba, Buonaparte has destroyed the only safeguard attached to his existence.   In reappearing in France with
designs of disorder and revolution, he has by his own act deprived
himself of the protection of the laws, and manifested to the world
that neither peace nor truce can be made with him.

The powers consequently declare that Napoleon Buonaparte
has placed himself beyond the pale of civil and social relations,
and that as the enemy and disturber of the world's peace, he has
delivered himself up to public justice.   They likewise declare
that, firmly resolved to maintain intact the treaty of Paris of
May 30th, 1814, and the provisions sanctioned by this treaty,
together with those which they have suspended, or will still
suspend with the view to complete and consolidate it, they will

---

[1] The Baron de Sémélé was born in 1773, served as a volunteer in 1792, and
became General of Division in 1811 ; he took service during the Hundred Days, and
was on this account put on the non-effective list under the second restoration.

[2] The Vicomte Dijeon, born in 1771, the son of a former general, became an
ensign in 1792.   He was made General of Division in 1813.   In 1815 he accompanied the Comte d'Artois to Lyons.   He was made a peer of France under the
second restoration, and War Minister in 1823.   He died in 1828.

[3] Jean Gabriel, Comte Marchand, born in 1765, was first a barrister, then enlisted ;
became a General in 1805 and took part in all the campaigns of the Empire.   He
was in command at Grenoble in 1815, tried to resist Napoleon, but was forced to
retire.   He was tried by court-martial in 1816, but acquitted.   Nevertheless he was
exiled.   He was created a peer of France by Louis Philippe and died in 1851.

[4] Nicholas-François Roussel d'Urbal, born in 1763.   Served at first in the
Austrian army and became Major-General in 1809.   Admitted into the French
service in 1811, he became General of Division in 1812, and Inspector-General of
Cavalry in 1815.   He died in 1849.

[5] Var. : " P.S.—*Je crois qu'après la déclaration il doit y avoir un trait bien
marqué qui la sépare du protocole à la fin duquel doivent être toutes les signatures comme
elles se trouvent dans la copie ci jointe*" = "I think that after the declaration there
ought to be a very marked line, so as to separate it from the protocol, at the end of which
all the signatures ought to come, the same as they are in the copy sent herewith."

employ every means and unite all their efforts, in order that universal peace, the object of Europe's prayers and the constant aim of her labours, shall not again be disturbed, and to secure her from all attempts which would threaten to again plunge the nations into the disorders and miseries of revolution.

And although thoroughly convinced that the whole of France by rallying round her legitimate sovereign, will completely frustrate this last attempt on the part of an impotent and mad criminal, all the sovereigns of Europe, animated by the same sentiments and guided by the same principles, declare that if, contrary to all expectation, any real danger whatsoever shall result from this event, they will be ready to give to the King of France and to the French nation, or to any other government that is attacked, and, as soon as they have been requested to do so, the assistance necessary to re-establish public tranquillity, and will make common cause against all those who would attempt to compromise it.

This present declaration, inserted in the protocol of the congress assembled at Vienna at the sitting of March 13th, 1815, will be made public.

Signed and approved by the plenipotentiaries of the eight powers who signed the treaty of Paris.

VIENNA, *March* 13, 1815.

(Here follow the signatures, in the alphabetical order of their courts).

> Austria.—LE PRINCE DE METTERNICH, LE BARON DE WESSENBURG.
> Spain (Espagne).—P. GOMEZ LABRADOR.
> France.—LE PRINCE DE TALLEYRAND, LE DUC DE DALBERG, LA TOUR-DU-PIN, LE COMTE ALEXIS DE NOAILLES.
> Great Britain.—WELLINGTON, CLANCARTY, CATHCART, STEWART.
> Portugal.—LE COMTE DE PALMELLA, SALDANHA, LOBO.
> Prussia.—LE PRINCE DE HARDENBERG, LE BARON DE HUMBOLDT.
> Russia.—LE COMTE DE RASOUMOWSKI, LE COMTE DE STACKELBERG, LE COMTE DE NESSELRODE.
> Sweden.—LOWENHIELM.

No. 35.—The Prince de Talleyrand to King Louis XVIII.

VIENNA, *March* 4, 1815.

SIRE,

The courier whom I am sending off to-day, carries into Switzerland to M. le Comte de Talleyrand, an order to take steps in concert with the ministers of Austria and Russia, as I had the honour of informing your Majesty yesterday, to remove Joseph Buonaparte from the French frontiers. This messenger will be much longer on the road than those who go direct to Paris, but I did not wish to despatch him without sending a letter to your Majesty, although I have nothing fresh to say, and the courier who is bringing me the instructions your Majesty has done me the honour to announce in your letter of the 2nd of this month, has not yet arrived.

I trust those instructions will not, as M. de Metternich flatters himself, be of such a nature as to put off indefinitely the decision respecting the fate of Murat. We cannot and must not believe any of M. de Metternich's promises *on this head*.[1] Only to-day I had a very emphatic explanation with him on this matter. My opinion is that if Murat's affair is postponed, it is lost to us, and thus the general opinion, which to-day is all in our favour, will be destroyed.

I have procured, and will send to your Majesty in the next letter I have the honour of writing to you, a document signed by the powers, who, at the time it was drawn up, still called themselves *allies*. It will enable your Majesty to judge of the position in which your ambassadors at the congress found themselves on their arrival in Vienna, as regards those powers, and how very different that position is to-day.

I send herewith one of the declarations which have been printed in Vienna and distributed all over Germany.

I have the honour to be. . . .

No. 36.—Prince de Talleyrand to King Louis XVIII.

VIENNA, *March* 15, 1815.

SIRE,

My letter No. 35 will not reach your Majesty until after that which I have the honour of writing to you to-day, as the courier who takes it goes round by Zurich.

---

[1] Suppressed in the text of the archives.

Although Buonaparte has only a handful of men with him, I have deemed it best to remove from him those in particular who, not being French, and finding themselves far from their own country, might for this double reason be more devoted to him. I have therefore requested that all the Poles who had followed him should be recalled by their government.

My proposal has been eagerly welcomed, and the order for their return drawn up at once under my directions.

The courier whom I now send, will take it, as well as a copy I have the honour of sending you. I entreat your Majesty to have the goodness to give orders that the necessary routes may be furnished to these troops. The Emperor of Russia and Prince Czartoryski were very gracious in this little matter.

A Prussian courier who arrived here about twelve hours before the one sent to me on the 8th brought the news, which is fully confirmed in all my letters from Paris. This news, which quickly became known, has excited general satisfaction here. Every one applauds the wisdom of the steps your Majesty has taken. Every one feels certain that Buonaparte cannot escape punishment, and is rejoiced thereat.

M. de Jaucourt speaks of the good effect a declaration from the congress would produce. He even speaks as if this came from your Majesty. Your Majesty knows by this time that your wishes on this point have been anticipated.

I sent by yesterday's courier the printed declaration for distribution on the Swiss frontiers; I have the honour to transmit to-day a few copies to your Majesty. The heading, Vienna, and the type of the Austrian chancellor's printing office, appeared to me very satisfactory.

The principles of legitimacy which it was necessary to recover from beneath the ruins under which they had been buried, as it were, by the overthrow of so many old dynasties and the growth of so many new ones, were at first coldly received by some and utterly rejected by others, but now under our guidance, they are at length better appreciated. Our [1] perseverance in defending them was not in vain. This honour however is entirely due to your Majesty, and the unanimity with which the powers have pronounced against Buonaparte's fresh attempt, is a proof of it.

I have often had the honour of telling your Majesty that the allies originally intended we should be mere spectators at the congress, but I thought that there was only a verbal understanding between them on this point, and never imagined they had agreed to it in writing. The two protocols I have the honour of sending your Majesty, prove the

---

[1] Text : = "our." Var. : "votre" = "your."

contrary, and also show how very little our actual position resembles that which it was intended we should take. These two protocols are copies of two originals which I have had in my own hands. Certainly the difference between what they desired on the 22nd of September and the declaration which has just been issued by all the powers, is immense.

I shall have the honour to reply to your Majesty by one of the next couriers, relative to the directions you have given me respecting the arrangements in Italy. I only received them this morning.

I have the honour to be. . . .

No. 37.—Prince de Talleyrand to King Louis XVIII.

VIENNA, *March* 16, 1815.

SIRE,

Finding I had to send another courier to Paris to-day with the order of recall for the Poles who are with Buonaparte, and which was inadvertently not enclosed in last night's despatches, I take advantage of this to have the honour of telling your Majesty how much I wish to be kept constantly informed, and as exactly as possible, of everything that takes place in France, also how very important this is.

However well disposed the sovereigns, and even the people of Vienna may be, it would be a marvel if there were not some evil-disposed individuals eager to proclaim alarming news, and many credulous persons ready to welcome and spread it. It is therefore important that your Majesty's legation should always be in a position to contradict them.

The news of Buonaparte's entry into France caused a fall in the funds here, but the declaration of the congress has made them rise again. I hope it will produce the same effect in France. Perhaps the news, received here this morning, will affect them again.

The Regency of Geneva wrote to the Federal Government at Zürich on the 8th, that it had that morning heard that a regiment sent against Buonaparte, having joined him instead, he had entered Grenoble at seven or eight in the evening and that the whole town was illuminated. The Regency therefore asked for assistance lest Geneva should be threatened by Buonaparte. The King of Würtemberg had sent these tidings to the Emperor Alexander [1] by express. I have endeavoured to combat this

---

[1] " Every one near him spoke of it that morning."

report by some, at least, possible explanations ; but they do not suffice to destroy an impression which, I believe, is entirely due to the alarm of the Genevese.

I have the honour to be. . . .

No. 38.—PRINCE DE TALLEYRAND TO KING LOUIS XVIII.

VIENNA, *March* 17, 1815.

SIRE,

I have the honour to send herewith a letter received this morning from Murat's minister here. I forward the original, so that there may be no delay in its transmission, and also because I no longer need it here. The Duc de Campo Chiaro has made the same communication to the Duke of Wellington, and also repeated it to the court of Vienna, to whose minister in Naples it had already been made. This step, coupled with the news which reached us here to-day, and the attitude of the plenipotentiaries of the great powers, enables me to foresee that if Buonaparte is making his way towards Paris, and if the powers unite their forces on our frontiers, it will be almost impossible, not only to get the congress to pronounce against Murat in favour of Ferdinand IV., but even to get Austria, and perhaps England, to take an actual and positive stand against him. I therefore pray your Majesty to graciously give me your final instructions on this point. We must think of ourselves before thinking of others.

News has been received to-day by M. de Metternich by way of Milan. It announced the defection of two regiments, Buonaparte's entry into Grenoble, and his departure thence on the 8th, for Lyons. It is added that the feeling in the provinces he has traversed is very bad.

This news appeared sufficiently serious to cause a *special*[1] conference of the Austrian, English, Russian, Prussian, and French legations to be summoned. The following questions were submitted for deliberation :

I. What political ground will the powers take, supposing that Buonaparte succeeds in re-establishing himself in Paris ?

II. What is the actual disposable military force ?

III. What are the means of preparation ?[2]

The political ground is already decided by the declaration of the congress. This will be adhered to.

A military commission has been appointed to consider the other two questions. It consists of :—

---

[1] Suppressed in the text of the archives.
[2] Var. : " proposer " = " proposed."

Schwartzenberg, Wellington, Volkonsky (Russian), Knese-beck (Prussian).[1]

The commission will assemble this evening. The Emperor of Russia wishes to be present. If by this evening I learn what they have decided, I shall not wait till morning to send off a fresh courier to your Majesty.

The Austrians having reason to suspect that M. Anatole de Montesquiou's visit here, ostensibly to see his mother (?)[2] had quite another object not without political significance, I have requested him to return to Paris without delay.

I have grounds for believing that the Emperor of Austria will take Buonaparte's son into his palace and under his charge, to prevent his being carried off. It has been affirmed that such an abduction was the object of M. Anatole's journey. We are led to believe this from the tenor of his mother's language, reported by the Austrian detectives placed over her.

I have the honour to be . . . . .

No. 39.—The Prince de Talleyrand to King Louis XVIII.

VIENNA, *March,* 19, 1815.

SIRE,

The Duke of Wellington is to-day sending a courier to London, who will take Paris on his way, if possible. I take advantage of it to inform your Majesty that at the military conference held the evening before last, and at which the Emperor of Russia was present, it was determined that Buonaparte, with whom none of the powers would ever treat again, must be stopped with prompt and strenuous measures. They have consequently stayed the renewal of the treaty of Chaumont, of which I had the honour to send your Majesty a copy. But it is solely against Buonaparte that this will be directed, and not against France, which, on the contrary, will accede to it. Sardinia, Bavaria, Wur-

---

[1] Charles-Frederic, Baron Knesebeck, born in 1768, went through the campaigns of 1792 and 1794, and subsequently that of 1806, with the Prussian army. Being an implacable enemy to France he took service in Austria in 1809, received in 1811 a secret mission to Russia and took part as a General in the campaigns of 1813 and 1814. He became later Field Marshal General, and died in 1848.

[2] Anatole, Comte de Montesquiou-Fezensac, born in 1788, enlisted in 1808, became in 1809 Orderly Officer to the Emperor, and Colonel in 1814. During the Hundred Days he went to Vienna to join his mother, who had accompanied the King of Rome, being his governess. Suspected, not without reason, of a desire to carry off the young prince, he received orders to withdraw. Being at first proscribed, at the second restoration he was pardoned and became attached to the household of the Duc d'Orleans. In 1830 he was charged with various diplomatic missions and became Brigadier-General, and subsequently peer of France. He died in 1867.

temburg and Baden will also agree to it, as well as Holland and Hanover.

The Ottoman Porte will not be asked to take part in the war, but merely not to receive either French rebels or their vessels.

Steps will also be taken as regards Switzerland. The question is one quite outside that of neutrality, the man who forces Europe to arm being nothing more than a brigand.

I have received a declaration from Austria relative to the Valtelline, Bormio, and Chiavenna, which declaration expresses that these places must enter into the arrangements for Italy and serve her as compensation.[1]

I have the honour to be . . . . .

THE DECLARATION SENT WITH THE PRECEDING DESPATCH.

VIENNA, *March* 18, 1815.

The undersigned has been commanded to make known to his highness, the Prince de Talleyrand, that their Majesties, the Emperor of all the Russias, the King of Great Britain, and the King of Prussia, have agreed with his Imperial and Royal Apostolic Majesty, that the valleys of the Valtelline, Chiavenna, and Bormio, which up to this date formed part of the kingdom of Italy, shall, under the denomination of the department of the Adda, be united to the Italian states of his Imperial and Royal Majesty. As these states, however, have been placed, by special negotiations between the courts of Vienna and the Tuileries, among the territories which might serve for exchange or compensation, in arranging the affairs of Italy, and particularly those which concern the future establishment of her Majesty the Infanta Marie Louise of Spain, and her son, the undersigned is authorized to give on this subject the most positive declaration, that the definite reunion of the said territories, which at this moment has become a matter of necessity prescribed by the most imperative circumstances, will not in any way derogate from the previous arrangements, and that they will none the less be given credit for, in estimating the lands which are to serve as compensation for the establishment claimed by the Infanta Marie Louise.

The undersigned begs his highness the Prince de Talleyrand to accept the assurances of his high consideration.

METTERNICH.

---

[1] The courier who left Paris on the 11th, has arrived without any difficulty.

No. 40.—Prince de Talleyrand to King Louis XVIII.

Vienna, *March* 19, 1815.

Sire,

No news whatever has reached us to-day. It is now six o'clock in the evening, when I have the honour of writing to your Majesty.

The affairs of Switzerland were concluded this morning. The deputation which was in Vienna, is to bear the declaration agreed upon and signed by all the powers. I am sending a copy to M. de Talleyrand.[1] The Swiss plenipotentiaries do not think it will completely satisfy one party, or greatly dissatisfy the other, thus the stipulations it contains, will, they believe, be generally adopted.

The first news received by us, will decide the day of Lord Wellington's departure. His courier ought to arrive on the 21st or 22nd, he will then decide what to do.

Here the feeling is excellent. Buonaparte alone is in every one's mind. All the documents will be in accordance therewith.

I have the honour to be. . . .

No. 41.—Prince de Talleyrand to King Louis XVIII.

Vienna, *March* 19, 1815 (*evening*).

Sire,

I have the honour to forward to your Majesty a letter I have just received from the Russian minister. It seems to me to leave nothing more to be desired on the subject of which it treats. The sentiments expressed therein are very good, and quite in accordance with the language held by the emperor under these circumstances. Everything that depends on him is done in the very best spirit.

It is proposed to have three armies in the field and two in reserve.

One, operating from the sea to the Main, will be composed of English, Dutch, Hanoverians, contingents from the north, and Prussians. They will all be under the orders of the Duke of Wellington.

The second will have its line of operations from the Main to the Mediterranean, and will be commanded by Prince Schwartzenberg. This army will be composed of Austrians, Piedmontese, Swiss and contingents from southern Germany.

The army of Italy has no commander as yet.

[1] M. Auguste de Talleyrand, Minister in Switzerland.

Of the two armies of reserve, one will be called the reserve army of the north, and commanded by Marshal Blücher. General Barclay de Tolly [1] will command the other, which will be the reserve army of the south.

All this has only been proposed, but seems to meet with the approval of Austria and England. We expect immediately to hear something as to the strength of each of these armies.

I have the honour to be. . . .

No. 42.—Prince de Talleyrand to King Louis XVIII.

VIENNA, *March* 20, 1815.

SIRE,

The Emperor Francis has just ordered Madame de Montesquiou to send him the child she has charge of. Her language in the present state of affairs is so opposed to the resolutions expressed by Austria and the other powers, that the emperor did not wish her to be any longer near his grandson. To-morrow she will receive orders to return to France. The child will stay at the palace in Vienna. Thus he cannot be carried off, which several circumstances seemed to render probable.

I have the honour to be. . . . .

No. 43.—Prince de Talleyrand to King Louis XVIII.

VIENNA, *March* 23, 1815.

SIRE,

M. le Duc de Rohan-Montbazon arrived here the night before last, and gave me your Majesty's letter which he had brought. All measures had been taken *several days* [2] before his arrival, and he saw the printed notice of the declaration of 14th [3] of this month near the Rhine. It ought to-day to be known all over France. I trust that its effect may be to destroy the confidence of the evil-disposed, and restore that of loyal men.

The troops which Austria, Russia, England, Prussia, Holland, the German States, and Sardinia will place in the field, will, including the garrisons, form a total of seven hundred thousand men, ready to act whenever required. The Prussians have already eighty thousand men on the Rhine; the English, Dutch,

---

[1] Michel, Prince Barclay de Tolly, Russian Field Marshal, born in 1755, of a Scotch family, settled in Livonia, became War Minister in 1810, and commanded the main body of the Russian army in 1812. He died in 1818.

[2] Suppressed in the text of the archives.

[3] Var. : "of 13th."

and Hanoverians a similar number, and two hundred and fifty thousand Russians will arrive there by the end of April with 590 pieces of cannon. I believe that, instead of three, there will be four armies in the field ; one of them will be under the command of General Blücher.

The powers themselves earnestly hope that no part of this force may be required, and that France will be able to do without their aid. But they only wait your Majesty's request to give it.

The papers received to-day from Paris, and which are up to the 14th inclusive, allow me to hope that your Majesty will not be obliged to quit Paris. If on the contrary this is found absolutely necessary, it is thought here, that it would be desirable for your Majesty to withdraw to some place in the north of which you are quite sure, followed by both Chambers, and that part of the army which has remained faithful, increased by a portion of the National Guard. It being most important to avoid as much as possible even the semblance of your Majesty's being isolated, or that your cause and that of the nation is separate, when in reality it is one and the same.

Lord Wellington would like even now to be in Belgium with the troops under his command, so as to be prepared for any emergency. This makes him quite ready to hurry on the affairs here that have still to be concluded.

There have been some difficulties respecting the departure of Madame de Montesquiou, and to-day they talk of sending her to Lintz.

Your Majesty will, no doubt, be grieved to hear that Madame de Brionne died last night. She was eighty years [1] of age.

I have the honour to be. . . . . .

No. 44.—PRINCE DE TALLEYRAND TO KING LOUIS XVIII.

VIENNA, *March* 23, 1815 (*evening*).

SIRE,

This letter is carried to your Majesty by a Prussian courier, who starts to-day.

I have just heard of a letter written by Buonaparte with his own hand to [2] Marie Louise. It is dated the 11th from Lyons, and announces that he will be in Paris about the 21st. This letter, which has been forwarded by General Songeon,[3] who has

---

[1] Var. : "eighty-one years."

[2] Var. : "*à l'archiduchesse*" = "to the archduchess."

[3] Jean-Marie-Songeon, born in 1771, enlisted in 1793, made General of Brigade in 1813. He retired in 1816, and died in 1824.

been false to your Majesty, was brought by an officer of the 7th Hussars named Nyon, to M. de Bubna,[1] who sent it on here. It is written with a double motive : the first to make his army and his partisans believe he is on friendly terms with Austria ; the second to persuade Austria that he has an enormous number of adherents in France. Added to this letter were a whole host of dreadful proclamations. He speaks of a previous letter, which, however, has not come to hand.[2]

At Lyons his force consisted of the 14th Hussars, and the 23rd, 24th, 5th, 7th, and 11th Regiments of the Line. None of these regiments were over a thousand strong. These, added to those he had already, gives him a force of about nine or ten thousand men. (I[3] am speaking of the date up to the 11th.)

It was stated that he was going towards Charolais, where the feeling generally is not supposed to be very favourable. He was still at Lyons on the 13th.

Here the good understanding is perfect ; on this your Majesty may rely. I can answer for it.

In order to hasten matters, the Emperor of Russia has proposed drawing up, in a special treaty between Russia, England, and Prussia, the stipulations relative to Poland. This was agreed to at the conference this morning. This special agreement will appear in the general treaty.

The Prince of the Netherlands takes the title of King of the Netherlands. The notification of this will be made to-morrow and signed the same day.

We are about to take in hand the affairs of Italy, in which we have gained ground greatly as far as Murat is concerned.

I have succeeded in getting M. de Schraut (the Austrian minister in Switzerland, who has used most unparliamentary language) recalled. It appears that his bad temper is owing to ill-health.

I am sending M. de Latour du Pin to France, as just now I have no use for him here. My object is to place him near Marshal Masséna, to encourage the marshal to take possession for your Majesty of all the places momentarily occupied by Buonaparte, and to tell him, without startling him too much, of the dispositions arranged by the powers, and to offer him whatever outside help your Majesty may consider needful. No steps

---

[1] Ferdinand, Comte de Bubna-Littiz, an Austrian Field Marshal then commanding at Turin. He had been, in 1805, President of the Aulic Council, and in 1813 Ambassador at Paris. In 1821 he became Governor of Italy, and died in 1825.

[2] Napoleon had written a previous letter to the Empress Marie Louise, dated Grenoble, March 8.

[3] Var. : "*il parle*" = "he speaks."

will be taken in this direction, except on receipt of a formal written order, signed by yourself.

I have the honour to be. . . . .

No. V.[1]—THE COMTE DE BLACAS D'AULPS TO PRINCE DE TALLEYRAND.

BRUGES, *March* 24, 1815.
(At 2 a.m., just as his Majesty is leaving for Ostend.) [2]

PRINCE,

The king was obliged to quit Lille yesterday at three in the afternoon. Marshal Mortier still held the garrison, though it had already declared for Buonaparte ; but his presence permitted his Majesty to quit the town, if not without danger, at least without any accident, and the king reached Menin, accompanied by an escort and followed by a picket of Chasseurs, many of whom did not wish to abandon him. The National Guard of Lille, which, like that of Paris and all other towns in France, is thoroughly loyal, accompanied his Majesty up to the gates of Menin, where they found some English troops, who probably will not delay in crossing the frontier. The entire population of France will join those troops who are coming to re-establish legitimate authority ; the opinion of the inhabitants is strongly pronounced in this respect, but the whole of France is domineered over by a rebel soldiery, and twenty-six millions of people are now enthralled by forty thousand troops.

The king slept the night at Bruges ; he hopes to reach Ostend this evening ; there he will await news of his household, who were to proceed to Dunkirk. His Majesty will join them there as soon as he hears that they have all arrived. It was not thought safe to go from Lille to Dunkirk either by Cassel or St. Omer, and I have already informed you that the king could no longer remain at Lille without exposing himself to great danger.

We do not know what has become of *Monsieur*, he, as well as the Duc de Berry, were to remain with his Majesty's household, but we have reason to believe that they have embarked at Dieppe, with the intention, no doubt, of going to the south, where M. le Duc d'Angoulême is already, or to the western

---

[1] This letter does not appear in M. Pallain's collection.

[2] Louis XVIII. left the Tuileries on March 19, at eleven at night. He arrived at Abbeville on the 20th, and there stayed the night and the following day. On the evening of the 21st he departed for Lille, where he arrived next day at noon. On the 23rd he left that town and reached Belgium. He passed through Bruges and arrived at Ostend on March 24. Thence he went back to Ghent and remained there.

provinces, which are now stirring, and are under the orders of M. le Duc de Bourbon.[1]

As soon as the king comes to any definite decision I will at once inform you of it, and will keep you acquainted with everything it is important that you should know. While at Lille, the king received the letter you sent him by General Ricard, also the Declaration of the Powers united in Congress at Vienna, which gratified his Majesty extremely. He expects the happiest results from the measures announced therein.

I will write to you from Ostend ; I have only time now to renew to you the assurance of my inviolable attachment and high consideration.

BLACAS D'AULPS.

P.S.—I could not post this letter till we reached Ostend, where we have found the Comte de Jaucourt, who will write to you more fully as to our position here.

No. 27.—KING LOUIS XVIII. TO THE PRINCE DE TALLEYRAND.[2]

OSTEND, *March* 26, 1815.

MON COUSIN,

I take advantage of an English courier who will probably arrive at Vienna before the letters written to you by the Comte de Blacas, and the Comte de Jaucourt. The total defection of the troops left me no choice as to what I must do. They say that my life is necessary to France. I therefore

---

[1] On the first news of the landing of Napoleon, all the princes of the royal family had been appointed to military commands. The Comte d'Artois arrived at Lyons on March 8th, but the defection of the troops on the approach of Napoleon, compelled him to leave on the 10th. He returned to Paris and left it again on the 19th, at the head of the king's household troops. He arrived on the 25th at Yprès in Belgium and went to rejoin the king at Ghent.

The Duc de Berry remained with the king, and eventually received the command of the forces they endeavoured to assemble between Melun and Paris. He followed his father into retirement.

The Duc d'Angoulême was at Bordeaux when Napoleon disembarked. Armed with full powers he organized and maintained the royal prestige in the south, and assembled his forces at Nîmes and Marseilles. But he was surrounded at Montelinart and forced to surrender to General Grouchy (April 8). He was put on board ship at Cette and reached Spain. During this time the duchess remained at Bordeaux where after vain efforts in the royal cause, she was compelled to embark on April 2. She rejoined the king at Ghent.

As for the Duc de Bourbon, he was appointed Governor of the Western Departments, hastened to Nantes and endeavoured to instigate a general rising in Vendée ; but seeing no chance of success, he fled into Spain.

[2] This letter, according to M. Pallain, is wanting in the manuscript at the Foreign Office.

deemed that its security might be risked if I waited some hours longer at Lille. Buonaparte has now all the armed force, but all the hearts belong to me ; of this I have had ample proof, all along my route. The powers cannot therefore be in any doubt this year as to the desires of France : there you have the text, I rely on you to enlarge upon it. I cannot too highly praise Marshal Macdonald and Marshal Mortier. The former behaved just in the same way as he did at Lyons, the latter, although he had received a telegraphic message to arrest me, insured my departure from Lille and my route as far as Menin. Whereupon I pray that God may have you, my cousin, in His safe and holy keeping.   Louis.

No. 45.—The Prince de Talleyrand to King Louis XVIII.

VIENNA, *March* 26, 1815.

SIRE,

The Emperor Alexander having sent last night to say that he wished to see me, I went to him this morning at eleven o'clock. He has never been so pleasant to me since I have been in Vienna. We must, he said, avoid all recrimination, *not go back to the past*,[1] but occupy ourselves in a straightforward and profitable manner with the present state of things, and not endeavour to seek causes, but to remedy them. He spoke frequently and enthusiastically of his attachment to your Majesty. He will give up if necessary his last man and his last coin for you, he even used the language of a valiant soldier who fears not to risk his limbs or his life, he would sooner sacrifice it, than abandon a cause to which he considers his honour is pledged. I on my side showed him the greatest confidence, and continue to do so through those who come more closely in contact with him, and with whom I am intimate. If the aid of a foreign power becomes a necessity, it is better for us that he, whose ambition cannot affect France, should play the principal part.

More than once he repeated to me " Tell the king that this is not the time for mercy, he has to defend the interests of Europe." He several times praised your Majesty for having decided not to quit Paris.

The forces ready for action, and of which he had a statement, amount to eight hundred and sixty thousand men.

The treaty of Chaumont, the conditions of which have been renewed, alone gives six hundred thousand men without counting

---

[1] Suppressed in the text of the archives.

the army of Italy, which will consist of one hundred and fifty thousand, and the Russian and Prussian reserves.

The Prussians have already seventy thousand infantry, seven thousand cavalry, and five thousand artillery on the Rhine. They are sending in addition, one hundred and fifty-nine thousand infantry, nineteen thousand cavalry, and six thousand artillery.

The Russians are beginning to persuade themselves that they cannot have entire confidence in Austria as long as she is not compromised as regards Murat. I have found the emperor very well disposed on this point.

We meet this evening to sign the treaty of co-operation. I yesterday suggested the insertion of the following article ;

" The sole object of the present treaty being to support France or any other country against the attempts of Buonaparte and his adherents, his most Christian Majesty will be specially invited to agree to it, and to make known in case he should require the aid of the forces mentioned in Article . . . . what assistance circumstances will allow him to devote to the object of the present treaty."

Although this article has not been definitely adopted, I have every reason to believe that it will be.

I have the honour to be . . . .

No. 46.—The Prince de Talleyrand to King Louis XVIII.

VIENNA, *March* 29, 1815.

SIRE,

There is no need for me to express to your Majesty the feelings with which I heard of the disastrous events which have succeeded each other with such incredible rapidity. You will judge of this from my attachment to your person, which is as well known to your Majesty as my zeal and my devotion. All the powers I possess will always be consecrated to your service. I say so now and I will not again repeat it to your Majesty.

The treaty of co-operation was signed on the evening of the 25th,[1] and was officially communicated to me on the 27th. I have the honour to send your Majesty herewith a copy of this treaty and of the memorandum transmitted to me at the same time by the plenipotentiaries, and my reply thereto.

This important matter finished, the Duke of Wellington did

---

[1] Treaty of the Quadruple Alliance, between Great Britain, Austria, Prussia, and Russia, to which France agreed by an official note from M. de Talleyrand of March 27.

not wish to delay any longer in joining his army, he therefore left Vienna at six o'clock this morning.

We are redoubling our efforts to get the affairs finished which the congress has still to arrange ; I think it will end in April.   I consider it is more than ever necessary that it should close with a solemn act, for such an act will prove to all the world that the powers are in accord and absolutely determined to maintain that order of things which Buonaparte's attempt tends to destroy.

As your Majesty might find it inconvenient just now to defray from the French chancellor's office the expenses of your embassy at the congress and also those of the couriers and persons sent to obtain information, I have made arrangements with England to see to this.   Your Majesty therefore need not give yourself any further concern in the matter.

I am most anxious to hear from your Majesty and to learn that you have arrived at the place where you have decided to stay.   I trust your Majesty has carried away with you all the letters I had the honour of writing to you, and that your Majesty has directed M. de Jaucourt to take away with him everything that relates to the congress.   There are many things in my letters which would certainly be displeasing to the powers, who now are willing to be friendly, but whose attitude six months ago may often have been severely censured.

I keep here with me two reliable couriers for communication between this place and wherever your Majesty may have to remain.   They will never enter France except across such frontier as your Majesty may consider safe.

I have the honour to be. . . .

TREATY OF THE 25TH MARCH, 1815, MENTIONED IN THE PRECEDING DESPATCH DATED 29TH MARCH.

In the name of the Holy and Indivisible Trinity, his Majesty the Emperor of Austria, King of Hungary and Bohemia, and his Majesty the King of the United Kingdom of Great Britain and Ireland, having taken into consideration the consequences which the invasion of France by Napoleon Buonaparte and the actual position of that kingdom may have on the security of Europe, have by common consent, together with his Majesty the Emperor of all the Russias, and his Majesty the King of Prussia, resolved to apply to this important circumstance the principles laid down by the treaty of Chaumont.   In consequence of which they have agreed to renew by a solemn treaty, signed separately by each of these four powers with each of the other three, the undertaking to preserve, against all attempts to the contrary, the order of affairs so happily re-established in Europe, and to decide upon the most efficacious means of carrying this undertaking into effect and of giving it all the possible latitude so imperiously demanded by present circumstances. With this view his Majesty the Emperor of Austria, King of Hungary and Bohemia, has for the purpose of discussing, concluding, and signing the conditions of the present treaty with his Majesty the King of the United Kingdom of Great Britain and Ireland, named the Sieur. . . . and his Britannic Majesty having on his side named the Sieur. . . . the said plenipotentiaries after having exchanged their full powers and found them in proper and due form, have drawn up the following articles :

Art. I.—The high contracting parties above named solemnly engage to combine in making every effort within their respective states, to maintain in all their integrity, the conditions of the treaty of peace concluded in Paris, May 30th, 1814, as. well as the stipulations drawn up and signed at the Congress of Vienna, with the object of completing the arrangements of that treaty, and guarding them against all attacks, and particularly against the designs of Napoleon Buonaparte. For this purpose they engage themselves, if required, to direct together and with mutual consent in the spirit of the declaration of the 13th of March last, all their efforts against him and against all those who have joined his faction or may do so later, in order to compel him to desist from his projects and place him beyond the possibility of disturbing for the future, the tranquillity and general peace under the protection of which, the rights, the liberty and the independence of the nations have just been established and assured.

Art. II.—Although it is impossible to estimate the measures necessary to attain so great and beneficent a result, and although the high contracting parties are determined to devote to it all those which according to their respective positions they can command, they are nevertheless agreed to keep permanently in the field a total of one hundred and fifty thousand men each, at least one-tenth of which shall be cavalry and a proper proportion of artillery, without reckoning the garrisons, and to employ these actively and jointly against the common enemy.

Art. III.—The high contracting parties reciprocally undertake not to lay down arms except by common consent and until the object of the war named in the first article of the present treaty has been attained, and so long as Buonaparte shall not have been placed absolutely beyond the possibility of raising fresh disturbances and renewing his attempts to seize the supreme power in France.

Art. IV.—This treaty being solely applicable to present circumstances, the stipulations of the treaty of Chaumont, and particularly those contained in Article XVI., will again come into full force as soon as the actual end has been attained.

Art. V.—All that which relates to the command of the allied armies, their maintenance . . . . . will be regulated by a special convention.

Art. VI.—The high contracting parties will have the power respectively, of accrediting to the generals in command of the troops, certain officers who will be at liberty to correspond with their governments, and keep them informed of military events and everything relating to the operations of the armies.

Art. VII.—The engagements entered into by the present treaty having for their aim the maintenance of universal peace, the high contracting parties have resolved between them to ask all the other powers of Europe to agree to them.

Art. VIII.—The present treaty having been solely entered into for the purpose of supporting France or any other country that may be invaded, against the attempts of Buonaparte and his adherents, his most Christian Majesty will be specially asked to give his consent thereto, and to make known, in case he should require the forces named in Article II., what assistance circumstances will permit him to bring forward towards the object of the present treaty.

Art. IX.—The present treaty shall be ratified, and the ratifications thereof shall be exchanged in two months, or sooner if necessary.

In witness whereof the respective plenipotentiaries have hereunto signed their names and set their seals.

Executed at Vienna, March 25, in the year of our Lord, 1815.

> THE PRINCE DE METTERNICH.
> THE BARON DE WESSENBERG.
> THE DUKE OF WELLINGTON.

On the same day the same treaty was concluded between Russia and Great Britain, and likewise between Great Britain and Prussia.

No. 47.—The Prince de Talleyrand to King Louis XVIII.

VIENNA, March 30, 1815.

SIRE,

General Pozzo is about to start and join your Majesty. I do not wish him to leave without taking a letter to you. All the powers are quite agreed on the destruction of Buonaparte ; they look upon it as a matter of personal interest. The Emperor of Russia is the most enthusiastic ; he is sending all his troops, and considers that this question is one on which he is bound to spend [1] his last coin. He will himself accompany them.

I trust the *corps diplomatique* has followed your Majesty. I am extremely anxious to receive news from you.

I have the honour to be. . . . .

No. 48.—The Prince de Talleyrand to King Louis XVIII.

VIENNA, April 3, 1815.

SIRE,

As Lord Clancarty is sending a courier to London who will pass through Belgium, I take advantage of it to make known to your Majesty the actual state of affairs. Some days ago we heard here that Murat [2] had entered the Papal States and that the Pope had to quit Rome. This event has at last opened the eyes of Austria and put an end to all her hesitation. We are now therefore almost entirely in accord with regard to Italian affairs, which will soon be arranged ; we shall then have only to combine all the articles agreed upon, in order to draw up the act which will terminate the congress ; for I strongly hold, and now more than ever, that there must be an act.

There is no change in your Majesty's embassy here. The same consideration is shown towards it, and it exercises the same influence as if your Majesty was still in Paris and your

[1] Var.: "son dernier homme et "="his last man and."
[2] Murat as soon as he heard of the landing of Napoleon, thought to profit by it, and put himself at the head of a similar movement and proclaimed himself King of Italy. He marched into Upper Italy, overran the Roman States and Tuscany, and drove back the Austrians as far as the Po; but he had soon to retreat, he was defeated at Tolentius and driven back on Naples. He embarked for France, and Queen Caroline was conducted to Trieste with her two children (May 20). As for Murat, after remaining some time in France, he passed over to Corsica, and there assembled a small number of followers, with whom he attempted a landing in his former states. He was captured almost immediately and shot at Pizzo (October 13, 1815).

authority was not ignored in any part of the kingdom. I can give your Majesty the assurance that this position is fully maintained.

I have not as yet received any news from your Majesty since you quitted Paris. I await it with the greatest impatience. I venture to say it is of the utmost importance that I should be kept informed as to your movements and intentions.

I have the honour to be. . . . .

P.S.—I much wish that your Majesty would acquaint me in detail of those who followed you and those whom you await. Only Christian names are necessary. Was the Archbishop of Rheims able to follow your Majesty?[1] I have heard nothing from M. de Jaucourt. May I take the liberty of enclosing a letter to him under cover to your Majesty?

M. de Vincent arrived this morning; the Austrian government will probably receive a letter from Buonaparte or the Duc de Vicence[2] through Lefebvre,[3] the secretary of the legation, but this communication will receive no reply and will have no effect.

My letter number 45, which has been returned to me, will show your Majesty those that are missing.

No. 49.—The Prince de Talleyrand to King Louis XVIII.

VIENNA, *April* 8,[4] 1815.

SIRE,

The events which have taken place in France have in no way altered the position of your Majesty's embassy at the congress, where the affairs concerning the future arrangements of Europe continue to be discussed as heretofore. I have reason to hope that what still remains to be decided will be carried out in accordance with the wishes expressed to me by your Majesty.

In several letters I had the honour of writing to your Majesty and which perhaps have not reached you, I mentioned that it seemed of the utmost importance to every one here, and also to myself, that your Majesty should not quit French territory, or, if that was unavoidable, that you should go no further away

---

[1] The Cardinal de Talleyrand-Perigord, the author's uncle.
[2] The Duc de Vicenre had just been made Minister of Foreign Affairs.
[3] M. Pallain writes "Lefeburo." He had been Secretary to the Embassy at Paris.
[4] This letter is dated 5th April in the text of the archives.

than was absolutely necessary. If I might venture to express my opinion, which is also that of the plenipotentiaries of all the powers, I should say that your sojourn in a town so near the sea as Ostend cannot but greatly injure your cause in public estimation, as it may lead people to think that your Majesty is desirous of quitting the continent and placing the sea between yourself and your country.

The place which under present circumstances would seem most suitable for your Majesty (provided the state of affairs permits), is the town of Liege, which the disposition of the troops seems to render safe.

We are occupied here with the second declaration of the congress, confirming the arrangements made by the powers in that of March 13th. It will answer all the proclamations issued by Buonaparte since he became master of Paris, and will, I feel sure, produce a great effect wherever it is made known. It has been specially written for the temper of the French people.

The only letter I have received from your Majesty since you left Paris is that with which your Majesty deigned to honour me dated March 26th. I have received none, either from M. de Blacas nor from M. de Jaucourt, and I must inform your Majesty that this neglect is extremely painful to me and very injurious to affairs here.

I have the honour to be . . . . .

P.S. I enclose herewith a letter sent by a courier which has come back to me, as well as a letter which the same courier carried to M. de Jaucourt.

No. 28.—KING LOUIS XVIII. TO THE PRINCE DE TALLEYRAND.

GHENT, *April* 10,[1] 1815.

MON COUSIN,

I have received by Prince Victor de Rohan[2] your letter No. 46. The expressions of your attachment are always agreeable to me, and perhaps even more so at such a painful moment, but I did not need them to count fully on them.

The treaty of March 25th, the sequel and completion of the declaration of the 13th, being solely directed against Buonaparte,

---

[1] Var.: "9th April."

[2] Victor, Prince de Rohan, born in 1764, was Grand Chamberlain in 1789; banished shortly afterwards, he entered the Austrian army and became Major-General and Field Marshal. He returned to France in 1814 and quitted it again in 1830, and died in Austria (1835).

I do not hesitate to charge you to adhere to it in my name. If you require a direction *ad hoc* you shall have it whenever you wish, but meanwhile I authorize you to act as if you had already received it.

The weight that I can throw into the scale is nineteen-twentieths of the French nation, whose sentiments neither I nor the powers need doubt. But this, powerful as it is, cannot be utilized without foreign aid. It will therefore be necessary for the allied armies to enter France, and that as soon as possible. Every moment's delay lessens my power. The nature of fierce enthusiasm is gradually to cool down, whereas delay, on the contrary, gives to the enemy facilities for concentrating his troops and the means, which he knows only too well how to employ, of turning in his favour those who to-day only ask to take up arms and fight for me.

The Duke of Wellington, whom I saw yesterday, and whose dispositions I cannot praise sufficiently, has sent off a courier to ask for permission to act without waiting till all the forces have joined. I need not impress upon you to support this request urgently. If we wait for the complete junction of the troops, it will be impossible to do anything before the first of June. I have no doubt as to our success, but Buonaparte will never be crushed except beneath the ruins of France, whereas speedy action, by more surely destroying him, might preserve her, and this should be the aim of every one, but especially ourselves.[1]

The Duke of Wellington tells me that the counter project which I sent you on March 7th, has been adopted. I was very pleased to hear this. I am also thoroughly satisfied with the arrangements you have made about the chancellor's office, the couriers . . . . . It is a relief to my finances, which are very low just now.

I have brought away with me all letters and documents you have sent me since you were in Vienna,[2] and have directed M. de Jaucourt to do the same. Your courage has not been crushed, as I felt sure it would not be, by these events. You see that mine is not affected either.

Whereupon I pray God that He may have you, my cousin, in His safe and holy keeping.

LOUIS.

----

[1] Var : "ce peut ne pas être le but de tout le monde, mais ce doit être le nôtre" = "this may not be the aim of all the world, but it must be ours."

[2] This passage in the king's letter proves that Buonaparte would not have found the treaty of January 3 in the escritoire in the Tuileries.

No. VI.[1]—The Comte de Blacas d'Aulps to the Prince de Talleyrand.

GHENT, *April* 10, 1815.

PRINCE,

The despatches which you sent by Prince Victor de Rohan reached us at Ghent ; you will have heard that the king went thither on leaving Ostend, where his continued residence seemed to him, to give colouring to the false reports of his embarkation. No one can deplore more than myself the necessity which obliged his Majesty to quit his country, but you will see by the very full account I have the honour of sending you herewith,[2] the imperative necessity with which he was forced to comply, and the painful duties imposed on those faithful subjects who dreaded everything for the king's honour, everything for the last resources of the Monarchy, during those critical moments, when counsel became so difficult.

The king had several marshals with him, by whose advice he was guided, respecting the troops, which in this sudden revolution, have become the sole arbiters of the destiny of France. Never has pretorian power exercised a more fatal ascendency. You would have been indignant at the irresistible violence beneath which the national will and inclination have been compelled to bow. It is fortunate that the European powers desire to maintain peace, and prevent the calamities ready to fall on themselves, for it is only on this interest and this assistance that we can count, to deliver our unhappy country from the extreme disorder into which France has been plunged.

M. le Duc d'Angoulême alone seems to have been able to rally some troops in the south. May God grant that treason does not baffle our efforts ! It seems that those of *Madame* were not able to preserve the town of Bordeaux.

You will no doubt think that under such circumstances you cannot too urgently hasten the measures already determined upon. It is above all most important to prevent the evil effects which the king's sojourn out of France might produce, and the powers, through their relations with his Majesty, can surround him with such a force, as will alone supplement the supremacy of which he has for the moment been deprived.

Lord Wellington, who arrived here yesterday, does not seem to have the least doubt about our future success, nor the slightest uncertainty respecting the restorative character that must be

---

[1] This letter is not in M. Pallain's collection.
[2] See this account further on.

given to the war, but he does not wish to commence operations until all his forces are assembled, and during this delay, France is suffering, and resistance becomes discouraged. This painful thought however must not weigh against the certain calculations which direct the aggressive preparations.

The treaty of March 25th is drawn up in the most satisfactory manner, and we may hope everything from the effect which its publication will produce in France.

The Paris journals have announced the approaching arrival in France of the Archduchess Marie-Louise. It would be very desirable to give the utmost publicity to any facts which contradict this assertion. As for the rest, prince, we cannot do better than rely on your zeal and your judgment. It is to you and to the centre of the European confederation, of which you are a member, that we must look for hopes of a happier future.

M. Pozzo de Borgo has reached Brussels, and will be here in the course of to-day. I do not know how long the king will remain here, his intentions in this respect depend upon the measures taken by the Duke of Wellington. We are trying to gather together the remains of the household troops; they are now assembled at Alost,[1] to the number of four or five hundred men.

Lord Harrowby and Mr. Wellesley Poole[2] have arrived on the part of their government to arrange the preliminary measures for the approaching campaign with Lord Wellington. They saw the king on their way through Ghent, and his Majesty has every reason to be satisfied with the dispositions they showed to him. M. de Chateaubriand,[3] and M. de Lally-Tollendal,[4] and M. d'Anglès,[5] are here now ; the king, I believe, means to consult them.

Accept, prince, the assurance of my most devoted attachment and highest consideration.

BLACAS D'AULPS.

[1] Alost, a town in Belgium near Ghent.

[2] Sir William Wellesley Poole, an English statesman, born in 1763, Master of the Mint and member of the House of Commons.

[3] Chateaubriand was about to be appointed Minister at Stockholm, when the Hundred Days interfered. He followed the king to Ghent, and became a Minister of State.

[4] M. de Lally-Tollendal, formerly member of the Constituent Assembly, was then a Privy Councillor.

[5] Comte Jules d'Anglès, born in 1778, Auditor to the State Council, Master of Appeal in 1809, Director of Police of the Departments beyond the Alpes, Police Minister under the Provisional Government in 1814, State Councillor under the first restoration. In March, 1815, he accompanied Comte d'Artois as Civil Commissioner, and then followed the king to Ghent. On the return of the king he became Minister of State, then Préfet of Police under the Decaze Ministry. He tendered his resignation after the assassination of the Duc de Berry, and died in 1828.

P.S.—General Pozzo de Borgo has just arrived. General Fagel[1] this morning presented his credentials to the king, as minister of the King of the Belgians.

NARRATIVE ATTACHED TO THE PRECEDING LETTER.

A catastrophe as baneful as it was unexpected, has just struck Europe with amazement. A king surrounded by the confidence and love of his people has been obliged to quit his capital, and soon afterwards his kingdom, which has been invaded by the man whose odious name recalls nothing but crimes and calamities ; and France, from the state of profound peace and progressive prosperity which she had regained, has in less than three weeks, been replunged into an abyss of ills which she believed had been closed for ever.

It is most important that it should be known by what process of irresistible causes, treason has, under these circumstances, been enabled to enslave public opinion and the national will.

On the 5th of March the king was apprised by telegraphic despatch, that Buonaparte had disembarked on French territory at the head of eleven hundred men. This attempt might be looked at from two different points of view. It was either the result of a plot supported by widely spread correspondence, or the act of a madman, whose ambition and passionate character would no longer suffer him to endure the inactivity, which only left him a prey to the uneasiness of remorse. Under this twofold supposition it was necessary to take every measure that prudence could suggest or the most imminent danger demand. Nothing was neglected. Orders were issued with all haste for the assembly of the troops at Lyons. Satisfactory accounts were received from the commandant at Grenoble, and the conduct of the garrison at Antibes inspired the hope, that Buonaparte had been mistaken in the belief that he would be able to gain over

---

[1] Robert, Baron de Fagel, born in 1772, of an ancient and illustrious Dutch family. Entering the army young, he took part in the campaigns of 1793 and 1794 against France. Being exiled by the fall of the House of Orange, he did not return to his country till 1813. In 1814 General Fagel was appointed Minister at Paris. He remained there until 1854.

the king's troops. Nevertheless, if he had some secret correspondents, they might favour his first progress, but a force stationed at Lyons would be able to check this. *Monsieur,* therefore, started at six in the morning, to assume the command ; he was followed the next day by M. le Duc d'Orleans.

All the marshals and generals employed in the departments received orders to rejoin their respective head-quarters, and started at once. Marshal Ney, who was in command at Besançon, and could from thence very efficiently second *Monsieur's* operations, came to take leave of the king, and on kissing hands, said to him, in a tone of devotion, and with an *élan* that seemed the outcome of a soldier's frankness, that if he came across the king's enemy and that of France, he would bring him back in an iron cage. Events soon showed with what base dissimulation a project of the blackest perfidy had even then inspired him.

Monsieur was enthusiastically received at Lyons ; everything was prepared for the most vigorous resistance, but unfortunately there were no munitions of war.

It was soon known that the garrison of Grenoble had opened the gates of that town to the enemy, and that a regiment from Chambéry, under the command of M. de la Bédoyère [1] had joined the rebels. Only a small number of troops had as yet arrived at Lyons, but *Monsieur,* whom Marshal Macdonald hastened to rejoin, nevertheless decided to make a stand behind the barricades that had been hastily thrown up. But the appearance of the first of the dragoons who preceded Buonaparte, caused general disaffection amongst *Monsieur's* troops. All the remonstrances of the Duc de Tarente were in vain ; and then, as ever since, the troops assembled to oppose the torrent, only served to increase it and add to its violence.

[1] Charles Huchet, Comte de la Bédoyère, born in 1786, enrolled as a volunteer in 1806, became Aide-de-Camp to Prince Eugène in 1809, and Colonel in 1814. In 1815 he commanded the 7th Regiment of the Line at Grenoble. It was known that he was one of the first to declare in favour of Napoleon and that he brought his regiment to him at Vizille. He became General of Brigade and peer of France during the Hundred Days. He was arrested on the 4th of August following, brought before a court martial and shot (August 19th).

On the tenth we learnt by a telegraphic despatch, and therefore without any details, that Buonaparte had entered Lyons that same day. The return of M. le Duc d'Orleans, who arrived in Paris on the twelfth, and also that of *Monsieur*, was speedily followed by information which raised to the highest pitch, the alarm which such a rapid succession of disasters could not fail to create.

But public opinion, excited by so many fears and suspicions, seeks elsewhere for the cause of his lamentable success, than in the fatal ascendency of a man so abhorred. No one believed it possible that the mere fascination of his presence could have such an effect on the troops. Marshal the Duc de Dalmatie, the war minister, had been the last to uphold in France by force of arms, the fallen fortunes of Napoleon. Some people seemed to see in this former proof of devotion an indication of present treachery. The public voice was raised against the marshal, who then sent in his resignation and tendered his sword [1] to the king. His Majesty with that reliance which has never failed him amid the most terrible treachery, summoned the Duc de Feltre, to whom public opinion pointed for selection, and handed him the portfolio of war minister, which post he had previously held under Buonaparte, until the restoration. This action has been fully justified by the Duc de Feltre's [2] fidelity.

There was nothing further to be done, than to withdraw the troops, which, when advancing towards the enemy, supplied him almost everywhere with auxiliaries. It was decided to form an army corps before Paris by assembling there as many of the National Guard and volunteers as could be got together. The Duc de Berry was on the 11th nominated general of this force, and Marshal Macdonald was on his arrival appointed to the command under the prince's orders.

But nevertheless the orders sent to hasten the organization of the volunteers and the mobile columns of the National Guard, could neither reach their destination nor be carried out for some days, and every moment brought forth fresh dangers. Buona-

---

[1] The marshal's resignation is dated 11th March. Some days after Napoleon created him peer of France and Major-General.

[2] The Duc de Feltre followed the king to Ghent.

parte marched with a rapidity the enormous advantage of which he foresaw, and several regiments, which were necessarily near his route, joined him, some even taking possession in his name of various towns in Burgundy. One of them preceded him into Auxerre.

There was still some faint hope that the regiments of the first military division, and those forming the garrison of Paris, might remain loyal. An imminent danger, just averted by the fidelity of the commandant of La Fère and the arrest of the traitors d'Erlong and Lallemand, likewise gave some little confidence as to the state of the departments in the north.[1] The Duc de Reggio, though deserted by the Old Guard, has succeeded in keeping the other regiments under his command faithful. It was decided to form an army of reserve at Peronne, where the troops, being together, would be less exposed to temptation and would be under the supervision of the Duc de Trévise, to whom was given the command of this army corps. The Duc d'Orleans went there shortly afterwards.

It was at this time that the king, impressed by the greatness of the danger, but equally sensible of the grave duties which the painful circumstances attendant on his situation imposed upon him, went to the representatives of the nation by whom he desired to be surrounded at the first approach of danger. His speech to the assembly of the two Chambers made a great impression in the capital, the inhabitants of which unanimously testified their sentiments of devotion to the king and the country ; but the National Guard, composed chiefly of fathers of families, could not furnish a sufficient number of volunteers to give any hopes of successful resistance ; and the Comte de Dessoles[2] who

---

[1] On the news of Napoleon's landing, a military rising broke out in the North. Generals Lallemand at Laon, Drouet-d'Erlon at Lille, and Lefebvre-Desnouettes at Noyon, who for some time had prepared a *coup de main*, wished to assemble their troops, march upon Paris, and keep the king a prisoner there. Lefebvre-Desnouettes gave the signal by endeavouring to carry off the depôt of artillery at la Fère, but he was prevented by the firmness of General d'Aboville (March 9). The conspirators then took possession of Chauny, but having been thwarted at Compiègne, they dispersed and the movement failed. At the second restoration these three generals were condemned to death in default.

[2] Jean Dessoles, born in 1767, enlisted in 1792, became General of Division and Chief of the Staff of the Army of Italy in 1798, and State Councillor in 1801. He remained a long time in retirement during the Empire, and then became Chief of the

commanded it, was so explicit on this point, that there was nothing left but to amalgamate the citizens with the troops of the line, in order to keep the latter faithful.

Every other plan of defence being impracticable, it became apparent that the principal means of resistance was reduced to some regiments, whose fidelity was more than doubtful, strengthened by a small number of brave and devoted volunteers, to whom would be added the body of cavalry belonging to the king's household.

On the 17th an overwhelming piece of intelligence rendered these preparations still less hopeful. Marshal Ney, who was supposed to be in pursuit of the rebels, had joined them; at the same time issuing a proclamation intended to spread the disaffection still further. This news struck terror into the departments adjoining Paris. The town of Sens declared itself unable to resist; the enemy would shortly be at Fontainebleau; and the troops in Paris, on whom every means had been exhausted in order to excite their patriotism, either remained perfectly silent or showed signs of a desire to abandon their colours.

Hardly had they started for the *rendezvous* assigned to them, than their evil inclinations degenerated into open rebellion. On the morning of the 19th it became known that there was not a single regiment before Paris which was not overtaken by this contagious defection; thus there was nothing to prevent Buonaparte's approach, and the only thing left for the king was to withdraw, accompanied by his household troops, on whose fidelity he could in future alone rely.

His Majesty, who had sent the Duc de Bourbon to the departments of the west, and who had given the Duc d'Angoulême the necessary powers for arming the southern provinces, deemed it best that he himself should go to the northern departments and endeavour to keep possession of the strongholds and use them as a *point d'appui* for the assembly of those faithful subjects who might rally there. The king left at midnight on the 19th, and

---

Staff to Prince Eugene in 1812. In 1814 he was appointed by the Provisional Government, General Commandant of the National Guard. At the first restoration he became a State Minister, peer of France, and Major General of the National Guard. In 1818 he was for some months President of the Council, and died in 1828.

was followed an hour later by his household troops under *Monsieur*, and by the Duc de Berry.

Reaching Abbeville on the 20th at five in the afternoon, the king rested there the next day to await the arrival of the household troops ; but Marshal Macdonald, who joined his Majesty at midnight on the 21st, pointed out to the king the necessity of leaving at once ; and after hearing his report his Majesty determined to retire to Lille, and sent orders to the household troops to rejoin him there by way of Amiens.

At one in the afternoon on the 22nd, the king, preceded by the Duc de Tarente, entered Lille, where he was received by the inhabitants with the most enthusiastic demonstrations of affection and fidelity. He had also been preceded by the Duc d'Orleans and the Duc de Trévise, who thought they ought to call out the garrison. This last circumstance, of which the king had not been advised, might greatly disconcert the plans of resistance which had been decided on. If the troops had not been called out, the national guards and the king's household troops, seconded by the loyalty of the inhabitants of Lille, might have secured to the king this last refuge on French territory. With a large and ill-disposed garrison the scheme seemed very difficult of execution ; his Majesty however determined to make the attempt. The enthusiasm of the people had already been roused to the highest pitch by his presence. An eager crowd followed him, making every effort to enlist the sympathies of the soldiers, and repeatedly shouting their cherished cry of " *Vive le Roi !* " The soldiers, dejected and indifferent, maintained a gloomy silence— an alarming warning of their approaching defection ; indeed, Marshal Mortier frankly told the king that he would not answer for the garrison.

When questioned as to the utmost expedients it might be possible to employ, he declared further that it would be out of his power to make the troops leave the town. In the meanwhile, the declaration published at Vienna on March 13th, in the name of all the European powers united in congress, arrived at Lille. The king directed it to be distributed and placarded at once, hoping, though in vain, thereby to show the troops the fatal results that would follow their defection, and the inevitable misfortunes it would bring on their country.

On the 23rd his Majesty heard that the Duc de Bassano, who had been made minister of the interior, had sent orders from Buonaparte to the prefet of Lille. On the same day, at one o'clock in the afternoon, Marshal Mortier came to inform the master of the king's household that a report having got abroad that the Duc de Berry was approaching with the household troops and two Swiss regiments, the whole garrison was prepared to rise. He entreated that the king would leave, in order to avoid the most terrible disasters, and added that he hoped by personally escorting his Majesty beyond the gates of the town, to keep a check on the soldiers, which it would be impossible for him to do if the departure was delayed for a single moment. The king therefore deemed it necessary to send orders to his household troops to proceed to Dunkirk, which order unfortunately never reached them ; but being unable himself to go straight to that town, he decided to proceed to Ostend. His Majesty left Lille at three o'clock, accompanied by Marshal Mortier, and followed by the Duc d'Orleans. At the foot of the *glacis*, the Duc de Trévise deemed it advisable to turn back to prevent any disturbance the garrison might commit during his absence. The Duc d'Orleans also returned to the fortress, and did not depart till several hours later. Marshal Macdonald did not leave the king till they reached the gates of Ménin, and to the last moment afforded to his Majesty, as did also the Duc de Trévise, the comforting proof that the sacredness of an oath and the fidelity of a man of honour are not scorned by all the gallant men on whom the French army prides itself.

A picket of the national guard of Lille, a detachment of cuirassiers and the king's chasseurs, followed his Majesty as far as the frontier. Some of the latter, together with several officers, did not wish to leave him, and accompanied him into Belgian territory. The king arrived at Ostend hoping to proceed to Dunkirk as soon as that town was occupied by his household troops. During this time, these unfortunate troops, who had been joined by a large number of volunteers of all ages and

ranks, had followed the route taken by the king on his way to
Lille. *Monsieur* and the Duc de Berry, always at the head of
this brave *élite* and sharing its fatigue, had good cause to admire
its heroic constancy. Young lads, who for the first time carried
heavy arms, and old men, had joined these faithful troops, doing
forced marches on foot on roads rendered almost impassable by
heavy and continuous rains, and were not discouraged either by
privation or the still more cruel uncertainty of a march, which
they were conscious the defection of the surrounding garrisons,
might render still more disastrous. In the absence of orders, which
the king could not prevent, and hearing also that his Majesty
had left Lille, the column marched straight to the frontier, but
in crossing a heavy country, over which the horses could only
pass with extreme difficulty, they were unable to defile quickly
enough to follow Marshal Marmont, who led them under
the orders of the princes, with an activity and zeal worthy of
better success, and a portion of these unfortunate men were
forced to remain behind, when *Monsieur*, fearing their devotion
would only lead them into useless perils, gave them leave to
withdraw. But being quickly surprised and shut up in Bethune
by orders received from Paris, they did not all succeed in dis-
persing, and left to *Monsieur* only the hope of rallying round
him by degrees, those amongst them whom he could collect on
the frontier ; for which purpose he remained there.

At eight o'clock on the morning of the 25th, the king heard
that *Monsieur* had reached Yprès, and the news of what had
befallen his household troops added fresh weight to the sorrows
with which he was already overwhelmed.

In the midst of this terrible disaster, his Majesty has received
the most gratifying tokens of fidelity, but they in a measure
serve only to increase his regrets. He is forced to leave his
people, good and devoted as they are, to the tender mercies of
an excited soldiery, and he cannot gather round him his staunch
and brave followers. There are evidences of unswerving fidelity
among many of the chiefs of that army which the king would
like to call his own, and yet he cannot offer any other recompense
than that esteem and praise which France and posterity will one
day acknowledge as their due.

Among the memories which are indelibly engraved on the king's heart and the honourable sentiments of which he has received the most convincing proof, those which he retains of the conduct of Marshal Mortier occupy the first rank. Since the arrival of his Majesty at Ostend he has heard through the Duc d'Orleans that an order to arrest him and all the princes had reached the marshal; a staff officer carrying a despatch from Marshal Davoust, in which the same order was enclosed, arrived at Lille after the king had left it; but the Duc de Trévise arranged matters so that nothing transpired until after the departure of the Duc d'Orleans.[1]

This brief narrative of the principal events which mark the short and unfortunate period just described, will enable you to judge of the sudden and innumerable difficulties by which the king sees himself surrounded. Never have such unexpected and rapid events changed the aspect of a vast monarchy; but never before has the marked difference between the disposition of the soldier and the citizen so completely paralyzed patriotism, weakened authority, and invested with a magic terror the man, who, arriving almost alone on French soil, was enabled two days later to array a mass of armed men against a defenceless people.

Moreover this simultaneous and general defection of the army has not, it is evident, been based on any motive that could for a length of time attach it to the fate of the man who has resumed so baneful an ascendency over it. The tacit compact he has made with it, will quickly be broken by the reverses that await him. It is not Buonaparte proscribed, rejected and shortly to be overwhelmed by the whole of Europe, whom this credulous soldiery desired to follow. They saw before them the devastator

[1] . . . . "I then decided to leave (*Lille*) in the night. It was not until I had come to this determination that I learnt from Marshal the Duc de Trévise (who had had the extreme delicacy to hide it from me as well as the king) that a telegraphic despatch of fifteen lines, had been sent him, by which he was enjoined to arrest the king and all the Bourbons who might be at Lille. He told me besides, that since the king's departure one of Marshal Davoust's aides-de-camp had presented himself at the gate, that he had sent for him and found that he brought orders to arrest the king and myself. He assured me that he could trust this aide-de-camp, and begging me to take no notice of what I had just learnt, he asked me to stay at Lille as long as if I had known nothing about it. I already appreciated all the qualities of Marshal the Duc de Trévise, for whom I had a sincere friendship, and I had no need of this fresh proof of loyalty to do justice to the nobleness of his character."—*My Journal. Events of* 1815, by Louis Philippe d'Orleans (i. 256).

of the world, ready to give them up the spoil.   His *prestige* once
destroyed, Buonaparte will soon lose his borrowed strength ; it
is for this, for the reflex which follows the intoxication of a great
illusion, which the king waits, with all the impatience to which
the happy results he expects from it, give rise.

No. 50.—The Prince de Talleyrand to King Louis XVIII.

Vienna, *April* 13, 1815.

Sire,

As Buonaparte has made himself master of Paris, the
powers consider that it might be advisable to renew by a second
declaration, the manifestation of the sentiments expressed in
that of the 13th of March.   There is every reason to believe,
that with the exception of a few individuals, every one in France
of whatever shade of opinion, desires the same thing, the downfall
of Buonaparte.   It would be well therefore to utilize this general
feeling, in order to annihilate him.   This object once accomplished,
the particular opinions of each party will find themselves without
support, without strength, and without means of action, and will
no longer present any obstacles.

The declaration has therefore been drawn up in such a
manner as to induce the representatives of all parties to compel
Buonaparte to retire.   Though fully agreed as to the basis of the
declaration, we have not yet come to an understanding as to its
form ; and its publication is for the moment delayed.   It is even
suggested to substitute for a declaration by the congress, a proclamation, to be issued simultaneously by all the commanders-in-
chief of the allied troops, at the moment that those troops enter
French territory, and I am not disinclined to adopt this idea,
which seems to me to possess many advantages.

All I hear from France proves that Buonaparte finds himself
greatly embarrassed.   I also judge of this from the two emissaries
he has sent here.

One of them, M. de Montrond, with the help of the Abbé
Altieri attached to the Austrian legation in Paris, has come as
far as Vienna.   He had no ostensible mission nor any despatches,
and he has most probably been sent by the party which favours
Buonaparte, not by Buonaparte himself.   That at least is my
impression.   He was the bearer of messages to M. de Metternich,
M. de Nesselrode, and myself.   He was to ascertain whether the
foreign powers were seriously determined not to recognize

Buonaparte, but to go to war with him ; he had also a letter for Prince Eugène. What he was told to ask me was, How I could possibly resolve on stirring up a war with France ? " Read the declaration," I replied ; " it does not contain one word which I do not fully endorse. Besides, it is not a question of war against France, it is war against the man of the island of Elba."

He asked M. de Metternich whether the Austrian government had completely lost sight of the views they held in March, 1814. " A regency ? " replied M. de Metternich, " we do not want one." Finally he tried to find out from M. de Nesselrode what were the Emperor Alexander's views. " The destruction of Buonaparte and all his people," was the reply, and there the matter ended.

It was decided to make M. de Montrond at once acquainted with the number of troops that will immediately take the field, and likewise with the treaty of March 25th. He has returned to Paris carrying this information and these answers back with him ; it will give those who have attached themselves to Buonaparte's fortunes, something to think about.

The second emissary he sent was M. de Flahaut.[1] When he arrived at Stuttgart the King of Wurtemburg had him arrested and conducted back to the frontier. He carried despatches for the Emperor of Austria, the Emperor Alexander, the Empress Marie-Louise, and for your Majesty's legation at Vienna. They were we presume (the despatches being all separate) letters to annul the powers of your Majesty's embassy.

The sovereigns continue very well disposed. I can assure your Majesty that it is an extremely difficult matter to get so many people all to go the same way ; I never cease in my efforts to prevent any of them from turning aside. The territorial arrangements for the north of Germany were concluded yesterday ; in a few days more I hope the congress will have finished all that it has to do.

I shall have the honour to send your Majesty by the first English courier, who leaves on Saturday the 15th, the declaration of war (very badly drawn up) by Austria, against

[1] Comte de Flahaut de la Billarderie, born in 1785, enlisted in 1798, took part in all the campaigns of the Empire, and became a General in 1813, and Aide-de-Camp to the emperor. In 1814 he adhered to the restoration, but was one of the first to rally round the emperor at the period of the Hundred Days. On his return from his fruitless mission to Vienna he was made a peer of France. He was exiled at the second restoration, and tendered his resignation in 1817. The Revolution of July gave him back his rank and his peerage. In 1831 he was for a brief space Ambassador at Berlin, and became in 1837 equerry to the Duc d'Orleans. In 1841 he was appointed Ambassador at Vienna, and held this post till 1848 ; he was created senator in 1853, and Grand Chancellor of the Legion of Honour in 1864. He died in 1870.

Murat. This matter will very shortly I trust be concluded to your satisfaction.

I have the honour to be . . . . .

P.S.—This letter is taken by M. Fauche Borel.[1]

No. 51.—THE PRINCE DE TALLEYRAND TO KING LOUIS XVIII.

VIENNA, *April* 15, 1815.

SIRE,

I have returned the three letters which your Majesty desired M. de Jaucourt to send me. I ventured to tell him (owing to some questions put to me the object of which was to ascertain whether your Majesty approved of the declaration) that the emperors expected to find in these letters some expressions of satisfaction on this subject. Nevertheless their words and their actions all show that the greatest unanimity reigns among them, and I will do my utmost to foster this feeling to the end.

M. Pozzo will have told your Majesty how, under even less difficult circumstances, it was no easy matter to make interests, apparently at variance, take the same line.

The Russian troops arrived in Bohemia four days before they were expected. It would not surprise me if, although going by way of the Vistula, they reached the Rhine before, or at any rate as soon as, the Austrian troops.

Reports here as to the actual force and position of the army under the command of the Duke of Wellington vary so considerably, that I should much like your Majesty to order M. de Jaucourt to send me positive information on this point, especially as to the time when they may be expected to enter France.

Marshal de Wrède leaves here in two days.[2] The force under his command, and also the Prussian troops, are much excited.

The Austrians have received news from Italy dated April 7th, with which they are on the whole satisfied; but then, they are

---

[1] Louis Fauche-Borel, a Swiss political agent of French origin. Born at Neufchâtel in 1762 he rendered great services to the *émigrés*. In 1795 he acted as intermediary between the Prince de Condé and Pichegru, and was mixed up in all the royalist intrigues and conspiracies in France up to 1801. He was then arrested in Paris and detained for eighteen months. At the intervention of the King of Prussia, he was liberated. He then retired to Berlin in 1805. Owing to the demands of Napoleon, he was compelled to take refuge in London. In 1814 and 1815 he received numerous missions and travelled frequently between Ghent and Vienna. He was at length arrested at Ghent by order of M. de Blacas. In 1816 he received from the King of Prussia the title of Councillor to the Embassy; but soon after, abandoned by all and quite forgotten, he was reduced to want, and ended by killing himself (1829).

[2] Var. : "he will stop four days at Munich and go thence to his army corps."

satisfied with very little. The reason of this satisfaction is that Murat's army corps, after having in vain tried to force the bridge of d'Occhiobello, has retired, and his whole army is now between Modena, Ferrara, and the sea. General Frimont hoped to be in a position to attack about the 12th.

I have the honour to send your Majesty the declaration against Murat, which has been communicated to me officially by M. de Metternich.

I have the honour to be . . . . .

No. 29.[1]—KING LOUIS XVIII. TO THE PRINCE DE TALLEYRAND.

GHENT, *April* 22, 1815.

MON COUSIN,

I was about to answer your letter No. 49, enclosing No. 38, when I received your letter No. 50, inclosing No. 44. You have without doubt influenced the declaration of the sovereigns. I hope, if there is still time, you will likewise influence that of the generals, which will be a very important document. If it is wished that it should produce all the effect desirable, it is necessary that, in conformity with the declarations of March 13th, and Article III. of the treaty of the 25th, Europe should declare herself the ally of the king and the French nation, and against the invasion of Napoleon Buonaparte, the friend of all those who declare for the former, and the enemy of all those who arm in favour of the latter, at the same time excluding all ideas of conquest and of all intermediate parties, the possibility of which must not even be supposed.

---

[1] M. Pallain here inserts another letter of the king's to M. de Talleyrand, dated 21st April. According to the number of the prince's despatches to which the king says he has replied, it is probable that the letter of the 22nd is the only one that was sent. The contents are besides almost similar, one phrase being identical. However here is the letter :—

GHENT, *April* 21, 1815.

MON COUSIN,

I have received your letter numbered 49, and also 38 which was enclosed. After you had despatched it you would have received my letters which I have continued to send, but which in default of the means I possessed when in Paris, necessarily cause unpunctuality in the correspondence.

I am very anxious to get the declaration which you mention, and in the drafting of which, according to your letter, I hope you have assisted. The Chevalier Stuart has just told me it was signed on the 11th. For my part, I am busy with the proclamation which I must publish when I again enter France. I will send it to you as soon as it is drawn up, and been seen, by the Duke of Wellington and General Pozzo di Borgo. If the sovereigns are still in Vienna when it arrives, I hope you will gain their goodwill for it. Nevertheless, I trust it may not find them there ; speed in all the operations is what is now most needed ; all the reports from the interior are excellent, but we must not give the enemy any time.

LOUIS.

For my part, I am preparing the declaration, or proclamation I shall have to issue, when I again set foot in France. I will send it to you as soon as it is drawn up, but I sincerely hope that it may no longer find you in Vienna.

Your letter No. 50, speaks of the termination of the congress. It will of course be necessary for you to sign in my name, the treaty which will end it ; but I long greatly to have you near me, especially in the present state of affairs.

You will have heard of the unfortunate issue of my nephew's [1] brave enterprise and also that even my niece was unable to save Bordeaux. Public opinion in France is not changed, all the reports are unanimous on this point. It is essential to act promptly, and this is both the wish and the opinion of the Duke of Wellington.

I will only say one word as to your letter No. 38, viz., that the letter of the Duc de Campo-Chiaro is worth preserving as a record of the notorious perfidy of his master.

Wherefore I pray God to have you, my cousin, in His safe and holy keeping.

LOUIS.

No. 52.—THE PRINCE DE TALLEYRAND TO KING LOUIS XVIII.

VIENNA, *April* 23, 1815.

SIRE,

Something has just occurred here which I would fain keep from your Majesty, as it will I fear greatly vex you, but which it is important you should know, being closely connected with your Majesty's present position, and a matter you would without fail hear from others without perhaps being informed of circumstances which would tend to ameliorate and counterbalance it.

For some time past I have had occasion to notice, that if the Emperor of Russia was often opposed to what your Majesty wished done, he was sometimes influenced, not merely by what he himself desired, but because he was often offended as well.

1st. Because your Majesty had not offered him the *cordon bleu*, having given it to the Prince Regent.

2nd. Because of the futility of his intercession and entreaties in favour of the Duc de Vicence, in whom he takes a great interest, and who was excluded from the chamber of peers.

3rd. Because of the firmness with which your Majesty, on

---

[1] This refers to M. le Duc, and to Madame la Duchesse, d'Angoulême.

CHARLES MAURICE DE TALLEYRAND-PÉRIGORD, PRINCE DE BENEVENTO

FROM A BUST BY MICHELET

the subject of the marriage, refused to accede to his wishes on the religious point.

4th. and lastly. Because the constitutional charter differed in many respects from the views he had expressed in Paris on this subject, and which, from his attachment to liberal ideas, he regarded as very beneficial and of great importance.

I knew that for some time he had complained of this privately *in pretty strong terms,*[1] but I did not then think it of much importance. Now however I am convinced, that these feelings influence his judgment as to the situation of France and that of your Majesty.

According to the news from France and the reports of those who come thence, the whole bulk of the nation is for your Majesty ; and against you are two parties, that of the army, which is entirely for Buonaparte (those in it who are well-intentioned being subjugated or carried away by the mass); and the party composed of what remains of the old revolutionary factions. The latter has only joined the former, because the first having taken the lead, the second[2] found itself obliged to follow. They are only agreed on the one point, that both wanted a change, but not for the same reasons nor for the same end. The army, tired of the long peace, wanted a chief who would give them back the chances of danger, fortune, and fame, to which they had been accustomed for the last twenty-two years. Buonaparte was evidently therefore the man for them. The chiefs of the other party know Buonaparte and hate him ; they know his insatiable love of power, they are aware that civil liberty has no more cruel enemy, they know well that wherever a rebel army is invested with supreme authority, only the merest shadow of a civil government can exist ; that outside this civil government, they are as nothing, and that passive obedience will be their fate as well as that of the rest of the people. They are perfectly aware of the motives which induced Buonaparte to approach them, they know that his union with them is a forced union, that the ties by which they will try to hold him and which at this moment he acknowledges, will only be binding so long as he has not the power of breaking them, and that victories, if he gains any, will give him this power. They do not conceal from themselves, that what the army has done once, it may do a second or a third time, and that in such a state of affairs there would be no security either for the master or the slaves. Undeceived as to their old chimeras, they no longer dream of a republic ; the titles and the fortunes they have

---

[1] Suppressed in the text of the archives.
[2] Var. : " ennuyée du répos " = " tired of inactivity."

acquired, bind them to the monarchical system. They were not opposed to the legitimate dynasty, but they could not endure a system of government, which by excluding them from holding any office, they believed[1] deprived them of all political existence, and menaced them for the future with even still greater losses. Their aversion to this state of affairs is such, that they would gladly remove it at any price, and rather than relapse into it again, they will plunge themselves into the horrors and dangers of revolutionary rule.

Buonaparte's first object is to nationalize the war he will have to carry on. The first aim of the Powers is to prevent this. He well knows he cannot attain this end by persuasion, and that he can only arrive thereat by means of terrorism. But his army which he must unite on the frontier, and which will be fighting with a foreign power, will not suffice him; he must have other means, and these he can only find in that party to which he himself once belonged, on the ruins of which he has raised himself, which he has for a long time oppressed, and from which he is now seeking support.

The Powers thought that this party (if it was deemed best to calm its fears) might be induced to separate itself from a man whom it does not love, and that thus Buonaparte would be deprived of his chief resource and of that which can make his resistance much longer and more dangerous.

A scheme for a declaration on these lines has been drawn up.

When it was only a question of Europe arming herself, not against France, but for France, that she recognized no enemies but Buonaparte and his adherents, that she would never negotiate with him, that she would grant him neither peace nor truce, and would not lay down her arms till she had overthrown him, all opinions were unanimous; but when it became a question of further expressing in the declaration, that the final aim of the war was the re-establishment of the legitimate dynasty, opinions were divided.

"If you do not mention this re-establishment," said some, "those who in the provinces armed themselves, and whom the declaration of the 13th of March induced to take up arms for the King's cause, will consider themselves abandoned, you will deprive yourself of a certain support, in order to obtain an uncertain one. If you merely announce your intention of overthrowing the usurper, and allow it to be supposed that this object accomplished, France may do as she likes, you will hand her

---

[1] Var. : "vu" = "saw."

over to Jacobinism and to factions more dangerous to Europe
than Buonaparte himself."

"The re-establishment of the legitimate dynasty," said
others, "is a matter with respect to which the intentions of the
Powers cannot be mistaken. The declaration of March 13th
expresses them sufficiently. By insisting on them afresh in too
absolute a manner, the original aim (that of detaching those
from Buonaparte who cannot be brought back, except by such
concessions as the Powers might hint at, but which the king
alone can promise and perform) will be destroyed."

Matters were at this stage when the Emperor Alexander sent
for Lord Clancarty, who, since the departure of Lord Castlereagh
and the Duke of Wellington, is at the head of the English embassy.
The account of their conversation was given me partly by Lord
Clancarty, but in much further detail by Lord Stewart and M. de
Metternich.

The task of having to relate it to your Majesty is the more
painful to me, that finding myself placed, from various causes,
between respect and devotion, I fear that what I give to the one,
I may seem to withhold from the other. But your Majesty,
whose interest it is to know the feelings of your most powerful
ally, could but imperfectly judge of them, if you were not acquainted with the reasons he gives, as well as the objections by
which he pretends to justify them. The exigency of this consideration alone constrains me to relate them.

The emperor first asked Lord Clancarty why he did not
approve of the draft declaration.[1] "Because, in my opinion,"
replied Lord Clancarty, "I do not think it says all it
should say. It is not enough to overthrow Buonaparte; the
door must not be thrown open to the Jacobins, who would be
still less to my taste than Buonaparte himself." "The Jacobins,"
replied the Emperor Alexander, "are only to be feared as
Buonaparte's auxiliaries ; and it is on that account one must try
to separate them from him. If he falls, it will not be they who
will recover his heritage; the first point therefore is to overthrow
him ; on this we are all agreed. As for me, I will devote all my
strength and will never rest until this has been accomplished.
However, I am quite willing to consent to put off a declaration
or proclamation, until our troops are close to France, indeed
I should advise this. But Buonaparte's overthrow is not
the sole point on which it is necessary for us to understand each
other. In such a huge enterprise as that in which we are now
engaged, it is necessary from the very beginning to keep the
end in view. Buonaparte's overthrow is only half of the work ;

[1] Var. : "and what objection he had to make to it."

I 2

the security of Europe must be provided for, she cannot be at peace so long as France is not, and France cannot be so, except with a government that suits all parties."

" France," said Lord Clancarty, " was happy under the King's government ; all the votes of the nation are for him."

"Yes," replied the Emperor, " of that portion of the nation which has always been passive, which for twenty-six years has put up with all the revolutions, which only bewails them but does nothing to prevent them. But the other portion, which apparently is the entire nation, because it alone is in evidence, or makes any stir and takes the lead, will it willingly submit itself and be faithful to the government which it has betrayed ? Would you impose it upon them, whether they like it or not ? Would you, for this, carry on a war of extermination, and perhaps an endless one, and have you any certainty of success at last ? "

" I feel," replied Lord Clancarty, " that duty ends where impossibility begins ; but until impossibility has been reached, I hold it to be the duty of the Powers to support the legitimate sovereign and not even raise the question of his abandonment."

" Our first duty," answered the Emperor, " is towards Europe and ourselves. Even if the re-establishment of the government were an easy matter, as long as there is no certainty as to its stability, what would its re-establishment do, but prepare fresh misfortunes both for France and Europe ? If what has once occurred should happen again, should we be all united as we are now ? Should we have nearly a million of men under arms ? Should we be ready at the very moment that the danger broke forth, and what probability is there (the elements of disorder being the same) that the government of the king will in future be more stable than it has been ? However, whatever opinions others may have on this matter, I hold that the re-establishment of the King, which we all desire and which I particularly wish, is likely to meet with so many unsurmountable obstacles when it does take place, that we ought to look ahead, and arrange in advance, what will then have to be done. Last year a regency might have been established ; but the Archduchess Marie-Louise, to whom I have spoken, will not return to France at any price. Her son must have an establishment in Austria, and beyond that she does not seek anything more for him. I have also ascertained that Austria no longer desires a regency. Last year it seemed to me that such a measure would have reconciled all opposing interests ; but the situation is no longer the same. It is therefore no use thinking any more about it. I see no one so fitted to conciliate all parties as the Duc d'Orleans ; he is a Frenchman, a Bourbon ; he has married a Bourbon, and he has sons. He also, when young, served the constitutional cause. He has worn the tricolor cockade, which I often maintained, when in Paris, ought never to have been discarded. In him all parties would be united. Do not you agree with me in this, my Lord, and what would be the opinion of England about it ? "

" I cannot possibly say," answered Lord Clancarty, " what would be the opinion of my government on an idea which would be as new to them as it is to me. As for my personal opinion, I do not hesitate to say, that it seems to me extremely dangerous to abandon the legitimate line and rush into any kind of usurpation. But your Majesty will surely wish me to acquaint my government with that which you have done me the honour to communicate ? "

The Emperor told him to write, and after pointing out how necessary it was to ascertain as far as possible what might be the result of so grave an undertaking, withdrew.

Lord Clancarty did write, but dwelt very strongly on the reasons why England should remain firm to your Majesty's cause.

M. de Metternich, to whom Lord Stewart and Lord Clancarty had communicated this conversation, thought that the question raised by the Emperor was quite out of place. That it was wrong to wander off into hypothetical questions which would never present themselves, and that it was necessary to wait till they did so, and grapple with each in turn.

He has instructed the Austrian embassy in London to express itself in this sense.

The Emperor Alexander, who hardly understands the principle of legitimacy, has, without waiting to hear the opinion of the English cabinet, inserted an article in the *Gazette de Francfort,* which I have now before me, and which declares, that all that the Powers desire, is the overthrow of Buonaparte, but that they have no intention of interfering with the internal government of France or of imposing a government upon her ; and that she will be at liberty to choose that form which she prefers. But up to the present he is alone in this view. Even Prussia, accustomed as she is to consult her own wishes alone, is favourable to your Majesty ; she has even expressed the wish that your Majesty should issue a proclamation, and that this proclamation should precede the meeting of the assembly of electors, which Buonaparte has summoned to Paris. This also is the wish of the greater part of the Powers. It is considered important that your Majesty should endeavour to rally all parties round you, by assuring to all, without distinction, the advantages of a constitutional government. The Powers believe that a declaration from your Majesty, made in this spirit, would prove an admirable auxiliary to the forces they are about to deploy. Several indeed think that your Majesty should lay the blame of any faults that may have been committed on your ministers, and form a fresh ministry, as if you were in France, in the composition of which each party would find the guarantee it desires. I have been asked to write to your Majesty about this, and have even been informed that this wish will be hinted at by the ministers about to be accredited to you, and I therefore hope your Majesty will be beforehand with them.

To all that which the Emperor of Russia told Lord Clancarty, I have to add utterances on his part, that have reached me from sources which I have every reason to believe are reliable. On several occasions he repeated, that when he was in Paris a year ago, all he then saw and heard, made him fear that the government could not hold its ground. It seemed to him that it would be difficult for the ideas and opinions of the princes to harmonize with the opinions and habits of a generation which had arisen during their absence, and which had not, on many points, either the ideas or customs of their fathers. " Now," he observed, liking always to deal in general views, " one cannot govern in opposition to the ideas of the times."

He said that his fears had increased when he found that your Majesty had summoned men to your council and ministry who, though no doubt very estimable, had been away from France or in retirement, during the period of the Revolution, and not knowing France or being known to her, were consequently wanting in that experience of affairs which even genius cannot supply. He considers they have done the royal cause great harm, although he believes that a similar evil will in future be avoided because your Majesty would make a different choice. I ought to mention that he made the remark, that the minister, concerning whom there were most complaints from every one, was more in your Majesty's confidence than any one else.[1]

He even went so far as to say, that the greatest harm has been done by the amount of power your Majesty has given to, or allowed to be assumed by the princes, who were ever near you ; that the prejudices that have arisen against them seemed to him an evil without a remedy ; that those to which your Majesty would have been personally exposed, would have produced a far less vexatious effect, seeing that the dissatisfaction against him who reigns is tempered and softened by the hopes placed on his successor, whereas when it is the successors who are feared, this hope falls to the ground.

[1] It was with reference to the Comte de Blacas that the Emperor Alexander made this remark.

The Emperor in general conversation, says that he is quite willing to believe that if your Majesty were alone, you would suit France and be both beloved and respected, but as you cannot be disconnected from all your surroundings, he fears you will never be firmly established. I notice with great satisfaction that the Powers are all sincerely interested in your Majesty ; even the utterances of the Emperor of Russia are the outcome of temper and the philosophic ideas which predominate his character, rather than from any premeditated design. I should be pleased if I could add that this interest extends to *Monsieur* and the Duc d'Angoulême and the Duc de Berry. But power once exclusively placed in the hands of your Majesty and with some responsible ministers possessing your confidence and that of the nation, the exaggerated views, both at home and abroad, caused by errors or inadvertencies, will gradually disappear.

The Baron de Talleyrand[1] arrived here with the letter your Majesty has honoured me with, dated April 10th. I never cease stirring up enthusiasm here, and pointing out how important it is to hasten matters. But the Duke of Wellington, in a letter of later date than that which your Majesty has done me the honour to mention, writes, that after the vexatious news received from the south, he feels the necessity of not commencing operations until a general attack can be made everywhere by all the forces. Yet with the best will in the world, the distances to be traversed are so great, that the Austrians could not place a hundred thousand men on the Rhine before the end of May.

Your Majesty will be pleased to learn that the Austrian troops in Italy have had successes, which promise still greater ones. Prince Leopold[2] will leave here in a few days to join the Austrian army. The Vienna papers have at last left off talking of *King Joachim*, they simply say *Murat*.

M. de Bombelles,[3] the former Portuguese ambassador, canon

[1] Alexandre-Daniel, Baron de Talleyrand, cousin-german to the Prince, Councillor of State, afterwards Minister at Florence (1832) and Copenhagen (1835), peer of France (1838). He died in 1839.

[2] Leopold, Prince of Salerno, second son of King Ferdinand. Born in 1790, married in 1816 the Archduchess Marie-Clementina. He arrived at Teano, the Austrian headquarters, on the 21st of May, and took possession of the country in his father's name.

[3] Marc-Marie, Marquis de Bombelles, born in 1744, belonged to a family of Portuguese origin settled in France, and afterwards entered the service of Austria. He at first took to diplomacy, and became French Ambassador to Portugal. Being exiled in 1792, he served in Condé's army.

He then entered holy orders, and was made Canon of Breslau. Under the restoration he became almoner to the Duchess de Berry, and Bishop of Amiens. He died in 1821.

of Glogau and father of Bombelles, who was in Paris, wishes to re-enter the diplomatic service ; he believes he would in this last capacity be of great use at Munich, and 8,000 francs would, he considers, be enough for him to live upon.

I am taking advantage of the zeal of the Comte Alexis de Noailles, who will have the honour of carrying this despatch to your Majesty. He has been most useful here in every way, and I fancy no one could better inform your Majesty as to the political and military situation of all the cabinets, whose assistance we now so greatly need. I entreat your Majesty to have the goodness to let him be the bearer of the despatches you will have to send me. He ought to be back here before the close of the congress ; and the affairs of Germany and Italy, which we must conclude, progress so slowly, that he will arrive here in ample time to append his signature to them.

I have the honour to be. . . . .

No. 53.—The Prince de Talleyrand to King Louis XVIII.

VIENNA, *May* 1, 1815.

SIRE,

The Baron de Vincent leaves to-day to join your Majesty, and has offered to take charge of the letter I have the honour of writing to you. When commencing hostilities, Murat counted on an insurrection in Italy, but in this expectation he was completely disappointed. Full of confidence, he advanced as far as the banks of the Po, where the first engagements took place. Since then he has met with nothing but defeat. He is retiring in haste to the kingdom of Naples, dreading lest his retreat should be cut off by an Austrian corps occupying Tuscany. The last engagement of which we have received official accounts took place near Cesena, where he repassed the Ronco, suffering considerable loss. His army, already much weakened by the number of prisoners taken, amounting to 7,000, is diminishing every day, owing to numerous desertions. There is every reason to hope, that before long this war will have come to an end.

Replacing Ferdinand IV. on his throne will not be the only advantage resulting from Murat's overthrow. By freeing the troops now employed against him, and removing all anxiety as to the maintenance of peace in Italy, our operations against Buonaparte will be greatly aided. It will also produce a very favourable effect in France, by proving to every one that Europe will not tolerate these new dynasties, founded on violence and injustice, and is determined to upset them.

This is the result of the efforts we have made here to uphold the principle of legitimacy. This principle is now fully recognized. A treaty has just been signed by M. de Metternich and Commander Ruffo,[1] King Ferdinand's minister at Vienna. This treaty covenants for the assistance to be given by Sicily in the war against Murat, and instead of the 20,000 men your Majesty had designed for this war, King Ferdinand, from what I hear, has undertaken to send 25,000.

My next despatches will acquaint your Majesty with all the stipulations of the treaty, which I have not yet seen.

Leopold, prince of the Two Sicilies, leaves here on the 4th of this month for the headquarters of the Austrian army.

Although matters respecting Parma are not yet concluded, the Emperor of Austria has issued an order by which he assumes positive control of the three duchies[3] in his daughter's name. Thus your Majesty will perceive that the arrangements to be settled by the congress are being carried out before they have been decided, which does not greatly matter, but which we have not the power to prevent.

The Austrian and Russian troops continue their march. The headquarters of Prince Schwarzenberg are at Heilbronn, in Wurtemberg. He himself proceeded there yesterday, passing through Bohemia, where he will remain a few days.

The arrangements with Bavaria, which I informed your Majesty were finished but not signed, are, after having caused fresh discussions, at last concluded. Nevertheless they are only provisionally so. They will not be definitely completed till after the war, because being dependent on the negotiations with the courts of Baden and Darmstadt, which have concessions to make to Bavaria, and to receive indemnities on the left bank of the Rhine, these courts will not accept any compensations which the chances of war (supposing it to be a disastrous one) might take from them.

Genèral Walterstorff,[4] the Danish minister, is to leave to-morrow for your Majesty's court. He, as well as M. de Vincent, are accredited commissioners to the Duke of Wellington.

I have the honour to be . . . .

[1] Commander Ruffo, an Italian diplomat, was the King of Naples' Minister at Paris in 1797. Returning to Naples in 1798, he followed the Court to Sicily in 1805, and was charged with a mission to Portugal. In 1815 he went to Vienna as a plenipotentiary to the Congress. He died in 1825.

[2] See d'Angeberg, *Congrès de Vienne*, p. 1156.

[3] Parma, Placentia and Guastalla.

[4] Ernest Frederick de Walterstorff, born in 1755, Lieutenant-General and Chamberlain to the King of Denmark, Minister-Plenipotentiary at Paris from 1810. He died in 1820.

No. 54.—The Prince de Talleyrand to King Louis XVIII.

VIENNA, *May* 5, 1815.

SIRE,

A former chamberlain [1] of Buonaparte's, who having accompanied the Archduchess Marie-Louise hither was made chamberlain to the Emperor Francis, and who had some time ago returned to Paris, has been lately sent here with a letter from Buonaparte to the Emperor, and another from M. de Caulaincourt for M. de Metternich. By virtue of his title as an Austrian chamberlain, he got as far as Munich, where, however, he was stopped, and the letters he carried were sent on here. Both letters demand the return, for various reasons, of the Empress and her son. The tone adopted by Buonaparte and his minister is moderate, but injured. The letters remained sealed until the conference assembled, and were then opened in the presence of the ministers of the allied Powers. It was decided not to reply to them ; this opinion was unanimous. Your Majesty will see, therefore, that Buonaparte's attempts to establish [2] some kind of relations with the foreign Powers, have been repulsed and proved abortive.

The English ministers, with whom I communicated relative to defraying the expenses of your Majesty's embassy at the congress, and who showed themselves quite willing to do so, have received letters from their government, authorizing them only to advance 100,000 fs. in the course of six months.

The credits we had on France, and which were far from being exhausted, have been suspended since March 21st. This leaves us to meet expenses incurred, and which ought to have been paid on April 1st. Moreover, no one attached to the embassy has received pay from Paris since the month of January.

The most reduced expenditure for the months of April and May, even without paying off all that is still owing, will take

---

[1] Baron de Stassart. Born in 1780 at Malines, he had been under the Empire Auditor to the State Council, then Intendant of the Tyrol (1805) and of West Prussia (1807). In 1810 he was appointed Préfet of Vaucleuse, and in 1811 of the Bouches de la Meuse. After the fall of Napoleon he was received by the Emperor of Austria, whose subject he was, and appointed his chamberlain. Having returned to Paris during the Hundred Days, he left it again on the 17th April with despatches from Napoleon. He was stopped at Lintz, and retired to Weltz, whence he sent his despatches to Vienna. He returned to his native country after Waterloo, and was several times elected to the States-General. In the reign of Leopold he became President of the Senate. M. de Talleyrand makes a mistake in calling him a former Chamberlain of Buonaparte's : he never held that office.

[2] Var. : "obtenir" = "obtain."

a considerable portion of the sum promised me by the British minister ; the balance will not reach us before the beginning of August, at which date your Majesty will have to consider what steps it will be possible for you to take in this matter.

I have the honour to be . . . .

No. 30.—King Louis XVIII. to the Prince de Talleyrand.

GHENT, *May* 5, 1815.

MON COUSIN,

I have received by M. de Noailles your letter No. 52. I enclose with this despatch the proclamation I intend to issue, with which I flatter myself the sovereigns will be as fully satisfied as the ministers who are resident here, have been. But this matter, although an important one, is not the most so. There is another point in your despatch, which, since its receipt, has been, and still continues to be, the subject of my most serious consideration.[1] In order to solve it I need the very best advice, and this cannot be given in writing. I therefore requested you to join me here as soon as you had signed the final act of the congress in my name, but now I still more urgently need your presence. If therefore this signature will detain you more than two or three days, leave without waiting for it. It is really a matter of indifference which of my plenipotentiaries signs the treaty, but it is most important I should have you here. Wherefore I pray God to have you, my cousin, in His safe and holy keeping.

LOUIS.

No. 55.—The Prince de Talleyrand to King Louis XVIII.

VIENNA, *May* 14, 1815.

SIRE,

The Comte de Noailles has arrived and delivered the letter of May 5th with which your Majesty has honoured me. His arrival is so closely followed by the departure of the courier of whom I wish to take advantage, that I can only send your Majesty a very short reply.

---

[1] These were the representations which, under the guise of a conversation with the Emperor Alexander, M. de Talleyrand made to the King with regard to the interior policy of his government. The King himself and several members of his government—M. de Lancourt in particular—anxiously desired M. de Talleyrand's return to combat the influence of what was then called the *parti resté émigré.*

My anxiety to be with you would make me leave to-morrow, if matters were sufficiently advanced to require only a signature, or if the close of the congress were still distant. But Italian affairs are not yet concluded, though nearly so. The delay caused thereby has kept M. de Saint-Marsan and Commander Ruffo some days longer here, although the departure of the latter is very urgent, and the former has been recalled to Turin, where he has been appointed war minister. On the other hand, the sovereigns are about to leave, and as in a coalition every step is subject to a thousand interpretations, I could not hasten the period of their departure without causing more harm than benefit to your Majesty's affairs. However, I shall make all preparation, so that the difference can only be a matter of forty-eight hours more or less. Besides, I do not think it would be well in our present circumstances to leave just at a time when every one else is necessarily hurried.

I had a rather long interview[1] with the Emperor Alexander to-day, which I shall have the honour to relate to your Majesty. I confine myself now to telling you that his utterances were very satisfactory, and that he expressed himself in the most spirited and favourable manner as to our affairs. His opinion is, that just at present very little action should be taken either by your Majesty or those around you. He is very desirous to have it understood, that any steps that might be taken by a single Power in connection with a common danger, ought to be undertaken by the unanimous desire of all. This is the chief object in despatching ministers to all the army corps, and I think this rule will have to be adopted by your Majesty.

I have the honour to be . . . .

No. 56.—THE PRINCE DE TALLEYRAND TO KING LOUIS XVIII.

VIENNA, *May* 17, 1815.

SIRE,

It has been decided to substitute, for the proposed declaration, which I had the honour of mentioning several times to your Majesty, a statement which will fulfil the same object. This will be published in the *Gazette de Vienne,* and will immediately after appear in the different journals of Germany and also in those of other countries, having first been printed at the Austrian Chancellor's office. I have the honour to send your Majesty several copies.

---

[1] Var. : "*un assez long entretien*" = "sufficiently long interview."

You will see that this statement fully confirms the arrangements come to by the Powers in the declaration of March 13th; that the sophistry of Buonaparte is refuted, and his impostures brought to light. But you will specially notice that Europe does not appear as if making war for your Majesty, and at your request, but that she does so for herself, because her interests require it, and because her safety demands it. Not only is this view of the war alone accurate, but every one thinks it is the only one suited to your Majesty. It is the only one that does not place you in a false position, as regards your own subjects, for nothing might contribute more towards alienating their affection, than if they were left in any doubt as to the cause of the war. They must never be able to attribute to your Majesty the evils which it will bring upon them.

I have the honour to be. . . .

P.S.—I have according to your Majesty's orders, written to the sovereigns and archdukes who are here, asking for permission to take my leave.

I have sent to M. de Jaucourt the letters from M. de la Tour du Pin, which may interest your Majesty. That of M. d'Osmond [1] which encloses them, gives the latest details respecting Italian affairs.

No. 57.—THE PRINCE DE TALLEYRAND TO KING LOUIS XVIII.

VIENNA, *May 25,*[2] 1815.

SIRE,

At my farewell audiences, I received from all the sovereigns the warmest expressions of esteem for your Majesty. These audiences were not merely formal, they were much longer than is usually accorded under similar circumstances. I shall have the honour to tell your Majesty about them.

Although everything is not yet completed, the anxiety I felt to be with your Majesty had decided me to leave to-morrow, but M. de Metternich, M. de Nesselrode, and the Chancellor de Hardenberg, having begged me to sign, together with the heads of the other cabinets, the protocols which comprise the arrangements decided on by the congress, I felt I ought to accede

---

[1] M. d'Osmond was the King's ambassador at Turin. It has been mentioned previously that M. de la Tour du Pin had gone from Vienna to the south of France where he flattered himself he might be of use to the royal cause.

[2] Var. : "May 23, 1815."

to their request, as it will only retard my departure by two or three days.

The protocol will contain the final draft, with the exception of a few modifications, which can only affect the expressions of the articles which are to form the deed of congress. A commission consisting of a plenipotentiary from each of the Powers, will remain here to put these articles into suitable form, and separate those which determine special relations, from those which concern general interests. I shall leave M. de Dalberg here to represent France on this commission. This business will only last nine or ten days, if the delegates work with a little more assiduity than their chiefs have done.

I have the honour to send your Majesty two letters from the Duc d'Angoulême. I had the honour to write one to him which is probably lost. We shall perhaps see it in a few days in some of the French journals. I have to-day sent a letter by courier to Lady Castlereagh for Madame la Duchesse d'Angoulême. In order that your Majesty may have a complete collection of my voluminous correspondence, I have the honour to send you copies of those numbers which I presume have not reached you. If no unforeseen obstacles arise, I shall be at your Majesty's orders in Ghent on Sunday, June 4th.

I have the honour to be . . . .

No. 58.—The Prince de Talleyrand to King Louis XVIII.

VIENNA, *May 27*, 1815.

SIRE,

I can now tell your Majesty of the great anxiety I have experienced during the last eight days. A question arose as to whether, under the circumstances, which necessitated leaving some points undecided, the signing of the Act of Congress ought not to be postponed to some future date. A rather deep intrigue lay beneath this. Its object was to make doubtful, matters which had already been decided, and to frustrate decision on several others which ought to be decided.

Nothing was of greater importance to your Majesty's interest, than that your name should be appended to an act which announced the union of all the Powers. All my efforts therefore were concentrated towards this end. In this I have been well supported by the English and Austrian embassies. The act will be signed to-morrow or the day after.

I have the honour to transmit to your Majesty a declaration by the Helvetian Diet to the ministers accredited to it ; and also

·a convention signed between these ministers and those of Switzerland. Your Majesty will see that, if, in the declaration, Switzerland seems to wish to preserve her neutrality, her intention (which is clearly explained in the convention) is nevertheless to do all that can possibly be expected of her for the cause of Europe. And in case of necessity (of which the allied generals are to be the judges) she will authorize the passage of the allied troops through Swiss territory.

In all the letters received here yesterday by the ministers of the Powers in Vienna, great praise is given to M. Auguste de Talleyrand for his efforts in attaining this advantageous end. Both from a moral as well as a military point of view, this action on the part of Switzerland, is looked upon by the allies as being of the greatest possible use.

I shall not have the honour of writing again to your Majesty from Vienna. I start at once to lay at your Majesty's feet my most respectful homage and devotion. I take no papers away with me.

END OF THE CORRESPONDENCE OF THE CONGRESS

AND OF PART VIII.

PART IX.

THE SECOND RESTORATION—
ADDENDUM—TALLEYRAND'S REPLY TO HIS ACCUSERS.

1815.

MY departure from Vienna was retarded several days beyond the date mentioned in my letter to the king of May 27th. The intrigue which had been started to prevent the signature of the final Act of the Congress, had not been put down ; they hoped to exhaust my patience. But I felt the importance of not yielding too strongly, to give in. I considered it absolutely necessary to have written, signed, and irrevocable pledges from the Powers, before commencing a war, the issue of which might for a long time be doubtful. No one could foresee that these same Powers would, after their victory, fail in their engagements, and that we, on our side, should have erred in leaving them the means of doing so. Be that as it may, my duty seemed plain, and I performed it. I did not quit Vienna till June 10th, the final Act of the Congress having been signed the evening before. Thus, as has been seen, when I reached Belgium, I heard the result of the battle of Waterloo.

The king had left Ghent before I arrived in Brussels, and I could not join him till I reached Mons. He was following the English army ; it was this I wished to prevent. When I presented myself he was just about to step into his carriage. He said a few kind words to me ; I did not conceal from him how grieved I was to see the manner in which he intended returning to France, that I felt he ought not to appear there among the ranks of foreigners, that he was ruining his cause, that in wounding the national pride he would damp the attachment felt for his person, and that my advice was, that he should proceed with some kind of escort, or better still without any at all, to some part of the French frontier which the foreigners had not yet reached, and there establish the seat of his government. I named the town of Lyons as suitable for the execution of my scheme, both from its importance and its position. "The king," I said to him, "could from thence exercise his power quite independent of all the allies. I would precede him there if he liked ; and return to acquaint him with the feeling of the town. That, once in Lyons, he could make an appeal to his faithful subjects; that those who had been led astray would probably be the first to return ; that he could there convoke the Chambers ; that there would be time to make all organic laws ere party spirit stepped in to introduce obstacles ; that from Lyons he could protect France, whereas from Paris he could not ; that it was necessary to provide for the chance of the allies turning round both in intention and language, after the victory they had just gained, and using against France those successes which they had solemnly declared they only wished to obtain for her. " There are several indications," I added, " which make me dread such a change. Their return to the principles of legitimacy is too recent, to prevent our having nothing to fear from people accustomed to found their rights on their pretensions, and their pretensions on their power. But if from allies they turned to enemies, and the king had then to treat with them, he would nowhere be so much at their mercy as in his capital." I therefore insisted that the king should not return there, until he could reign as undisputed sovereign, and until Paris should be equally rid of factions and all foreign troops. I wound up these explanations by telling the king that if he decided to act differently, it would be impossible for me to continue to direct his affairs. I placed my resignation in his hands and then withdrew, having given him the subjoined memoir.[1] It is a *résumé* of our labours at the congress, and a statement of the measures I deemed necessary, to repair the faults committed during the first Restoration.

REPORT MADE TO THE KING DURING HIS JOURNEY FROM GHENT TO PARIS.

SIRE,

In April, 1814, France was occupied by three hundred thousand foreign troops, with five hundred thousand more ready to follow them. She had but a handful of her own soldiers left, who had performed prodigies of valour, but who were now fairly worn out. Abroad she had large armies, but these dispersed and without communications could no longer be of any use to her, nor even assist each other. One portion of these forces was shut up in distant towns, which they could hold for a longer or shorter period ; but which would inevitably fall if simply invested. Two hundred thousand Frenchmen were prisoners of

[1] This resignation did not take place then. M. de Tallyrand did not resign till September 24th.

war. In such a state of affairs it became necessary at any price to cease hostilities by concluding an armistice. This was done on the 23rd of April.[1]

The armistice was not merely a necessity, it was an act of great policy, for it was necessary above all, that the power of the allies should be succeeded by a feeling of confidence, and for this it was essential to inspire them with it. The armistice moreover deprived them of nothing which they had the least hopes of preserving. Those who believed that by delaying the surrender of the fortified towns until the conclusion of peace, better terms could have been made, either ignored or forgot the fact, that, setting aside the impossibility of obtaining an armistice for France without surrendering those towns, any attempt to prolong their occupation would have excited the suspicion of the allies, and consequently changed their intentions.

The arrangements agreed upon were such as France could well be satisfied with. They were much more favourable than she had any right to expect. The allies were welcomed as liberators, and the praises lavished on their generosity stimulated them to show more. It was necessary to profit by this sentiment while it was favourable, and not allow it to cool. It was not enough to obtain, cessation of hostilities ; it was necessary to induce them to evacuate French territory. It was imperative that the interests of France should be fully settled, and that there should be no uncertainty as to her fate, so that your Majesty could then and there take the position which was yours by right. To make peace on the best possible terms, and to draw therefrom all the advantages that it would bring, its immediate signature was essential.

By the treaty of May 30th France only lost what she had conquered, and not even all that she had gained in the course of the conflict which it brought to an end. It took nothing from her that was essential to her safety. She lost the means of ruling which were foreign to her happiness, and which she could not retain, coupled with the advantages of a durable peace. In order to form a fair estimate of the character of the peace of 1814, it is necessary to consider the impression it made

[1] Var. : 22nd April.

K 2

on the allied nations.　At St. Petersburg and Berlin the Emperor Alexander and the King of Prussia were not only received with coldness, but with murmurs of discontent, because the treaty of May 30th did not fulfil the expectations of their subjects. France had everywhere levied heavy war contributions, and it was quite expected that these in return would be levied on her. She was required to pay none ; she remained in possession of all the art treasures she had acquired ; all her monuments were respected, and it is not too much to say, that she was treated with a degree of moderation which under similar circumstances has no parallel in history.

All the direct interests in France had been provided for, while those of other states remained subordinate to the decision of the future congress.　France was summoned to assist at this congress, but when the plenipotentiaries arrived there, it was found that the rancour, which the treaty of May 30th ought to have extinguished, and the prejudices which it ought to have dispelled, together with the possible regrets which still lingered with the Powers, had, since its conclusion, sprung up afresh, therefore the Powers continued to call themselves allies as if the war was still going on.

Being the first to arrive in Vienna, these Powers had undertaken by written protocols (the existence of which the French legation suspected from the first, but was unable to make sure of till four months afterwards) not to admit the intervention of France, except as a matter of form.

Two of these protocols, which are before your Majesty, and which are dated September 22nd, 1814,[1] stipulated in substance— " That the allied powers will take the initiative in all matters that have to be discussed ; [under the name of allied powers only Austria, Russia, England, and Prussia were named, because these four powers were more closely allied together than any others, as much by their treaties as by their views].

" That they alone should arrange between them the distribution of the disposable provinces, but that France and Spain should be allowed to give their opinions, and bring forward their objections, which would then be discussed with them.

---

[1] See d'Angeberg's *Congress of Vienna*, p. 249.

" That the plenipotentiaries of the four Powers would not confer with those of the two Powers on any matter relating to the territorial distribution of the duchy of Warsaw, that of Germany or that of Italy, until they had fully decided and were perfectly agreed among themselves on these three points."

It was intended, in fact, that France should play a purely nominal part at the congress. She was simply to be a spectator of what was being done by the others, instead of taking part in it herself ; she was still an object of distrust, nourished by the recollection of her numerous invasions, and of animosity excited by the many evils with which she had only recently overwhelmed Europe. She was still feared ; her power was still dreaded ; and it was thought that peace could only be secured by forming a European union against her ; in fact, the coalition still existed.

Your Majesty will permit me to recall the earnestness with which, on every occasion, I maintained and tried to persuade even the highest officers in the army, that it was for the interest of France, as well as their own glory, to renounce willingly all thoughts of regaining Belgium and the left bank of the Rhine. I believed that unless this patriotic sacrifice was made, there could be no peace between France and Europe, and as a fact, although France no longer owned these provinces, her power and grandeur held Europe in such a state of terror, that she was obliged to preserve a hostile attitude.

So great is our power, that now, when Europe is at her maximum strength and France at her minimum, the former still doubts the success of the struggle she has undertaken. My opinions on this matter were only the expressions of your Majesty's sentiments, but most of your principal statesmen, the worthiest writers, the army, and the greater part of the nation did not share these moderate views, without which any durable peace or even the semblance of it was impossible ; and these ambitious views, which with some reason were looked upon as those of France, served still further to increase and justify the terror her strength inspired.

It was on this account that the public journals teemed with insinuations and accusations against France and her plenipoten-

tiaries.   They remained isolated, no one ventured to approach
them ; even the few ministers who did not share these prejudices,
avoided them lest they too should be compromised.   Everything it
was proposed to do was carefully hidden from us ; conferences were
held without our knowledge ; and when at the commencement of
the congress a commission was appointed to organize the German
federation, all the ministers who composed it were pledged on
honour, not to communicate to us anything that passed there.

Although your Majesty's government had none of the views
imputed to it, although it had nothing to ask for itself and had
no wish to ask for anything, all that was to be arranged by the
congress was of the utmost importance to it.   But if its interests
in these arrangements differed from the actual or momentary
interests of some of the Powers, it was happily in conformity with
those of the majority, and even with the permanent interests of all.

Buonaparte had overthrown so many governments, added so
much territory and so many diverse populations to his empire,
that when France ceased to be the enemy of Europe and
returned within the limits beyond which she could not preserve
friendly relations with other states, there were, in almost every
part of Europe, vast countries without any governments.   The
states which he had despoiled without wholly destroying them,
could not recover the provinces they had lost, because these had
in part passed under the rule of princes who had since then
become allies.   It therefore became necessary that the countries
without rulers (owing to their renunciation by France), should have
some kind of government, and in order to indemnify the states
which had been despoiled by her, that these countries should be
divided among them.   However repugnant or degrading to
humanity such a distribution of men and countries may be, it
was rendered indispensable through the violent usurpations of
a government, which, using its strength merely to destroy, had
brought about the necessity for reconstruction from the *débris*
it had left.

Saxony was conquered, the kingdom of Naples was in
possession of a usurper, and it was necessary to determine the
fate of these states.

The treaty of Paris declared that these arrangements would

be carried out in such a manner as to establish a real and durable equilibrium in Europe. None of the powers denied the necessity of having to conform to this principle, but the special views of some, deceived them as to the means of accomplishing this object. On the other hand it would have been useless to establish this equilibrium, without at the same time constituting those principles, which alone could ensure the domestic tranquillity of the states, while at the same time preventing their being solely under the dominion of the strongest, in their relations one with another.

Your Majesty on re-entering France, desired that principles of political morality should return with you, and become the rule of your government. Your Majesty felt it was also necessary they should pervade in the cabinets, and show themselves in the relations between the different states, and you had commanded us to use all the influence your Majesty possessed and to devote all our energies, to obtain their complete recognition by the whole of Europe.

This task presented many difficulties. The effects of the revolution were not confined merely to French territory, they had spread themselves abroad by force of arms, by the encouragement given to every kind of passion, and by general licentiousness. Holland and several parts of Italy had, at different periods, seen revolutionary governments replace legitimate ones. Since Buonaparte had become master of France, not only was the fact of conquest sufficient to do away with sovereignty, but people became accustomed to seeing sovereigns dethroned, governments annihilated, and whole nations disappear entirely by simple decrees.

Although such a state of affairs, if allowed to continue, must necessarily lead to the total destruction of civilized society, custom and fear made people still endure it, and as it was favourable to the momentary interests of some of the powers, the others did not sufficiently dread the reproach of taking Buonaparte for their model.

We pointed out all the dangers of this false policy. We showed that the existence of all the governments was compromised in the highest degree by a system in which their

preservation depended either on faction or the fate of war.
We at last made them see that it was above all necessary, in
the interests of the nations, to establish the legitimacy of
governments, because legitimate governments can alone be
stable, while those that are illegitimate, having no other support
than that of violence, fall as soon as this support is withdrawn,
and the nation falls a prey to a succession of revolutions of
which it is impossible to see the end.

These principles were long in being understood, being too
severe for the politics of some courts ; they were opposed to the
policy followed by the English in India, and perhaps irksome to
Russia, as she had disowned them in several important and
recent contracts. Before we succeeded in making their importance felt, the allied powers had already made arrangements
which were quite opposed to them. Prussia had demanded the
whole of Saxony, Russia had asked this for her. England had
by official notes, not only consented unreservedly to this transfer,
but even tried to make out that it was fair, and a matter of
necessity. Austria had also officially given in her adhesion to
this measure, excepting only some frontier stipulations. Saxony
was thus completely sacrificed by special arrangements entered
into between Austria, Russia, England and Prussia, to which
France was a complete stranger.

Nevertheless the language of the French embassy, its reasonable, serious, and uniform attitude, free from all ambitious aims,
began to make itself felt. Confidence began to spring up
around it. It was felt that its utterances were not more in the
interests of France than in those of Europe and of each particular state. People's eyes were opened to the dangers France
had pointed out. Austria was the first to desire to withdraw
from what had, if I may say so, been decided upon relative
to Saxony, and declared in a note sent to Prince Hardenberg
on December 10th, 1814, that she would not consent to the
destruction of that kingdom.

This was the first advantage obtained by us in following
the line laid down by your Majesty.

I blame myself for having so constantly, in the letters I had
the honour of writing to your Majesty, complained of the

difficulties we had to contend with and of the delays which constantly impeded the progress of affairs. Now I am thankful for these delays, for if matters had been concluded with greater rapidity, the congress would have terminated before the end of March, the sovereigns would have returned to their capitals, the armies would have been disbanded, and then what difficulties there would have been to encounter !

M. de Metternich having officially communicated to me his note of December 10th, I could make known the views of France, and I therefore sent both to him and to Lord Castlereagh, a full profession of political faith. I declared that your Majesty desired nothing for France, that you only asked for simple justice for every one, and that what you wanted above all, was that revolutions should be put an end to, that the doctrines these had given rise to should no longer be allowed to enter into the political relations of nations, so that each government could either prevent or crush them completely, if menaced or attacked by them.

These declarations served to dissipate the doubts of which we were at first the victims. But these soon gave place to very different sentiments; nothing was done now without our concurrence, not only were we consulted, but our approbation was sought after. Public opinion was completely changed respecting us, and shoals of people, who before had shown themselves timid, now hastened to put an end to the isolation in which we had at first been left.

It was more difficult for England than it had been for Austria, to go back from her promise to Prussia, of giving up to her the whole of Saxony. Her notes were more decided ; she had not, like Austria, given in to the surrender, because of the difficulty of finding any other means of indemnifying Prussia, by possessions equally conveniently situated, for the losses she had sustained since 1806. Moreover, the position of the English ministers obliged them, under pain of losing what is called in England their *character,* not to diverge from the path they have once entered upon, and in choosing this road, their politics must always conform to the probable opinions of Parliament. Notwithstanding this, the English legation was also brought to reconsider its promise, to change its line of action, to withdraw its acquiescence in the destruction of the kingdom of Saxony, to improve its relations with France, and even to join her in a treaty of alliance with Austria. The treaty, specially remarkable as being the first conciliatory step whose joint interests would sooner or later oblige them to support each other, was signed on the 3rd of January. Bavaria, Holland, Hanover and the Netherlands also joined, and it was only then that the coalition, which in spite of the peace had continued to exist, was finally broken up.

From that moment the greater number of the Powers adopted our principles. The others showed, plainly, that they would not hold out much longer; it therefore only remained to press the point.

Prussia deprived of the support of Austria and England, though still backed by Austria, found herself under the necessity of limiting her pretensions to receiving only a portion of Saxony. Thus this kingdom, whose fate seemed irrevocably settled and whose destruction had been pronounced, was saved from ruin.

Buonaparte after having taken possession of the kingdom of Naples by force of arms, had given it, (in defiance of the law of nations, and as if it were a private possession of his own, or as he would have done with an ordinary estate,) to one of his generals as a reward for services rendered. It would have been nothing less than a violation of the laws of legitimacy to allow the possession of that kingdom under such a law. His downfall was inevitable; it could no longer be doubtful, when he himself accomplished it by his aggression. Seven weeks have scarce elapsed since this aggression, and the usurper no longer reigns; Ferdinand IV. has already remounted his throne. In this important question the English minister had the courage to side completely with the policy of France, despite the indiscreet and misplaced clamours of the opposition, and the foolish and inconsiderate utterances of English travellers on all matters relating to Italy.

France has also to congratulate herself on the way in which most of the other arrangements of the congress have been carried out.

The King of Sardinia having no male heir in the actual reigning branch of his house, there was some fear lest Austria should attempt to get the succession passed on to one of the Archdukes who had married one of his daughters, by which the whole of upper Italy would then be placed in the hands of Austria or one of her princes. The right of succession of the branch of Carignan to the states of the King of Sardinia, has been acknowledged. These states, increased by the district of Genoa, and being the heritage of a family whose every interest attaches to France, will thus form a counterpoise to the power of Austria in Italy, necessary to maintain the equilibrium in that country.

If it was not possible to prevent Russia from obtaining some portion of the duchy of Warsaw, the half at least of that duchy will go back to its ancient owners.

Prussia has not got either Luxemburg or Mayence. She does not anywhere border on France ; on all sides she is separated by the Netherlands, whose natural policy since her territory has been augmented, gives France the assurance that there will be nothing to dread from her.

The benefits of perpetual neutrality have been assured to Switzerland, an advantage almost as great for France, whose frontier on that side is perfectly open and undefended, as to Switzerland herself. But this neutrality does not prevent Switzerland from joining Europe to-day in her efforts against Buonaparte. What she has desired and what has been assured to her for ever, she will enjoy during any wars that may take place between the different states. But she herself felt that she ought not to claim this privilege in a war which is not made against a single nation ; a war which Europe has been forced to undertake for her own safety, and which concerns Switzerland herself as much as it does other nations. She is, therefore, desirous to join in the cause of Europe in such a manner, as her position, her organisation, and her resources will allow her to do.

France has, by the treaty of Paris, undertaken to abolish the slave-trade at the expiration of a given date, which may be considered as a sacrifice and a concession she would have made, even if the other maritime Powers which do not share in the sentiments of humanity which dictated this measure, had not also adopted it.   Spain and Portugal, the only ones among these Powers who joined in this treaty, undertook to abolish it as well as France. It is true they reserved to themselves a longer period of delay, but this delay is proportionately less, when the needs of their colonies are taken into consideration, and when it is remembered that in these somewhat backward countries, opinion on such a matter has to be educated.

The navigation of the Rhine and the Schelde has been placed under proper regulations, equally the same for all nations. These regulations prevent the states bordering on the rivers, from placing any special obstruction in the way of the navigation, or imposing upon it any dues other than those which have been established for their own people.   These arrangements give back to France, by the facilities which they afford to her commerce, the greater part of those advantages which she formerly derived from Belgium and the right bank of the Rhine.

All the principal points have been arranged to the satisfaction of France, as much and more, perhaps, than we could have hoped for.   Even in details quite as much consideration was shown for her special convenience, as that of any other country.

Having got rid of their prejudices, the Powers found that in order to establish a permanent order of things, it was necessary that each state should feel it had gained those advantages it had a right to expect.   All therefore worked together with goodwill to procure for each, what would not harm the other.   This was a stupendous undertaking ; it meant the reconstruction of that which twenty years of disorder had destroyed ; it meant the conciliation of contradictory interests by equitable arrangements, the compensation of partial [1] inconveniences by greater advantages, and to subordinate even the idea of absolute perfection in political institutions and in the distribution of the forces, to the establishment of a durable peace.

The principal obstacles had been successfully overcome, the most thorny questions had been settled, every effort was made to leave nothing undecided.   Germany was to receive a federal constitution resulting from the deliberations of the

---

[1] Suppressed in the text of the archives.

congress, which would have arrested the tendency observable among some, to form a league of the north and a league of the south. The powers were about to oppose by wise and just measures in Italy, an efficient barrier to the recurrence of those frequent revolutions which have harassed the people of that country for centuries. Wise measures were being concerted to insure the reciprocal interests of the different countries, and to multiply their points of contact, as well as the revenues of their industries and commerce, and all useful intercourse was perfected and facilitated, according to the principles of a liberal policy.

We flattered ourselves in fact that the congress would crown its labours, by substituting for these fleeting alliances (the result of necessities and momentary calculations) a permanent system of universal guarantees and general equilibrium, the advantages of which we had succeeded in making all the powers appreciate. Lord Castlereagh had drawn up a very good document on this subject. The Ottoman Empire entered into this great scheme of preservation, and probably the information given her by England and ourselves, contributed in determining her to repulse all Buonaparte's advances ; thus the order established in Europe would be placed under the perpetual protection of all the parties interested, who by wisely concerted plans, or by sincerely united efforts would crush at the very outset, any attempt to compromise it.

Then revolutions would be prevented, and governments would be able to devote their time to home administration and real reforms, in conformity with the needs and wishes of the people, and in the execution of numerous salutary schemes, which, owing to the dangers and convulsions of past times, had unfortunately been in abeyance.

The re-establishment of your Majesty's government, whose interests, principles, and wishes were all directed towards the preservation of peace, afforded Europe the means of placing her happiness and tranquillity on a solid basis. The maintenance of your Majesty on your throne was necessary to the success of this great work ; the terrible catastrophe which for a time has separated you from your people has acted as a check. It has been found necessary to bestow less care on the prosperity of nations, and devote more to finding measures for the safety of their existence, which was menaced. Many matters ready planned, had to be adjourned, and others less matured and less thought out, than if full care and attention could have been given them, had to be substituted.

The congress having thus been forced to leave uncompleted the work it had undertaken, it was suggested that the signature of the Act that would ratify it, should be put off until such time as the business should be completed.

Several of the cabinets were of this opinion, probably with the secret hope of taking advantage of the coming events. I looked upon this adjournment as a very great misfortune for your Majesty ; less on account of the uncertainty that would remain as to the intentions of the Powers, than as to the effect such an act would have on public opinion in France, affecting as it would, all the highest interests of Europe, and in which, despite the actual circumstances, your Majesty appears as one of the principal actors. I therefore did my utmost to accomplish the ratification, and I consider myself fortunate that it was finally agreed to.

The great consideration in which your Majesty's government ought to be held at all foreign courts, would not be complete, except by securing to your subjects that esteem which belongs by right to the members of a great nation and of which the fear inspired by the French had deprived them. Since the month of December, 1814, not a single Frenchman has come to Vienna, no matter on what business, without receiving the greatest possible attention, and I may inform your Majesty that on March 7th, 1815, the day on which the news of Buonaparte's arrival in France became known, the fact of being a Frenchman became a passport to the kindness of every one in Vienna. I knew the great stress your Majesty laid on this evidence of good feeling and I am happy to be able to inform you, that your wishes in this respect have been thoroughly carried out.

I entreat your Majesty to allow me to bring to your notice the great assistance given me by the Duc de Dalberg, the Comte de la Tour-du-Pin, and the Comte de Noailles, whom your

Majesty sent here with me as ambassadors ; likewise M. de la Besnardière, who accompanied me, in bringing the negotiations to a successful issue. They have not only been of the greatest use by their work on the different commissions to which they were attached, but also by their social qualities, their language and the pleasant impression they gave of themselves as well as the government they represented. It is owing to their skilful co-operation, that I was enabled to overcome so many obstacles, to change so many adverse dispositions, and destroy numerous false impressions, and finally to restore to your Majesty's government all the weight and influence it ought to have in the affairs of Europe. It was only by firmly maintaining the principles of legitimacy that we attained this important end. The presence of all the sovereigns who were in Vienna and likewise all the members of the congress, at the expiatory ceremony of the 21st of January, was a striking homage rendered to this principle.

But while it triumphed at the congress, it was attacked in France. What I am about to say to your Majesty on this subject, was probably more evident at a distance than it was in Paris. Outside of France, attention being less distracted facts became known *en masse*, and being separated from surrounding circumstances could, to a certain extent, be judged more fairly ; nevertheless I would not rely implicitly on any observations that were merely my own. Having filled a position abroad for a long time, my duty to your Majesty obliges me to do what the Foreign Office enjoins on all those in its employ. They are bound to render an account of the opinions formed by the countries to which they are accredited, of the various acts of their own government, and the different impressions produced by these acts, on enlightened and able men.

It is quite possible to become reconciled to a settled state of affairs, even if it jars somewhat with one's principles, because one need not dread the future ; but not to an unsettled state of things, which changes every day, for in this latter case, each day brings forth fresh fears, to which one can see no end. The Revolutionists took their stand against the first acts of your Majesty's government, then they became alarmed at what was done in the course of ten days, a month—six months—and resigned themselves to the expulsions in the Senate,[1] but could not tolerate those of the Institute,[2] although these latter were far less important. The changes made in the *Court de Cassation*[3] since your Majesty considered them necessary, ought to have been effected eight months before.

The principle of legitimacy suffered still further, and in perhaps a still more dangerous manner, from the faults of the defenders of legitimate power, for they confused two things so completely opposite, as the source of power, and its exercise, persuading themselves (or acting as if they were so persuaded) that as the power was legitimate, it must therefore necessarily be absolute.

But however legitimate power may be, its exercise must vary according to the object to which it is applied, both as regards time and circumstance. Furthermore the spirit of the times in which we live, requires that in all civilized states, supreme power is never to be exercised, except in concert with certain bodies from the midst of the society it governs.

To contend against this opinion would be to contend against universal opinion ; and a great number of those persons placed near the throne, were essentially injurious to the government, because their views were in opposition to it. All your Majesty's power was based on the opinion formed by the people of your virtues and good faith. This some acts tended to weaken. I

[1] The Chamber of Peers created by Louis XVIII. consisted of 504 members, of whom eighty-four were old senators ; fifty-three senators were excluded—twenty-three as being no longer Frenchmen, and the other thirty for political reasons. Among the latter the best known were Cambacérès Chaptal de Lapparent, Curé Fouché, Siégès Roger-Ducos, François de Neufchâteau, the Abbé Grégoire, Gorat, Lambrechts Roederer, Cardinal Fesch, &c.

[2] By the proclamation of the 10th of March the fourth class of the Institute—that of the Fine Arts—was suppressed. In addition, Prince Lucien, Cardinal Fesch, Cardinal Maury, Cambacérès, Gorat, Marlin, Roederer, and Siégès were excluded from the French Academy ; the Emperor Napoleon, Mouge, Guyton de Morneau, and Carnot from the Academy of Sciences ; King Joseph, Lakanal, and the Abbé Gregoire from the Academy of Inscriptions.*

[3] The highest Court of Appeal in France. By the proclamation of February 16th, 1815, the composition of this Court underwent the following modifications :—The first President, the Comte Muraire, was replaced by M. Desèze. Of the three presidents two remained—M. Barris and M. Heurion de Pensey. The third, M. Mourre, was made Attorney-General, in place of Merlin de Douay, dismissed, and was replaced by M. Brisson. As for the judges, fourteen of them were deprived of their seats.

* The Academy of Inscriptions and *Belle Lettres*, was founded by Colbert. Translator.

will only cite as an instance the ˙forced constructions and subtilties, by which some of the conditions of the constitutional charter seemed to be evaded ; particularly in the ordinances which subvert the institutions founded on the laws.[1] Then arose doubts as to the sincerity of the government ; it was thought that the charter was only regarded as a temporary act, granted under the exigencies of circumstances, and which it was proposed to allow to fall into disuse, if representative vigilance would permit it. Reactions were dreaded, and some nominations justified these fears ; for example, the appointment of M. de Bruges[2] to the Chancellorship of the Legion of Honour (whatever his personal qualities might have been) displeased every one in France, and I may tell your Majesty, also astonished every one in Europe.

The general state of uneasiness attracted all those to the revolutionary party, who without sharing its errors, were attached to constitutional principles, and also all those who were interested in the maintenance, not of the doctrines of revolution, but of that which had been effected by their influence.

It is more owing to this cause than from any real attachment to his person, that Buonaparte succeeded in finding some partisans outside the army, and even a great number of those he possessed in the army ; because having been brought up in the midst of the Revolution, they were attached by various ties[3] to the men who were the chief actors in it.

However great the advantages of a legitimate government may be, it is impossible to deny the fact, that it is also liable to great abuses, and on this point, opinion is very strong ; for during the twenty years that preceded the Revolution, the tendency of all political writings has been to make them known and to

---

[1] This alludes to the police proclamation of June 7th, 1814, respecting the observance of Sundays and fêtes, as being a violation of the charter which had guaranteed religious freedom.

[2] Henry Alphonse, Vicomte de Bruges, born 1764, became Naval Lieutenant in 1789. He emigrated, and served in Condé's army ; later on he was attached to the English army. In 1815 he was appointed Brigadier-General and Grand Chancellor of the Legion of Honour, in place of M. de Pradt. He died in 1820.

[3] Text : " Parce que élevés avec la revolution ils etaient attachés par toutes sortes de liens " = as translated. Var. : " Parce que *élevé* avec la revolution *il etait attaché* par toute sorte de liens " = " because having been brought up in the midst of the revolution, he was attached by various ties."

exaggerate them. Few people really know how to appreciate the advantages of legitimacy, for they are still in the future. Whereas all the world can see abuses, for they crop up at any moment and show themselves on every occasion. Who, during the last twenty years, has given time enough to reflection, to realize, that if a government is not legitimate it cannot be stable ; that in offering to all ambitious spirits the hope of over-throwing it, in order to replace it by another, it is always being threatened and bears within it a revolutionary ferment ready to burst forth at any moment ? The impression unfortunately exists in people's minds, that legitimacy in assuring the crown to the sovereign, no matter how he governs, gives him too great facilities to place himself above the laws.

With this disposition, which is now found in every nation, and at a time when all things are examined, discussed, and analysed, political subjects above all, people ask themselves, what is legitimacy, whence has it sprung, and what constitutes it?

During the period when religious sentiments were deeply engraved on human hearts, and when they exercised an all-power-ful influence on the mind, men might have believed that the sovereign power was indeed a divine gift. They might have believed that the families placed by Heaven on thrones which they had occupied, by its will, for a length of time, reigned over them by divine right ; but in these days, when there hardly remains the faintest trace of these sentiments, and the bonds of religion if not entirely broken, are at least[1] relaxed, such a theory of legitimacy is no longer tenable.

The general opinion of the present day (and it would be vain to try to weaken it) is that governments exist only for the people ; a necessary consequence of this opinion is, that the only legiti-mate power is that which can best secure their happiness and peace. Hence it follows that the only legitimate power is that which has existed for a long succession of years, in fact a power strengthened by the respect due to the recollection of the past, and by the attachment which is natural among men for the dominant race (having for it the old feeling of possession which is a right in the eyes of every one, being that of the law which

---

[1] Var.: "*bien*" relâché = "much relaxed."

governs private property), and therefore exposes the people more rarely than any other, to the fatal risks of revolution. It is to such a power therefore that their dearest interests compel them to submit ; but if unfortunately any cause is given to induce the belief, that the abuses of this power are greater than the advantages derived from it, legitimacy is then looked upon as a chimera.

What then is needed to give people confidence in legitimate authority and to preserve to this authority the respect which insures its stability ? It is sufficient, but also indispensable, that it should be constituted in such a manner that all causes for fear which it may inspire should be eliminated. It is no less in the interests of the sovereign than of his subjects that it should be thus constituted, because absolute power in these days would be as heavy a burden to him who wields it, as to those who are under its influence.

Before the Revolution, power in France was restricted by ancient institutions, it was modified by the action of the large body of the magistracy, the clergy, and the nobility, who, were necessary elements to its existence, and of whom it made use for the purpose of governing. Now that all these institutions are destroyed, and these great means of governing are annihilated, others must be found, of which public opinion will not disapprove ; and it is even necessary it should itself point them out.

Formerly, religious influence could support royal authority ; it can do so no longer, now that religious indifference has pervaded all classes, and become almost universal. Royal authority can therefore only derive support from public opinion, and to obtain this it must be in accord with that opinion.

It will have this support, if the people see that the government, though all powerful to do good, can do nothing to the contrary. But they must also have the certainty that there is nothing arbitrary in its proceedings. The mere desire to do good will not suffice ; such a desire might change, or mistaken measures might be employed, to achieve its end. It is not enough that confidence should be based merely on the virtues and noble qualities of the sovereign, which like himself are perishable, it is necessary to found it on the strength of permanent institutions ;

it needs even more than this.   No institutions, no matter what their nature, could insure happiness to a nation, or even inspire it with any confidence, if they did not establish such a form of government, as would in the general opinion of the times be considered the only fitting one to attain the end in view.

Guarantees are required, both for the sovereign and for the people, but they will not be believed to exist unless :

(*a*) " Individual liberty is legally safe from all attacks."

(*b*) " The liberty of the press is fully assured, and the law does not hesitate to punish its misdemeanours."

(*c*) " The judicial bench is independent, and on that account composed of persons," permanently appointed.[1]

(*d*) " Legal judgments are not in certain cases reserved to be dealt with by the administration or any bodies other than the courts of justice."

(*e*) " The ministers are fully responsible for the proper exercise of the power with which they are intrusted."

(*f*) " No other persons except those actually responsible, are permitted to influence the councils of the sovereign."

Finally, " Unless the law is the outcome of a will formed by the union of three distinct wills."

In large and ancient communities where the intellectual capacity is developed with the needs, and the passions with the intelligence, it is necessary that public authority should acquire a proportionate strength, and experience has proved, that it is strengthened by being divided.

These opinions are no longer confined to one country.   They are common to almost all.   It is for this reason that constitutions are asked for everywhere, the need is everywhere felt of establishing something analogous to the more or less advanced state of political society, and preparations are everywhere being made to this end.   The congress did not give Geneva back to Sardinia, Lucca to the Infanta Marie Louise of Spain, restore Naples to Ferdinand IV., nor return the legations to the Pope, without stipulating for such arrangements for those states, as their actual condition seemed to permit or require.   I have not met a single sovereign or a single minister, who dismayed by the results,

---

[1] Text : *inamovibles* = irremovable.

that must befall Spain under the system of government carried out by Ferdinand VII., did not bitterly regret that the latter should have been allowed to regain his throne without the condition being made by Europe, that he should give his states such institutions as were in harmony with the ideas of the times. I have even heard sovereigns, whose people were too little advanced in civilization, to appreciate institutions suitable to a high degree of culture, lament over this, as if it were a misfortune from which they suffered themselves.

I have gathered these opinions in the midst of the deliberations of assembled Europe, I have come across them in every conversation I have had with the sovereigns and their ministers. They are expressed in all the letters written by the Austrian and Russian ambassadors to London, and also in those of Lord Castlereagh. It was my duty therefore to submit this report to your Majesty. I felt I could still less avoid doing so, when the sovereigns in the farewell audiences accorded to me, all advised my telling your Majesty that they were perfectly convinced that France would never be at peace, if your Majesty did not fully share these opinions and take them as the sole rule for your government. That everything in France must, without exception, be obliterated, that any exclusion would be dangerous, and no guarantees would be found for the sovereign, until he gave them to all parties, and that these guarantees would not be sufficient unless they were accepted as such by all classes of society ; that it seemed absolutely necessary to adopt some complete system which would restore and render evident, the sincerity of each party ; which would from the commencement clearly show the object the government had in view, and which would enable every one to understand his proper position and leave no one in any uncertainty. They added, that if your Majesty was interested more than any one else in maintaining the tranquillity of France, they in reality were no less so, for the emergency in which your Majesty is now placed, compromises the existence of all Europe ; and finally that all the efforts made during the past year would be very difficult to renew, when once they had returned to their own countries.

After having read the declaration which your Majesty lately

addressed to your subjects, the sovereigns further informed me
that they had noticed with regret a phrase by which your Majesty
implied (though expressed with much circumspection) that you
had consented to accept their help, from which it might be
inferred that even if you had refused it, peace could still have
been maintained. They fear that from this it may appear to
the people of France, as if your Majesty had wrongfully yielded
to pressure from the sovereigns. They think therefore that in
order not to confirm an opinion so opposed to the interests of
France, it will be advisable for your Majesty as well as for those
around you, to take very little action in the matter. Your
Majesty will have some difficulty in carrying this out, for it means
restraining zeal and even repressing it. According to their view,
your Majesty ought to lament over what is being done, instead of
co-operating with it ; you will have to place yourself (or be
placed by them) between the allied sovereigns and your people,
to lessen as much as lies in your power the evils of war, and to
assure the allies of the loyalty of the fortresses which have been
surrendered, and which according to the arrangements which I
presume your ministers will make with the Duke of Wellington,
will be handed over to persons chosen by yourself. Lastly, they
consider that in order not to appear as provoking a war, or even
desiring to make it yourself, neither your Majesty nor any prince
of your family should be seen with the allied armies. Never
before have politics required such delicate handling.[1]

---

[1] M. de Talleyrand here alludes to the following proclamation, which the king
had signed on June 25th, when he returned to France :—

"FRENCHMEN,

    "From the time when the most wicked of enterprises, seconded by the most
inconceivable defection, obliged us to temporarily quit our kingdom, we have warned
you of the dangers which menaced you if you did not hasten to throw off the yoke of
the tyrant usurper.

    "We did not wish to join our arms or those of our family, to those of the instru-
ments which Providence has used to punish this treason. But, now that the powerful
exertions of our allies have dispersed the tyrant's adherents, we hasten to re-enter our
country, in order to re-establish the constitution we have given to France, to repair
by every means in our power the evils which are the necessary result of revolt and war,
to recompense the good, to enforce the law against the guilty, and finally, to gather
round our ancestral throne that large body of Frenchmen, whose fidelity and devotion
have brought such comfort and consolation to our hearts.

    "Chateau Cambrésis, 25th June, 1815.

                                                                "LOUIS.

    "In the name of the King.
    "Secretary of State for War, Duc de Feltre."

If owing to the events about to take place, any portion of France should succeed in escaping from Buonaparte's yoke, I believe your Majesty could not do better than go thither at once, take your ministry with you, convoke the chambers and assume the government of your kingdom, just as if it was entirely subject again. The plan of an expedition to Lyons (which I earnestly desire on account of the effective result it would produce on the southern provinces) might allow this idea to be carried out with much advantage.

The announcement of the large number of commissioners to be sent to the armies has not been well received. I believe that all the steps which your Majesty may take, will have to be in concert with the allies, almost indeed with their consent. This deference should aid in placing clearly before them the object of the war, which I may say, is not quite the same with all the cabinets. For though England particularly and really desires your Majesty's return, I am not so sure that Russia would not prefer some other combinations; nor can I say that Austria, though I believe she sides with us, is very eager about it, while Prussia's first consideration is certainly her own aggrandisement.

Would it not be possible for your Majesty, just as the foreign troops are about to enter France, to address a second declaration to your subjects, carefully guarding the French *amour propre* which wishes, and with reason, that nothing, not even that which it most desires, should be due to foreign aid. This declaration first pointing out that Buonaparte is endeavouring to mislead the people as to the actual cause and object of the war, might then go on to state, that it is not on your Majesty's account that the foreign powers have undertaken it, because they know that France only needs to be protected from oppression, but that it is for their own individual security; that they would not have undertaken it had they not felt convinced that Europe would be menaced with the most terrible disasters, as long as the man who has for so long oppressed it is master of France; that the

It was this manifesto which had alarmed M. de Talleyrand, and which, having been laid by him before the Council and the *Corps diplomatique*, became the subject of strong representations, which were afterwards submitted by him and the Duke of Wellington to the king, who gave in, and three days later, on June 28th, issued a second proclamation, countersigned by Talleyrand, which will be found on p. 156.

return of this man to France is the sole cause of the war, and its immediate and principal object to wrest from him the power he has thus usurped.   And in order to mitigate the evils of war, and prevent the disasters and arrest devastation, should such occur, that your Majesty surrounded by Frenchmen, will place yourself as an intermediary between the foreign sovereigns and your people, in the hope that the consideration which is accorded to you, may be utilised for the benefit of your country; that this is the only position your Majesty intends to occupy during the war, and that you do not wish any of the princes of your house to take service with the foreign armies.

Then passing on to the interior arrangements of France, your Majesty might make it known, that you are prepared to give whatever guarantees may be deemed necessary.   As the choice of your ministers is one of the most important you can offer, you will at once announce a change of ministry.   Your Majesty ought to say that the ministers thus selected will only be temporarily appointed, because you desire to reserve the formation of a cabinet until you return to France, so that it may be one adapted to all parties, all opinions, and calculated to remove all uneasiness.

Lastly, it would be well if this declaration made some reference to national property, and in such a manner as to convey a more positive and more absolute assurance on this subject, than that contained in the charter of constitution, the provisions of which have not been sufficient to allay the uneasiness of the purchasers of such property.   As the sale of the public forests (the produce of which will become much more necessary than heretofore) has been thereby prevented, it is important just now to allay all doubts and to give no pretext whatever for them, but rather to afford every encouragement.

It is generally considered that it would be wise and even necessary for your Majesty to address your people in this sense, and I confess to your Majesty that such also is my opinion.   I also think it indispensable that with regard to the guarantees, your Majesty should make them thoroughly satisfactory.   If, as I venture to hope, your Majesty shares this opinion, you will no doubt depute some persons who are honoured with your confidence, to prepare and submit to your Majesty the draft of this declaration.

I have now given your Majesty a full and exact account of the result of the negotiations that have taken place during the Congress and the impressions French affairs have made in Vienna. It only remains for me to speak of a few details of no great importance. Since I have been here a mass of papers has accumulated on my hands. The greater part are not of sufficient importance to be required again. Your Majesty has copies of all the others, so that I need not take them away. I have therefore burnt a great many and have left the rest in Vienna in safe keeping.

I am happy to be able to wind up this long business (which the nature of the matters I had to submit to your Majesty often rendered very painful to me) by bringing to your notice the zeal and devotion quite beyond praise, of which your ambassadors and ministers to the various courts, have given you increasing proofs during the whole course of the congress. Their position, difficult at first, from the same causes which threw so many obstacles in my way at Vienna,[1] became still more so later on, in consequence of the disastrous events which have succeeded each other since the beginning of March. They however only saw in these difficulties a further occasion to exhibit the attachment they feel towards your Majesty. Several of them also have already[2] for some time past been placed in pecuniary difficulties; they did their very utmost to live in accordance with the different posts your Majesty had confided to them. Some arrangements will surely have been made, to mitigate the circumstances in which they find themselves.[3]

PRINCE DE TALLEYRAND.

This memoir produced as little effect as my words upon the king, who ordered his horses and proceeded towards France. I had suggested Lyons as his residence, because it was the second town in the kingdom and I knew we should not on that side

---

[1] Suppressed in the text of the archives. [2] *Ibid.*
[3] Var. : " Plusieurs éprouvent des besoins très pressants "= " Many experience very pressing needs."

come in contact with the Austrian troops. Lyons could also be quickly reached by the Rhine and Switzerland.

I remained twenty-four hours at Mons, during which time messages arrived for me from all parts; among others I received the following letter from Prince de Metternich which quite confirmed me in my opinion.

MANNHEIM, *June* 24, 1815.[1]

Here, dear Prince, is an address to the French nation which I have drawn up, and to which Prince Schwartzenberg has attached his signature. I flatter myself that you will find it correct both in principle and language, and above all quite in accordance with our proceedings.[2]

M. de Vincent, and in default of him M. Pozzo, received orders to draw attention to the objection raised to the nomination of royal commissioners to our armies. The matter went entirely against the king. I refer in this report to what I send to de Vincent, and I inclose herewith for your private information a copy of a letter I wrote to Lord Wellington in answer to one, in which he desired to prove to me the great benefit that would result from requisitions made in the name of the king. I can see nothing in such a step but great inconvenience and useless complications with the allied generals, besides serious difficulties as regards home policy. Remain firm to *your* idea, make the king go to France, to the south, to the north, to the west, no matter where, provided only that it is in his own country, surrounded by Frenchmen, and away from foreign bayonets and foreign aid. It is sufficient to follow Buonaparte's system of government to be convinced, that the great weapon he means to make use of, is *emigration.*

The king will cease to be an *émigré*[3] the day he returns home to his own people. It is necessary that the king should rule and that the *Royal* troops should act at a distance from the allied armies. As soon as the king has formed a nucleus at home, we will send all those who desert to our armies, to him.

Vincent's[4] wound troubles me greatly. I am in hopes of hearing from him to know whether I should send you a

---

[1] The allied sovereigns were at that time at Mannheim.
[2] See the *Moniteur* of July 10th, 1825.
[3] Refugee.—*Translator.*
[4] The Baron de Vincent was at the time Austrian minister accredited to King Louis XVIII., and commissioner with the Duke of Wellington; he was wounded in the hand on the morning of the battle of Waterloo, which he believed at first to be lost, and hastened to carry the news to Ghent, and it was not until late in the night of the 18th and 19th of June that they learnt the victory of the allies.

substitute, for it is in every way necessary that you should have some one near you who can act as an intermediary.

Here all goes well; now that the Russian troops are in line (and this step is a wise and most necessary one) the operations will be carried on with much vigour. The main body of the Austrian army will pass the Rhine at Basle on the 25th, that of Frimont will be in Geneva on the 26th, another army will on the same day cross the Mont Cenis, and a third will disembark without ceasing in the south. The advance-guard yesterday passed the centre of the frontier.

The accounts that have reached us from the interior show that the fermentation increases everywhere; Fouché's reports are sufficient to prove this. I trust soon to see you again, somehow or other mon Prince.

Always yours,
METTERNICH.

But at Mons the king's friends harassed me by representing the dangers he ran, and I was not a little surprised to find among these ardent followers M. de Chateaubriand, who while in Vienna, in the end of 1814, had so bitterly complained of what was being done in France. He was then dissatisfied with all the world and with everything; thought it strange that he should be sent back to Stockholm as the king's minister, and ended by declaring that he intended to apply to enter the Russian service. His letter ought to be in the archives of the Foreign Office among the papers relating to the Congress of Vienna. At last, pestered and pursued by those who described to me the absolute desolation to which the king would be reduced by his craze to return to the Tuileries, and by the fears that the strangers amongst whom he would be alone would take advantage of his position adverse to France, I gave up my own convictions, and followed the king to Cambray, to become like him, part of the baggage of the English army.

My arrival at Cambray had at least the result of obtaining from the king a second public declaration, fitted to allay, if not to do away with, the evil effects of the unfortunate one which had been issued on June 25th, at Chateau Cambresis.

This is what I drew up, which the king signed, and which I countersigned. I even now believe that it was the best that could be uttered under the circumstances.

DECLARATION OF KING LOUIS XVIII.

Given at Cambray June 28th, 1815.

Learning that one of the gates of my kingdom is open to me. I hasten to present myself. I do so in order to recall my misguided subjects; to mitigate those evils I had desired to prevent ; to place myself a second time between the allied armies and the French, in the hope that the feelings of regard of which I may be the object, may benefit my people. In this way only have I thought fit to take part in the war. I have not suffered any prince of my family to appear in the ranks of the foreigners, and have restrained the ardour of those of my servants who were able to marshal themselves around me.

Now that I have returned to my native land, I feel great satisfaction in speaking to my people as a friend. When I reappeared among them, I found men's minds were disturbed and carried away by opposing passions. Whichever way I looked, nothing but difficulties and obstacles presented themselves. My government may have made mistakes and probably has done so, for there are times when the purest motives are insufficient to guide, and may even occasionally mislead ; experience alone can teach us ; it will not have done so in vain. The preservation of France is the object of all my wishes. Severe trials have taught my subjects that the principle of the legitimacy of sovereigns is one of the fundamental bases of social order, the only one on which a great nation and a moderate and well ordered liberty can be established. This doctrine has now been proclaimed as that of the whole of Europe. I had already consecrated it by my charter, and I purpose to add to this charter all the guarantees which can ensure its success. The unity of the ministry is the strongest that I can offer. I intend that it shall be permanent, and that the frank and decided policy of my council shall secure all interests and quiet all apprehensions. Of late the re-establishment of the tithe and feudal rights has been spoken of ; this fable invented by the common enemy needs no refutation. It will not be expected that the King of France should stoop to refute calumnies and falsehoods, the success of which only too clearly betrays their origin. If the acquirers of national property are under any apprehensions, the charter should have sufficed to reassure them. Did I not myself propose to the Chambers sales of these properties, and cause them to be completed ? This proof of my sincerity needs no comment.

I have of late received from all classes of my subjects equal proofs of affection and fidelity; I would have them know how deeply I appreciate this; and it will be my pleasure to select those who are to be around my person and my family from among all classes of Frenchmen.

I only intend to exclude from my presence those men whose reputation is a source of grief to France and of terror to the rest of Europe. In the conspiracy hatched by these men, I see many of my subjects who have been misled and a few who are culpable. I, who as all Europe knows, never promised anything without fulfilling it, now promise as regards those Frenchmen who have been misled, to pardon everything that has taken place from the day when I left Lille in the midst of so many tears, up to the time when I entered Cambray amid so many rejoicings. Nevertheless the blood of my subjects has been shed through treachery such as the annals of Europe afford no example. This treachery has brought foreigners into the heart of France, and each day reveals some new calamity to me, therefore I owe it to the dignity of my throne, to the interest of my people, and to the repose of Europe, to exempt from pardon the authors and agents of this detestable conspiracy. They will be handed over to be dealt with by the two Chambers which I propose to summon at once.

Frenchmen, these are the sentiments with which I again appear among you: he, whose sentiments which time cannot change, misfortune wear out, nor injustice depress, your king, whose fathers reigned over your fathers, for more than eight centuries, now returns to devote the rest of his days to defend and to comfort you.

LOUIS.

THE PRINCE DE TALLEYRAND.

I nevertheless admit, that I was much disheartened in having to abandon the hope I had conceived, that by prevailing upon the king to go to Lyons, an order of things would have been established by which a recurrence of the events of the 20th of March would have been averted. I was convinced that France could only find quiet and freedom in a constitutional monarchy. The organic law known as the charter, consisting only of a collection of maxims, applicable to every kind of government, appeared to me to require for its interpretation a body of institutions fitted to regulate the affairs of the country. Yet how was a true constitution to be framed in Paris in the presence of sovereigns, either absolute or aspiring to be so, and of necessity not very anxious to see a great country offer an example they had no wish to follow? Far from being able to hope that they would be found favourable to the constitutional system in France, there was only too much reason to fear, that the party still holding the principles of the *émigrés*, would make use of them, if not for the immediate accomplishment of their purposes, at any rate as a preparation for future triumphs.

The king, by only treating with the foreigners at a distance, and keeping his family about him, would have cut the thread of every intrigue, and would at any rate, only have returned to Paris soon enough to have tendered his thanks to the allied sovereigns, if indeed they had not demanded a price for their services, which would have freed him from showing any gratitude. The king would have appeared in his capital with a ministry already formed. The choice of M. Fouché as minister of police, which, as I told the king, appeared to me a weakness, would not at Arnouville [1] have received the support of *Monsieur* to whom he presented himself, introduced by the *bailli* of Crussol as representing the royalists who had remained in Paris. The Duke of Wellington would not have considered it necessary, that in order to check the savage enterprises of General Blücher, and to have the glory of being the first to enter Paris, he should both at Senlis and afterwards at Neuilly have to confer with M. Fouché, and other intriguers,[2] who only thought of making capital of the power which they no longer

---

[1] A country house near St. Denis where the king spent some days before his entry into the capital.

[2] The provisional government on the 27th of June appointed an Armistice Commission, composed of General Comte de Valence, peer of France ; General Comte Andreossy ; M. Flaugergues, deputy ; Comte Boissy-d'Anglas, peer of France ; and M. de la Besnardière. Their instructions, drawn up by M. Bignon, Minister for Foreign Affairs, authorized them to offer the Somme, with a strong fortress, as the line of demarcation during the armistice. They were forbidden to respond to any overtures that might be made to them respecting the future government of France. The negotiators quitted Paris on the 28th, met Blücher, who escorted them at Noyon, and rejoined Wellington on the 29th at Estrées Saint Denis, a village situated ten miles north-west of Compiègne, and not at Senlis. This mission had no result whatever.

Respecting the conferences at Neuilly, M. de Talleyrand has in view the negotiations which preceded the nomination of Fouché to the Ministry. Fouché several times met Wellington at Neuilly. He had persuaded him that the obstacles which prevented the re-establishment of royalty obliged the king to have recourse to men of the Revolution. The result of these conferences was to induce Wellington to bring Fouché favourably to the king's notice.

possessed, and could only give him such advice as tended to relieve them from their personal embarrassment.[1] No sooner

[1] This is the letter written to me by the Duke of Wellington on the subject. I retain all the faults of style in this letter, recollecting that the commander-in-chief of the British army was not bound to write French like a member of the Academy.

PRINCE,

M. Boissy d'Anglas and General Valence, General Andréossy, M. de la Besnardière, and M. de Flaugergues, have been sent to me from Paris to ask for a suspension of hostilities, and I have had an interview with them of so much interest to the king, that I think it advisable to write to you without loss of time.

I explained to them that in my opinion the abdication of Napoleon does not offer such security to the allied powers as would justify a suspension of hostilities ; and after some further discussion I said to them that I could only look upon our object as secured, if Napoleon was delivered up to the allies, and Paris occupied by our outposts ; and if such a government was established as would give confidence not only to France but to Europe.

After some hesitation these gentlemen requested me to explain what I meant by such a government. I told them I had no authority to speak on this subject, but my private advice would be, to recall the king without any conditions, and that the honour of France demanded this step, before anyone could suppose that the intervention of the powers had been the sole occasion of his recall.

All these gentlemen agreed with me, and though apparently they think that some changes in the constitution would be necessary, especially as regards the ministry and the framing of the laws, they admitted it would be better to let the king make these changes rather than impose them upon him as conditions.

M. de Flaugergues said he did not believe that the two chambers would agree to the king's recall without conditions. Our conversation then turned upon the manner of bringing about what everyone desired, without infringing the principles respecting the quiet, natural and unconditional restoration of the king. During the discussion we received the king's declaration, dated the 28th, and countersigned by your highness, and these gentlemen consider it admirably fitted to fulfil all our intentions, if the two articles herewith appended are withdrawn, or at any rate made clearer.

The individuals indicated in article No. I. are the persons included in the late conspiracy ; but this not being sufficiently explained, it is thought, or it might be thought, that you therein include the regicides. I opposed this view, because the king having consented, before his departure, to the principle of employing Fouché, could not actually refuse to employ either him or any other minister, and the preceding sentence explains this clearly enough. Nevertheless it would be well to explain it, or to withdraw it altogether.

Article II. is displeasing to these gentlemen, because it contains a threat. It appears useless to them because it comprises too many persons, and above all, because the expressions are stronger than becomes the king, and their opinion is that it should be suppressed.

They strongly feel as to the words marked in No. III., and they are of opinion that the recall of the king will not be effected in the manner most advantageous to his majesty, and the public welfare, if the chambers learn that they are to be dismissed at once. I therefore recommend that the words underlined be omitted ; the king will then have the means of summoning a new assembly or of continuing the present chambers if he thinks proper. He could not admit, à priori, that the present chambers constitute a lawful assembly, but there is no necessity for his informing them to begin with, that they are to be dismissed. Your highness will perceive from all that has passed, that my wish is to restore the king—1st, unconditionally, 2nd, in such a manner that it may not appear to be the effect of compulsion by the allies, and probably you will agree with me that such a result is well worth a few sacrifices.

I am about to see General Blücher, and will try to persuade him to agree to the armistice on the conditions stated below. I earnestly hope to receive your reply early to-morrow. Meanwhile I think the king should come to Roze, leaving a garrison in Cambray.

WELLINGTON.

therefore had we arrived at Paris, than we met with nothing but difficulties. We had in the first place to contend against the outrages and depredations of the Prussians, who, filled with a long-cherished animosity which they had been unable to gratify the year before, were now making up for the constraint which had then been laid upon them. We were unable to preserve many warehouses which they plundered, but we saved the bridge of Jena which they purposed destroying on account of its name. An admirable letter from the king however saved it.[1]

A compromise was made, and the bridge of Jena took the name of the bridge of *l'Ecole Militaire*, a designation which satisfied the savage vanity of the Prussians, and which as a play of words, is perhaps even a more pointed allusion, than the original name of Jena.

The Duke of Wellington himself I am sorry to say, headed those who wished to despoil the museum. Monuments of art ought perhaps never to have been included in the spoils of our conquests, and if we were to blame when we carried them off from other nations, it might have been perfectly just to recover a portion of them from France in 1814, when she was an enemy; but to recover them from France in 1815, when she is an ally, would be an act of violence. At least it would have been right to distinguish those works which had been yielded to us by treaty, apart from those which had not. No distinction was however made, and all was taken; and this is what the Duke of Wellington pretended to justify in a letter in which he lectured France in the name of morality, of which he constituted himself the champion, as no doubt he had done, when he served in India, where his government of course does nothing which is not highly moral.

---

[1]   King Louis XVIII. to the Prince de Talleyrand.

Paris, *July* 15, 1815.   *Saturday,* 10 *o'clock.*

I have just learned that the Prussians have mined the bridge of Jena and that probably they intend to blow it up this very night. The Duke of Otranto has told General Maison to prevent it by every means in his power, but you know well that he has none. Do all that is in your power, either by yourself or through the Duke of Wellington or Lord Castlereagh. As for me, I shall if necessary go to the bridge, and they can blow me up with it if they choose.

I was very well satisfied with the contribution from the two lords.

Louis.

If nothing further had been intended, than taking pictures and statues back from France, this letter was unnecessary, and the Duke of Wellington need not have taken the trouble to write it ; but it had another object, which was to let us know, that our deliverers were not so much our allies, as to preclude them from justly exercising over us all the rights of conquest, and to prepare us for the demands which the allied Cabinets were meditating, but which they felt a difficulty in broaching, because they knew not what name to give to their intentions.

I pause here, as I do not wish to treat of the negotiations I had to carry on with the allied powers, before reverting to certain points relating to the home affairs of France, during the month of July, 1815.

The day after the king's return to Paris, July 9th, a royal proclamation announced the formation of the new ministry, to the head of which I was called as President of the Council and Minister for Foreign Affairs. I had procured the nomination of Marshal Gouvion [1] as War Minister, and the Comte de Jaucourt as Minister of Marine, [2] Baron Pasquier as Minister of Justice and Baron Louis of Finance. It was necessary to counter-balance the unfortunate choice of the Duke of Otranto, who had been appointed Minister of Police, in consequence of Louis XVIII. yielding to the solicitations of *Monsieur* and the Duke of Wellington. M. Fouché, during the Hundred Days, had

---

[1] Laurent, Gouvion-Saint-Cyr, born at Toul in 1764, joined in 1792, became General of Division in 1794, Commander-in-Chief of the Army of Rome in 1798, and of that of Naples in 1803. He was but little in favour during the Empire. Nevertheless he received the Marshal's *bâton* in 1812. In 1813 he capitulated at Dresden, and was kept a prisoner. In 1814 he again served under Louis XVIII., and from 1815 to 1821 was several times War Minister. He died in retirement in 1830.

[2] Etienne Denis, Baron, afterwards Duke Pasquier, born in 1767, became Parliamentary Counsel at Paris in 1787. Was imprisoned during the Reign of Terror, and was saved by the 9th Thermidor. In 1806 he was appointed Master of Appeal to the Council of State, then State Councillor and Préfet of Police (1810). Under the first Restoration he became Director-General of Roads and Bridges ; held aloof during the Hundred Days, became Keeper of the Seals in 1815, then Minister of State, Privy Councillor, Grand Cross of the Legion of Honour, and President of the Chamber of Deputies.

On the 12th January, 1817, he was again made Keeper of the Seals. He quitted the Ministry in September, 1818, and re-entered it in 1819 as Minister of Foreign Affairs. He retired in December, 1821, and was then made a Peer of France. In 1830 he became President of the Chamber of Peers, then Chancellor of France (1837), and received at the same time the title of Duke. Duke Pasquier retired into private life in 1848 and died in 1862.

engaged in secret correspondence, first with M. de Metternich,[1] then with the Court of Ghent, and finally with the Duke of Wellington, persuading them all, that he was indispensable to the restoration of the monarchy, because he held the threads of all the intrigues that had overthrown it. The confidential friends of *Monsieur*, thought they had achieved a great success in securing for the king so able a man, not seeing that his very name would be a disgrace to the royalist party, rather than a terror to the revolutionists.

The Duke of Wellington, deceived by the prejudices current in England, as to the immense influence of the Duc d'Otranto, thought him alone capable of establishing the king on his throne, and M. de Metternich was also inclined to this opinion. While however this choice was pleasing to both the English and Austrian Cabinets, it could not fail for the same reason to displease the Emperor Alexander, who moreover bore me a grudge, for having so strongly defended the interests of legitimacy and of France, at the Congress of Vienna. It had therefore become essential to smooth down the susceptibilities of this sovereign, who played so important a part in the coalition, and it was with this view, that I had proposed to the king, not to fill up the appointments of Master of his Household and Minister of the Interior, in order that he might give these posts later on, to two men who would be acceptable to the Emperor of Russia, namely, the Duc de Richelieu and M. Pozzo de Borgo, who were both still in the Russian service. M. Pozzo de Borgo is a very clever man, and as much a Frenchman as Buonaparte, against whom he cherished a hatred—the hatred of a Corsican which till then had been the ruling passion of his life. He had been a member of the Legislative Assembly in 1791, and had thus been associated with the first events of the French Revolution ; his presence in the ministry therefore, would only have a reassuring tendency for all parties with whose views he was in accord, either on one or another particular point. But this combination fell through after various consultations had been held. M.

---

[1] For the intrigues between Fouché and M. de Metternich, and the curious negotiation of Basle, consult Thiers (vol. xviii., p. 488, *et seq.*) and the *Mémoires* of M. Fleury de Chaboulon (vol. ii., p. 1-42).

Pozzo preferred to remain in the Russian service, and as for the Duc de Richelieu, I will insert here the correspondence interchanged between us on the subject, which will show the grounds of his refusal.

THE DUC DE RICHELIEU TO THE PRINCE DE
TALLEYRAND.

PARIS, *July* 20, 1815.

MON PRINCE,

His Majesty the Emperor of Russia has been pleased to inform me of the conversation he has had with the king respecting myself. Feeling assured after what your Highness did me the honour to tell me the other day, that you, Prince, are the cause of the request addressed by the king to the emperor, I have thought it my duty to submit to you the reason for the irrevocable determination at which I have arrived, and which I will ask you to be good enough to lay before the king.

I have been absent from France for twenty-four years. During this long period I have only appeared there for a very short time on two occasions ; I am a stranger there, both to men and things, I am ignorant of how public affairs are managed, everything connected with the administration is unknown to me. At no time, would it be more indispensable for me to know all that of which I am ignorant, than in the times in which we now live. No one is less fitted than I am, to fill a place in the ministry anywhere, and above all here. I, Prince, know, better than any one else, what I am worth and for what I am fitted ; it is perfectly clear to me that I am in no way suited for the post which is offered me ; so much so, that were I to occupy it, I feel sure that I could not keep it six weeks. It would be very painful to me to think that my refusal might produce an unfavourable impression in the public mind, but I cannot take blame to myself in the matter, since the nomination was made without my knowledge, and while I was still at Nancy.

Excuse my frankness, Prince, but I prefer to speak openly to you as to the resolution I have taken. I must also add further, that having been for twenty-four years in the Russian service, and for twelve years employed in a department to which I am much attached, I could not think of throwing it up at present.

Be good enough, Prince, to lay my excuses and my regrets at the feet of the king, and accept the homage of those respectful sentiments with which I have the honour to be your highness's most humble and obedient servant.

RICHELIEU.

THE PRINCE DE TALLEYRAND TO THE DUC DE RICHELIEU.

PARIS, *July* 28, 1815.

MONSIEUR LE DUC,

In informing the king of the resolution which you assure me you have irrevocably taken, I must confess I could have wished to have been able to justify your grounds for it, better than you have put me in a position to do.

You have been long you say, *a stranger to men and things in this country ;* but since revisiting it, you must have observed, that there is a large number of persons, who though they have never been away from it, are all the more out of harmony with the ideas of moderation and prudence, which the king has conceived, and with which it is his purpose henceforth to inspire his ministry, and you have the advantage over them of having conceived these ideas, and carried them out intelligently in practice, in countries far more strange and new to you, than France. You foresee great difficulties, but I do not hesitate to tell you, Monsieur le Duc, that in accepting the confidence of the king, we are none of us blind either to the present, or the future. We too have seen the immeasurable, and innumerable difficulties, which every day and every instant must put our zeal and our ability to the proof.

This outlook has alarmed us and still does so ; but we have seen France overwhelmed with evils, Europe encompassed with peril, the king's mind a prey to cruel anxiety, and under these circumstances we felt we had no longer the right to choose. Finally, Monsieur le Duc, you say that *you are bound by interests* and engagements to a country you have long served, but permit me to remind you, that the name you bear has shone with lustre during two of the most brilliant centuries of our history ; and do you not think that this glory which is for ever attached to it, imposes obligations on you, with which other duties can never effectually compete, and from which at this present time you dare no longer try to free yourself ?

.I have, as you see, delayed answering the letter you did me the honour of writing ; you will readily understand my reason for so doing. I had hoped some of these ideas would have presented themselves to your mind, and would have suggested some other decision.

I have the honour to be . . . .

PRINCE DE TALLEYRAND.

I will only make one remark on the Duc de Richelieu's refusal, in which he persisted. Either the reasons he alleged for refusing the comparatively less important post of master of the king's household were insufficient, or they were valid; how then could he, two months later, become President of the Council and govern France?

The refusal of M. Pozzo and the Duc de Richelieu rendered it necessary to appoint M. Pasquier, Keeper of the Privy Seal, *ad interim* Minister of the Interior, and the Comte de Pradel Master of the Household. The king had returned to Paris on July 8th, and on the 13th, a royal proclamation announced the dissolution of the Chamber of Deputies, and convoked the Electoral Colleges for August 25th.

This proclamation is conceived in such a liberal and prudent spirit, that it deserves to be recorded.

PROCLAMATION DISSOLVING THE CHAMBER OF DEPUTIES CONVOKED BY THE ELECTORAL COLLEGES, AND MAKING PROVISIONAL REGULATIONS FOR THE ELECTIONS.

Louis, by the grace of God, King of France and Navarre, to all whom these presents may concern, greeting:

We had announced that it was our intention to propose a law to the Chambers, for the proper regulation of the election of the deputies of departments. Our purpose was to modify, in conformity with the lessons gained by experience, and the well-known wishes of the nation, several articles of the charter, concerning the qualifications and number of the deputies, and some other dispositions respecting the formation of the Chambers, the initiation of legislation, and the mode of its deliberations.

The misfortunes of the time having interrupted the session of the two Chambers, we have thought, that as the number of deputies of departments, had, through divers causes, become so greatly reduced, the nation is insufficiently represented. Under these circumstances, it is above all things necessary, that the national representatives should be numerous, that their powers should be renewed, that they should emanate more directly from the electoral colleges, and finally that the elections should express the actual opinion of our people.

We have therefore determined to dissolve the Chamber of Deputies, and to summon a new one without delay.   But as it is impossible to regulate the mode of election by a law, or to make modifications in the charter, we have deemed it within our province, to admit the nation to enjoy the advantages at once, which it will derive from a more numerous representation, and one elected under less restricted conditions, it being more-over our pleasure, that in no case should any modification of the charter become definite, except under constitutional forms.   The regulations of this present proclamation, shall be the first object of the deliberations of the Chambers.   The entire legislative power will settle the law of elections, and the alterations to be made in the charter with reference thereto, alterations as to which we only take the initiative, in respect of the most indis-pensable and urgent points, while pledging ourselves to keep as much as possible to the charter, and the forms, previously in use.

For these reasons we declare and have declared, ordained and have ordained, the following :

Art. I. The Chamber of Deputies is dissolved.

Art. II. The electoral colleges of districts shall assemble on the 14th of August of the present year.

Art. III. The electoral colleges of departments shall meet eight days after the opening of the electoral colleges of districts.

Art. IV. The number of departmental deputies, is fixed in conformity with the schedule hereto annexed.

Art. V. Each district electoral college shall elect a number of candidates equal to the number of deputies of the department.

Art. VI. Our *préfets* shall transmit to the president of the departmental electoral colleges, the lists of candidates prepared by the district electoral colleges, which lists shall be transmitted to them by the presidents of these colleges.

Art. VII. The departmental electoral colleges shall choose at least one half of the deputies from these candidates.   If the total number of the deputies of the department is uneven, the division shall be made in favour of that portion which is to be chosen from among the candidates.

Art. VIII. The electors of the district electoral colleges may take their seats, provided they are of the full age of twenty-one years.   The electors of the departmental colleges may also do so at the same age, but they must have been chosen from the list of those who are rated the highest.

Art. IX. If the number of members of the Legion of Honour, who, in conformity with the decree of February 22, 1806, may be added to the district or departmental colleges, is not complete, our *préfets* shall, at the request of the members of the Legion of Honour, propose further nominations, which shall be provisionally confirmed. Nevertheless all members of the Legion of Honour, who are admitted to the departmental colleges, must, in conformity with Art. IX. of the Charter, pay at least three hundred francs in direct taxes.

All nominations made since March 1st, 1815, are null and void.

Art. X. Deputies may be elected at the full age of twenty-five years.

Art. XI. Conformable to former laws and regulations, every election in which the half of the college plus one, shall not have taken part, shall be null. The absolute majority of the members present, is necessary to the validity of the election.

Art. XII. If the district electoral colleges have not completed the election of the number of candidates they are entitled to choose, the departmental college shall nevertheless proceed to exercise its function.

Art. XIII. The election returns shall be examined in the Chamber of Deputies, which shall pronounce as to the regularity of the elections. The elected deputies shall be required to produce to the Chamber, their certificate of birth, and an abstract of their assessments, showing that they pay at least one thousand francs in taxes.

Art. XIV. Articles 16, 25, 35, 36, 37, 38, 39, 40, 41, 42, 43, 44, 45, and 46, of the charter shall be submitted for revision to the legislative power at the next session of the Chambers.

Art. XV. The present proclamation shall be printed and affixed to the place of meeting of each electoral college.

The articles of the charter above mentioned shall be printed conjointly with it.

Art. XVI. Our minister of the interior is charged with the execution of the present proclamation.

Given at the palace of the Tuileries this 13th day of July, in the year of grace, one thousand eight hundred and fifteen, and the twenty-first year of our reign.

(Signed) LOUIS.

The proclamation having been published, the selection of the *préfets* who were to be charged with its execution in the departments had to be provided for, and this selection was not an easy one. It was necessary that the new *préfets* should be moderate as well as energetic men, in order to carry out the views of the government, and to resist as far as possible, the exactions of the allied troops in the departments occupied by them, and also the reactionary tendencies of certain departments in the south.

The greater number of the *préfets* appointed during the Empire, inspired the royal government with no confidence, and the men recommended by the advisers of *Monsieur* and the princes, were dangerous from the violence of their opinions. It was not easy under these circumstances to find eighty-six men, possessing the qualities necessary to carry out so delicate a mission as that of the new *préfets*, and there is the less reason for surprise, that the result has been to give France a Chamber of Deputies, which even while I am now writing,[1] distinguishes

---

[1] I will only cite one letter from a *préfet* of that time, to show how difficult was the task of the government and of its agents.

M. DE BOURRIENNE,* PRÉFET OF YONNE, TO THE
PRINCE DE TALLEYRAND.

AUXÈRRE, *August* 20, 1815.

PRINCE,
Four days ago this department was in despair ; the public funds were seized and carried off, there were enormous requisitions and exaggerated demands of every description ; maltreatment and threats of military executions, and a studied contempt for the king's agents. Such was the conduct of the Bavarians, when I made my complaint to Comte de Rechburg,† brother of the minister of that Court, at Paris. He told me that, not having been invited to assist in drawing up the memorandum of the 24th of July,‡ and perceiving that there was an intention to exclude them from a share in the war contributions, the Bavarians were under the necessity of looking after themselves, and taking their share of what they could get. Then, loudly expressing his hatred of the Austrians, Comte de Rechburg added : " We have sixty thousand men under arms, and we could soon give a good account of one hundred thousand Austrians in a pitched battle."

However, as I spoke to him with some determination and above all with much show of reason, he told me that although administrative measures were not his business, he would confer on the matter with the Commissary of the army.

All this took place on the eighteenth, and on that day no rigorous measures were taken. Yesterday the news of the arrangements made on the seventeenth, arrived from Paris, and the circular to the *préfets* has produced a great change, both in the situation of the country people, and in the conduct of the Bavarians. Please God that they do not come again, and tell us *that they know nothing of the arrangement and have nothing to do with it.* Up to now *hostilities* have ceased, and we are awaiting the arrival of Prince de Wrède on the twenty-second, to see if their first system of isolation is to be continued, or if they will range themselves under the general standard of the allies, to plunder us in a regular and methodical fashion.

Together with the news of the announcement of the seventeenth, came the royal

---

* M. de Bourrienne was not *préfet* of Yonne. He was at that time candidate for the post of deputy of this department and was elected a few days afterwards.

† Count Joseph de Rechburg (1769 to 1833), general in the Bavarian Army 1814 to 1815, and afterwards minister at Berlin.

‡ This note, addressed by Austria, Russia, Prussia and England, to the French cabinet, had for its object the regulation of the government of the territories occupied by the allies in France. Article VIII. particularly specifies that no contribution was to be levied singly by the commissaries of the different armies.

itself by its reactionary spirit and its want of prudence and moderation.[1]

The appointment of extraordinary royal commissioners, which had been previously made, in the departments of the South, either by the Duc d'Angoulême, or the king himself, would still further have complicated the situation of the new *préfets ;* but the council advised the king to recall the powers of all these commissioners by proclamation. This proclamation became one of the principal grievances of one part of the court,

proclamation as to the war contribution of a hundred millions. I may tell you, prince, that it has been almost received *with pleasure ;* not a single complaint has been raised. The general expression was : *shedding one's money is not like shedding one's blood.*

Here payment will be prompt, and also in the other departments, because men are grateful to the government for having considered how much these departments have suffered through sacrifices and losses. I think I may assure you, prince, that every demand for money will be received without murmuring, provided it is justly apportioned and its destination is known. It is almost certain that we shall not have Dumolard * as deputy. As for Desfourneaux,† I am not quite sure of him. It is true, I have already succeeded in excluding him from the list of candidates, but since then, he has redoubled his intrigues and solicitations. He presents himself in all the communes of his department, his big red ribbon outside his coat, and a huge new badge on his left side, and when it is represented to him, that this royal favour is of last year's date, and that it only brings his treachery more prominently forward, he at once answers, by showing two letters dated August 1815, one from the Duc d'Otranto, the other from the Duc d'Havré,‡ both of them describing him as the man most worthy to represent the department of the Yonne. On the one hand, the government desires, and with reason, to remove such intriguers ; and on the other hand, one of the ministers and a captain of the guards, solicit the good will of the authorities and the public, on his behalf.

I have been obliged to inform you, prince, of this circumstance, so that you may not blame me too much if I am unsuccessful. I have read with as much pleasure as gratitude, the name of the Marquis de Louvois § on the list of peers ; this choice has given general satisfaction. I like to believe, prince, that you have remembered what I told you about him. I shall always gratefully acknowledge the great kindness you have shown me, by unbounded devotion and unshaken fidelity. I am, with the greatest respect, Your Highness's very humble and obedient servant,

BOURRIENNE.

[1] It is to be observed that this portion of the Memoirs was written in 1816 at the time the *Chambre introuvable* was sitting.

* Bonvier-Dumolard, born in 1781, at first auditor to the Privy Council ; then commissary of Corinthia in Saxony and charged with the organization of the Venetian States. In 1810 he was appointed *préfet* and again during the hundred days, when he was also elected a deputy. At the second restoration he was ordered to leave Paris.

† Comte Etienne Desfourneaux, born in 1769, became sergeant in 1789, went to St. Domingo in 1792, where for his successes, he was appointed General-in-chief in 1793. In 1798 he became governor of Guadeloupe. In 1802 he commanded a division in the Expedition to St. Domingo. He returned shortly afterwards to France, and retired to the department of Yonne and was elected deputy in 1813 and again during the hundred days. He was not elected in 1825.

‡ Joseph Anne Auguste Maximillian de Croy, Duc d'Havré, prince of the Holy Empire and grandee of Spain, born in 1744, lieutenant-general in 1749. Deputy from the bailiwick of Amiens to the States-General peer of France at the Restoration, and captain of the king's guards. He died in 1839.

§ Auguste-Michel Le Tellier de Sonoré. Marquis de Louvois, born in 1738, was chamberlain to the emperor in 1809 and peer of France under the Restoration. He took no part in politics, but held an important position in trade. He died in 1844.

against the ministry, and it accordingly encountered opposition on all sides.

We had infinite trouble in inducing the king to issue another proclamation respecting the press, which, except as regards the journals, gives it complete freedom,[1] but I was less fortunate in another very serious question, in which M. Fouché carried his point against me. I wanted the king to dispense with all measures of severity, excepting that all those peers of the Chamber of 1814, who had consented to form a part of the Chamber of peers created by Napoleon during the hundred days, should forfeit their seats. I believed that by thus striking at the highest persons in the state, a sufficient example would be made to punish the abettors of the revolution of the 20th of March, and to secure in future the sanctity of the oath, so unworthily betrayed by those who, within so short a space of time, had abandoned the royal cause. But this measure did not satisfy the royalist reaction, which demanded legal persecution, and proscriptions. In vain I urged waiting for the meeting of the Chambers, to whom if it were necessary, might be left the responsibility of pointing out the guilty. I hoped that by retarding the measure, time would aid us to soften it down, if not to get rid of it altogether; but my efforts were in vain. Pressure was put on the Duc d'Otranto, who, embarrassed by the close relations he had entered into with the extreme royalist party, and with the foreign courts, laid a list before the council of more than a hundred persons, who he demanded should be either proscribed or tried by court-martial.

After a painful struggle, which lasted several days, and the king having declared himself for the odious measure, it was necessary to yield; but the list was reduced to fifty-seven persons. Nineteen of these, almost all military men, were to be brought before a court-martial, or the court of assizes, while the other thirty-eight, were to leave Paris in twenty-four

---

[1] The first proclamation, dated 20th July, 1814, ordered the chief librarian and the *préfets* not to make use of Articles III., IV. and V. of the law of October 21st, 1814. These articles gave them the right to submit all writings of less than twenty printed leaves, to a preliminary inspection of the censors. A second proclamation, dated 8th August 1815, subjected all the journals to fresh authorization from the minister of police, and all periodical literature had to be submitted to examination by a committee.

hours, and betake themselves to places appointed them by the police. Those comprised in the first category, were all warned in time, so that they might escape if they thought proper ; but the measure was nevertheless an act of blundering folly, calculated only to create difficulties and dangers for the government.[1]

Notwithstanding this proclamation, the proposal I had made respecting the Chamber of Peers, could no longer be put aside, and I had in my turn, to draw up the list of peers, who, having sat in the chamber of the hundred days, could no longer form part of the Chamber of Peers which had been constituted on a new basis, since I had induced the king (much against his will) to admit, that the peerage should henceforth be hereditary. The list of peers eliminated, comprised the Count d'Aboville, the Marshal Duc d'Albuféra, the Comte de Barral, the Archbishop of Tours, the Comte Belliard, the Comte Boissy-d'Anglas, the Duc de Cadore, the Comte de Canclaux, the Comte de Casabianca, the Comte Clément de Ris, the Comte Colchen, the Marshal Duc de Conégliano, the Comte Cornudet, the Comte de Croix, the Marshal Duc de Dantzig, the Comte Dedeley d'Agier, the Comte Dejean, the Marshal Prince d'Essling, the Comte Fabre de l'Aude, the Comte Gassendi, the Comte de Lacépède, the Comte de Latour-Maubourg, the Comte de Montesquiou, the Duc de Plaisance, the Comte de Pontécoulant, the Duc de Praslin, the Comte Rampon, the Comte de Ségur, the Marshal Duc de Trévise, the Comte de Valence.

This proclamation also bore the date of the 24th of July ; but on the 17th of August following, the king issued another at

[1] This is the list of the persons comprised in the proclamation of the 21st of July, 1815.

Category of the nineteen who were prosecuted and brought to trial : Marshal Ney, Labédoyère, both brothers Lallemand, Drouet D'Erlon, Laborde, Lefebvre—Desnouttes, Ameille, Brayer, Gilly, Mouton-Duvernet, Grouchy, Clausel, Debelle, Bertrand, Drouot, Cambronne, Lavalette, Rovigo ;

Category of the thirty-eight, ordered to leave Paris in three days and proceed to places appointed by the police.

Marshal Soult, Generals Alix, Exelmans, Vandamme, Marbot, Lamarque, Lobau, Piré, Dejean junior, and Hullin, M. Felix, Lepelletier, Boulay de la Meurthe, Mehee-Latouche, Fressinnet, Thibaudeau, Carnot, Harel, Barrère, Arrighi (of Padua) Arnault, Pommereuil, Regnauld de Saint-Jean-d'Angély, Réal, Garrau, Bouvier-Dumolard, Merlin de Douai, Durbach, Dirat, Defermont, Bory, de Saint Vincent, Felix Desportes, Garnier de Saintes, Mellinet, Cluys, Courtin, Forbin-Janson the elder and Lelorgne d'Idevile.

my suggestion, by which ninety-two new peers were created, and which restored the Comtes D'Aboville and de Canclaux, who proved that they had not sat in the Chamber of the hundred days, and also M. Boissy d'Anglas, as a reward for his noble and courageous conduct at the Convention, and the special services he had rendered the king.

I also added to this list, the three sons, still minors, of the Duc de Montebello, and Marshals Berthier and Bessières.

The king, in signing this proclamation, made some objection to the name of M. Molé, who had served during the hundred days ; but I persisted, saying, " May the king be pleased to restore this name.   It is Mathieu Molé,[1] who asks it of you," and the king, who had at first erased it, replaced it with his own hand.

At last, on the 20th of August, the proclamation constituting the peerage appeared ; it had been discussed in the Council for several days.

The king vigorously opposed the hereditary peerages, as depriving him of all personal influence over the members of the Chamber ; but I argued against this view, as being in comparison, secondary to the weight and stability the heredity of its members would give to the Chamber.   Accordingly in the preamble of the proclamation, the king declared that, " Wishing to give his subjects a fresh pledge of the value which he attached to founding those institutions, on the most permanent basis on which a government can rest, and convinced that nothing secures the quiet of the State more than that heredity of feeling, which in families is joined to heredity of high public functions, and thus creates an uninterrupted succession of subjects, whose fidelity and devotion to their king and country, are guaranteed by the principles and examples they have inherited from their fathers. . . ."

The harsh measures introduced by M. Fouché were not long in bearing fruit.   Frightful tumults and bloody scenes broke out in various places in the south, where the royalist reaction, deem-

---

[1] M. Molé the fifth descendant in the direct line from the first President, Mathieu Molé.   During the hundred days he refused the portfolios of the Interior and of Foreign Affairs.   He was appointed peer of France, but never sat in the Chamber.

ing itself encouraged by these measures, indulged in horrible massacres ; the government made every effort to put a stop to them, and the king published the following declaration, in which he said :

"We have learnt with grief, that in the departments of the south, many of our subjects have recently been guilty of the most criminal outrages ; that under pretence of making themselves the instruments of public vengeance, Frenchmen have shed the blood of Frenchmen, to gratify their private hatred and revenge, even after our authority had been universally re-established and acknowledged throughout our kingdom. That horrible treachery and great crimes have been committed, which plunged France into an abyss of evils, is doubtless an indisputable fact ; but the punishment of these crimes must be a national, solemn, and regular one. The guilty persons must fall by the sword of justice, and not under the weight of vengeance. All social order would be upset, if men were allowed to constitute themselves both judge and executioner, either as regards the injuries they have received, or the outrages committed against our person.

"We hope that this odious attempt to forestall the action of the law, has already ceased. It is an offence against France and ourselves, and however deeply it may pain us, nothing shall be left undone to punish such outrages. We have therefore strictly enjoined our ministers and magistrates, to enforce absolute obedience to the laws, and to show neither weakness nor indulgence in prosecuting those, who have offended against them."

This declaration, however natural under the circumstances, nevertheless offered a pretext to the extreme royalist party to censure the ministry ; while M. Fouché, alarmed at the mischief he had done, by flattering the evil passions of that party, wished to retrace his steps and get out of the difficulty, by an act of perfidy, calculated, as he thought, to bias public opinion in his favour, and to still further weaken the government. He made two confidential reports to the king, one in which he depicted the deplorable condition to which the conduct of the allied troops was reducing the population of the provinces they occupied, and the consequences that could not fail to result therefrom. The second report was no less emphatic than the first, in the picture it drew of the outrages committed in the

south, and the violent party rancour displayed in every part of
France. Up to this point there was nothing to find fault with.
M. Fouché had but done his duty, and we are quite ready to admit that the contents of these reports were not far from the
truth. But these reports were confidential and should only
have been communicated to the king and his Council.

This, however, was not what M. Fouché did. He at first
concealed them from the ministry, and after having given a copy
to the king, he made them public, while asserting that they had
been stolen from him, and that it was not he who had published
them. It was impossible to maintain any relations with a man
who had recourse to such measures. I asked the king for his
dismissal from the ministry, and it was not long ere he was
removed. [1]

But the greatest and most painful difficulty that affected the
situation, was the conduct of the allied sovereigns and their
troops. This is a point on which I must now touch, leaving it
to historians to relate the events of this period, which are
universally known. For my part I shall confine myself to exposing the painful negotiations I was condemned to carry on,
as well as some of the occurrences connected with them. I
hasten to finish these odious recollections.

The most urgent point in these negotiations, and the one to be
first treated of, was that which settled the allowances that were
to be made for the services of the innumerable armies who had
invaded France and were devouring her ; while at the same time,
insisting everywhere on the most scandalous exactions, in the
name of the Powers, who at Vienna had signed the agreement,
to arm themselves in aid of their ally the King of France.

I have already quoted the letter of the *préfet* of Yonne, on
the conduct of the Bavarian generals. I wish also to record an
order of the Commissary-General of the Austrian Army, to show
how far the revolutionary spirit (for I can call it by no other
name) had carried these governments, who loudly proclaimed
that they only made war against revolution in the person of
Buonaparte.

[1] 19th September.

The Imperial, Royal, and Apostolic Army of Italy.

We, Count de Wurmser, Chamberlain, Privy Councillor of State to his Imperial, Royal, and Apostolic Majesty, Commander of the Royal Order of Saint-Stephen of Hungary, President of the Aulic Commission, charged with the superintendence of the survey of the monarchy, and Commissary-General of the Imperial and Royal Army of Italy.

Considering, on the one hand, that the general and subordinate receivers of the departments and districts, have been compelled to sign bonds to the order of the treasury, for the payment on fixed dates, of the sums received from direct and indirect taxation, and that, on the other hand, these payments and taxes in those parts of the French territory, occupied by the troops of the allied armies, have, according to military law and the law of nations, devolved on the said powers, we order and decree as follows :

Article I.—That all bonds payable to the French treasury by the general and subordinate receivers, and other revenue officers of those parts of French territory occupied by the Imperial Austrian Army of Italy, or which shall be so occupied in future, are not available, either for arrears or for current payments of any public taxes or imposts whatever. The said receivers and revenue officers are therefore forbidden to discharge them on any pretxt whatsoever.

Article II.—Any infraction of this prohibition will involve not only the personal responsibility of each receiver and revenue officer, but will further be punished with all the rigour of martial law, as an act of connivance with the enemy.

Article III.—These dispositions apply to the bonds and drafts delivered by the purchasers of national and communal property, and those who have acquired the right to fell timber in the State forests.

Article IV.—The courts are forbidden to entertain any suits for payment of the said bonds or drafts, under pain of being dissolved, and being further dealt with according to the rigour of military law.

Article V.—All *préfets* and *sub-préfets* are charged with the immediate printing and placarding of the above order, wherever it may be necessary.

Given at headquarters, Nantua, July 18th, 1815.

(*Signed*) COUNT DE WURMSER.

By order of his Excellency the Commissary-General,

CUVELIER,

Commissary.

King Louis XVIII., who had discovered when too late, the grave error he had committed in not following the advice I had given him, not to return to his capital before he had settled everything with the foreign governments, now strove vainly to repair this fault, by addressing the following letter to me, which I communicated to the allied plenipotentiaries.

KING LOUIS XVIII. TO THE PRINCE DE TALLEYRAND.

PARIS, *July* 21, 1815.

The conduct of the allied armies will very soon drive my people into arming themselves *en masse* after the example of the Spaniards. Were I a younger man, I would place myself at their head ; but if age and infirmities prevent my doing so, I will not at any rate even seem to connive at the outrages I lament. I am therefore resolved, if I cannot obtain justice, to retire from my kingdom, and ask the King of Spain for an asylum. If those, who even after the capture of the man against whom alone they had declared war, continue to treat my subjects as enemies, and who consequently must regard me also as such, wish to interfere with my freedom, they are at liberty to do so. I would rather be a prisoner, than remain at the Tuileries, a passive spectator of the miseries of my people.

LOUIS.

In consequence of this letter and a proposal for an arrangement made by Baron Louis, Minister of Finance, the allied plenipotentiaries addressed a note to me on the 25th of July drawn up in these terms :

" The undersigned ministers have carefully considered the proposals transmitted to them by the ministers of the king, through his Excellency Baron Louis. They are too firmly convinced of the necessity of taking the most speedy and effectual measures, as regards administrative action, not to accept, with the utmost readiness, the views which are expressed in these overtures. They are therefore of opinion that the following arrangements, which have just been adopted, will be the most efficacious for reconciling the king's wishes with the position in which the allied armies will be placed during their stay in France."

The arrangements referred to in this note, laid down, that in exchange for a contribution of a hundred millions, conceded by the French government, it was agreed that a line of demarcation should be traced, to fix the departments that would be occupied by the allied troops and assigned for their maintenance. The royal authority was to be restored, and the *préfets* and *sub-préfets* re-established in their official functions. Military governors were to be appointed by the departments, within the radius of each army. They were to protect the authorities, ensure the supplies to the armies, and supervise their relations with the French officials. An administrative commission was to sit in Paris to transact direct all affairs between the king's government and the foreign authorities. Orders were immediately to be given to put a stop to all the irregular contributions which had been levied on the departments.

This point settled, the remainder would have been soon arranged, if the sovereigns had been true and faithful allies of the King of France. But, as I have already stated, when speaking of the arrival of the foreign armies in Paris, the allied cabinets were puzzled how to bring forward their demands, as they could find no name for their wishes. At first they only used the word *guarantees*. They wished for general guarantees without specifying for what purposes, upon which I addressed the following note to them, dated July 31st, 1815 :

"The king's minister has the honour to communicate to their Excellencies the ministers and secretaries of State of the allied powers, three proclamations by his Majesty. One issued at Lille for the disbanding of the French army, and two others, which are as yet only drafted, and relate to the organization of a new army; it being no less necessary for Europe than for France herself, that she should have an army. The king has tried, and believes he has succeeded, in reconciling this necessity with the still greater one, common to both parties, that of coming to some decision, without reverting to revolution.

"It is now twenty-six years since France, seeking guarantees against the abuses of an uncontrolled ministerial power, exercised without unity or supervision, strayed from the true path, and lost herself in that species of equality, the inevitable consequence of which, is the dominion of the multitude, that is to say, its tyranny, which is the most frightful of all tyrannies, and for that very reason the least durable. This tyranny gave place, as it always has and always will do, to the despotism of a single individual, who, by temperament and clever calculation, carried the revolution into another channel, by altering its motive power, and transporting it from the interior to the exterior, and substituting the spirit of conquest for the spirit of equality.

"The late events have proved, how greatly both these had been weakened, since the usurper, who had summoned both to his aid, did not obtain sufficient support from either, to counteract the effect of a first and single reverse.

"But as the chances of revolution can never cease, unless they are both entirely extinguished, or so controlled, that they never can again become dominant, all the thoughts of the king during his retreat into Belgium were concentrated on the best means of obtaining this result, and every act of his, since his return, has been in furtherance of this end.

"The doctrine of complete equality may, no doubt, still have its apostles and partizans among those speculative minds, who set up theories for an imaginary world, and among a certain number of men, to whom this doctrine alone gave a temporary power, which they then abused, and which they now regret. But the masses themselves have long been undeceived by the cruel experiences they have undergone. This doctrine will never make proselytes, and its spirit will never be formidable, so long as every man's civil rights are secured against all arbitrary measures, by a political constitution, which excludes from power all those who are not in the position, in which the sense of preservation, is not stronger than the necessity and desire of acquisition.

"Such is the character of the political system by which France will be governed.

"The Chamber of Peers will be hereditary. The Chamber of Deputies will be formed on the only principle which can bring it into harmony with the two other branches of the legislature, a principle which it will be our endeavour to re-establish and to enforce in all civil institutions. It will share with the king, the right of framing the laws, a right which previously he had reserved to himself.

"The manner in which the laws will be framed, gives the strongest possible assurance of their impartial equity, since it will be the expression, not of the will of a single person, or a single body, but of a will arising from the concurrence of three distinct wills.

"A ministry is already constituted, each of whose members have their own special province, which has been decided on after joint discussion. It has therefore all the active force which unity gives, and it is also responsible, which is a preservative against the abberations of power.

"The judges will be irremovable, which assures the independence of the courts.

"In criminal matters the trial by jury, now existing, will be maintained. Confiscation is in all cases and for ever abolished.

"Finally the restrictions laid on the freedom of the press have already been removed.

"This institution, by placing the state, equi-distant between absolute power and anarchy, will not afford either means or pretexts to the latter, wherewith to assert its power.

"This same institution will no less happily repress the spirit for conquest, which has arisen under circumstances, and supported by causes, which will never occur again.

"There will no longer be a revolutionary dynasty in France, interested in the overthrow of legitimate sovereigns, in order to set up others in its own likeness.

"There will no longer be a tyrannical dynasty in France, which requires to withdraw the attention of the people from the evils it permits, by soothing them with the delusions of a glory purchased with their noblest blood.

"Buonaparte is in the power of the allies, and has ceased for ever to be formidable.

"The instigators and principal supporters of his late crimes, have been handed over to justice. The principal instruments of his despotism, the most ardent of his admirers, have either gone from France, or left the capital, and been deprived of all public functions.

"The spirit of conquest was not that of France ; for her it has been nothing but a cruel calamity. It only reigned in the army, for it requires success to sustain it, and it perishes under reverses. The preceding campaigns had gradually weakened it, nor does it seem possible that it should survive this last one. Those who are still infected by it, cannot conceal from themselves, that they will no longer, as heretofore, find Europe divided, and that against united Europe they can hope for nothing ; no man persists in hoping where there is no hope. The spirit of conquest was further maintained by the almost unlimited duration of military service, which caused the soldier at last to recognise no other home and no other country, than the army. This cause will be removed by the present scheme of organization, which by frequently restoring the soldiers to the habits and affections of civil and domestic life, will no longer dispose them to encourage interests and feelings opposed to those of their country.

" The king believes that this conjunction of facts, dispositions, and measures, will give to France, to Europe, and himself, all the guarantees of security that can be desired.

" The king's ministry are of the same opinion. They therefore request their Excellencies, the ministers and secretaries of state of the allied Powers, to be good enough to inform them, whether they share this opinion, or if in their judgment anything else ought to be added to these dispositions, and in that case what they believe to be desirable to be so added.

" The Prince de Talleyrand has the honour to. . . ."

PARIS, *July 25th*, 1815.

Under the given circumstances, and with honourable allies, the observations contained in the following memorandum could have admitted of no reply, but I had already discovered that it was not with such allies, that I had to deal. I refer to the occasion of the spoliation of our art galleries, which gave rise to an interchange of Notes, which I omitted to mention when speaking of this matter before. I will here make good this omission, so as to complete the documents connected with the negotiations of this sad period. I shall begin with the first Note on this subject, addressed to me by Lord Castlereagh, 11th of September, 1815.

Translation of a Memorandum from Lord Castlereagh to the Prince de Talleyrand.

" Representations having been made to the ministers of the allied Powers, by the pope, the Grand Duke of Tuscany, the King of the Netherlands, and other sovereigns, reclaiming (through the intervention of the high allied Powers,) the restoration of the statues, pictures, manuscripts, and other works of art, of which their respective countries have been systematically and persistently despoiled by the late revolutionary government of France, contrary to every principle of justice, and the established and accepted rules of war, and these representations having been submitted to the consideration of his Court, the undersigned has received instructions from the Prince Regent, to call the attention of his allies, to the following remarks on this engrossing topic.

"It is now for the second time, that the European Powers have been compelled to invade France, in defence of their own liberty and to insure the tranquillity of the world, and their armies have by conquest, twice taken possession of the capital of the country, in which the art treasures and the spoils of the greater part of Europe have been accumulated.

"Twice also has the legitimate ruler of France been enabled, under the protection of these armies, to re-occupy his throne, and to obtain from the signal indulgence of the allies, a peace for his people, which their conduct to their own sovereigns and to other states, gave them as a nation no right to expect. That the purest feelings of regard for Louis XVIII., deference for his ancient and illustrious name, and respect for his misfortunes, invariably guided the councils of the allies, has been amply proved by the care they took last year, to lay down, as the express basis of the treaty of Paris, the preservation of the complete integrity of France, (and more especially after having lately seen their hopes so cruelly deceived,) by the efforts they are still making to definitely combine the actual integrity of France, with an equivalent measure of temporary precautions, which may satisfy what they owe to the security of their own subjects.

"But it would be the height of weakness (and the effect of it would be far more likely to mislead the French people than to bring them back to moral sentiments and peaceable views), if the allied sovereigns, from whom the world expected protection and repose, were to refuse a just and generous application of this principle of integrity to other nations who are their allies (and above all to those who are weak and defenceless), when they are on the point of granting it a second time, to a nation against which they have so long fought.

"By what right can France at the termination of such a war, expect to retain the same extent of territory as before the Revolution, and at the same time wish to keep the *chefs d'œuvres* robbed from every other country ? Can there be a doubt as to the issue of such a controversy, or of the power of the allies to carry out what justice and policy demands ? If not, then by what right is France deprived of its late territorial acquisitions, and at the same time left in possession of the spoils of those very territories, which all modern conquerors have invariably respected, as inseparable from the country to which they belong?

"The allied sovereigns have perhaps to justify themselves before Europe, as to their conduct in this matter, when they were at Paris last year. It is true they never made themselves accomplices of the criminality, involved in such wholesale robberies, so far as to sanction them by any stipulation in their treaties: such an acknowledgment they always steadily refused, but it is certain that they used their influence to repress the expression of these reclamations, in the hope that France, subdued as much by their generosity as by their arms, would be disposed to maintain inviolable a peace, which had been carefully established, in order to serve as a bond of reconciliation between the nation and the king.

"But now the question is a very different one, and to act in the same manner under circumstances so essentially altered, would, in the opinion of the Prince Regent, be as imprudent for France, as it would be unjust towards the allies, who have a direct interest in the question.

"His Royal Highness however, in giving this opinion, feels that it is necessary to protect himself against the possibility of misinterpretation. While deciding that it is the duty of the allied sovereigns, not only not to hinder, but even to facilitate the restoration of these art treasures to the places whence they have been taken, he deems it no less suitable to their good feeling, not to permit the position of their armies in France, or the removal of these objects from the Louvre, to be the direct or indirect means, of taking back to their own dominions, a single article, which at the time of their conquest, did not belong to their respective family collections, or to the countries over which they at present reign.

"Whatever value the Prince Regent might attach to such perfect specimens of the fine arts, if they had been otherwise acquired, he has no wish to become possessed of them at the expense of France, and above all, by following a principle in warfare, which he holds to be a reproach to the country which adopts it. And so far from desiring to profit by the opportunity, to acquire from the lawful owners, any object which they might have resolved to give up for pecuniary considerations, his Royal Highness wishes on the contrary to give them the means of replacing them, in those temples and art galleries, of which they have so long been the ornaments.

"If it were possible that the sentiments of his Royal Highness for the person and the cause of Louis XVIII. could be doubted, or that the position of his Most Christian Majesty, with respect to his own people could suffer from it, the Prince Regent could not but arrive at this decision with the greatest possible repugnance.

"But on the contrary, his Royal Highness is firmly convinced that the affection and respect of his Most Christian Majesty's subjects, for his person, will increase in proportion, as he separates himself from these memories of a system of Revolutionary warfare.

"These spoils which are an obstacle to the moral reconciliation of France with the countries which she has invaded, are not necessary to recall the exploits of her armies, which despite the cause in which they were achieved, must always make the arms of the nation respected by others. But so long as these objects remain in Paris, constituting as it were the *title-deeds* of the countries which have been surrendered, the desire to re-unite them to France will never become extinct and the spirit of the French people, will never be able to accustom itself to the diminished territorial extent assigned to the nation reigned over by the Bourbons.

"In giving this opinion, the Prince Regent has no intention of humiliating the French nation. The general policy of his Royal Highness, the conduct of his troops in France, his anxiety immediately after Buonaparte's surrender, to restore to France the freedom of her commerce, and above all, the desire he has recently testified, to definitely preserve to France with some slight modifications, her territorial integrity, are the best proofs that no ungenerous feeling towards her, but a wish to do justice to others, and the desire to heal the wounds inflicted by the Revolution, have been the sole motives of this decision.

"The whole question reduces itself to this : Are the powers of Europe now arranging a true and lasting agreement with the king, and if so, on what principles shall it be concluded ? Shall it be on the retention or the abandonment of the spoils of the Revolution ? Can the king suppose that he increases his own dignity, by surrounding himself with monuments of art, which only serve to recall the sufferings of his own illustrious house, no less than those of the other nations of Europe ?

"If the French wish to retrace their steps, can they reasonably desire to retain this source of animosity between themselves and other nations ? and if they do not, is it politic to flatter their vanity and to keep alive those hopes, which the contemplation of these trophies must arouse ?

"Can even the army itself reasonably desire it ? The recollection of its campaigns can never perish ; they are recorded in the military annals of Europe, they are engraved on the public monuments of its own country. What need therefore to associate with the glory acquired on the field of battle, a system of pillage, contrary to the present laws of warfare, and by which the chief who led them to battle, has in reality tarnished the lustre of his arms ?

"If we really wish to return to peace and the old maxims, it cannot be prudent to retain so many vestiges of past abuses, and the king cannot wish, when escaping from the shipwreck of the Revolution, of which his family have been the principal victims, to perpetuate in his house this odious monopoly of the fine arts.

"The rich collections which France possessed before the Revolution, augmented by the Borghèse collection (one of the finest in the world) which has been since purchased, will give the king ample means to suitably beautify the capital of his kingdom, and the king can safely give up these valuable objects derived from an impure source, without prejudicing the culture of art in France.

"In applying a remedy to this dangerous evil, it does not seem possible to adopt a middle course, that would not tend to recognize various spoliations made under the form of treaties, and the character of which is, if possible, still more startling, than the acts of open plunder, by which these relics have in general been collected.

"The principle of property, regulated by the reclamations of the countries whence these works of art have been taken, is the surest and the only guide, which justice must follow ; and there is nothing perhaps, which can at present contribute further to establish public feeling in Europe, than such homage offered by the king to the principle of virtue, of conciliation, and of peace.

" CASTLEREAGH."

To this note I answered :

"The king's minister has received the note, which his Excellency Lord Castlereagh has done him the honour to write, respecting the art treasures which belong to France. His Majesty, to whom the note has been submitted, has ordered him to return the following reply.

"The protestations made by his Excellency, were not required to convince the king of the disinterestedness shown by the Prince Regent, in the demand which he has thought it his duty to direct his minister to address to the French government. His Majesty has even pleasure in recognizing, in the reasons which have dictated this step, those feelings of goodwill which his Royal Highness has always shown towards the king. But the arguments on which these reasons are founded, seem to him to be based only on inaccurate suppositions, or on mistakes ; in fact his Excellency seems pleased to imagine, that the wars of 1814 and of 1815, are both of the same nature, and that the second, ought to be terminated by a treaty of peace, as was the first. But these two wars are of a perfectly different nature; the first was really a war with the French nation, because it was a war with a man, who was recognised as its head by all Europe, in whose name everything was administered, to whom all were subject, who, in a word, disposed of all the resources of France, and who disposed of them legitimately. The war being made against the nation, a treaty of peace was necessary ; in 1815 on the contrary, this same man, against whom Europe has made war, was not recognized by any Power as ruler of France. If he partly used the same instruments, he did not use them lawfully, and submission was far from being complete. It was against him alone, and the factions which recalled him, and not against the nation that Europe, as her own declaration showed, has made war. The war therefore was brought to a close, and peace was restored, by the sole fact of the overthrow of the usurper, the dispersion of his adherents, and the punishment of their leaders. It is therefore not easy to see how the war of 1815, could be a valid ground for changing the state of affairs established by the peace of 1814.

" His Excellency Viscount Castlereagh, has furthermore laid it down as a fact, that objects of art cannot be acquired by conquest. The king's ministry are very far from wishing to apologise for any kind of conquest. Would to God that the name or the thing had never existed ! But since after all, this form of acquisition by nations, is sanctioned by the usages of all people and all times, the king's minister does not hesitate to express his conviction, that the conquest of inanimate objects, the sole use of which is to produce physical or intellectual enjoyment, is far less objectionable, than that by which people are separated from the society to which they belong, are subjected to new laws and customs which are not their own, united to people whom their natural dispositions make uncongenial to them, and lose even the surname which they have always borne.

" As regards the art treasures, which have from time to time been brought into France, a distinction should have been made, which appears not to have been done. Among the countries which France gave up in 1814, many belonged quite legitimately, to her, or to her former ruler, because they had been ceded to her. She had the right therefore to dispose of the art treasures which were there. When she gave up these countries, she restored them just as they were at the time of their restitution, and it is difficult to see by what right their present possessors could now claim articles, which were not included in the surrender that France then made.

"Lastly, other art treasures also belong to France, by a title no less legitimate. They belong to her in virtue of the cessions made under solemn treaties.

"As to the moral considerations dwelt upon in the note of his Excellency Viscount Castlereagh, his Excellency has every reason to believe that the king would be glad to be able to yield to them, and that he would hasten to restore all that has been carried away and brought to France during the course of the Revolution, were he free to follow only his own inclination ; but his Excellency is mistaken in supposing, that the king is now in a position to do so, any more than he was in 1814, and the ministry has no hesitation in affirming, that if, which they do not doubt, any cession of the ancient territory (supposing the king were to consent to it) would be imputed to him as a crime, cessions of the works of art would be no less so, as giving a severer blow to the national self-esteem.

"Prince de Talleyrand, president of the ministerial council has the honour to be . . . .

"PARIS, *Sept.* 19*th*, 1815."

It was the Duke of Wellington, as I have already said, who undertook to reply to this note. He did so with the roughness, I might even say, with the brutality of a soldier. This was his reply :—

"That at the time of the conferences for the capitulation of Paris, the French negotiators had wished to have an article inserted, with reference to the art galleries and the preservation of the works of art. That Prince Blücher had opposed this, seeing that there were pictures in the museums which had been taken from the King of Prussia, and which Louis XVIII. had promised to restore." The Duke of Wellington added, "that being as it were, the representative of the other nations of Europe, at the time of the capitulation, it was his duty to reclaim, all that had been taken from the Prussians ; that though he had no instructions relative to the art galleries, nor any official knowledge of the opinions of the sovereigns on this point, he must nevertheless presume, that they would strongly insist on the fulfilment of the promises of the King of France, in accordance with the obligations they were all under, to cause the restoration to their dominions, of those pictures and statues which had been removed from them, contrary to the regular usages of war, during the terrible period of the French Revolution. The sovereigns could not be unjust to their subjects, in order to satisfy the pride of the army and of the French nation, who must be made to feel, that notwithstanding some partial and temporary advantages, over several European States, the hour for restitution had arrived, and the allied sovereigns could not permit such an occasion to pass, for giving the French a *great moral lesson.*"

What could be done in the face of such language, supported by force? An armed resistance, with the help of the national guard of Paris, would only result in a useless struggle and certain defeat, solely calculated to justify the vengeance of our infuriated enemies, and to irritate those, who, like the Duke of Wellington himself, desired to show themselves more kindly disposed towards us in the general negotiations. We were forced therefore to bow our heads beneath this act of violence, more damaging to those who committed it, than to those who had to submit to it, and on this point history will be in accord with the general sentiment of France, and, I dare venture to say, of Europe.

A passage in the Duke of Wellington's answer, reveals one of the most serious difficulties with which the French negotiators had to contend, and which it will be best to describe here. It will have been seen, that the Duke of Wellington resented my demand in favour of our art galleries, on the plea, that the assent to this demand had already been refused on the capitulation of Paris; this capitulation, agreed to by the Chamber of Deputies of the Hundred Days, after they had in vain asked for an armistice from the Duke of Wellington and Marshal Blücher, preferring to treat with strangers, rather than with the legitimate King of France. The Chamber of Representatives had even done worse. A deputation chosen by themselves, had gone to the foreign sovereigns at Hagenau, and there, carried away by hatred to the house of Bourbon, had all but consented to a cession of territory, if Louis XVIII. had not been re-established on the throne! And it was these people, who called themselves staunch patriots, who dared to suggest such proposals!

If they were not accepted, they left a no less deplorable impression, which I found fatally adverse all through the negotiations. When I rejected the first overtures made to me by the allied plenipotentiaries, as to cession of territory, declaring that the whole of France would oppose such cession in the strongest manner, I was informed that the interviews at Hagenau showed quite a different spirit, since it was the party which claimed to be most devoted to the interests of France, which had itself brought forward this cession of territory.

While the so-called patriotic party had thus weakened our means of resistance, against the demands of the allies, the *émigré* party, who had secret relations with the foreign diplomats, all declared that the concessions claimed by the allies ought to be admitted, since the restoration of the house of Bourbon was entirely due to them.

On the other hand, the four Powers, notwithstanding all our efforts, were unanimous in imposing the severest conditions on us. The Emperor Alexander, terribly annoyed that he was not, as in 1814, the principal author of the second restoration, did not forgive me, either for having while in Vienna, defended the cause of the people and of legitimate governments, nor for having brought about the treaty of the 3rd of January, 1815. The Prussians, more violent than ever in their hatred and vengeance, hotly demanded the dismemberment of several French provinces. M. de Metternich, who at first seemed inclined to keep to his engagements, and side with the more moderate views of England, ended by dreading lest this moderation should prejudice him with Germany, and espoused the intense feelings of hatred of Prussia. England therefore alone remained, represented by the Duke of Wellington ; and from her sense of fairness, some help might be hoped for. But even in this direction the Russian, Austrian, and Prussian Plenipotentiaries, had found a mode of action detrimental to us. They had persuaded the English that the new kingdom of the Netherlands, their own creation, would require to be fortified against France, whom it would be necessary to deprive of several of her frontier fortresses, and thus weaken her, by giving to the Netherlands, what would consolidate that kingdom.

What contributed still further to embarrass and compromise the situation of the French negotiators, was the fact, that mysteries were made about everything with them ; they were not admitted to the conferences where the allied plenipotentiaries mutually discussed their projects, and it was only by hints and insinuations, that the views which were guiding them, could be guessed at.

In this manner the whole of August and part of September were spent, when at last, in the middle of the latter month, I received the following note from the plenipotentiaries of the four Powers, which they presented to me, as a sort of *ultimatum of the guarantees* they demanded from France :—

NUMBER I.

"The following document which is here tendered, is the result of the obligations due to their people by the allied sovereigns, and of their desire to reconcile these obligations to the sentiments which they have pledged to H.M. the King of France.

"It is in this form that they present their united views, which they have agreed to hold with regard to France."

NUMBER II.—*Bases of the final Arrangement proposed to France*

"1st. The confirmation of the treaty of Paris in all those particulars, which shall not be modified by the new treaty.

"2nd. Rectification of the frontiers as established by the treaty of Paris. By this article, nearly two-thirds of the territory that the treaty of Paris had added to that of ancient France, will be separated from her.

"The King of the Netherlands will receive back the greater number of the districts which formerly belonged to Belgium, and the King of Sardinia will again come into possession of the whole of Savoy. There will also be several changes in the direction of Germany. The towns of Condé, Philippeville, Marienburg, Givet, Charlemont, Sarrelouis, and Landau are comprised in the cessions demanded of France.

"3rd. The destruction of the fortifications of Hüningen, with the understanding that they are never to be rebuilt.

" 4th. A contribution of six hundred millions, as indemnity for the expenses of the war.

" 5th. The further contribution of a sum of two hundred millions, to cover in part the expenditure, devoted to the construction of new fortified places in the countries adjacent to France.

" 6th. The occupation for seven years of a military line on the northern and eastern frontiers, by an army of one hundred and fifty thousand men, under the command of a general, to be nominated by the allies, and which army will be kept up at the expense of France."

Number III.—*Project of the Treaty.*

" The allied powers having by their united efforts, and the success of their armies, delivered the French nation from the calamities with which it was being threatened, by the last attempt of Napoleon Bonaparte, and having preserved Europe from the upheavals which menaced her, in consequence of the revolutionary system which had been reproduced in France, in order to ensure the success of that attempt;

" And now sharing with His Most Christain Majesty, the wish to offer to Europe, by the inviolable maintenance of the Royal authority, and by putting into force the constitutional charter, the most reassuring guarantees for the stability of the order of things happily re-established in France, and to consolidate the friendly relations and great harmony, which the treaty of Paris had restored between France and the neighbouring countries, and to remove everything that might alter or compromise these friendly relations ;

" Their Imperial and Royal Majesties have promised to His Majesty the King of France and Navarre, the bases of an arrangement, which would insure to them, full indemnities for the past, as well as solid guarantees for the future, these being the only conditions by which it would be possible to arrive at a prompt and durable pacification; and His Most Christian Majesty having acceded to the said propositions, it was agreed to insert them in a definite treaty.

" To this effect, the high contracting parties have named. . . .

" Who, after exchanging their full powers, which were produced in good and due form, have signed the following articles :—

" Article No. I.—The treaty of the 30th May, 1814, is confirmed, and will be carried out in those particulars which will be found not to be modified by the present treaty.

"Article No. II.—The high contracting parties having learnt by experience, the drawbacks which are attached in several particulars both military and administrative, to the designation of the limits of French territory, that had been established by Article No. II of the treaty of the 30th May, 1814, and desiring in this particular, to adopt a system for the future, which would be equally favourable to the maintenance of general tranquillity, and the welfare of their subjects, have definitely fixed the line of demarcation, between the said territory and the neighbouring states, in the following manner.

"On the North, this line will follow the demarcation fixed by the treaty of Paris, as far as the point where the Schelde enters the department of Jemmapes, and from this river, as far as the frontier of the canton of Condé, which will remain outside the French frontier. From Quiévrain, the demarcation will be traced along the ancient frontier of Belgium and of the former bishopric of Liége, as far as Villers near Orval, leaving the territory of Philippeville and Marienburg, which are both enclosed therein, and the canton of Givet, outside the limits of France.

"From Villers to Bourg, to the right of the road leading from Thionville to Tréves, the demarcation will remain as it has been fixed by the treaty of Paris. From Bourg it will follow a line which will be drawn over Lannsdorf, Waltwich, Schardorf, Niederlingen, Palweiler, as far as Houvre, leaving all these places and their appurtenances in the hands of France. From Houvre, the frontier will follow the ancient limits of the district of Saarbruck, leaving Sarrelouis and the course of the Sarre, with the places situated on the right of the above-named line and their appurtenances in the hands of Germany. From the limits of the district of Saarbruck, the demarcation will follow that which actually separates the department of the Moselle, and that of the lower Rhine from Germany, as far as the Lauter, which will serve as a frontier up to its confluence with the Rhine, in order that Landau, enclosed in the projection formed by the Lauter, shall remain German, whereas Lauterbourg and Weissembourg, both situated on this river, shall remain in the hands of France. On the east the demarcation shall remain as it was established by the treaty of Paris, from the mouth of the Lauter as far as Saint-Brais, in the department of the Upper Rhine. This demarcation will then follow the Doubs as far as fort Joux, in order that the town of Pontarlier, situated to the right of the Doubs, and the land adjacent may belong to France, and the fort of Joux, situated to the left of the same river, to the Helvetian confederation. From the fort of Joux the boundary line will follow the crests of the Jura as far as the Rhone, leaving the fort of the Ecluse beyond the French frontier.

"From the Rhone, as far as the sea-coast, the line of demarcation will be made by that of the frontiers, which in 1790 separated France from Savoy and the country of Nice.

"France shall resign any claim to keep a garrison in the principality of Monaco.

"The neutrality of Switzerland shall be extended as far as the territory, north of a line traced from Ugine—including this town—to the south of the lake of Annecy, past Taverge, as far as Lecheraine, and from thence to the lake of Bourget to the Rhone, in the same way that it has been extended to the provinces of Chablais and Francigny by article 92 of the final act of the Congress of Vienna.

"Article III.—The fortifications of Hüningen being an element of perpetual disquietude to the town of Basle, the high contracting parties, wishing to give a further proof of their good-will and solicitude to the Helvetian confederation, have agreed to abolish the fortifications of Hüningen, and for the same reasons, the French government pledges itself never to replace them, nor to replace them by. any other fortifications within a distance of three hours from the town of Basle.

"Article IV.—The responsibilities of the allied sovereigns towards the people they govern, having compelled them to demand a compensation for the pecuniary sacrifices, which the late general armament had imposed on countries, already heavily drained by this long succession of wars, carried on against the revolutionary powers of France, and His Most Christian Majesty not being able to refuse to admit the principle on which this claim is founded, the sum of six hundred millions of francs will be furnished by France, by way of indemnity. The manner and the terms of this payment, to be regulated by a special convention, which will have the same force and weight, as if it had been actually inserted in the present treaty.

"Article V.—Considering, furthermore, that, in the course of the wars brought about by the events of the Revolution, all the countries adjacent to France, notably the Netherlands, Germany, and Piedmont, have successively witnessed the demolition of those fortified places which formed their barriers, and that the security of these countries and the future peace of Europe render it equally desirable, that an equilibrium, essentially favourable to the maintenance of general peace, should be established between them, for their mutual means of defence, the allied Powers believed they could not better attain this object, than by proposing to France to take upon herself, a part of the expenses connected with the construction of a certain number of fortified places on the frontiers opposed to her own, and to facilitate and complete this measure, by giving up in favour of the allies all claim to some of those places situated on the most advanced points of the line of fortifications ; and His Most Christian Majesty, fully sensible of the advantages that France, after such long and continued agitations, will reap, by the consolidation of a general peace, and ready, in order to obtain so great a benefit, to submit to any sacrifice which does not compromise the substantial integrity of his kingdom, having acceded to the propositions of the Powers, it is agreed, that, independently of the pecuniary indemnity stipulated for in the preceding article, the French government shall furnish the allies, with a sum of two hundred millions, to cover in part the expenses resulting from the re-establishment of their defensive system, and shall cede the fortified towns of Condé, Givet, Charlemont and Saarlouis, with sufficient radius of territory, as has been designated in Article II.

"Article VI.—The state of disquiet and ferment, which France must experience after so many violent upheavals, and more especially after the last catastrophe, the duration of which, in spite of the paternal intentions of her king and the advantages secured by the constitutional Charter it is difficult to determine, demanding, for the security of the neighbouring states, precautionary measures and temporary guarantees, it has been judged indispensable, to occupy provisionally, by a body of troops, certain military positions along the French frontier, with the express understanding, that this occupation shall cause no prejudice to the sovereignty of His Most Christian Majesty, nor to the state of possession, such as is recognized and drawn up in this present treaty.

"The number of these troops shall never exceed one hundred and fifty thousand men. The commander-in-chief of this army shall be nominated by the allied powers.

"This army corps shall occupy the towns of Valenciennes, Bouchain, Cambrai, Maubeuge. Landrecies, le Quesnay, Avesnes, Rocroi, Longwy, Thionville, Bitche, and the entrance of the bridge of fort Louis.

"The town of Strasbourg shall be evacuated by the troops of the line, and committed to the civic guards, the citadel remaining occupied by the allies.

"Or it will be entirely evacuated, disarmed, and entrusted to the local guards.

"The line which will separate the allied and the French

armies, shall be specially indicated. The towns comprised in this line, and unoccupied by the allied troops, shall be entrusted to the civic guard.

"The maintenance of the army destined for this purpose, falling on France, a special convention will also regulate the relations of the army of occupation, with the civil and military authorities of the country.

"The duration of this military occupation will be limited to seven years. It will come to an end before the expiration of this time, if, at the end of three years, the assembled allied sovereigns, taking into consideration the state of France, agree, that the grounds which necessitated this measure, have ceased to exist. But at the expiration of seven years, all the towns and positions occupied by the allied troops shall without further delay be evacuated and restored to His Majesty Louis XVIII., or to his heirs and successors.

"PARIS, September 1815."

(Here follow the signatures.)

I was filled with the profoundest indignation on the receipt of this communication, which was more insolent in its form, than in the actual demands it contained.

There was only one opinion in the council as to the reply that I proposed to make to it, and the king fully shared this opinion. I therefore addressed the following note to the allied plenipotentiaries, regretting deeply that I was unable to express in it the indignation that I felt ; the circumstances however demanded a painful reticence and prudence :—

NOTE OF THE FRENCH PLENIPOTENTIARIES IN REPLY TO THE PROPOSITIONS MADE BY THE ALLIES.[1]

"The undersigned plenipotentiaries of His Most Christian Majesty, have immediately brought to his knowledge the communications made to them in yesterday's conference, by their excellencies, the plenipotentiaries of the four Powers assembled regarding the definite arrangement, for the basis of which their excellencies have proposed :

"1. The cession by His Most Christian Majesty, of an amount of territory equal to two-thirds of that which had been added to ancient France by the treaty of the 30th May, and

---

[1] The reply is dated 21st September.

which would comprise the towns of Condé, Philippeville, Marien-bourg, Givet, Charlemont, Saarlouis, Landau, and the forts of Joux and of the Ecluse.

" 2.   The destruction of the fortifications of Hüningen.

" 3.   The payment of two sums, one of six hundred millions, as an indemnity, the other of two hundred millions, wherewith to construct fortified places in the countries adjacent to France.

" 4. The occupation for the space of seven years, of the fortresses of Valenciennes, Bouchain, Cambrai, Maubeuge, Lan-drecies, le Quesnay, Avesnes, Rocroi, Longwy, Thionville, Bitche, and the head of the bridge of fort Louis, as well as a line, following the northern and eastern frontiers, by an army of one hundred and fifty thousand men, under the command of a general to be nominated by the allies, and subsidised by France.

" His Majesty being extremely anxious, to hasten as far as in him lies, the conclusion of an arrangement, the delay of which has caused such innumerable evils to his people—which he daily deplores—and has prolonged, and continues to prolong, the internal agitation in France, which have excited the solicitude of the great Powers : and, being still further animated by the desire to communicate his friendly dispositions to the sovereigns his allies, has desired that the undersigned should communicate to their excellencies the plenipotentiaries of the four courts, without loss of time, the principles on which he believes that the negotiation relating to each of the proposed bases, should be carried on, and by ordering them to submit the following observations on the first-named basis, which concerns the territorial cessions, in which this important subject is viewed under the twofold aspect of justice and of utility, which it would be dangerous to separate from it.

The absence of any common arbitrator, possessing authority and power to put an end to the dissensions of the sovereigns, would leave no other course open to them, when they can no longer adjust these differences amicably, than to resort to arms, which would thus constitute a mutual state of war.

If therefore under such circumstances, the possessions of one party were occupied by the adversaries' troops, these possessions would be in occupation ; and by right of conquest the full enjoyment and possession of the same, would be acquired by the occupants, during the entire period of occupation, or until peace be re-established

Justice demands that, as a condition of this re-establishment of peace, the territory thus occupied, should be ceded to the occupier in whole' or in part, and that as soon as the cession has taken place—the character of the tenure being changed from temporary to actual possession,—the occupier should become its sovereign. This way of acquiring territory is authorized by international law.

But the state of war, conquest, and the right to demand territorial cessions, are facts which precede and depend on each other, so that the first named is a necessity for the existence of the second, and the third an absolute sequence of the second, as, apart from a state of war, no conquest can take place, and where there has been or is no longer, any conquest, the right to demand cessions of territory could not exist, as no nation can demand to keep that which it never possessed or ceases to possess.

No conquests can be made excepting in a state of war, and as from those who have nothing, nothing can be taken, conquests can only be made over those who have possessions ; from which it follows that there must be war between the occupiers and the possessor or sovereign of a country, before any conquest can ensue, the rights of possession and the sovereignty of a state, being inseparable or rather identical.

If therefore war is made in a country, and against a number more or less great of the inhabitants of that country, but that the antagonism is not extended to the sovereign thereof, it is clear that war is *not* made against this state, this last expression only signifying that the domain is taken for the possessor. Therefore a sovereign is excluded from a war which foreigners make in his territories, as long as they recognize him and interchange ordinary peaceful relations with him. War is then made against the people, to whose rights their antagonists could not succeed, they having no rights over which any conquests could be made.

The aim or effect of such a war could not be to conquer, but only to recover : therefore those who recover what does not belong to them, can only do so with the object of restoring it to whomsoever they recognize as the legitimate owner.

For a state to believe itself to be at war with any other country, without including the sovereign of that country, who had formerly been recognized as such, would necessitate one of two things : either the sovereignty must be regarded as being transferred from the sovereign to those who are being fought against, by the act itself for which they are being fought ; that is, sanctioning and recognizing those doctrines, which have overthrown so many thrones, and which have been the cause of the general war made against them by the whole of Europe ; or else to believe that such an anomaly as a double sovereignty could exist ; whereas a sovereignty is essentially one, and can never be divided. It may exist in various forms : either collective or individual, but never in both forms in the same country, which cannot acknowledge two sovereigns at the same time.

The allied powers did not however take either of these two views.

They considered Bonaparte's enterprise as the most heinous crime that man could commit, the mere attempt of which puts him outside the pale of international law. In his adherents, they only saw the accomplices of this crime—accomplices whom it was their duty to fight, quell and punish, which effectually excluded the supposition, that they could possess, acquire, confer, or transfer any rights whatsoever.

The allied powers have never for an instant ceased to recognize His Most Christian Majesty as king of France, nor consequently denied to him the rights which appertain to him in this capacity. They have never ceased to be on friendly terms with him, which fact alone binds them to respect his rights. They took upon themselves, formally as well as implicitly, to respect these rights by their declaration of the 13th of March, and in the treaty of the 25th. This engagement was further circumscribed by including the king, through his accession to the treaty, in their alliances against a common enemy. If therefore no conquests can be made over a friendly power, they can still less be made over an ally. It cannot be said that the king could only be allied with the other powers, by co-operating with them actively, and that he failed to do so. If the total defection of the army, which was already known and reputed inevitable at the time of the treaty of 25th March, prevented his making use of the regular forces, those Frenchmen, who to the number of sixty or seventy thousand took up arms for him in the Southern and Eastern departments, and those who showed themselves disposed to bear arms (forcing the usurper into the necessity of dividing his forces), as well as those who, in lieu of the resources of men and money, he required after his defeat at Waterloo, only left him the alternative of totally abandoning the enterprise, were very real and useful auxiliaries to the allies.

Finally the allied powers, as their forces gradually advanced into the French provinces, re-established the authority of the king, which measure would in itself have annulled any conquests in these provinces, even if any such had in reality been made.

It is therefore evident that the territorial cessions demanded cannot be based on any conquests made.

Neither can they be based on the sums disbursed by the allied powers, as if it be just that the sacrifices they were forced to make for a war, entered into for the general good, though for the more especial good of France, should not be at their expense ; it would, on the other hand, be equally fair that they should be satisfied with a compensation commensurate with the sacrifices made. The allied powers have not, however, sacrificed any territorial possessions.

We live in times in which, more than in any others, it is important to strengthen confidence in the promises of kings. The cessions required from His Most Christian Majesty would produce quite the opposite effect, after the declaration, in which the powers announced, that they were only armed against Bonaparte and his adherents, and after the treaty in which they undertook to maintain, in their integrity, *the stipulations of the 30th May*, 1814, which cannot be maintained if that of France be abandoned, after the proclamation of their commanders-in-chief, in which the same assurances are renewed.

Any cessions demanded of His Most Christian Majesty would deprive him of the means of extinguishing completely and for ever, the spirit of conquest amongst his people; that spark, which fanned by the usurper into a flame, would infallibly burst forth again, in the desire to recover that which the French nation would never believe it had been justly deprived of.

Any cessions exacted from His Most Christian Majesty, would be regarded as a crime committed by him, as if he had thereby bought the succour afforded by the allied powers, and would thus be an obstacle to the strengthening of that royal prerogative, which is so essential to legitimate dynasties, and so necessary for the peace of Europe, in as far as this peace depends on the internal tranquillity of France.

Lastly, the cessions exacted from His Most Christian Majesty, would destroy, or at any rate alter, the equilibrium, to the establishing of which the powers have devoted so much care and made so many sacrifices and efforts. They themselves were the arbitrators of the boundaries of France. How therefore can the measures they considered necessary, only a year ago now, cease to be so regarded ? On the European continent, there already exist two powers, surpassing France in extent and population; their relative greatness would necessarily increase in proportion to the actual decrease of the greatness of France. Would this be in conformity with the interests of Europe ? Would this eventuality even be in accordance with the interests of those two states, taking into consideration the relations which they occupy to each other ?

If in a small democracy of ancient times, the mass of the people, learning that one of their generals was about to propose a measure, which, though beneficial, was not in accordance with strict justice, all rose in a body and declared unanimously that they did not desire even to know what this measure was, can it be doubted that the monarchs of Europe would unanimously deprecate a step, not only unjust in itself but also pernicious?

It is therefore with the greatest confidence that the undersigned have the honour to submit the preceding remarks to the allied sovereigns.

His Majesty, however, in spite of the grave inconvenience attaching to all territorial cessions, will consent to the re-establishing of the former limits at those points, where an accession was made to the boundaries of ancient France, by the treaty of the 30th May.

He also consents to the payment of an indemnity, but of such a nature as would leave him the means to supply the want of the home administration of the kingdom, in default of which it would be impossible to achieve the establishment of that order and tranquillity, which were the sole aim of the war.

He will also consent to a provisional occupation.

The duration of this occupation, the number of fortresses, and the extent of country to be occupied, will be the subject of further negotiations.

But the king does not hesitate to at once declare, that an occupation of seven years' duration, being incompatible with the tranquillity of the kingdom, is utterly inadmissible.

The king therefore admits primarily, the cession of any territory which did not form part of ancient France; the payment of an indemnity; a provisional occupation by a number of troops, and for a certain period, to be determined later on.

His Most Christian Majesty is impressed with the belief, that the allied sovereigns will consent to establish negotiations on these three fundamental principles, and that they will introduce into the negotiations that spirit of justice and moderation, by which they are actuated, in order that the arrangements may be promptly concluded, to their mutual satisfaction.

If these principles be not adopted, the undersigned are not authorized either to entertain or to propose any others.

> (Signed) PRINCE DE TALLEYRAND.
> THE DUC DE DALBERG.
> BARON LOUIS."

I am still firmly convinced, that by clinging with energy and decision to the principles and ideas developed in this Note, we should have triumphed over the demands of the plenipotentiaries of some of the allies, and that we should have maintained our position, conceding only (1), an insignificant cession of territory under pretext of a rectification of the frontier ; (2), a contribution of at most three or four millions of francs ; (3), a temporary occupation by foreign troops of a few fortresses, in order to give time to reorganize the army.   But those foreign cabinets which were animated by the greatest spirit of revenge and rapacity, and who besides, were informed of the network of intrigues by which the king's weakness was surrounded, insisted on the pretentions formulated in the Note of the 15th September, and replied to the Note of the 20th by the following :—

Reply of the Ministers of the Allies.

22 September, 1815.

" The undersigned plenipotentiaries of the four allied courts, have received the Note in which the plenipotentiaries of France have replied to the communications which had been made to them in the conference of the 20th of this month, relating to a definite settlement of affairs.   They have been surprised to find in this draft, a long series of remarks on the right of conquest, on the nature of the wars to which it may be applied, and on the grounds which should have prevented the Powers from resorting to it in the present instance.

" The undersigned believe themselves to be all the more exempt from prosecuting this argument with the French plenipotentiaries, that none of the propositions that they made, by order of their august sovereigns, to adjust the present and future position of France with Europe, were based on right of conquest, and that they studiously avoided anything in their communications which could lead to a discussion on this right.

" The allied courts, always taking into consideration the re-establishment of order and the consolidation of the royal authority in France as the principal object of the steps they had taken, but being also convinced that France could never enjoy a permanent peace, if the neighbouring countries continued to nourish either feelings of bitterness or continual alarm towards her, consider that the principle of due compensation for the losses and sacrifices incurred in the past, as well as that of a sufficient guarantee for the future safety of the neighbouring countries, is the only proper means of putting an end to all discontent and fear : and that this consequently is the sole and true basis of any permanent or durable arrangement. It was on these two principles only, that the allied courts based their propositions, and the drawing up of the project itself, which the undersigned had the honour to hand to the French plenipotentiaries, stated the same most distinctly in each article.

"The French plenipotentiaries themselves, whilst maintaining complete silence with regard to the second of these principles, recognize the justice of the first.

"It is however evident, that the necessity of guarantees for the future, has become more perceptible and more urgent than it was at the time of the signing of the treaty of Paris. Recent events have struck terror and alarm throughout the whole of Europe. At a time when sovereigns imagined they were about to enjoy a long interval of peace after numerous troubles, these events have provoked agitation, changes, and sacrifices in all quarters, such as are inseparable from a general upheaval.

"It is impossible immediately to efface, from the minds of contemporaries, the recollection of such an upheaval. What might therefore have satisfied them in 1814, would entirely fail to do so in 1815. The line of demarcation which sufficed to reassure the states contiguous to France at the period of the treaty of the 30th May, can no longer answer to the just claims they now make. France is now bound to offer them some further pledge of security. This she should determine to do as much from a feeling of justice and expediency, as with a view to her own personal interests ; and in order to compass the happiness and tranquillity of the French nation, it is imperatively necessary that their neighbours should be in the same state.

"These are the powerful motives which have actuated the allied courts, when making their demands of territorial concessions from France. The inconsiderable extent of these cessions, the choice of the positions on which they bear, sufficiently prove that they are not in keeping with any views of aggrandizement or conquest, and that the safety of the adjoining states was their sole and single aim in making these demands. These cessions are not of a nature to attack the substantial integrity of France ; they only embrace detached portions of land and very advanced points of her territory ; they could not weaken her materially in either her administrative or military position ; her system of defence would not be affected by them ; France will remain none the less a state which is one of the best defined, best fortified in Europe, and the richest in resources of all kinds, to enable her to resist any danger from invasion.

"Without entering into these major considerations, the plenipotentiaries of France, however, admit the principle of concessions relating to those points which the treaty of Paris had added to the limits of ancient France. The undersigned have some difficulty in comprehending on what this distinction could be founded, and in what the essential difference between the former and present territory would consist from the point of view of the allied powers. It is impossible to suppose that the French plenipotentiaries would wish to insinuate in these present transactions, the doctrine of the *pretended inviolability of the French territory*. They are only too well aware that this doctrine was brought forward by the chiefs and apostles of the revolutionary system, and formed one of the most revolting chapters of the arbitrary code they wished to impose upon Europe. To assert the principle that France is able to extend her dimensions, acquire provinces, unite them to her territory by conquests or treaties, whilst she alone enjoys the privilege of never losing any of her ancient possessions, either through the misfortunes of war, or by those political arbitrations which would ensue therefrom, would completely destroy all notion of equality or reciprocity between the great powers.

"With regard to the last portion of the Note of the French plenipotentiaries, the undersigned reserve to themselves a complete explanation, until they meet at a conference they have the honour to propose to the French plenipotentiaries.

"(This last paragraph related to the duration of the stay of the foreign troops in French territory.)"

(Here follow the signatures.)

When I took this Note to Louis the XVIIIth, I found him much alarmed as to the results it might have. The *emigrant faction,* who above all dreaded being abandoned to their own resources, had so convinced the king, that to irritate the allies by any peremptory refusals, would compromise both himself and the kingdom of France, that his courage at last gave way. He informed me that negotiations must still be continued, that various temperaments must be gauged, and that although only at the last extremity must the present position be abandoned, yet when that point was reached, full concessions must be made. But to treat with a demand for cessions was virtually to admit that they were legitimate ; it meant reducing the dispute merely as to the amount to be considered ; in short, rendering us powerless to do anything but concede.

For my part I felt convinced that this measure would stultify all my former proceedings at Vienna, and would cancel all the precautions I had taken, lest at any time the alliance then formed against Bonaparte, should be turned against ourselves. I was therefore immovably determined never, under any plea whatsoever, to recognize a right which the allies could not possibly have, nor to affix my signature to any act treating of the concession of any portion of territory. The other ministers were of the same mind. The king, however, placed between the allies who were reiterating their demands, the courtiers who feigned an anxiety for the safety of his person which they did not really feel, and a minister whose views were immovable, and who did not fear to oppose himself to the princes of the council, found himself in so hopeless and cruel a dilemma, that I felt obliged to relieve him, by tendering him my resignation, the other ministers also offering to retire from office.[1]

I would not listen to the entreaties of M. de Metternich, Lord Castlereagh, and his brother Lord Stewart, who all three came to beg me not to separate myself from them. Lord Castlereagh went so far as to say, " Why will you not become minister of *Europe* with us ? " " Because," I replied, " I wish only to be minister of *France,* and this you will see by the manner in which I have replied to your Note."

My resignation was irrevocably tendered. The king accepted it with the air of a man greatly relieved. My retirement was also a relief to the Emperor of Russia, who did me the honour to hate in me, not, as he said, the friend of the English (he knew well enough, that if I had made auxiliaries of the English against him, when he had flattered himself that he would carry the frontier of his empire as far as the banks of the Oder, I was on that account no more their friend than the interest of Europe in general and those of France in particular demanded) but the man, who having seen him in close proximity in many different situations, in good and in bad fortune, knew exactly how far to count on the generosity of his character, on his former liberalism, and on his recent devotion ; he required a dupe, and this I could not be. But what pleased him most

[1] 24th September.

was, that the man who succeeded me in the double functions of President of the Council and Minister of Foreign Affairs, was a Russian Lieutenant-General, formerly governor of Odessa, the Duc de Richlieu, an undoubtedly good man, but a novice in diplomacy, and somewhat credulous. Fully persuaded, that among the images of the divinity on earth, there was none nobler than the Emperor Alexander, he thought he could not do better, when assuming charge of the affairs of France, than secure the abilities and support of this monarch.

I retired from office without very great regret; truth to say, the honour of governing France ought to be the aim of the noblest ambition, but circumstances at that time were such, that the gratification of this ambition would have been too dearly purchased by me.

Independent of the sacrifices demanded by our allies (now become our enemies), I should have had to encounter difficulties which affected me personally, and which would have made the exercise of power almost impossible for me. Louis XVIII., even whilst granting the Charter, only admitted with regret the consequences in what related to the independence of his ministers, and bore with scarcely concealed dislike, the burden of gratitude be felt he owed to me. His courtiers, encouraged by the success of the elections which had resulted in a Chamber of deputies eager for reaction, would have constantly endeavoured to undermine the cabinet over which I presided. The Chamber, itself, supported by the secret opposition of the king, would not have failed to exhibit even more animosity and violence, than it did in the presence of a ministry which had chosen moderation for its badge. I had sufficiently appreciated the value of the inflammatory battles of the tribune during 1789 and 1791, to know that in France they can but end in disorder, if there is not sufficient authority to confine them to the simple and calm discussions of the affairs of the kingdom. My age too, and the fatigue I had undergone through past events, would have prescribed the retirement for which I yearned. I can therefore say that it was without regret that I withdrew from public affairs, fully determined never again to take their leadership.

It will only be by my votes, that I can in future serve my

country and the government I have desired for her, because I believe it to be the one best adapted to her happiness and her actual needs. If our new institutions are really understood and sincerely carried into effect, I have the firm hope that France will again very speedily take the place which she ought to occupy in Europe, both for her own glory and the interests of civilization and the world.

I here finish these recollections which must close the end of my political career. In writing these last lines I am happy in being able to bear witness to myself, that if I have committed faults, and errors during this perhaps too protracted career, they have only been to my personal disadvantage, and that, animated by the most profound love for France, I have always served her conscientiously, seeking for her that which I honestly believed would benefit her most. Posterity, rather than contemporaries, will judge more liberally and more independently of those, who, placed like myself on the great stage of the world, during one of the most extraordinary epochs of history, have by this fact the right to be judged with greater impartiality and greater equity.

VALENCAY, *August*, 1816.

ADDENDUM.[1]

I FIND myself obliged to add a few words to these recollections, while at the same time regretting the necessity of having to recall so painful and sad an event, which I did not even wish to touch upon in the preceding pages.

I have always disdained to reply to the libellous and wicked accusations, which in times like those I lived in, could not fail to reach the persons who devoted themselves to any great public work. But there is a limit to this disdain, and when *bloody* questions are raised, such silence (at least as regards posterity) is no longer possible. The wickedness and the crimes of my accusers, shamelessly exposed by their own recitals, would possibly in ordinary cases be a sufficient refutation of their accusations. But in this actual affair, the nature of the facts, their historical importance, the fraction of truth in the recitals themselves, the high position of the persons concerned, the honour of my name and family—all force me to throw off the stigma of blood, that cupidity and passionate hatred would fain cast upon me.

I have been accused by M. Savary, Duc de Rovigo, of being the instigator, and consequently the author, of the horrible outrage (of which he confessed himself to have been the instrument) perpetrated twenty years ago upon the Duc d'Enghien. M. le Marquis de Maubreuil[2] on the other hand, declares that in 1814

---

[1] This addendum was written in 1825, to answer the accusations of the Duc de Rovigo. The duke had published in 1823, an extract from his memoirs relative to the Duc d'Enghien, in which he formally accuses M. de Talleyrand of having proposed and advised the arrest and execution of this prince. M. de Talleyrand herein defends himself.

[2] Marie-Armand Guerri de Maubreuil, Marquis d'Orsvault (1782-1855), belonged to an ancient Breton family. At the Revolution he followed his family abroad, and returning to France in 1797, served in the ranks of the Vendéans. Later on he entered the army, and became equerry to King Jerome. Falling into disgrace, he led from that time a most exciting existence, and launched into numerous speculations. In 1814 he became mixed up in the singular adventures related in this ad-

subject of almost any one who will read it with the attention it deserves."— *The Independent.*

" The author presents some novel propositions which he argues forcibly. His chapter, the ninth, on 'State Sovereignty and Right of Secession,' is among the ablest and best essays in the book. Our author does not believe in the assertion that 'governments are instituted among men, deriving their just powers from the consent of the governed,' as declared in the Declaration of Independence. He says : ' Not only is it true as a fact that governments do not derive their just power from the consent of the governed, but it is not even believed in by the people, except as a part of their philosophy.' He declares ' that the exercise of the right, claimed in the American Declaration of Independence, to alter or abolish any government which fails to secure to the individual protection of life, liberty, and the pursuit of happiness, however justifiable in morals it might be at times, is never legal, always illegal.' That ' revolutions are nothing more than successful rebellions, while rebellions differ from revolutions only in the fact that the former are successful. Both have their beginning in unlawful acts, even though the cause be righteous.'

" Whether the reader agrees with Professor Tiedeman or not in all his propositions, he will be interested in the fine clear method in which he backs up all his propositions. Some of them are revolutionary in their tendency, but the writing in the main is sound and reasonable, and, we may add, is lively and profoundly interesting."— *The Inter-Ocean.*

" The leading thought in this able treatise of Professor Tiedeman is expressed by him at the close of his first chapter, viz. : that the same social forces which create and develop the ethics of a nation create and develop its law ; that the substantive law is essentially nothing more than the moral rules commonly and habitually obeyed by the masses, whose enforcement by the Courts is required for the public good, while ethics are the rules of morality set forth by our moral teachers as their highest conceptions of moral development. A legal rule, therefore, is the product of social forces reflecting the prevalent sense of right. . . . The author evolves the idea of what he calls ' The Unwritten Constitution.' His point is that the present will of the people is the living source of law, and we should in construing the law follow and give effect to the present intentions and meaning of the people. We have not the space to follow the author through all the ramifications of his argument, which he develops with great skill and ability. But we commend his volume to the attention of all students of law and politics. . . . ' The Unwritten Constitution of the United States ' is not the least important of the works with which he has enriched the literature of his chosen profession."— *Charlestown News.*

G. P. PUTNAM'S SONS

NEW YORK   LONDON
27 WEST TWENTY-THIRD ST.   27 KING WILLIAM ST., STRAND

The Knickerbocker Press

1891

THE UNWRITTEN CONSTITUTION OF THE UNITED STATES.

A PHILOSOPHICAL INQUIRY INTO THE FUNDAMENTALS OF AMERICAN CONSTITUTIONAL LAW.

BY

CHRISTOPHER G. TIEDEMAN, A.M., LL.B.,

PROFESSOR OF LAW IN THE UNIVERSITY OF MISSOURI,

Author of Treatises on " The Limitation of Police Power," " The Law of Real Property," etc., etc.

16mo, cloth .   .   .   . $1 co

CONTENTS.—Origin and Development of Municipal Law in General—The Origin and Development of Constitutional Law —The Electoral College—The Re-eligibility of the President —The Inviolability of Corporate Charters and Charter Rights —The Doctrine of Natural Rights in American Constitutional Law—The Constitution in the War of Secession—Citizenship in the United States—State Sovereignty and Right of Secession—The United States Government One of Enumerated Powers—Cardinal Rule of Interpretation and Construction of Written Constitutions—The Real Value of Written Constitutions.

COMMENTS.

" This small volume of only 165 pages is remarkably full of meat, and is of interest not only to the student of law, but to every thinker and to every man fit to cast a vote. The author does not accept the ' social-contract ' theory, but insists that governments were of natural rather than of conventional origin, and that laws are rather an expression of public conviction than agents informing it—a result rather than a cause. He discusses Municipal Law, Constitutional Law, Secession, Citizenship, and the Government of the United States, and shows how gradual changes are going on, bringing both legal enactments and legal decisions into harmony with public opinion—the consensus of the right-minded, intelligent portion of the citizens of our country."—*Public Opinion*.

" Mr. Tiedeman writes well, in a clear, strong, and simple English style. He grasps all sides of a subject, and thinks broadly and justly. Without the affectation of originality he pursues his own line boldly, as in Chapter IX., where he expresses himself on the right of secession as one which was not decided by the Constitution, and, depending of right, theoretically and practically, on the will of the people at the time constituting the State, could not be decided except as the issue of the appeal made by the people to force decided it. Chapter VI., on ' Natural Rights,' is a piece of sound thinking and writing which will be likely to give a new form to the thoughts on this

I attempted to bribe him, to assassinate the Emperor Napoleon while in the island of Elba. Madness has strange aberrations sometimes! That is all I have to say about this last accusation, which is so absurd and so senseless, that it could only have been invented by a fool or a madman. But M. Savary is neither the one nor the other, and I wish therefore to reply to him first.

All M. Savary's accusations, it is true, are lost sight of in those he has made against himself. Never did a man cognisant of a crime, more imprudently and shamelessly unmask himself. Is it necessary to follow him into the abyss into which he has voluntarily thrown himself, in order to answer vain and false accusations? These allegations are however connected with publications which come from a different source. Documents have come or are said to have come from St. Helena, and have been published with the sole object of re-establishing a great reputation, defiled by the studied and impassioned calumnies, of all the most celebrated contemporaries. I therefore feel honoured, in seeing my name continually associated with those of all the princes and ministers of the day. I cannot but congratulate myself that so large a share should have been reserved for me, in the expressions of anger, the chief motive of which was to satisfy implacable and jealous hatreds, and to punish France for her past glory, her recent misfortunes, and her hopes of the future. Nothing that has been found in these crude collections of idle discourses, vain boastings, pedantic dissertations and libellous calumnies, could be brought forward as a proof against any one.

In these writings, the same as in M. Savary's pamphlet, two letters of mine have been mentioned; they have not however been correctly reported. I will now give them word for word as they ought to be in the archives, and I assume all the responsibility of them to this day. These letters however do not represent the painful part of the duty I had then to perform; I have nothing to hide about this shocking catastrophe, for the share I had in it has been made public, and if it inspires me with painful regrets, it leaves me without any remorse.

dendum, and which have not yet been cleared up. Being arrested in April, 1814, released in March, 1815, and re-arrested by the emperor's orders, he managed to escape into Belgium, but was there seized by Louis XVIII. He was released by order of the King of the Netherlands, and returned to France. In 1816 he was again arrested, and again escaped, it is said by connivance of the police. After many vicissitudes, he revisited Paris in 1827. He assaulted M. de Talleyrand, whom he blamed for all his misfortunes, in the cathedral of Rheims on the 21st of January, for which he was condemned to five years' imprisonment. Nothing more was heard of him after this.

Let me briefly recall the facts ; it will be the best way to refute the lying imputations of M. Savary.

It is well known that in the end of 1803 and the beginning of 1804, there were numerous plots against the life of the first consul. Grave proceedings were instituted during the first months of 1804 against George Pichegru, Moreau, and others, who were accused. During the course of the investigations made by the police at home, traces of other plots abroad were discovered, and it was but natural to connect the one with the other. The head of the general police had been vacant for several months ; one of the state councillors had been put in charge of this department, which had thus been placed under the direction of Chief Justice Regnier.[1] This minister on the 7th of March 1804, (16 Ventôse year XII) made the following report to the first consul :

CITIZEN FIRST CONSUL,

There is a society in Offenburg in the electorate of Baden, and in all the departments of the Rhine, paid by the English government. This society is composed of French *émigrés*, retired general officers, knights of St. Louis ; their object is to try and stir up disaffection in the heart of the republic, by all possible means.

Their principal agent is an *émigré* called *Mucey*, a man well known for some time past for his intrigues and the implacable hatred he has sworn against his country.

This miserable wretch is charged by his party, to introduce into France and to circulate freely, the incendiary mandates of the rebellious bishops, as well as the infamous libels which are concocted abroad, against France and her government.

A man called *Trident*, postmaster at Kehl, is the individual employed by the society, to transmit their correspondence to their confidential agents at Strasburg. These agents are known, and orders have been given for their arrest.

I do not think however that these measures will suffice. Public tranquillity as well as the dignity of the nation and its chief, require the destruction of this nest of intriguers and conspirators, who are in Offenburg, and who come to brave the republic and its government at its very gates, as it were ! It is

---

[1] Claude-Ambroise Regnier, Duc de Massa, born in 1736, was a barrister at Nancy in 1789, when he was elected deputy to the States-General. In the end of year III. he seconded Buonaparte on the 18th Brumaire, became State Councillor, Supreme Judge, Minister of Justice, and was for a short time Minister of Police (in 1804). Later on he became a senator, and was appointed President of the *Corps Legislatif* in 1813. He died in 1814.

necessary that both should be avenged, by their prompt punishment.

I therefore propose, Citizen First Consul, that you at once demand from his Serene Highness the Elector of Baden the extradition of Mucey, Trident, and his accomplices.

With salutations and respects. . . .

(Signed) REGNIER.

Certified correct.

Secretary of State, HUGUES MARET.

The First Consul, when showing me this report, told me to forward it to the government of the Electorate of Baden, and to demand the extradition of the persons therein named.

Here is the note I thereupon wrote to M. le Baron d'Edelsheim, Minister of Foreign Affairs to his Serene Highness the Elector of Baden :

PARIS, 19 *Ventôse, Year* XII. (10 *March*, 1804).

" The undersigned, Minister of Foreign Affairs to the French republic, has the honour to send to M. le Baron d'Edelsheim, a copy of a report which the chief justice has made to the First Consul. He begs your Excellency will place this important document before his Serene Highness the Elector of Baden. His Highness will therein find fresh and undeniable proofs, of the kind of warfare the English government pursues towards France ; and he will learn, with grieved astonishment, that in his own state of Offenburg, there exists an association of French *émigrés* who are among the most active instruments in all these horrible plots.

The undersigned is charged to formally demand, that the individuals who form this society in Offenburg, should be arrested and delivered up with all their papers to the French officers ordered to receive them at Strasburg.

The official demand, which the undersigned presents with regard to this matter, is founded on the text of Article I. of the treaty of Luneville. And when it is a question of a state conspiracy, the known facts of which have already roused the indignation of Europe, the individual feelings of friendliness that exist between France and his Serene Highness the Elector, leave no room to doubt that he will, at the request of the French government, hasten to execute this chief stipulation of the treaty of Luneville, and also in other ways further assist to unveil these machinations, which menace at the same time, the life of the First Consul, the safety of France, and the peace of Europe.[1]

The undersigned is ordered to demand, that sweeping and irrevocable measures should be taken, to send away all the French *émigrés* from the lands that form the Electorate of Baden. Their stay in the part of Germany nearest to France, cannot but be a source of disquietude and of trouble, as well as a temptation to themselves, to enter into intrigues, by which England profits and which she utilizes to further her own detestable schemes.

And when it is remembered that the *émigrés*, who are still out of France, are all men, plotting against the present government of their old country, men whom it has been impossible to reconcile to any changes or circumstances, and who are in a perpetual state of antagonism against France, it is evident that they are among those persons who in accordance with the terms of the treaty of Luneville, should find neither refuge nor protection in the German states. Their exclusion is therefore a stern right. But even if it only depended on the well-known principles and feelings of his Serene Highness the Elector, there could be no doubt that he would make every effort to drive forth from his states, such dangerous characters, and thus give another proof to the French government, of the great value he attaches to the friendly relations which so many circumstances have combined to establish between France and the Electorate of Baden.

The undersigned therefore awaits with full confidence the decision that will be made by his Serene Highness the Elector on the two demands he has been charged to convey to him, and he takes this opportunity to renew the assurance. . . ."

This note and the memorandum that accompanied it, fully prove that it was only on the information furnished by the police, that the French government demanded the extradition of some persons and the expulsion of others from the Electorate of Baden ; and it will also be seen that the information, on the strength of which the prosecutions against the Duc d'Enghien were instituted, did not emanate from the Foreign Office.

My note was despatched on the 10th of March : a few hours later I was summoned to the presence of the First Consul. I found him in a state of violent excitement. He reproached M.

---

[1] The article of the treaty of Luneville which covenants for peace between the Empire and France, lays down : "That no assistance or protection shall be given, either directly or indirectly, to those who desire the injury of either of the contracting parties."

Réal,[1] State Councillor in charge of the general police arrangements, and who was present, for not having known that the Duc d'Enghien was at Ettenheim with General Dumouriez,[2] and plotting against the safety of the republic and against his, the Consul's, life, and that the chief centre of these plots was at Offenburg. Then quickly turning towards me, he reproached me in the same way, asking how it was that the French *chargé d'affaires* at Carlsruhe, M. Massias,[3] had not notified such a state of affairs. As soon as I could put in a word, which was not easy (for his passion was such that he gave no opportunity for a reply), I reminded him that he had been for some time perfectly aware that the Duc d'Enghien was in the Electorate of Baden, and that he had even told me to inform the Elector of Baden that the prince might reside at Ettenheim ; that as to the intrigues that were planned at Offenburg, the *chargé d'affaires* at Carlsruhe, M. Massias, might have forgotten or neglected to mention them in his correspondence, either because he attached no importance to them, or because he feared to compromise the Baroness de Reich, who it is said, was a relation or friend of his wife's.

I tried, but in vain, to soften the wrath of the First Consul. He showed us the reports sent to him by General Moncey, Chief Inspector-General of *gendarmerie*, which in fact announced the presence of Dumouriez at Ettenheim. These reports, like all those of a similar nature, were founded more on inferences than on positive facts, save only that of Dumouriez's presence, which was asserted, and which nevertheless was not true.

But the First Consul was filled with apprehension; nothing would persuade him that these intrigues were not connected with the plots, inquiries into which were being prosecuted in Paris. Consequently he then and there took the fatal step, to order the arrest, by French troops on Baden territory, of all the

---

[1] Pierre François, Comte Réal, born in 1765, attorney at Châtelet in 1799, was Deputy Attorney to the Commune, and Public Prosecutor to the revolutionary tribunal. He became Commissary of the department of the Seine under the Directorate. After the 18th Brumaire he was appointed State Councillor, and attached to the Police Ministry. He was Prefect of Police during the Hundred Days, and was exiled at the second restoration, but returned shortly after to France, and died in 1834.

[2] The *émigré* Thumery, who was then with the Duc d'Enghien, was mistaken for Dumouriez. The resemblance of manner, added to a German accent, caused this error on the part of the police agents.

[3] Nicolas, Baron Massias, a man of letters and a French diplomat, born in 1764, was first an officer, then professor of polite literature. He entered the diplomatic service under the Directorate, was appointed *chargé d'affaires* to the district of Suabia, at Carlsruhe, and then to the Grand Duke of Baden. In 1807 he became Consul-General at Dantzig. He retired in 1815, and devoted himself entirely to literature until his death (1848).

émigrés who were then at Offenburg and Ettenheim. He himself dictated the orders to the war minister for the execution of these instructions, and ordered me to make known to the Elector of Baden, when too late, the steps he had deemed it necessary to take. I therefore wrote the letter which I here insert, to the Baron d'Edelsheim.

PARIS, *20th Ventôse, Year* XII. (11 *March*, 1804).
3 o'clock in the morning.

" M. LE BARON,
I had just written a note to you the object of which was to demand the arrest of the society of French *émigrés* residing at Offenburg, when the First Consul became aware, through the arrest of the numerous robbers with which the English government has deluged France, and also from the result of the investigations that have taken place here, of the large share taken by the English agents at Offenburg in the horrible plots devised against his person and against the safety of France. He has also learnt that the Duc d'Enghien and General Dumouriez were at Ettenheim, and as it is impossible that they should be in that town without the permission of his Serene Highness the Elector, the First Consul has seen with the deepest grief, that a Prince to whom it has pleased him to show the most special marks of the friendship of France, should have given refuge to his most cruel enemies, and allowed them quietly to hatch such unheard-of conspiracies.

Under such extraordinary circumstances, the First Consul considered it necessary to send two small detachments to Offenburg and Ettenheim, to seize the instigators of a crime, which from its nature, place those who have been convicted of taking part in it, outside the pale of the law of nations.

General Caulaincourt is charged with the orders of the First Consul in this respect. You may feel assured that he will exercise all the consideration that his Serene Highness the Elector could possibly wish in their execution. He will have the honour to convey the letter to your Excellency which I have been ordered to write.

Receive, M. le Baron, the assurance . . . "

In sending this letter to General Caulaincourt, I wrote him the following lines :—

PARIS, 21 *Ventôse, Year* XII. (11 *March*, 1804).

" GENERAL,
I have the honour to send you a letter for Baron d'Edelsheim, Prime Minister of the Elector of Baden, which ⱽou

will have the goodness to send him as soon as your expedition to Offenburg is completed. The First Consul desires me to say, that if you are not in a position to take the troops into the Electoral states, and if you hear that General Ordener[1] has not either done so, this letter is to remain in your hands, and must not be placed in those of the Elector. I am directed to give you special orders to take possession of and carry away, the papers of Madame de Reich.[2]

I have the honour . . ."

I have given these three letters in their entirety, as they constitute the only real share I had in the deplorable affair of M. le Duc d'Enghien. It will be easy to judge of my share in all this, by examining these letters with a little care.

The First Consul had been for some time aware of the presence of the Duc d'Enghien in the Electorate of Baden, the French *chargé d'affaires* at Carlsruhe had informed us of it in the name of the Elector of Baden, and he had been informed in reply, that the inoffensive conduct of the prince, of which he had given an account, placed no obstacle whatever to his remaining there. The Minister of Foreign Affairs took no part whatever in the investigations made at that time by the French police, in the countries adjoining our Rhenish frontier. These investigations were made, either by the *préfet* of Strasburg, in compliance with the orders of State Councillor Réal, in charge of the general police of the Republic, or by the officers of the local *gendarmerie*, in accordance with the orders of General Moncey, chief inspector of *gendarmerie*. M. Réal and M. Moncey sent the reports they received direct to the First Consul. I never heard anything about these matters, except what the First Consul told me, when he had any orders to give me. Thus, as has been seen, I transmitted to Baron d'Edelsheim the report of the chief judge, M. Regnier, in which no mention whatever was made of M. le Duc d'Enghien, when on the receipt of fresh information, the authenticity of which I tried to disprove, I received the peremptory order to write a second time to Baron d'Edelsheim. My letter could not have, in any way, had a share in the arrest of the prince, as it was

---

[1] Michael Ordener (1755–1811) enlisted at the age of eighteen, became a non-commissioned officer in 1789. On the 18th Brumaire he was appointed Commandant of the Consular Cavalry Guard. He it was who commanded the detachment ordered to carry off the Duc d'Enghien. In 1805, Ordener became a general of division, then a senator (1806), and first equerry to the Empress.

[2] The Baroness de Reich had already been arrested at Offenburg by order of the Baden government, delivered up by it to the French authorities, and with her papers carried off to Strasburg.

only intended to inform M. d'Edelsheim of the arrest, after it had been already effected. The letter to General Caulaincourt still further proves, that I had provided against the violation of the Baden territory, thereby clearly showing that I was ignorant of how precise, imperative, and unavoidable of execution, were the orders given by the War Minister for the entry of the troops into the states of the Elector. A still further reason why I must have been ignorant of the sanguinary project, which the First Consul had in his own mind decided upon.

I lay stress on these facts, which are supported by all published and unpublished documents, for they refute, in the most peremptory manner, M. Savary's perfidious assertions and insinuations. With the exception of the letters cited above, I was in complete ignorance of everything, and M. Savary, without knowing it, and certainly against his own wishes, had taken care to confirm this.

It will be seen, that in one of the most important paragraphs of his libel, he tries to prove that during this time, the police investigations were not extended beyond the frontiers, and that my office was alone responsible for foreign matters.

Nevertheless, further on, he states that the first Consul was ignorant of the name and even the very existence of the Duc d'Enghien, thus not hesitating to remove all semblance of truth in his recitals, by putting forth such an absurdity. He then goes on to show, in fullest detail, all the police measures and devices, and the means taken by State Councillor Réal and the head of the *gendarmerie*, in order to obtain correct information as to the sojourn, the departures, the various correspondents, and the journeys of this unfortunate prince.

It was in fact on the strength of their reports, and those of their agents, that the villainous and fatal determination was taken, and neither I, nor the representatives of my office abroad, took part either in the premeditation or execution of any of these measures.

State Councillor Réal and the First Consul knew perfectly well that they would not suit my character, any more than the principles of my office; that to expect my intervention in the matter would be useless, and that therefore it was better to keep me in total ignorance.

As to the two letters addressed to Baron d'Edelsheim, I do not think they require any apology; but if such is deemed necessary, it will be found in the official position I held at this period, in the critical position in which great events had then placed France, and finally in the new and entirely unexpected relations, which these same events had created, between the government lately established, and the other governments on the Continent.

I must also here be allowed to make some remarks on the duties of men in official positions during those calamitous times, when it pleases Providence to interpose violently between the personal fate of kings and that of their people.

Then the monarch is absent, his future is hidden, and his special adherents cling to his fate and share his misfortunes, his dangers, his hopes. In leaving their native soil, they bind themselves indissolubly to his lot, and I do not refuse either my respect or my admiration to this self-devoted party. But as for the others, their country still remains to them. She has a right to be defended, and to be governed. She has also incontestably another right, that of claiming from them the same services they owed to and gave her before the departure of the sovereign. It was according to this view that I tried to regulate my conduct.

At this period France, though again engaged in war with England, was at peace with all the rest of the world. It was therefore the duty of the Minister of Foreign Affairs to do all that lay in his power, within the limits of right and justice, to preserve this peace.

With regard to this, it is almost impossible to describe the very complicated nature of such a duty. Standing between governments which were terrified, touchy, and uneasy as to their danger, though all more or less reconciled to each other, and a powerful sovereign, whose genius, character, and ambition only gave too just cause for disquietude and umbrage, the Minister for Foreign Affairs had constantly to exercise an equal degree of vigilance on the policy he had to restrict, and on that which he had to combat.

His negotiations with his own government were often much more difficult, and much longer, than those he had to carry through with governments which he had to tranquillize.

The letter addressed to General Caulaincourt, which I have given above, throws a vivid light on this matter.

It plainly shows that the First Consul had guarded himself against all such negotiations, and this fact of itself proves, that I had done everything to prevent occurrences which must inevitably have led my office into great and inextricable difficulties. My letters to the Minister of the Elector of Baden were the prelude to this ; which must not be lost sight of, if the true view of the matter is desired, that, fortunately for myself, I had only to justify those measures of which I was cognizant.

To prevent a weak prince from drawing on himself the

enmity of a powerful neighbour, to remove from the French frontiers the assembly of enemies, who could not harm the existing government except by imprudent attempts, as fatal to the peace of Europe as to that of France ; to prevent, in fact, all causes of misunderstanding between the French Government and the neighbouring states, this was the object of my first letter.

It is true the second, contained a scarcely founded justification of an act which attacks one of the principles of public right. And for this error I blame myself, but that is altogether different from more or less plausibly justifying or counselling such an act and taking part in its execution. The former only enforces a painful and unhappy necessity, the latter is a crime.

I speak too strongly in describing an infraction of public right as a crime, when it only means the simple violation of a neighbouring territory. During this war, and in the course of all other wars, much graver crimes have been committed by the enemies of France, by France herself, and by the governments that ordered them. They were not described as criminal, nor were their ministers, who undertook to carry them out, and then had to apologize for committing them.

In the present instance it was a crime, but only as regards the aim in view, when thus violating strange territory ; and my ignorance of this aim is my exculpation. Here the crime consisted in the fatal consequences brought about by this violation.

But is it fair in my accusers to assert, without proof, that I was cognizant of them ? Such horrible knowledge could only have been possessed by accomplices.

I must add some further observations to those I have already made above, on the duties of men in office during exceptional times. When through force of circumstances a man finds himself obliged to live under and serve a government, which has no other guarantees for the safeguard of its power, than the events which have caused its rise, and the need of the nation, many conjunctions may arise in which he has to decide as to the nature of the duties connected with the position he occupies. Should the government under which he lives order him to commit a crime ? Incontestably and without hesitation he must disobey; he must at all risks incur its displeasure and submit to all the consequences. But should the government, without his knowledge commit a crime ? In that case an argument may be raised on a double hypothesis. If the crime is against public order, if it draws or may draw the country into great danger, if it tends to social disorganization, contempt of the laws, or the ruin of the state, there can be no doubt that not only must it be resisted, but the yoke must be thrown off, and arms taken up against a power which has become the enemy of the country it has lost the power of governing.

But if the crime is of an isolated nature, if it is circumscribed in its object, as well as in its effect, if it has no other result than to tarnish the name of the man who has committed it, and to hold up to public condemnation the names of those who have been its instruments, its executioners, or its accomplices, then one is forced to grieve over the mixture of grandeur and feebleness, of exaltation and abasement, of energy and perversity, that flash forth in some characters which it has pleased nature to produce ; but the distribution of the share of glory or of infamy, which is their respective due, must be left to the justice of future ages. Only the fame of those who have committed these crimes is compromised, and if the law of nations, general morality, the safety of the state and public order are not affected by them, then it is right to continue in office. Were it otherwise, picture the position of a government suddenly deserted by all the capable, generous, enlightened, and conscientious men in the country, and all its departments filled by the scum and the dregs of the population ! What terrible results would not arise from such a state of affairs, and which could only be attributed to the neglect of that principle which has just been referred to, and which not only justifies the engagements which men most inimical to legitimate governments may find themselves voluntarily obliged not only to make but also to be faithful to, so long as the maintenance of social order and the defence of national rights against foreign enterprises are thereby preserved ?

Herein we can find an apology for the French administration during the whole of this period. It must not be forgotten, that only a short time previously, social order at home and the political system abroad, had both been a prey to anarchy. It was left to the French government to put an end to these excesses, and this noble task it has performed with as much zeal as success. It will be for historians to relate all that was then done to calm down the disturbed spirits, to place a curb on unbridled passions, and to restore order, regularity, moderation, and justice, in all the branches of the services. A good financial system, the establishment of *préfectures*, the formation and proper composition of a large army, the keeping up of the roads and the publication of the civil code, all date from this period, and attest the good services done during that time by the civil and military branches of the French administration. The peace of Amiens, the political organization of Italy, the Swiss mediation, the first trial of the establishment of a German

Federal system, all bear witness to the activity, the wisdom, and the high standing of the government which I had formed and which I directed. If later on, the rules of prudence and moderation, which with indefatigable patience I established, maintained, and defended, were allowed to fall into disuse, my decision to give up office and the period when that decision was taken, will exculpate me in the eyes of posterity from all participation in this change. But what was possible to me in 1807 was not so in 1814, for in the latter case I should have deserted the great duties that I felt myself called upon to render to my country. This view of matters was shared by many others as well as myself, and it is needless to recall that not a single voice was raised in the country to protest against the frightful outrage of which M. le Duc d'Enghien was the victim. It is sad to have to say this, but it is the actual truth, and can only be explained by the dread possessed by every one of disturbing a government which had succeeded in rescuing France from anarchy.

Whatever may be thought of the reasons I have given, and which I believe to be just and well founded, I will sum up the points which bear on this deplorable affair, and go over those which concern myself.

1. That it was neither through the Foreign Office nor consequently through me, that the First Consul was informed as to the plots, real or pretended, that were being hatched at that period on the other side of the Rhine.

2. That I had nothing further to do with the whole business of the Duc d'Enghien, than transmitting to the Minister of the Elector of Baden, first the report of the minister of justice, and later on to inform him, when too late, of the orders given by the First Consul, to Generals Ordener and Caulaincourt, orders over which I had not, and could not have had, any influence whatever.

Then as touching the sentence and execution of M. le Duc d'Enghien, it will not, I think, be difficult for me to prove that I had no share in it whatever. As Minister of Foreign Affairs, I could have nothing to do with the selection of the council of war, nor with the execution, of which M. Savary so boldly accepts the responsibility.

For me therefore to have taken any part in this bloody drama, it must be supposed that I had done so voluntarily, and that I had interfered for no other reason than the love of bloodshed. If my character and my antecedents did not place me above such an odious and infamous suspicion, there is another question I could put before my accuser, which he is in a better position to answer than any one else, namely, What interest could I have in the murder of the Duc d'Enghien ? I had taken no part in any of the crimes of the French Revolution, I had given sufficient proofs to the First Consul, of my devotion to the order of things he had established, not to need to inflame his passionate anger, in order to obtain a confidence which I had fully possessed for the last five years. Posterity will judge between me and M. Savary, and all those who, like him, for one reason or another, seek to throw on me the responsibility of a crime which I repudiate with horror. I have not, and will not accuse any one, and have confined myself to writing the subjoined letter to the king, which is followed by M. de Villèle's answer :—

To King Louis XVIII.

SIRE,
I am not telling your Majesty anything fresh when I say, that I have a great many enemies, both near the throne and also far removed from it. Some of them have not yet forgotten that I took a different view to theirs, of the first troubles of the Revolution, but whatever their opinion may be, they must know that it is due to the stand I then took, that I owe the happiness of having, during a time specially marked by Providence, contributed so fortunately to the restoration of your august throne and the triumphs of legitimacy. It is this same restoration and this same triumph that my enemies have not and never will pardon. Hence all those libels, those voluminous recollections from St. Helena, in which during the last two years I have incessantly been insulted and defamed by men who, in selling the true or imputed words of a deceased celebrity, make capital out of the famous personages of France, and who by this shameless traffic have constituted themselves the testamentary executors of Napoleon Buonaparte's revenge.

Sire, in this latter class I must place the former minister of the Emperor, the only one whose name I dare not even pronounce before your Majesty ; this man who, in an access of insanity, has recently denounced himself to public prosecution, as the actual perpetrator of a horrible assassination ; happy if, by plunging himself in blood, he can, by joining my name to his, drag me down with him, and dishonour the chief agent of both Restorations ! Yes, Sire, of both Restorations ! In me they persecute the days of the 30th of March, 1814, and the 13th of April, 1815 ! Days of glory for me and of happiness for France ; days which have joined my name to the constitutional charter that we owe to your Majesty. But it is in vain that envy hatred, and baffled ambition, coalesce to deprive me of my right to contemporary esteem and historical justice ; I shall be enabled to defend and transmit these intact to the inheritors of my name.

During the numerous storms that have marked the past thirty years, calumny has heaped many insults upon me. But there is one which up to now has been spared me. Not a single family has felt itself entitled to demand from me the blood of any of its members ; and now a madman imagines that, suddenly giving up these peaceful habits, these moderate views, which even my enemies have never disputed, I should have become the author and instigator of a most horrible assassination ! I, who have never—and I thank heaven for it—spoken a word of hatred or counselled revenge against any one, not even against my most bitter enemies, that I should choose to make a single exception, and that exception, whom ? A prince of the family of my sovereigns. And that he should be the victim to signalize my *début* in the career of an assassin ! And that not only should I have advised this atrocious crime, but that, in addition, I used every endeavour to subvert the First Consul's clemency, and that in spite of, and against Buonaparte's orders, and at the risk of the greatest and most awful responsiblity, I should have hurried on the execution of the sentence !

And who is the man who dares to accuse me of such atrocities ? My accuser has made himself sufficiently well known.

Nevertheless, Sire, my name, my age, my character, the high position I owe to your goodness, do not permit me to submit to such an outrage without seeking satisfaction. As a peer of France, I must not ask this satisfaction from the tribunals entrusted by law with the punishment of calumny ; I shall therefore indite my accuser before the Chamber of Peers ; from it I shall obtain an inquiry and judgment. This trial, Sire, which I claim from your sense of justice, you will no more dread for me, than I do for myself. Then calumny will be confounded, and its impotent rage will expire before the great light of truth.

I have the honour to be, with the most profound respect . . . .

PRINCE DE TALLEYRAND.

PARIS, *8th November*, 1823.

M. DE VILLÈLE TO PRINCE DE TALLEYRAND.

PRINCE,

The king has read your letter of 8th November with great attention.

His Majesty desires me to say, that he notices with surprise, that it is your intention to call for a special investigation in the

Chamber of Peers of the facts just published by M. le Duc de Rovigo. His Majesty wishes that the past should be buried in oblivion, excepting always as regards the services rendered to France and to himself.

The king could not therefore approve such a needless and unusual step, which would give rise to vexatious debates, and revive the most painful recollections.

The high place which you continue to hold at court, Prince, is a convincing proof, that the imputations which hurt and vex you have made no impression whatever on his Majesty.

I am, Prince, your Excellency's most humble and obedient servant,

JOSEPH DE VILÈLLE.

PARIS, 15*th November*, 1823.

This letter imposed silence upon me ; I have observed it ; for though I have deemed it necessary to expose what has just been read, it is only because it will not be published until long after my death, when it will establish the truth of the facts, without provoking the scandals dreaded in 1823.

An announcement inserted in the papers of the 17th March, 1823, stated :

"The king has forbidden the Duc de Rovigo to enter the palace of the Tuileries."

A few days after the receipt of M. de Vilèlle's letter, when I presented myself at the palace, to pay my respects to the king, his Majesty on seeing me said : " Prince de Talleyrand, you and yours can come here without fear of any unpleasant encounters."

I have nothing further to add to this recital.

And now one word as to M. de Maubreuil's accusation. This is so utterly absurd, that it will suffice, I think, to speak of it in the words used by its author, to cause it to fall to the ground. It is necessary first, however, to know who M. de Maubreuil was.

Descended from an old and honourable family in Brittany, M. de Maubreuil entered the military service, under the Empire, in 1807. After serving for some time with the army in Spain, he was dismissed at a time when no one was removed from the army, unless for a very grave fault indeed, every soldier being urgently needed. His name, and the introductions he contrived to get, secured him a place at the court of Jerome in Westphalia. This court, as is well known, was not over scrupulous in its choice of those who composed it ; the appointment of M. de Maubreuil as equerry to the king, after the incident in Spain, would be proof enough if this were

needed.   Nevertheless, Maubreuil contrived to get again dismissed, even from this court.   Returning to Paris, and being in
possession of a considerable fortune, Maubreuil next launched
into business, but into business with people of his own stamp,
as an army contractor.   Whether through too great sharpness
on his part and that of his associates, or else through their dis-
honesty, differences soon arose between them and the government, resulting, as he declared, in heavy losses to himself, which
irritated him greatly against the Emperor Napoleon.   Such was
his position at the fall of the Empire, and it was then, according
to himself, that in the beginning of April 1814, he was several
times sent for to my hotel by M. Roux Laborie,[1] who filled the
post of secretary to the Provisional Government, and who, in
my name, had suggested to him the assassination of Napoleon ;
that rewards were offered to him to carry out this *secret
mission* as he calls it, but always through M. Roux Laborie, for
Maubreuil states that he has never spoken to me.   These
rewards were to be (I quote his actual words) " horses, carriages,
the rank of Lieutenant-General, the title of Duke, and the
government of a province."   He avows that he accepted them
all, and took measures to carry out his *secret mission.*   It was
only after leaving Paris, and when already *en route,* that he experienced some scruples, and began to realize the horror of the
crime he was about to commit.   He thereupon generously
resolved to abandon it, but as he wished to mark his return to
virtue by a good action, he took advantage of the first occasion
that presented itself.   On his road, he encountered Queen
Catherine, princess of Wurtemburg, and wife of Jerome Buonaparte, his sovereign in Westphalia.   Stopping her carriage, he
ransacked the waggon which followed it, robbed her of all her
money, jewels, and other effects, and returned in triumph to
Paris, where he was greatly astonished at being pursued and
arrested as a common highway robber.   This is the abridged
history of my accuser, M. de Maubreuil.

I ask, is not this sufficient in itself to refute the accusation ?

There is only one point upon which I have not touched.   I
wished, ere mentioning it, to say that even now I cannot quite
understand it, and can only bring forward conjectures to explain
it.   At the moment of his arrest, Maubreuil was in possession

---

[1] Antoine Roux Laborie, born in 1769, Secretary to the Minister of Foreign
Affairs in 1792, took refuge abroad after the 10th of August. Returning to France, he
was made Chief Secretary of Foreign Affairs, after the 18th Brumaire ; but, compromised in the Royalist conspiracies of that date, he had to conceal himself, and lived
in retirement till 1814.   Later on he was made Secretary-General to the Provisional
Government ; followed the Court to Ghent in 1815, and at the second Restoration
was elected Deputy of the Somme, but was not re-elected in 1816. He died in 1840.

of passports and regular safe-conducts, given by the allied armies and by the French authorities, in which he was described as charged with a mission, which required the utmost expedition.

It will be remembered that in the beginning of April 1814, the Provisional Government sent emissaries into all parts of France, to announce the overthrow of the Imperial Government and the accession of the legitimate government. It became necessary to choose persons at haphazard, to carry out these missions, and I can easily believe, that a loudly expressed hatred to Napoleon would, at that moment, have been a sufficient recommendation to obtain one of these appointments, which were those of a courier. There was not much time to make inquiries as to the moral status of those who were thus employed ; and a man presenting himself under the name of the Marquis de Maubreuil, and as a victim of the Emperor's persecutions, would have been accepted without any further inquiries. The words *secret mission,* mentioned in his passports, are quite naturally explained by the circumstances of the case, for the persons so entrusted with orders from the Provisional Government, were liable to meet detachments of the French army, or other authorities, who might have been disposed to hinder their mission, if aware that its object was to proclaim everywhere the overthrow of the Imperial Government. I can see no other possible explanation of these passports and safe-conducts which were in Maubreuil's possession when he was arrested.

Then, even as to the grounds for the supposition, that I could have conceived the idea of assassinating the Emperor Napoleon (putting quite aside, for the moment, the revolting nature of such an idea), I would fain ask, what possible interest would it be to me, to burthen myself with so odious a crime, when there was no necessity whatever for it ? Before his abdication, the Emperor was at Fontainebleau, surrounded by the glorious remains of his army, and it would not, I fancy, have entered into any one's head to go there to assassinate him. After the abdication, he was a fallen enemy, whose existence was no longer dangerous to any one. Finally, who would ever believe that the title of duke, and the government of a province would be offered to a base assassin, and that such a man as M. de Maubreuil could credit the reality of any such offers ? But I have already said more than enough to refute an accusation, if possible even more absurd than it is infamous. Therefore, in conclusion, I again repeat, that it could only have been invented by a fool or a madman.

END OF THE NINTH PART.

PART X.

THE REVOLUTION OF 1830—APPENDIX.

1830—1832.

Effect of the Revolution of July in Europe—Louis Philippe's anxiety to get his Government recognized by England—Talleyrand recalled to public life—Is sent as Ambassador to London—His arrival at Dover—Contrasts his present journey to England, with his previous one thirty-six years before, when an exile from France—Satisfactory interviews with Lord Aberdeen and the Duke of Wellington—Favourable attitude of the English Ministers towards France—Talleyrand laments the inefficiency of his staff—This is counterbalanced by the presence of his niece, the Duchesse de Dino—She becomes a great favourite in English society —Outbreak of the Revolution in Belgium—Will England maintain her policy of non-intervention ?—Lord Aberdeen thinks France and England should mediate between the King of the Netherlands and the Belgians —Mediation is not intervention—Talleyrand's sketch of William IV.— England will act in concert with France respecting Belgium and Portugal —Animated correspondence as to the seat of the Conferences—Decided eventually to hold them in London—State of affairs in Portugal—Great disquietude in France—Russia continues her war preparations—Is anxious to support the King of the Netherlands—Considers England is pledged to do the same—Copy of Count Nesselrode's secret despatch to the Russian Ambassador in London—Talleyrand's account of the opening of Parliament, after William IV.'s accession—Popular demonstrations in England in favour of Louis Philippe—Excitement over the " Reform Bill "—The Duke of Wellington's ministry resign—Formation of the new Cabinet under Lord Grey—The Princess de Lieven, wife of the Russian Ambassador—Her great influence in politics—Sketches of the different members constituting the Conference—Arrival in England of M. de Flahaut—He brings a scheme from the French Cabinet, for dividing Belgium between the powers—Talleyrand's reply—Points out the fatal policy to France of such a measure—England determines to maintain the independence of Belgium—Various names brought forward for the Belgian throne—The Belgians ask for the Duc de Nemours— Louis Philippe refuses—The rising in Poland hastens the solution of the

CHARLES MAURICE DE TALLEYRAND-PÉRIGORD, PRINCE DE BENEVENTO

FROM AN ENGRAVING BY NAPIER

Belgian question—Talleyrand's views as to the restoration of the kingdom of Poland—Letter from Mdme. Adelaide announcing the result of the trial of Charles X.'s ministers—Futile protest of the King of the Netherlands against the decision of the Conference—Prince Leopold of Saxe-Coburg refuses the Crown of Greece—It is offered to Prince Otto of Bavaria—M. Van de Weyer sent to London to offer the crown of Belgium to Prince Leopold—Efforts of M. de Celles to secure the union of Belgium with France, or the crown for the Duc de Nemours—Close of the eventful year of 1830—Appendix containing some of Prince Talleyrand's *private* correspondence.

I NEVER imagined when, in 1816, I finished the recital of some of the events of my life, and my times, that I should ever again take part in public affairs, and that, consequently, I should have reason to take up my pen again to complete this narrative. It is true, I was not wholly satisfied as to the wisdom and ability of those who then had the direction of affairs in France, but I did not think that they would lead her to ruin. For a long time, I confess, I flattered myself with the hope, that I should die peacefully in the shadow of that throne which my efforts had in some degree contributed to restore ; and if from 1816 to 1829, I was often disquieted, by seeing into what dangerous paths the government was sometimes led, my fears never went so far as to imagine the possibility of another Revolution. I tried, at different times, to give such warnings as I was able. I expressed my views, sometimes in the Chamber of Peers, sometimes in private conversation, but while doing so with caution, I nevertheless did not hesitate to point out the perils of the home and foreign policy, that had been adopted by the government, or rather had been imposed upon the government, by a party more imprudent than culpable.

When Charles X. took the foolish step, in 1829, of changing his ministry, and summoning the most unpopular men to his council, men who had no other merit than that of obedience, an obedience that was as blind, as was the obstinacy of the unfortunate king. It was impossible to conceal from ourselves, that we were hastening towards destruction.

I can here honestly declare, that I never ceased to desire the continuance of the Restoration, and this was only natural, considering the part I had taken in it ; I did nothing to disturb it, and utterly repudiate all connection with those who boast that they helped in its downfall. In 1814 and 1815 I believed, and I think so still, that France could have no solid and durable institutions, except such as were at the same time based on legitimacy, and on those liberal and wise principles, of which the Revolution of 1789 had shown the practical possibility. Such will always be my opinion and my political faith ; but from the moment that legitimacy herself betrayed her own principles, by breaking her vows, it became necessary to look to the safety of France at all hazards, and at least rescue, if it were possible, the monarchical principle, independent of legitimacy, in the great tempest thus raised. The idea of substituting the younger for the elder branch of the Royal family, similar to what had been done in England in 1688, had, as it were, become common town-talk ever since the formation of Charles X. last ministry. The newspapers, both those that were friendly and those that were inimical to this ministry, discussed it openly, it was in everyone's thoughts ; and it was by no means one of the least foolish acts of this said imbecile ministry, to have thus influenced public opinion. There was no lack of warning in this respect, but there was a decided want of that courageous loyalty and firmness, which might have arrested a feeble and credulous prince on the downward path. And that was a crime, it can be called by no other name, for it was the cause of the Revolution of July 1830. If Charles X. had not had cowardly servants, ready to sign the fatal proclamations of that period, they would necessarily have remained unpromulgated.

But be that as it may, as it is not my intention to make this a history of the faults of the Restoration, I will confine myself to the simple facts of the necessity France was under, in consequence of these faults, of choosing another government. It is the more easy for me to declare, that the choice she then made was the best possible, under the given circumstances, as I took no part whatever in its formation. I accepted it, I clung to it as to a sheet anchor, and I served it energetically ; for if this government fell, I saw nothing before us but another Republic and the terrible consequences it would entail—anarchy, a revolutionary war, and all the other evils from which France had been rescued with so much difficulty in 1815. I did not even go into the question as to whether Louis Philippe would have done better, if he had simply taken the title of lieutenant-governor of the kingdom, and refused the crown. It had been decided by the men, who had placed themselves at the head of the movement set on foot by the proclamations, and who believed that legitimate royalty would never pardon them for the part they had taken. Those men placed Louis Philippe in the dilemma, either of accepting royalty, or delivering France over to a Republic. His acceptance decided the conduct of those who wished to save their country above all things. It is easy to reason when the danger is past ; that is the only answer I will give to those who, on the day of danger, kept quietly aloof, and on the morrow appeared in public, loudly blaming and criticising, what they had not had the courage to prevent.

I saw King Louis Philippe soon after the vote of the 8th of August, which had assigned the crown to him.[1] The first subject we touched on was naturally the impression which this new Revolution would produce in Europe ; we both realized that the first step to be taken, was to procure the recognition of the principle of this Revolution by the foreign governments, and obtain, if not their good-will, at least their absolute non-interference with the home affairs of France. We naturally looked first to England, our nearest neighbour, and who, by her institutions and her past revolutions, ought to be the power best disposed towards us. The king at once sent over his aide-de-camp General Baudrand,[2] who soon returned bringing a recognition of our government by that of Great Britain, and with fairly friendly sentiments from the the English Ministry. This first step gained, the king felt, and so did I, that though this recognition would probably bring about that of the other cabinets,[3] it was in London, that the new government must seek for directions as to its foreign policy. It was therefore indispensable that an experienced ambassador should be sent there, and one already well known in Europe. The king at once offered me this somewhat difficult post. I objected on account of my great age, the activity that such a mission required,

---

[1] The voting of the Chamber took place on the 7th August.

[2] General Comte Baudrand (1774 to 1848) entered as a volunteer 1792, and served in the corps of engineers. He became colonel in 1815, and, after the Revolution of 1830, lieutenant-general and peer of France.

[3] England recognized the new French government in the end of August. In the end of October, Russia, Austria, Prussia, and Spain, and all the secondary powers of Europe likewise acknowledged it. *See* Appendix, Letter No. 6.

and the endless difficulties that were necessarily connected with it ; but I was forced to give in to the solicitations of the king and his Ministry,[1] particularly of M. Molé, at that time Minister of Foreign Affairs.   I therefore in this instance, like in so many others during the course of my life, made up my mind to be guided by the feeling of duty, and the thought of serving my country.   I thought the new government could only gain stability by the maintenance of peace, and although at that time everyone was against me and was of opinion that war was inevitable, I felt assured that my name, the services I had rendered Europe in former days, and all my efforts, would perhaps succeed in averting that most terrible of all evils, a revolutionary and general war.   I am happy to think I succeeded in this before my career was ended.

We were in the month of September, and on the 3rd, I received the following note from M. Molé :—

" It is half-past six ; I have just returned from the *Palais Royal*, dead with fatigue and with a bad headache.   The king is determined, *insists* on it more than I can tell you.   You will see and judge for yourself.   It will be discussed this evening at the council at eight o'clock.   Were I less exhausted and in less pain, I would come and tell you all about it.

" I am yours in everything and for everything.

" MOLÉ.[2]

" *Friday, 8th September,* 1830, 6.30 P.M."

Two days later the king wrote to me : " I wish to have the gratification of telling you myself, that the *Moniteur* of to-morrow will announce an appointment which I have had great pleasure in making.   If my London ambassador is disengaged to-morrow at 4 o'clock, I shall be delighted if he will come and see me.   L. P.

" *Sunday, 5th September,* 1830, 9.30 P.M."

[1] The following formed the Ministry of the 11th of August :—M. Dupont de l'Eure had received the portfolio of Minister of Justice ; Comte Molé, that of Foreign Affairs ; M. Guizot, of the Interior ; the Duc de Broglie, of Public Instruction, Religion, and President of the State Council ; Baron Louis, of Finance ; General Gérard was War Minister ; General Sebastiani, Minister of Marine, and MM. Lafitte, Casimir Perier, Dupin, and Bignon were ministers without portfolios.

[2] My reason for inserting this note will be seen later on.   I wish to say here, once for all, that I shall intersperse my Memoirs with as many letters and notes as I can, for I think the best recital in the world does not equal the articles actually written at the time when the events occurred.—(*Note by the Prince de Talleyrand.*)

Thus I was Ambassador at London, and it behoved me to make all my preparations with the utmost despatch. Lord Aberdeen[1] was Minister of Foreign Affairs in the Cabinet presided over by the Duke of Wellington. I had had intimate relations with both in 1814 and 1815, and I informed them of my appointment, by writing to Lord Aberdeen, who at once replied to me.

FOREIGN OFFICE, 20*th September*, 1830.

MON PRINCE,

I am too much flattered by your recollection of me, not to feel the necessity of expressing my feelings to you. If, during a most remarkable period, I was fortunate enough to be in accord with your Excellency, it is truly not for me to ignore this privilege and pleasure.

Allow me therefore to assure you, mon Prince, that when you arrive in England, you will find me eager to renew these friendly relations,—the more so, as I hope I am not deceived in thinking, that the principal object of your mission, is to confirm the good understanding between our two countries.

Accept . . . .

ABERDEEN.

Assured that I was understood by the man with whom I should have to do with principally, I had only to prepare for my departure. I left Paris on the 22nd of September reaching Dover on the evening of the 24th. When I heard the noise of the guns from the fortress, announcing the arrival of the French Ambassador, I could not help remembering the time, when, thirty-six years before, I had quitted these same English shores, exiled from my country by revolutionary troubles, and repulsed from British soil by the intrigues of the *émigrés;* now I returned filled with hope, and above all with the wish, to bring about at last that alliance between France and England, which I had always considered to be the most solid guarantee for the happiness of both nations, and the peace of the whole world. But what obstacles there would be to overcome, ere this end

[1] George Gordon, Earl of Aberdeen, born in 1784, was Ambassador at Vienna in 1814 at the Congress. In 1828 he became Minister of Foreign Affairs in the Duke of Wellington's Cabinet, and retired with that ministry on the 16th November, 1830. He returned to public life in November 1834 under the short Wellington ministry, as Colonial Secretary, and again in 1841 in the Peel Cabinet. In 1852 he was head of the ministry that made an offensive and defensive alliance with France. He retired in 1855, and died in 1860.

should be attained ! But if I hid them from others, in order not
to discourage them, they were none the less apparent to myself :
they were numerous, grave, and of a two-fold nature ; on the
one hand was France, with a hastily-constituted government,
fighting daily for its existence, and unable therefore to inspire
foreign powers with any real confidence. On the other hand, I
was quite aware that a Conservative and Tory ministry governed
England, and that notwithstanding its ready recognition of our
Revolution, it could not look upon it in a favourable light, more
especially after this rising in Belgium, the news of which had
reached me at Calais.[1] These were my reflections as I traversed
the rich, beautiful, and peaceable country of England, and
entered London on the 25th September, 1830. Fortunately,
however, they did not shake either my resolutions or
convictions. And this was as well, for ere long I received
letters from France which were anything but reassuring. M.
Molé wrote as follows :

PARIS, *26th September*, 1830.

MON PRINCE,
    I received your kind letter from Calais yesterday. I
saw with much pleasure, that you had borne the journey comfort-
ably. The papers, incorrect as their accounts have been, will
have informed you of what has happened here since your departure. At one time, I feared that our official correspondence
would have ceased ere it had begun. Now, I believe that it will
commence, though I cannot say how long it may continue.
Madame de Dino, whom I saw yesterday, and with whom I dine
this evening, will tell you more.
    Accept . . .

The Duc de Dalberg also wrote to me on the date of 27th of
September :—

You have but just quitted Paris, my dear Prince, and
the papers will have made known to you, the various matters
that have occupied us for the last few days ; I should there-

---

[1] On the 25th of August, the people of Brussels rose in the name of National
independence. On the 1st of September, the Prince of Orange, the eldest son of the
king, arrived beneath the walls of the town, but he was recalled by his father, who
feared that he might side with the insurgents. On the 23rd of September, his
brother, Prince Frederic, entered the town, but was forced to evacuate it after a
struggle of four days. On the 3rd of October following, a Provisional Government
proclaimed the independence of Belgium.

fore have deemed it unnecessary to write to you, if Madame de Dino had not wished to bring you something more, than the mere expressions of my sincere devotion to you.

I have sent word to you, that we were on the verge of a democratic anarchy. The ministry was about to be dissolved. Lafitte[1] was to have formed another ministry, from which I am assured the king has excluded General Lamarque[2] and Mauguin.[3]

Lafitte withdrew, when he found that ninety deputies were ranged in opposition, that petitions were being signed at the Bourse, and that the reports from the departments were unfavourable to a power that took so low a stand. It remains to be seen whether matters will continue as they are, until the end of October. The important question now is, will Belgium come to some arrangement with her sovereign, who seems to me to be very obstinate, and who does not speak out frankly and positively? If Belgium rises and resists, you will have a change of government here, followed by a war. Marshal de Trevise said to me this morning, " The Belgians have begun six months too soon," and Marshal Soult, who was next him, remarked that here we were behindhand. If diplomacy is to be carried on by opinions such as these, I would counsel you, mon Prince, to retire. You could never do anything. . . .

So much for France. The following extract from my second letter to M. Molé, will give a correct idea of the views of the English ministry with regard to us.

[1] Jacques Lafitte, born in 1767, entered the office of the banker Perregaux in 1788, whose confidence he gained completely and became his partner in 1800. At his death, he succeeded him, became governor of the bank of France in 1814, and deputy of the Chamber of Representatives in 1815. He was re-elected in 1816-17. After the Revolution of July, he joined the ministry of the 11th August, and was president of the Cabinet of the 3rd November, 1830. He retired in March, 1831. He was re-elected each time to the Chamber, except during a short interval in 1837 ; he kept his seat in the ranks of the opposition until his death (1844).

[2] Maximilien, Comte Lamarque, born in 1770, served as a volunteer in 1791, became a Brigadier-General in 1801, Chief of the Staff of the army of Naples in 1807, and General of Division the same year. During the hundred days, he was made governor of Paris, and later, Commander-in-Chief of the army of Vendée. He was exiled during the second restoration, returned to France in 1818, and was elected deputy in 1828, becoming one of the most active members of the opposition. He died of cholera in 1832. His funeral gave rise to great disturbances and occasioned much bloodshed (5th and 6th of June).

[3] François Mauguin, born in 1785, called to the bar of Paris in 1813, defended M. de Labédoyère in 1815, and was pleader in most of the political trials on the restoration. In 1827 he was elected deputy for Cote-d'Or, and from that time forth kept his seat in the Chamber, until 1851. He sided with the advanced opposition in 1830, and was the friend of General Lamarque. He died on the 4th of June, 1854.

LONDON, *September 27th,* 1830.

M. LE COMTE,

Lord Aberdeen having returned to town to-day, I have requested M. de Vaudreuil [1] to inform him of my arrival and to ask him at what time I could see him. He answered immediately that he was ready for me, and would not go out. I had every reason to be satisfied with this first interview. He most kindly told me, that when he heard of my arrival in London, he had shortened his stay in the country and hastened back to town. Although my visit was a lengthy one, we touched only (as I intended we should) on general topics, into which I could easily introduce those principles which govern the policy of France. To do this I had only to remember the instructions the king had given me. I could see at once, that his Britannic Majesty's minister was far more ready to praise, than to combat them. I could not but be satisfied with what he said on this subject.

On leaving Lord Aberdeen, I went to the Duke of Wellington, who had also returned this morning. Here also I had every reason to be well pleased with the reception accorded to the king's minister. The Duke's sentiments were quite favourable to the state of things which *fortunately,*[2] now exists in France. Nevertheless, as in the course of our conversation, he made use of the word *unfortunate* in speaking of the Revolution, brought on by the foolish actions of the late government, I thought I ought to take notice of this expression, and said that no doubt it had been suggested to him, by a very natural feeling of pity for those, whom this Revolution had dethroned; but that he must feel convinced that it was not a misfortune, either for France—saved by it from the terrible position in which the policy of the late government had placed it—or for the other States, with whom we are desirous of remaining on friendly terms, and from which we shall never deviate, if, as we have the right to demand, the dignity of France is always respected.

After this observation of mine, made in a somewhat excited tone, the duke rather withdrew the expression he had used, by hastening to endorse the view I had suggested to him.

I believe, M. le Comte, that I can certainly augur, from these first interviews, that the personal feelings of the English ministers will not complicate the difficulties that may arise from the very nature of the matters I shall have to treat of with them.

Lord Aberdeen has not yet been able to tell me at what date

---

[1] Victor Louis Rigaud, Vicomte de Vaudreuil, was born in 1799, entered the diplomatic service in 1815 and had been secretary at the Hague, at Cassel, at London, and at Lisbon. In 1830 he was Chief Secretary in London. He was soon after appointed minister at Weimar, and then at Munich, where he died in 1834.

[2] Suppressed in the text of the archives.

the king can grant me an audience, nor whether it will be in London or at Brighton.

These letters and despatches will suffice to prove the great delicacy of my position here. The future (which fortunately for man is hidden from him) did not reveal to me, how greatly this position would be still further embarrassed by fresh complications, and I therefore set to work with good courage.

My staff at the embassy was but a mediocre one ; it had been in great part arranged for me ere I left Paris, and I was forced to make many changes, before it was as effective as it afterwards became. But, on the other hand, my niece, the Duchesse de Dino, had consented to accompany me to London, and I knew that her charming manner and disposition, would greatly assist me in conciliating that very exclusive English society, the goodwill of which, I saw with pleasure, she very quickly gained. It was no easy matter, however, for the majority of the English aristocracy had not accepted our revolution as readily as the ministry had done ; and in this aristocracy, there were besides outside influences at work (to which I shall have occasion to refer to later), which were in active operation against us on our first arrival, but which we succeeded, though not without some trouble, in overcoming.

Events rapidly took a more serious aspect in Belgium. The revolt in Brussels, changed into a general rising over the whole country, and partly through the fault of the government and its unpopularity, and partly from the desire to imitate what had taken place in France, a revolution, as complete as ours, had taken place, with only this marked difference ; that whereas in France, the revolution was partly the result of the ungodliness of the clergy, in Belgium it was the clergy themselves who instigated it. A serious lesson given to all governments, who had once again, to learn the double danger, of favouring one religion more than another (as was done in the Netherlands), or of vesting the religion in the government, as was attempted in France.

This incident of the Belgian revolution, singularly increased the difficulties of our first relations with the English Government ; for if I was obliged, from the commencement, to utilize in favour of our revolution, the principle of non-intervention, generally adopted by this Government, I nevertheless could not forget, that the creation of the kingdom of the Netherlands,[1] by the union of Belgium and Holland, had, in 1814, been the work of England, and of those same English statesmen, whom I now again found in power in 1830. Would these men consent to accept the consequences of the principles of non-intervention, the result of which would be the overthrow of a combination, adopted out of hatred or fear of France, when this same France must appear still more dangerous to them, after the revolution she had just effected? A very delicate primary question to lay before the English ministers!

I nevertheless did not hesitate to do so, as soon as the news reached London, that the Dutch had been repulsed from Brussels, and that the King of the Netherlands was quite unable to re-establish his power in Belgium.

I must do the English Government the justice to say, that it at once and most loyally, recognized the rights of the principle of non-intervention; but its application to the present case, presented certain considerations which were not without force. The following was the view taken by the Cabinet:

"If it is proved that the King of the Netherlands cannot possibly restore order in his country, it is none the less important to the interests of Europe, that matters should not remain in the state they are in at present. We cannot, neither can you any more than we, remain indifferent to what is happening there. Thus, while supporting the principle of non-intervention, it is necessary that we should together, find means to prevent those States, which fear the spread of the revolutionary spirit, from taking such violent action, as would render a war inevitable. Would it not be possible by judicious advice, to effect a reconciliation, advantageous to both Holland and Belgium, by which each, in making some sacrifice, would obtain the essential part of what she had a right to demand? Giving advice is not interfering, if he who gives it, makes no attempt to follow it up by coercion. By not overstepping this friendly position, the

---

[1] Since the year 1815 the Dutch Constitution, which had been extended to Belgium, had been submitted for approbation to the leading men of Belgium. It was rejected by 796 votes against 527, and among the members of the majority, 126 had specially given, as the reason for their vote "*the articles relating to religion.*"

independence of the State so counselled is not hurt, and no other
Government could possibly take umbrage at it. All Europe
agreed to the formation of the Netherlands in 1814. It would be
a great mistake to suppose, that if the dismemberment of that
kingdom is allowed, the peace of Europe would not be disturbed."

Lord Aberdeen said in conclusion, that it was the duty of
the Powers who could in any way influence the King of the
Netherlands, to use that influence now, but only in the way of
persuasion, and carefully avoiding any steps which might be
interpreted as having a different character, in order to prevail
upon the two parties, frankly to make concessions, so that an
understanding might be arrived at ; and that as France and
England were alone in a position to act, they should do so at
once, the urgency of the circumstances requiring it ; and he therefore thought it fell to them, to offer their advice in this matter.

These considerations had the more weight in my eyes, that
having no reason to doubt the sincerity of the intentions of the
English Government, I saw herein from the very first, the
necessity it felt of concerting with us in a matter in which its
interests were involved. It therefore seemed to me quite out
of the question that we should entrench ourselves behind the
general principle of non-intervention, and take up a passive
attitude, which was not without danger to the peace of Europe,
and by which we should lose part of the influence the English
Government seem desirous we should possess. I therefore supported in Paris, the views that Lord Aberdeen presented through
Lord Stuart of Rothesay, the English ambassador there.

On the 6th October, while awaiting the answer from Paris
to these proposals, I had an audience of the King of England, at
which I presented my credentials.[1] On that occasion I addressed
the following speech to him :

Sire, His Majesty the King of the French has chosen me
as the interpreter of his feelings towards your Majesty.

I gladly accepted a mission which gave so noble an object
to the last days of my career.

Sire, of all the vicissitudes that my great age has witnessed,
of all the divers changes that forty years teeming with events,
have mingled in my life, perhaps none has so completely fulfilled
my wishes as the selection which brings me back to this happy

[1] See Appendix, Letter No. 6

country. But what a difference between the two periods ! The jealousies, the prejudices that have so long divided France from England, have now given place to feelings of esteem and enlightened affection. Common interests will draw the ties between the two countries still closer. England repudiates abroad equally with France, the principle of intervention in the home affairs of her neighbours, and the ambassador of a sovereign chosen unanimously by a great nation, feels himself at ease on a soil of liberty, and near a descendant of the illustrious house of Brunswick. I appeal with confidence to your goodwill, sire, with reference to the matters I am charged to bring to your notice, and I pray you to graciously accept the homage of my profoundest respect.

William IV., to whom I was accredited, had been in the navy, and had retained the tone and manners which that service generally gives. He was an honest man, rather narrow-minded, and whom the Whig party had always counted in its ranks ; nevertheless, since his recent accession to the throne (26th June, 1830) he had retained the Tory ministry of his brother and predecessor, George IV. He received me very kindly, stammered a few friendly phrases in his incorrect French about King Louis Philippe, and expressed the pleasure he had felt on hearing that the *Sociétés populaires*[1] had been closed in Paris. I wish to say here, so that I need not refer to it again, that during the four years of my embassy in London, I have nothing but praise to record of the behaviour of the King and Queen of England, who eagerly took every opportunity of making themselves pleasant both to me and to my niece, the Duchesse de Dino.

Before M. Molé's answer to the proposals of the English Cabinet reached me, I received two letters from him, which contained some quite unfounded reproaches.[2] The following extract from the despatch which I sent him on the 6th of October, after seeing the king, will sufficiently explain both the nature of the reproaches, and the small foundation for them :—

. . . . We must not reproach Lord Aberdeen for not having made known to me, a demand for assistance which

---

[1] It is not quite right that the *clubs* were shut up at this date (6th October). It is true that on the 25th of the preceding September, a discussion had taken place in the Chamber on this subject, and MM. Guizot and Dupin had urged the Cabinet to take vigorous action, but the ministers had refused to discuss it. Nevertheless the same evening the *Société des Ami du Peuple*, situated in the Rue Montmartre, was invaded and dispersed by the inhabitants of that quarter of the town.

[2] See Appendix, Letters Nos. 3 and 5.

he was said to have received from the Government of the Netherlands. I can give you the assurance that no such step had been taken, and that nothing of the sort has occurred. Fears have been expressed, needs have been revealed, troubles and difficulties have been spoken of, but no positive demand had been made. The actual request for support and assistance only arrived this evening at midnight. Lord Aberdeen has just confirmed what I have written to you on this subject. The English Government will not reply until it has come to some arrangement with us. This arrangement is now eagerly desired by the English cabinet, and it seems to me that to arrive at such a result, not much time has been lost between the 27th of September and the 3rd of October, *when I wrote to you.*[1] I deemed it preferable that the proposal should come from the English Government, and I am still of this opinion, without however greatly insisting on it, since I have seen the letter—I mention this in passing—which you wrote to the Duke of Wellington, without informing me of the fact, that overtures were being made on our side. This, however, is not a point of real importance. The affair is on the right road, and the favourable dispositions here are on the increase. Every means are sought in thorough good faith, to solve the difficulty, and you will meet with very few obstacles on the part of the English government. Those which it will make, will have reference to undertakings named in special treaties, but objections of this nature are not insurmountable when a powerful government really wishes to settle matters.

Lord Aberdeen told me some days ago, that we were to have a conference on the affairs of Portugal, but he added that there was no immediate hurry. I will therefore write to you later on as to this matter. It will be difficult for you,[2] to get the English Government to recognize (according to my instructions) the government of Terceira as an actual government;[3] for it is an undoubted fact that it emanates from Dom Pedro, that it is paid by him, and that he nominates its members. When you come to treat of this question, this is the objection that England will probably raise.

When going away the King said to me, "*Au revoir à Brighton,*" and I think I shall go there, as soon as I find that affairs no longer require my presence here. . . .

As I was informed that it was thought in Paris I had not written frequently enough during the weeks I had been in

---

[1] Suppressed in the text of the archives.   [2] Var.: "*nous*"="us."
[3] The island of Terceira (Azores) was the seat of Queen Donna Maria's government during the usurpation of Dom Miguel (1829—1833).

London, and that uneasiness was expressed thereat,[1] I did not rely on my despatch of the 8th October having been read, but wrote a private letter to M. Molé, which I here insert, in order to show in what spirit I intended carrying out the mission entrusted to me.

LONDON, *8th November*, 1830.

We know one another, we love one another, we desire the same things; we understand them in the same way, we wish them to be carried out similarly, our point of departure is the same, our goal is the same. Why then, being on the same road, do we not understand each other? There is something here which I cannot comprehend, and which I trust, is but of a passing nature.

Our correspondence is neither friendly nor official; I think that it should be otherwise between us, and I come, with all my old friendship, to pray you, that it may be so. A less complete confidence, a less intimate understanding, might seriously harm, impede, or delay affairs; our friendship would suffer, and this would grieve me greatly. If my way of carrying on affairs is out of date, it would be better to tell me so frankly. Let us then be quite open with one another; we can do no real good, unless we treat affairs with that ease and frankness, which begets confidence. You will find that I shall always tell you everything, except what I think is of no importance; it was thus I carried on affairs with the emperor, as well as with Louis XVIII. I know that modern France does not hold with this old style; that she is, what is called *progressive;* but standing here on the soil of ancient Europe, I feel that we must leave these matters to time, and that undue haste is too much opposed to English habits not to somewhat lessen the degree of weight which we must give to all our proceedings. The English Government, you may rest assured, is well inclined towards us.

With kindest regards. . . .

Together with this letter, I sent a despatch, giving a full account of what the ministry knew and thought of Belgian affairs. Prussia, to whom the King of the Netherlands had also appealed for help, replied that she would only act in concert with England. It was thought that Austria would do the same, but nothing of course was as yet known, as to the views of St.

---

[1] Madame Adelaide had made herself the interpreter of the prince's sentiments (see Appendix, letter 7, written to him on the 8th of October. M. de Talleyrand replied to it on the 29th, justifying himself, letter 11).

Petersburg, on this question. Much uneasiness has been felt at Prince Frederic of the Netherlands'[1] march on Brussels.

The same day these letters were sent off, M. Bresson,[2] chief clerk at M. Molé's office, arrived in London, having been made first secretary of my embassy, in place of M. Challaye, who had been sent to Smyrna as consul-general. I had need of such reinforcement for the daily work, which required much time.

The reply from Paris to the overtures of the English Government arrived at last : the answer was virtually an acceptance of the English proposals, but at the same time expressing a resolute desire, that the conferences on the Belgian question, should take place in Paris. M. Molé's reply to my letter was written in a very friendly spirit, and all appeared to be going on smoothly.

When I acquainted Lord Aberdeen with the wishes of the French Government, relative to the locality for the conferences, he said he must consult his colleagues on this matter, though he himself saw no objection. He soon however informed me, that at a cabinet council, at which the proposal of the French Government had been submitted, he and his colleagues had decided that it could not be accepted. The Duke of Wellington, whom I saw after this communication, told me the reasons which had decided them to reject our proposal. They considered, he said, that under the circumstances, the question of time was everything ; that it was all important to discuss and decide matters quickly, and that everything was ready in London, for arriving at a prompt and definite decision. He considered that this was quite in our interest, for our position, notwithstanding the recognition of the powers, would not be assured, until after the pacification of Belgium, and he added, that it was now also important for England, that this position should not only be assured, but that it should also be great and powerful. He thought he was sure of the foreign ministers who would be

---

[1] Frederic-Guillaume-Charles, Prince of the Netherlands, son of King William I., was born in 1797, made administrator-general of the war department and admiral, by his father. In 1830 he was placed at the head of the army, that was to operate against Brussels. He entered that town on the 22nd of September, but was forced to evacuate it after a struggle of four days.

[2] Charles Comte Bresson, born in 1798, entered the diplomatic service under the Restoration. In 1830 was appointed chief secretary at London, and in 1833 *chargé d'affaires* at Berlin. In November 1834 he became Minister of Foreign Affairs, and was created a peer of France. In 1841 he went as ambassador to Madrid. and in 1847 to Naples, and committed suicide a few days after his arrival there.

summoned to the conference, if it was held in London ; many indeed had their credentials already, and those who had not yet got them, would follow the lead of the others, and all would sign what France and England wished. He greatly doubted whether it would be the same in Paris, where the foreign ministers would not venture to sign anything, without first consulting their respective courts. A few days lost now, might complicate matters to such an extent, that it would be extremely difficult to remedy them, or come to any mutual understanding.

I tried in vain to combat these views, according to the instructions I had received from Paris. I pointed out specially, the word *resolute* contained in those instructions ; but I could gain nothing, and was only able to write to Paris, that from whichever side the concession came, whether from France or England, France would find the English cabinet equally well disposed towards her.

I must nevertheless admit that on this point I agreed with the English Cabinet for reasons hardly yet realized. It did not seem to me advisable to assemble the conference in the midst of Paris, given up either to riots or daily disturbances, and when the precarious position of the Government, disquieted by the coming trial of the ministers of Charles X.,[1] could not inspire any confidence in the foreign ministers, charged with maintaining the peace of Europe. Besides I knew that in Paris M. Pozzo[2] would be the leading spirit at the conference, owing to the influence he had over M. Molé : and the Duke of Wellington's reputation in Europe seemed to me preferable to that of Pozzo. Nevertheless I did my utmost, to induce the English ministers to agree to Paris, as the scene of the negotiation. But I still believe that they did wisely in refusing to comply with this request.[3]

There was, besides, another question, which at that time complicated the relations between the new French Government and England, *i.e.*, the affairs of Portugal. I have already alluded

---

[1] The trial of the Ministers was to commence on the 15th of December before the Chamber of Peers.

[2] Count Pozzo de Borgo was at that time Russian ambassador at Paris.

[3] M. de Talleyrand in his private correspondence insists repeatedly on the great influence of the Duke of Wellington, on his European reputation, and on the necessity of fixing the seat of the conferences in London. (See Appendix, letters No. 8 and No. 10.)

to them, but it is necessary here, briefly to recall the facts, in order to understand the question better.[1]

It will be remembered that Dom Miguel, having returned to Portugal, had, with the consent of the powers, taken up the government of the country until his niece, Dona Maria, whom he was to marry, came of age. It was thought, that in this way the difficult question as to the rights of Dom Pedro (Dona Maria's father, who on being made Emperor of Brazil, had renounced the crown of Portugal) and the pretensions of Dom Miguel, who after this renunciation had claimed the crown of Portugal, might become reconciled. Dom Miguel however had no sooner entered Portugal, than he threw aside the mask, and broke all his promises. He abolished the constitution, governed the kingdom in his own name, and relentlessly persecuted his nieces' partisans, who were at the same time the partisans of the constitutional institutions granted by King John VI. The emperor Dom Pedro, enraged at this conduct, sent an expedition

---

[1] In order to understand the position of Portugal, it is necessary to refer to events some little way back. King John VI. died in 1826, after having accepted, and actively worked out the constitution imposed by the Cortes in 1821. He left two sons, the eldest Dom Pedro remained in Brazil, when his family returned to Lisbon (in 1821) and was proclaimed Emperor of Brazil (1822) having, together with his father, signed a treaty in 1825, according to the terms of which, the separation of the two states was recognized, and the two crowns were never again to be united. The second son, Dom Miguel, had always protested against the constitutional tendencies of his father, and had even stirred up plots against him.

Before King John died, he instituted a provisional regency under the presidency of his daughter, Isabella Marie, until *the wishes of him to whom the crown belonged were made known.* This ambiguous wording was the cause of long-continued troubles. On the one hand, Dom Pedro declared himself King of Portugal, notwithstanding the treaty of separation of 1825. He, however, abdicated very soon after, having granted a new constitution, in favour of his daughter Dona Maria da Gloria, whom he destined to marry Dom Miguel, thinking by this union, to reconcile the two branches of the family. But Dom Miguel, after making a pretence of submission, and with the concurrence of his mother and his uncle Ferdinand VII., King of Spain, as well as the moral support of the principal courts of Europe, who looked with displeasure on the establishment of constitutional ideas in Portugal, raised the standard of absolutism October 1826. The Miguelists were at first victorious: the Regent Isabelle Marie resigned her power in favour of Dom Miguel, and the Cortes proclaimed him King of Portugal, July 1828. Then a general civil war broke out. The town of Oporto declared in favour of Queen Maria, and the greatest terror was spread all over the country. Meanwhile the Emperor Dom Pedro wished to uphold his daughter's rights by force of arms. The Azores having declared for her, became the rallying point of the Constitutionalists. A regency was established there in the name of the young queen in 1830, but it was not recognized by the continental courts. Dom Miguel was even able, as legitimate sovereign, to negotiate a loan of fifty millions. Such were the respective positions of the two parties, when the revolution of July, by a counter-stroke, changed the whole face of matters in Portugal. Dom Miguel lost the support of France and England. He was forced to resign. And the Queen, Maria da Gloria, ascended the throne in 1834.

from Brazil, composed entirely of Portuguese, who had settled in Terceira and who, not being powerful enough to land in Portugal with any chance of success, had proclaimed Dona Maria's government in the island, together with the charter which Dom Pedro had given to Portugal, before abdicating the throne of that country in favour of his daughter.

Up to the time of my arrival in London, Dom Miguel's government, and the changes he had made, were not recognized by the Powers, neither was the government established in the island of Terceira.

The new French government would have liked England to pronounce in favour of the Regency installed at Terceira, whereas the cabinets of the other great powers, with England at their head, leant towards Dom Miguel. It is easy to understand the motives which influenced both one side and the other. France, having just ended a liberal revolution, naturally wished to support her political principles wherever she saw they existed ; she might have met with sympathy from England on this point had not the interests of the latter placed an obstacle in the way. The truth was that England was not at all sure that the majority of the Portuguese nation did not prefer the rule of Don Miguel, and above all she felt convinced that any struggle would cause great disturbances between her commerce and that of Portugal, a commerce of such great importance that the latter country might almost be looked upon as an English colony. The Duke of Wellington's Tory ministry, even while blaming Dom Miguel's infamous conduct, would have preferred to uphold his government and thus avoid civil war, fresh revolutions, and all those changes so hurtful to commercial relations. The cabinets of Vienna, Berlin, and St. Petersburg were all influenced by the same motives as England, and Dom Miguel, cruel despot as he was, had gained their favour, as representing a monarchy without a constitutional government. Thus it was not easy to reconcile such very opposite views.

I thought therefore, that troubled as we were **at** home, both by our own affairs and those of Belgium, it would have been unwise to quarrel with England respecting Portugal. I determined to work according to my instructions, and urge the English cabinet to separate themselves from Dom Miguel's party and acknowledge the Regency of the island of Terceira, but to do so with moderation, in order not to compromise our good relations on other questions. I referred specially to the faults of Dom Miguel, which gave me fair grounds to work upon. In October 1830, Lord Aberdeen and his cabinet still believed that they would be able to obtain a general amnesty from Dom Miguel, as the price of England's recognition, and it was by means of this measure, that they hoped to justify themselves to the Liberals in England, for having recognized the odious tyranny of Dom Miguel.

On the 19th of October, in sending an account of the state of the Portuguese question to Paris, I wrote the following :

The news we have received from Portugal describes that unhappy country as given up entirely to the distrust and fury of Dom Miguel. The effect of this, however, will not be to retard the recognition of his government by the Powers, that is a matter which has already been pretty well decided, self-interest raising it above all other considerations. There is reason to believe even now, that the amnesty, insisted on from Dom Miguel, as a primary condition, will only be promised as it were, and not carried into effect, until a distant period, mutually agreed on, between the English government and Dom Miguel. The ordinary usages will not even therefore be observed. This morning I pointed out to Lord Aberdeen what a scandal would result therefrom. He assured me that the amnesty would necessarily follow the recognition ; but I do not feel disposed to put much faith in this.

Such was at this period, the state of the Portuguese question to which I shall have to refer several times. We will now revert to the Belgian affair, a much graver matter, since it threatened to disturb the whole of Europe. The French government, that is to say M. Molé, notwithstanding the necessity there was for urgency in this matter, vehemently insisted that the conferences should take place in Paris. I received still more urgent instructions on this point, which I was obliged to communicate to the English government. I will here give another extract from the despatch in which I

gave an account on the 25th of October, of the fresh explanations I had had with the Duke of Wellington :—

I have not lost a moment in pressing for a decision conformably to the wishes expressed in your despatch of the 20th
ult. I spoke again about it yesterday to the Duke of Wellington, who then discussed the subject with the Austrian ambassador and the Prussian minister. I brought forward your
arguments and developed and enlarged upon them ; I don't
think I omitted a single plea that could convince them. But
they all three took the same view. The late occurrences in
Paris seemed rather to have strengthened their opposition.
They see in our persistency to hold the conference there, somewhat of a desire to discuss the Belgian question in the midst of
what they call the revolutionary whirlpool ; and this opinion
they maintain, having the French journals in their hands. In
this they certainly do not sufficiently separate the king's
government, from the factious influences against which it has to
fight. But their disquietude explains their errors.

This disquietude is very great, and is fully justified by facts,
of the exact truth of which, you are better aware than I am.
They say they have been informed that some French officers who
are fighting in the ranks of the Belgians, have not been censured
in any way by the king's government, and that notwithstanding the promises given (for these were admitted) to repulse all
the overtures and solicitations of the Belgians, and to abstain from
all direct or indirect co-operation, in the success of their cause,
these officers (whose number no doubt is exaggerated) are
kept on the strength of the French army. The name of M. de
Pontecoulant is often brought up in connection with this
subject. They think that sufficiently effective measures have
not been taken, to put a stop to the expedition of the Spanish
refugees.[1] They have seen several French names, among
those sent them from Spain, which have awakened their
suspicions. I should be hiding the truth, if I did not tell you,
that the feelings of the cabinets and their ministers have changed

---

[1] The reaction which had followed the return of King Ferdinand to absolute
power, had decided several liberal Spaniards to seek refuge abroad. After the revolution of July, they formed themselves into revolutionary committees, with the view of
attempting a bold stroke and entering Spain by force of arms. The government of
Madrid appealed to the cabinets of Paris and London. The latter took some
stringent measures, but in France the government either could not or would not put
a stop to the enterprise. Colonel Francisco Valdès and the celebrated Mina, penetrated
into Navarre at the head of 500 men, and took possession of the town of d'Urdax.
This expedition failed. Beaten and driven back, the revolutionary troops were obliged
to re-pass the frontier.

somewhat towards us ; their anxiety has been awakened, now that their security seems likely to be endangered. The Duke of Wellington specially remarked, that the action of the king's government, should tend to reassure the different Powers as to the state of agitation in France which absorbs the attention of all Europe. The ministers would see in the concession made now, a common, and consequently conciliatory action, if you accede to their proposition to hold the conferences in London, where the five great Powers have men, fully possessing their confidence. They agree in saying, that these conferences ought to be held at the Hague. The former engagements of Europe have induced them to take this view : and in abandoning it, they specially take into consideration the urgency of the circumstances, and the great need of expedition, which according to them can only be effectually attained in London, where they again assert, every one is ready, while no one is so elsewhere. They declare that we shall isolate ourselves from the other Powers by insisting on taking a contrary step ; that much precious time will be wasted, and that the weeks or rather days, which change the state of affairs in' Belgium, also change the feelings and views of the cabinets.

You will perceive, M. le Comte, that I am reporting exactly what I have been told, and that I refrain from all personal opinions. The Duke of Wellington told me he had written a letter to you, in which he gave his reasons for his persistence. I have tried in vain to combat them ; the state of Paris too completely pre-occupies both his mind and that of the ministers accredited here ; and they cannot consider the centre of such great excitement a suitable place for diplomatic discussions. But these discussions, which according to them, cannot take place there, do not appear to them less urgently necessary elsewhere ; however quickly the events in Belgium may progress, whatever arrangements may be made between the Prince of Orange and the Belgians, the success either of the provisional government or of the prince, will not, according to them settle the question. The union of the Netherlands has been guaranteed by the great Powers ; *that is the state of affairs which has been recognized;* what still remains to be recognized is *the state of affairs which has been substituted ;* and then the important question of fortresses will inevitably reappear.[1]

---

[1] The treaties of 1815 in creating the kingdom of the Netherlands, only desired to place a barrier between France and the northern powers. To this effect they had given to the new kingdom, a strong line of fortresses ; Courtray, Tournai, Mons, Charleroi, Namur, Liège, Luxemburg, Philippeville, Marienbourg, and Bouillon, intended as a check against any enterprises on the part of France. These fortresses were to be kept in thorough efficiency by the King of Holland. The allied sovereigns

Amid the difficulties that such delicate deliberations will bring about, when concessions will be required on all sides, and previous engagements will have to be amended, they consider that many things will have to be settled by word of mouth, and that conferences therefore are worth more than memorandums, or any other political documents ; and this remark is perfectly true.

There remained another and still more powerful reason, concerning which the Duke of Wellington and the ministers spoke to me separately yesterday. They pointed out to me that the English parliament was about to assemble ; that the king would have to give his views on the Belgian question, and that his speech would have immense weight and importance. Should he say that conferences have, or have not, been opened in London, his declaration will, one way or the other, have either a tranquillizing or disquieting effect. They even go so far as to assert, that this announcement may entirely change the whole aspect of affairs, and that it is therefore most important his speech should be as reassuring as possible.

Here again, M. le Comte, I pray you not to believe that my opinion coincides with these observations of the English cabinet and the foreign ministers. I have not yielded a single point, I have tried to modify opinions which appeared to me too decided, but they are too important, and indicate too marked a change from the former views of the Powers, for me not to make them known to you, such as I found them. I send this despatch by M. de Chenoise, to whom I recommend all speed ; you will no doubt deem it necessary to send him back with a prompt and decisive answer. The English parliament opens on the 2nd November.

Four days later, on the 29th October I sent some further details to M. Molé, which, without having direct reference to the question of the seat of the conference, were nevertheless of a nature to cause some reflection as to the views of the Powers :—

. . . There is no doubt, that an unlimited credit has been opened for Charles X. with an Edinburgh banker.[1]   This

had even a right of watch and inspection over them. If the state of affairs created in 1815 was done away with, Europe would lose this precious guarantee against the still dreaded iniquities of France. What then would happen, if this line of fortresses were to fall into the hands of a new kingdom, the friend and ally of the very nation against which it had been directed?

[1] Var.: "chez le *premier banquier d'Edimbourg, dont le nom est, je crois, Forbes,*" = "with the principal banker in Edinburgh, whose name I believe is Forbes."

strange generosity has greatly astonished and occupied the English.[1] It is generally attributed to the Emperor Nicholas, and I am the less inclined to doubt this, knowing how very unfavourably he is disposed towards us.   He is passionately devoted to foreign matters, which in his own mind he mixes up with the home affairs of his kingdom.   In several instances he has expressed himself on the actual state of affairs in anything but pacific terms.   He believes that nothing but force will arrest the doctrines of disorder.   These prejudices might easily shake M. Pozzo, who has striven to lead the emperor's views[2] in another direction.   M. de Matusiewicz[3] who held the same opinions and worked in accord with him, is not himself at all sure about it now.   The strangest thing, and which yet is nevertheless a fact, is that M. de Metternich does not now take the same view as the Emperor Nicholas, but he could very easily be brought round again.   The Prussian cabinet is divided. The Prince Royal,[4] and M. Ancillon,[5] are all for war ; M. Guillaume de Humboldt,[6] brother of the *savant* in Paris, and M. de Bernstorff,[7] would like if possible, to avoid it.   This is a very critical period.   Events in Belgium are very complicated. Those of Spain add still further to the difficulties.   M. de Zea Bermudez[8] has received no news of any kind from his government for some days ; and his anxiety is great.

[1] M. de Talleyrand, kept the court of the Tuileries minutely informed as to the life of Charles X., the princes and their suites.   See Appendix, letters No. 4—No. 18.

[2] Variante, "*sur les evênements de Paris*" = "as to the events in Paris."

[3] André Joseph, Comte de Matusiewicz, at that time temporary Russian minister in England during the absence of Prince de Lieven.   He was the son of Thaddeus de Matusiewicz, a Polish noble, who had been Minister of Finance in the Grand Duchy of Warsaw in 1812.

[4] Frederick William (1795—1861) son of King Frederick William III., who ascended the throne in 1840.

[5] Jean Pierre Frederic Ancillon, descended from a Protestant family, originally of Metz, who had taken refuge in Berlin, after the revocation of the Edict of Nantes. Born in 1766, he decided to enter the Church, became known by his philosophical and historical works, and in 1806 was appointed governor to the Prince Royal of Prussia.   Later on he entered the Foreign Office, became leader of the political section (1825) and minister in June 1831.   He died in 1837.

[6] William de Humboldt at this time did not fill any public position.   He had just quitted the ministry.   His brother Alexander, the celebrated *savant*, had come to Paris after the July Revolution, commissioned officially to recognize King Louis-Philippe.

[7] Christian, Comte de Bernstorff, born in 1769, descended from a Danish family, was first Danish ambassador at Berlin and Stockholm, and Minister of Foreign Affairs in 1797.   He resigned in 1810, and in 1811, was appointed ambassador at Paris. In 1815 he represented Denmark at the Congress of Vienna.   In 1818 he entered the service of the King of Prussia, who made him Minister of Foreign Affairs, and whom he represented at the various conferences of the Holy Alliance.   In 1830 M. Ancillon was sent to assist him, and finally he replaced him in 1831.   M. de Bernstorff died a few months after.

[8] Francois Zea de Bermudez, born in 1772, was a Spanish statesman.   He began as Secretary to the Embassy, and was then made minister at Constantinople, and

I expect the answer to the despatch I sent you by M. de Chenoise, either to-morrow or Sunday.

At last this despatch arrived, which had only been written by M. Molé at the last minute on the afternoon of the 31st of October. I will give it here *in extenso*, that others may the better judge of the spirit that dictated it, and how little reassuring were the news it brought me :

PARIS, 31*st October*, 1830.
Sunday, 3 P.M.

I had retarded the departure of M. de Chenoise until I could announce the formation of the Ministry to you.[1] But the letter which I have this evening received from the Duke of Wellington, will not, mon Prince, allow me to delay. I would send you a copy of my reply, but that I had not even time to have it copied. The King has charged me to authorize you to join the conference at once, and take part in everything that may have reference to Belgian affairs. Were I still Minister I should perhaps send you either to-morrow or the day after, a plenipotentiary, fully instructed, and I need hardly say that I should have selected one as much as possible in conformity with your views. As however the urgency of the circumstances obliges you to commence negotiations by yourself, I believe that you will be able to carry them through to the end without any assistance. Many things may arise out of this Belgian question, without reckoning on war or peace. No one knows better than you, mon Prince, all that it embraces, and therefore it will be best to leave it entirely in your hands.

We have just passed through a most stormy week, and for no one, perhaps, has it been a more anxious time, than for me. I am not mistaken as to the source of the efforts made to aid me, but they were such that it would be impossible for me to

later at London. In 1824 he was appointed Minister of Foreign Affairs, but only kept this post one year. He went as ambassador to London in 1828, and remained there till 1832. He then returned to Madrid, and was Prime Minister there for a short time, but had to leave his country, when the Liberal policy of minister Martiney de la Rosa triumphed in 1844. Returning to Spain, he entered the Senate in 1845, and died in 1850.

[1] The Ministry was replaced on November 2nd by a new cabinet. It was composed as follows : M. Lafitte, President of the Council, and Minister of Finance ; Marshal Maison, Minister of Foreign Affairs ; Dupont de l'Eure, Keeper of the Seals ; the Comte de Montalivet, Minister of the Interior ; Mérilhon, Minister of Public Education and Religion ; Marshal Gerard, Minister of War ; General Sebastiani, Minister of Marine.

give you any idea of the situation in which I was placed. Nothing has yet been decided. Both parties of the Government have several times already refused to remain in office, but they have both always been obliged, owing to the state of affairs, to come in again and try the effect of a coalition ministry. M. de Broglie and M. Guizot are now quite out of the question, which greatly complicates it according to my view, and also as far as I, personally, am concerned. If I retire however, I shall leave our foreign relations on the best possible footing, or at any rate the least unfavourable. I have received very satisfactory assurances from Berlin ; they do us justice both as regards Belgium, and all other species of propaganda ; they show us entire confidence, and would be quite willing that the conferences should take place at Paris. The Berlin Cabinet would even have proposed this to the Cabinet of St. Petersburg, asking their consent thereto. Let the Duke of Wellington be informed of this, I pray you, that he may see that it is to his wishes we yield. The truth is, he has been far less accommodating than any of the others. My opinion, well thought out, and I believe fairly argued, is, that it would be better for everything and every body, that the conferences should take place here ; but, if they are to be held in London, they cannot, as far as France is concerned, do without you, and the second plenipotentiary would be entirely useless. I owe you several letters, but I do so everywhere, and to all who write to me. For the last six days I have been in consultation, from six in the morning till twelve at night, respecting the arrangement of the Ministry.

Adieu, mon Prince, you may, I can assure you, consider yourself fortunate not to be here. The elections are very satisfactory, but a Ministry will be formed anyway. I always thought this would be inevitable.

Accept. . . . . MOLÉ.

This letter requires some comment in order to point out its contradictions and errors. M. Molé, though with evident reluctance, gave in to the question of the seat of the conferences ; he agreed to their being held in London, nevertheless maintaining that it would have been better to have held them in Paris ; yet in the same breath what a picture does he draw of the state of that capital, of its government and its ministry, one portion of which disputes the power of the other ! And this is the spectacle he would like to exhibit to the plenipotentiaries of the great European Powers, who are charged with maintaining peace,

based on the strength of the opposition of the French Government to revolutionary tendencies.[1]   Truly it would be impossible
to understand such an idea, except by seeking the explanation
in a personal matter, namely the desire to carry through the
negotiations himself.   They would not however have remained
long in his hands, as forty-eight hours after he had written that
letter he was dismissed from the office of Minister of Foreign
Affairs, which post passed into the very inexperienced hands (as
will be admitted) of Marshal Maison.[2]

I put on one side all that is unpleasant as regards myself in
this letter, and his intention of sending me a second plenipotentiary if he had continued as minister.   All that is of small
interest ; but what is important, is the erroneous view he took
of the political position of France abroad.   Was it only in order
to praise himself, or did he really believe it, when he wrote on
the 31st October, 1830, *that he would leave our affairs abroad
on the best possible footing ?*   In order to prove how greatly he
was mistaken on this point, I am obliged here to insert the long
despatch which the Comte de Nesselrode, Russian Minister of
Foreign Affairs, addressed to Comte Matusiewicz, Russian
minister in London, on October 19th, 1830.   It is very curious in
every respect, and shows with how much friendliness the situation, considered so satisfactory by M. Molé, was regarded at
St. Petersburg !   This secret despatch I need hardly say is perfectly authentic, though it is not necessary to mention here, by
what chance it fell into my hands.

---

[1] The Chamber of Deputies had in the course of three months lost 113 of its
members through invalidation and resignations.   Complemental elections had taken
place on October 22nd.

[2] Nicholas Joseph Maison, born 1771, entered the army as a volunteer in 1792.
After going through all the campaigns of the Revolution he became Brigadier-General
in 1805, General of Division in 1812, and Commander-in-Chief of the army of the
north in the end of 1813.   At the first restoration he was made a peer of France and
governor of Paris.   He held himself aloof during the Hundred Days.   In 1828 he
commanded the expedition to the Morea, which gained him a Field Marshal's baton.
He became Minister of Foreign Affairs, November 2nd, 1830, was soon after nominated
Ambassador at Vienna (November 17th), then at St. Petersburg (1833), and returned to
Paris in 1835 to take his place as War Minister (April 30th).   He retired in 1836 and
died in 1840.

Despatch of the Comte de Nesselrode to the Comte de Matusiewicz.

St. Petersburg, *October 19th,* 1830.

Commodore Awinoff handed me on October 7th, your Excellency's despatches of September 26th and October 8th. I have not lost a moment in submitting them to the Emperor, and I now hasten to inform your Excellency, as to his Imperial Majesty's decision concerning them.

Your previous reports of September 9th and 12th, had already made known to us the point of view taken by the English Cabinet with regard to the Netherlands. The Duke of Wellington and Lord Aberdeen, both recognize King William's right to ask the assistance of the alliance, to maintain the union of Belgium and the Dutch provinces. They both seem quite convinced of the necessity of granting such assistance to the King of the Netherlands, should he be in a position to require it, rather than allow an edifice, erected in the interest of England as much as in that of Europe, to fall to the ground. Both, in fact, have protested loudly against the claims of the French Government, not to permit any foreign interference in the affairs of Belgium.

After so frank and so decided an avowal of the views of the English Government, we were quite prepared to come to a similar decision, when the time arrived, as we had foreseen, for the King of the Netherlands to make a formal demand for assistance, while, on the other hand, the French Government persisted in its extraordinary demands.

Nevertheless your Excellency's last despatches announce, that at this decisive moment, the Cabinet of London has deemed it necessary to adopt another line of conduct, and recognizing the impossibility of now coming to the assistance of the King of the Netherlands (seeing the inefficiency of the means at the disposal of the English Government) has exhausted every endeavour in order to preserve peace, by inviting France to take part in the negotiations, which the allied courts have agreed to open with that of the Netherlands, relative to the separate administration of Belgium and the Dutch provinces.

Every effort, the object which is to assure to Europe the benefits of peace, must on that account alone, be entitled to the suffrage of our august master. His Imperial Majesty would therefore be quite ready to approve the plan proposed by the Duke of Wellington, if it did not in its execution and results, present some difficulties, which the Duke, with that penetration and frankness which so eminently characterize him, himself pointed out in the interviews he had with your Excellency. We will not stop to inquire into the different possibilities that may arise, during the negotiations about to be opened with the concurrence of the French Government. Your Excellency has foreseen them all in your despatch. The difference of the interests of France, as regards the Belgian fortresses, and her refusal to consent to employing an armed force to carry out the arrangements agreed upon, may give rise to complications which would compromise the very aim of the negotiations. But what, in the Emperor's eyes, is a real and very serious difficulty is, that these negotiations, so far from at once deciding the principal question, namely, the submission of the insurgent Belgians, only puts it off; that much precious time, which ought to be efficiently employed, will thereby be frittered away, that the rebels will be enabled to complete their culpable enterprise, furnishing a baneful encouragement to the revolutionary spirits of other countries, and will thus add to the difficulties and obstacles which we shall have to combat, when, after *all is said and done*, it will be unanimously deemed indispensable to intervene by force of arms.

Fully convinced that such will be the inevitable result of the system of pacification, proposed by his Britannic Majesty's Prime Minister, the Emperor would have greatly desired that the Cabinet of London, should have been disposed to send a large force at once to act in concert with its allies, and thus maintain the combination to which it contributed so largely in 1814 and 1815.

Nevertheless, his Imperial Majesty wishes on this occasion, again to give a fresh proof of his constant desire to remain united with his allies, and to show his deference to their wishes.

Consequently you are invited, M. le Comte, to declare to the British Government:

"That if France consents to negotiate on the Belgian question, the Emperor will on his side consent to her being admitted to the conferences, which have for their object *the pacification of the kingdom of the Netherlands by means of a change in the conditions of the union of Belgium with Holland, but maintaining the integrity of this State under the rule of the House of Orange, together with the full security of the fortresses which are to protect her independence.*

"That in the event of these conferences being held in London, you are authorized to take part in them, M. de Gourieff[1] being

---

[1] Russian Minister at the Hague.

already provided with similar powers, to enable him to assist at these conferences if they were held at the Hague.

"That his Majesty hopes the result of the negotiations will be vigorously upheld by the allied Powers, and that, however great may be the opposition of France, they will if necessary *even employ force of arms*, in order to carry out the arrangements agreed on.

"That his Imperial Majesty accepts with the greatest satisfaction the positive assurances given you on this point by the Duke of Wellington.

"That if France, nevertheless, refuses to agree to the negotiations proposed to her, or will not take any part in them, except on condition that the hypothesis of an armed intervention be excluded, and that thereby the intentions of that Power are no longer subject to any doubts, the Emperor trusts the English Cabinet will take such energetic measures as the fulfilment of its treaties and its own dignity require.

"That as regards the first alternative, *i.e.* the consent of France to the negotiations in question, it must not be forgotten that if these negotiations have the advantage of preventing a universal war and *compromising the French in some way with the Belgian insurgents*, they would not, on the other hand, arrest the progress of the insurrection itself, and that, since England is not in a position to act at present, though she agrees with us as to the necessity of preserving Belgium and the allied fortresses to the House of Orange, it would at least be imperative to utilize the interval of the negotiations, in making important military preparations, lest the employment of an armed force should become indispensable : that the Emperor in this case counts on the foresight of the British Cabinet, and that on his side his Imperial Majesty will not only assemble his contingents on the frontier, but *a considerable army* ready to march as soon as military action shall have been agreed on by common consent."

Such, M. le Comte, are the decisions to which his Imperial Majesty has deemed it right to adhere for the present. As for the rest, M. le Prince de Lieven,[1] who will immediately return to his post as ambassador to his Britannic Majesty, *will have full powers to arrange with the English Government, and the representatives of the Courts of Vienna and Berlin, all military or other combinations* and all declarations, which the general conjunctures or the affairs of Belgium and the policy of France may indicate as being necessary.

Accept. . . . . . NESSELRODE.

---

[1] Christopher Andreiewitch, Prince de Lieven, descended from a noble family of Livonia. was made General in 1807. In 1801 he went to Berlin as Minister Pleni-

This despatch plainly shows Russia's disposition towards us at this period, and whether M. Molé had grounds for congratulating himself on the *footing on which he should leave,* as he said, *our foreign relations !* It is very plain to me that the Emperor Nicholas would never have consented to empower M. Pozzo to deal with Belgian affairs in Paris ; and that even while authorizing Prince Lieven and Comte Matusiewicz to deal with them in London, in conference with the five Powers, he by no means made the road smooth for the French plenipotentiaries.

If such was the state of affairs abroad, it was not any easier for me in Paris, where for eight days the split among the ministers had suspended all action, had prevented my receiving not only any instructions, but even the simplest information, and almost amounted to a complete change of ministry, but little reassuring to Europe.   Whatever might be the good intentions of the new Cabinet, presided over by M. Lafitte, one could not disguise the fact, that the names of some of its members, would not inspire Europe with any great confidence in the maintenance of peace ; a fresh obstacle for whoever was called on to negotiate in a conference of the plenipotentiaries of the Powers, who were disquieted by what had already occurred, and as to what might still occur in France. But I was not discouraged, and fortified at last with authority to begin the negotiations, I informed Lord Aberdeen that I was ready to take part in them.

The King of England had during this interval [1] opened the parliamentary session with a speech in which the following passages relating to foreign policy occurred :

" Since the dissolution of the last Parliament, events of the greatest interest and importance have taken place on the Continent of Europe.

" The senior branch of the House of Bourbon no longer reigns in France, and the Duc d'Orleans has been called to the throne, under the title of King of the French.

" Having received from the new sovereign a declaration of his ardent desire to cultivate the good understanding, and to

potentiary, passed thence to London as Ambassador (1812), and remained there for twenty-two years.   Recalled in 1834, he was made Governor to the Hereditary Prince Alexander, and died in 1839.

[1] November 2nd.

maintain intact the existing engagements with this country, I have not hesitated to continue my diplomatic relations and cordial intercourse with the court of France.

" I have seen with profound regret the present state of affairs in the Netherlands.

" I greatly deplore that the enlightened administration of the King has not guaranteed his States from a revolt, and that the wise and prudent measure, to submit the wishes and complaints of his people to the deliberations of an extraordinary session of the States-General, has not led to a satisfactory result. I am endeavouring, in concert with my allies, to re-establish peace by such means as may be compatible with the well doing and the good government of the Netherlands, as well as the future security of the other States. Scenes of tumult and disorder have produced great uneasiness in different parts of Europe ; but the assurances of a friendly disposition, which I continue to receive from all Foreign Powers, justifies the hope that I shall be enabled to preserve to my people the blessing of peace.

" Convinced of the necessity of at all times respecting the faith of national engagements, I am firmly persuaded that my determination to maintain, together with my allies, those general treaties, by which the political system of Europe has been established, will offer the best guarantee for the peace of the world.

" I have not yet accredited my ambassador to the court of Lisbon, but the Portuguese Government, having decided to perform a great act of justice and humanity, by according a general amnesty, I believe that the time will soon arrive when the interests of my subjects will require a renewal of those relations which have for so long existed between the two countries."

In transmitting this address to Paris, I was able to state that on leaving Westminster Hall I followed the king's carriage to the palace, that on my way there, I was the object of the kindest and most friendly demonstrations, having reference solely to the king whom I have the honour to represent, that cries of " Long live Louis Philippe ! " were heard on all sides, and that our national cockade attracted universal attention.[1]

The king opened Parliament on the 2nd of November, and Lord Aberdeen fixed the 4th of November for the first meeting of our conference. This I therefore attended, being authorized

---

[1] Mdme. de Dino sent the account of this ceremony to Mdme. Adelaide. See Appendix, Letter 12.

to do so by M. Molé's last letter, but I had no instructions whatever as to my line of conduct, either from M. Molé or from Marshal Maison, who succeeded him as Minister of Foreign Affairs on the 2nd of November.

Before entering into the deliberations of the conference at London [1] in detail, it is necessary to recall briefly the events which had taken place in Belgium and which were the cause of this conference.

As has already been stated, the King of the Netherlands had been beaten in his struggle with the Belgians, and with the exception of the fortress of Antwerp, which was still occupied by the Dutch troops, these latter had entirely evacuated the territory which formed the old provinces of Belgium; and the Dutch and Belgian troops found themselves face to face on their respective frontiers and quite ready to continue the war.

A provisional government had been established in Brussels, and although many of its members were honest and temperate men, there was such a diversity of opinions among them, that it was very difficult to foresee which would prevail in the end. In the actual country, the House of Orange had still many partisans, who nevertheless were not represented in the provisional government. This was composed of ardent Catholics, who would no longer hear of having the Protestant Princes of Nassau, of a few Republicans without weight or real support in the country, and lastly of men who anxiously desired the reunion with France. These last were old officials of the French Empire, mostly intriguers of not over good repute, and who had opened up relations with the Imperialists of Paris, some of whom had easy access to Louis Philippe. The greatest plotter among them was the Comte de Celles,[2] the grandson of Mdme. de Genlis. The

---

[1] At the Conference of London, which began on November 4th, only England, France, Prussia, Russia, Austria and the Netherlands were represented.

[2] Antoine Charles Fiacre, Comte de Wisher de Celles, born in 1779, was made Deputy to the States-General of Brabant, and member of the Municipal Council of Brussels. Napoleon nominated him Master of Requests to the Council of State and *préfet* of the *Loire Inférieure*, and also of Zuyder Zee. After the events of 1814, having again become a subject of the King of the Netherlands, he was elected for some time to the provincial states. In 1830 became the head of the French party in Belgium, who asked for the Duc de Nemours as king. Nevertheless, King Leopold sent him as Minister Plenipotentiary into France. After some time he there became naturalized, and was elected Councillor of State in 1833. He died in 1841.

Belgian provisional government was naturally the expression of the Chamber of Deputies which had created it, and it will readily be seen, that all this formed sufficiently discordant and unmanageable elements to contend with.[1]

The position of the King of the Netherlands was no less complicated. His eldest son, and heir to the throne, the Prince of Orange, working for his own ends, had tried to place himself between the revolted Belgians and his father the king. He would willingly have agreed to an arrangement, which, by provisionally separating Belgium from Holland, would have placed the former under his rule: trusting to again re-unite the two kingdoms after his father's death. He had allowed this scheme to become apparent, in a proclamation issued from Antwerp, which had greatly incensed both his father and the Dutch nation against him. Nevertheless, being finally rejected by the Belgians, the prince had to retire to the Hague, where it was no easy matter to reconcile him to the king, and appease the popular feeling that had manifested itself against him. In order to extricate him from the false position in which he found himself in Holland, the king shortly after sent him temporarily to England, under the pretext of upholding the interests of Holland at the conference.

Such was the position of this question, when the first meeting of the conference took place on the 4th of November, an account of which I sent to Paris on the 25th.

LONDON, *November* 5th, 1830.

M. LE MINISTRE,

Conformably to the authority given me by the king, and which was transmitted to me by M. le Comte Molé, under date of 31st October last, to assist at, and participate in, all the conferences which might take place respecting the affairs of Belgium, I went yesterday morning to Lord Aberdeen's, whither I had been summoned, together with the Austrian ambassador and the Prussian and Russian ministers.

We have held our first conference. The Duke of Wellington, who was present, spoke first, and expressed the sentiments of all the members of the conference, by pointing out that the

[1] The provisional government, called together on the 25th of September, was composed of the Baron d'Hooghworst, M. Charles Rogett, the Comte A. de Mèrode, MM. Gendebien, Van de Weyer, Jolly, Van der Linden, Nicholai, and de Coppin. M. de Potter joined it three days later.

Powers must endeavour to find the most persuasive and conciliatory means of arresting the effusion of blood in Belgium,
of calming the extreme irritation of the people, and restoring
national tranquillity. It seemed to us that humanity as well as
policy demanded that our first efforts should be directed to this
end, and that such would be more surely attained, if it were
possible, first to procure a provisional armistice between the two
parties, until the deliberations of the Powers were concluded.
This proposal was unanimously agreed to, and it was decided
that we should meet again this evening, to consult as to the
means of making known at the Hague and at Brussels the views
of the five great Powers represented at the conference.

M. Falck,[1] ambassador of the Netherlands, was present at
the evening conference, in accordance with Article IV. of the
protocol, agreed to on November 15th, 1818, at Aix-la-Chapelle,
which runs as follows :

"When special assemblies, either among the august sovereigns
themselves, or between their respective ministers and plenipotentiaries, shall have for their object any matters specially connected with the interests of the other states of Europe, such
meetings will not take place except in pursuance of a formal
invitation on the part of those States whom the said affairs
concern, and with the express reservation of their right to participate in them directly or by their plenipotentiaries."

M. Falck has agreed to the proposal of an armistice, which the
five ministers signed this morning, and which he has undertaken
to transmit to the King of the Netherlands. It will be sent to
Brussels this evening by two commissioners, and as I wished
France to appear prominently in this great humanitarian act, I
suggested that it would be both suitable and expedient if one of
the two commissioners was French, and I got the five Powers to
select M. Bresson. Mr. Cartwright,[2] the English minister at
Frankfort, was the other commissioner chosen.

I hasten to send you a copy of this protocol.

This proposal is advantageous in every way, and justice will
be done to the intentions which brought it about, even if it falls
short of the desired effect.

---

[1] Antoine Reinhard, Baron Falck, a Dutch statesman, born 1776, formerly secretary
to the Embassy at Madrid. On the accession of King Louis, he retired into private
life until after the evacuation of Holland by the French in 1813. He was then made
secretary to the provisional government, later on Secretary of State, and in 1818
Minister of Education and the Colonies. After the Revolution of 1830 he re-entered
the diplomatic service and was appointed Minister in London, and in 1840 at Brussels.
He died in 1843.

[2] Sir Thomas Cartwright, an English statesman, born in 1795. He was specially
attached to Lord Palmerston, whose secret foreign agent he became. He was
Minister at Stockholm when he died.

The speech of the King of England at the opening of Parliament occasioned some interesting debates. The opposition complained, that the principle of non-intervention in the affairs of Belgium was not made sufficiently plain. Active intervention is assuredly not the intention of the English Cabinet ; intervention by counsel and advice is not of an alarming nature, and the guarantee given by the five Powers to the union of Belgium and Holland, rendered this step necessary in presence of the events which had dissolved it. The opposition also raised the question of parliamentary reform, on which the king's speech had not touched. Contrary to general expectation, the Duke of Wellington, instead of trying to evade or adjourn it, declared that as long as he remained at the head of affairs he would never consent either to a radical or a partial reform. His friends had not expected that he would express himself thus plainly, and Mr. Peel, while the duke was addressing the House of Lords, replied to similar remarks in the House of Commons, but with greater caution and reserve. This declaration greatly vexed those who favour the present administration. . . .

The instructions from Paris for which I had asked with so much urgency, arrived at last. They were sent to me by Marshal Maison, together with a letter announcing his appointment as Minister of Foreign Affairs.

Here are these instructions :—

I do not know what can have retarded M. de Chenoise's arrival, but as I know that he was bringing you the authority to open the conferences and to take part in them, I have nothing further to write to you on that head, unless it is to say that the king impatiently awaits the details, which you will send me respecting all that has taken place.

As regards the instructions you asked for, I will occupy myself in drawing them up, and will meanwhile tell you their substance, without waiting to discuss what might have been possible at one time but is so no longer.

1st. That we believe that the only possible basis of arrangement in the present state of affairs is, that Belgium should be separated from Holland, and raised into an independent state under a sovereign prince ;

2nd. That this prince should if possible be the Prince of Orange ;

3rd. That if it cannot be the Prince of Orange, the Belgians should be called upon to declare their wishes as to the choice of the prince who is to become the head of the state ;

4th.   That you must set aside all demands that may be made to you, to entrust, even temporarily, any other fortress except that of Luxemberg, to any foreign garrisons whatsoever.

I have the honour moreover to inform you that what I am writing to you is strictly confidential and secret, and that no one in London must know that I have written it to you. I have only told you of it in order that you may know the special directions given in your instructions, and consequently the line your communications with the English Government must take in order to attain the end which the king has in view.   This end is to bring about an arrangement compatible with the equilibrium of Europe, as established by existing treaties, and at the same time to show that France is determined to maintain her engagements, to manifest her complete disinterestedness, no matter how great may be the sacrifices to which she resigns herself, in order to give neither motive nor pretext for war, and to ensure the continuance of universal peace.

The king desires that you will also inform the Duke of Wellington that his Majesty has seen with great pleasure the assurances given by him on this point, in his speech in the House of Lords.

I must also inform you that these instructions alter nothing, but on the contrary confirm whatever my predecessor sent you, and that you are not at present to make any special proposals at the Conference, but to accept those that will be made, *ad referendum*, and transmit the same to me, in order that I may take the king's instructions and make known his wishes to you.

It will be seen that these instructions had been dictated by the king himself to Marshal Maison, who was too little *au courant* with matters to have initiated and drawn them up.   Such as they were they sufficed me for the moment.

Simultaneous with the arrival of the Prince of Orange in London, without any other object than to conceal his awkward position in Holland, the provisional government of Belgium sent over a kind of agent, charged to find out whether the foreign Cabinets would be disposed to accept one of Eugène Beauharnais, sons as king of Belgium ; [1] these suggestions were not however even listened to. But another storm was gathering on the horizon,

---

[1] There had been a question of August Charles Eugène Napoleon, Duc de Leuchtenberg and Prince of Eichstadt, the eldest son of Prince Eugène, born 1810. The opposition of the French government put an end to his candidature. In 1834 he married Dona Maria, Queen of Portugal, but died shortly after in 1835.

and threatened to oppose fresh obstacles to the progress of affairs. No sooner had the late French Ministry been replaced by a Cabinet, tainted with the reputation of a revolutionary spirit, than the existence of the English Cabinet was in its turn shaken. It will be remembered that when giving an account of the debates in the House of Lords, on the king's speech, I mentioned that the Duke of Wellington had spoken with extreme warmth against any kind of reform in the electoral system of the House of Commons.

This warmth was to prove fatal to the Cabinet over which he presided.

The king had accepted an invitation to dine with the lord mayor, on which occasion the ministers and the whole *corps diplomatique* were to be among the guests, numbering over five hundred. It was natural that such a sight would attract a great crowd, which no doubt would take this opportunity to exhibit the feelings that agitated them, either for or against reform, and that if the king was cheered, the same feeling might not be shown towards the Ministry. This dinner was to take place on the 9th of November. On the 8th, Mr. Peel, the Home Secretary, wrote to the lord mayor, stating that their Majesties, the king and queen, would not be present at the dinner, as they feared the *cortège* might provoke disorder, and endanger the lives of his Majesty's subjects.

This decision caused great agitation all through the town. Large crowds gathered in the city; the funds fell on the exchange; and after much consultation the dinner was put off indefinitely.[1] But such an incident could not stop there, and necessarily increased the animation of the debates in Parliament, where Mr. Brougham,[2] on the 16th November, gave notice of a motion on Parliamentary reform.[3]

---

[1] See M. de Talleyrand's letter to Madame Adelaide, Appendix, No. 14.

[2] Henry, Lord Brougham, a writer, barrister, and statesman, was born in 1779, elected a member of Parliament in 1810. He sided with the Whigs. As a lawyer, he did most of the political law business of the House. It was he who defended Queen Caroline in the trial brought against her by her husband George IV. In the House, as at the bar, he stood equally in the first rank as an orator. In 1825 the University of Glasgow elected him Chancellor. Finally, in 1830, he took part in the Government. Created a peer of England and Lord Chancellor, he joined the Cabinet of Lord Grey, and helped to pass the Reform Bill. He retired in 1834. Up to his death in 1868 he often spoke in the House of Lords.

[3] The Reform Bill thrown out by Wellington, again brought forward by Lord Brougham, was finally brought forward in the Commons in 1831 by Lord John Russell.

While awaiting the results of the sitting of the 16th, the Plenipotentiaries met several times in Conference, without, however, making any marked progress, as we had not yet heard how the proposal for an armistice had been received at the Hague and Brussels. But during this interval I received a remarkable document which I had to consider as supplementing my instructions. This was a statement of the Belgian question drawn up by Louis Philippe himself, and which I will give here in its entirety. It was addressed to Marshal Maison, the Minister of Foreign Affairs, who sent it on to me just as he had received it. It is dated 11th November, 1830.

It seems to me to be most important, my dear Marshal, that M. de Talleyrand should be somewhat enlightened as to the present state of Belgium, in order that he may acquaint us what arrangements for the formation of a government could be obtained from the Belgians, and ratified by the Prussians ; for that is the problem which has to be solved, and the solution is not an easy one ; especially when you add thereto our predominant concern in the matter, so that the interests of France may not be injured, either in the present or in the future.

We have established as a primary basis, the separation of Holland from Belgium. This is what both the Dutch and the Belgians wish themselves, but which the King of the Netherlands does not want. Can he be compelled to accede to it ? That is the question, for force cannot be used to bring this about ; and yet, to arrive at it by negotiation, it would be necessary either to show him some special advantages, which we can find nowhere, or at least to obtain unanimity amongst the Powers as to what they require of him, and to accomplish this is more than doubtful.

If we had been, or were even now, able to induce the Belgians to accept the Prince of Orange as their king, I believe the Powers could have been brought (without encountering any insurmountable difficulties) to insist unanimously on this being ratified by the king his father, which he would have been compelled to do. A satisfactory arrangement of the limits of the two countries would, however, still have been necessary ; this would have been a source of great difficulty, and it is as

---

It did away with the representation of three hundred *rotten Boroughs*, increased that of the towns, and added largely to the number of members of Parliament. Thrown out in 1831 by the Lords, this Bill was not carried in both Houses till June 7th, 1832.

well to pause a little in order to look into it ere going any further.

In the proposal for an armistice, to which M. de Talleyrand very wisely agreed, the Conference decided as a first step, on a line of demarcation, which secured to the Belgians the evacuation of the fortress of Antwerp ; but this advantage is balanced by the preservation to the King of the Netherlands, of Maëstricht, Stephenswerdt, Venloo, that is to say, the line of the lower Meuse, which protects Belgium from the aggressions of Germany, and the inhabitants of which are attached to Belgium by their customs, habits, and ideas ; although they originally formed part of Holland, and not of the Netherlands. It is partly from knowing the moral disposition of the people, and partly from want of troops to form proper garrisons, that the king has already removed all the war material from Maëstricht by way of the Meuse. It also appears that the moral and political feelings of Breda, Bois-le-duc, and Dutch Brabant, are similar, and that they also wish to make common cause with Belgium and not with Holland.

As for that portion of Belgium which is on the right bank of the Meuse, and which was formerly part of Lower Austria, that is to say, Ruremonde, Virours, Limburg . . . the inhabitants of these places are entirely Belgian, and there is even reason to believe that all these districts have already sent their deputies to the National Congress at Brussels.

With regard to the more southern portion on the right bank of the Meuse, the inhabitants are still more Belgian than anywhere else. But here fresh complications, much more difficult of adjustment, present themselves.

These countries consist of the duchies of Buillon, Luxemburg, the ancient abbeys of St. Hubert, Stavelot, and Malmédy . . . the duchy of Luxemburg has been incorporated in the German confederation ; the fortress of Luxemburg has become a Federal fortress and has, under this name, been occupied for fifteen years by a Prussian garrison. It is needless to say anything further in order to show the difficulties that would be experienced, either by uniting these countries to the new Belgian state, or retaining them for the King of Holland, and re-establishing his authority, which has everywhere been annulled, except in Luxemburg itself, where it has been preserved if not in reality at least in name, by the Prussian garrison.

Doubtless all these complications would disappear were it possible to induce the Belgian National Congress to ask for the Prince of Orange as their sovereign, and it is the weight of these considerations which makes it so essentially desirable that he should be chosen, for then there would be nothing to arrange between Belgium and Holland except a question of boundary, which would be of very slight importance to Europe, and in which France would have no further interest, than to take care that the Prussian occupation should be limited, as it is now, to the fortress of Luxemburg only. It would have to be stipulated that neither Bouillon nor Maëstricht . . . could be occupied, except by the troops of the sovereign, to whom those places belong ; for it will not escape either your perspicuity or your patriotism, my dear Marshal, that if, for example, Maëstricht and Venloo were to be occupied by German garrisons, France would have the right to demand, in the way of security and compensation, that Bouillon and Philippeville should in their turn be held by French garrisons. But this is a useless and perhaps even a dangerous point to discuss, and every way it is preferable to arrange, that the fortress of Luxemburg shall continue to be the only one which can be occupied by a German garrison. It is necessary to try and eliminate from the discussion, everything that might lead to the supposition that France has ambitious views, which she has not, since her greatest wish is, that the general peace of Europe should not be disturbed, and that each Power should continue within its present limits.

The most important question at present, therefore, is to ascertain whether the Prince of Orange can still become King of Belgium, or whether he cannot. If he can, there is no doubt that he should have the preference, as much in the interest of France as that of the other Powers ; but if this is no longer possible, it will be necessary for the Powers to agree as to the choice of whoever becomes his substitute.

It is on this important point that it will be necessary to instruct M. Bresson to gain the most precise information in the shortest possible time. The choice of the Prince of Orange is, above all desirable, in order to *paralyze* the war party in the foreign Cabinets, especially that of St. Petersburg, where, it is said, this selection is the only one that will obtain the consent of the Emperor Nicholas. It is asserted that the King of the Netherlands is the more opposed to the choice of his eldest son, as he has no love for him, and that he is persuaded that if he can but succeed in stirring up a continental war, the result for himself would be, not only the recovery of Belgium, but also the addition of French Flanders and some other fortified towns to his states. These dreams, founded on the same chimeras with which the Cabinets deluded themselves in 1792, will probably have the same result now as they had then ; that is to say, the

King of the Netherlands will stand a greater chance of losing Holland by a war, than of regaining Belgium and of adding French Flanders to his states ; but we must expect him to oppose every obstacle he can to the choice of his eldest son, and still more to that of any one else.

It appears that the composition of the National Congress of Brussels is almost analogous to that of 1790, under Van der Noot and Van Eupen,[1] that is to say, it is composed principally of the aristocracy and the clergy of the country. It is even said that more than one-fourth of its members are ecclesiastics. This circumstance will make the selection of a Protestant prince still more difficult, and it is even asserted that they have decided upon the total exclusion of the House of Nassau, not only of the Prince of Orange, but of his son, who, some people flattered themselves, they might proclaim under the regency of some distinguished Belgian, such as, for instance, Comte Felix de Mérode,[2] a member of the provisional government, to whom so much influence is attributed, that he might, if he chose, be elected hereditary Grand Duke of Belgium, or even king. He is the grandson of M. de La Fayette, and his relatives in Paris, as well as his friends, speak openly of the *possibility*, or even according to them, the *probability* of such a choice. They consider him a triumph over the republican party of Potter[3] and Theilmann[4]

[1] Henry Charles Nicholas Van der Noot, a Belgian politician, born in 1735, distinguished himself in 1759 by his energy in throwing off the Austrian yoke. He tried to interest England, Prussia and Holland in the Belgian cause, placed himself at Breda, together with the Abbé Van Eupen, at the head of a committee of Belgian *émigrés* and on the 24th October, 1789, proclaimed the independence of Belgium. His attempt seemed likely to succeed. He entered Brussels and called a Congress together, over which he exercised a powerful influence ; but in November, 1799, the approach of the Austrians obliged him to fly. He took refuge in Holland and was no more heard of till his death in 1827.

[2] Philippe Felix Comte de Mérode, born 1791, was descended from an old and illustrious Belgian family. He married Mademoiselle de Grammont, and was living in Franche Comté when the news of the revolution called him to Brussels. He entered the provisional government. His name and his influence placed him foremost for the regency, and even for royalty. Nevertheless he furthered the election of King Leopold and was several times Minister during his reign. He retired in 1839, and died in 1857.

[3] Louis Joseph Antoine de Potter, a political writer and Belgian historian, born 1786. He did not begin his political career till 1828. The attitude he took caused him to be greatly censured. He was condemned to eight years exile when the revolution of 1830 broke out. Returning to Brussels he placed himself at the head of the Republican party. Seeing that his efforts were ineffectual, he returned to Paris in 1831, whence he energetically combated the policy of King Leopold. He went back to Brussels in 1838, and lived there in retirement till his death in 1859.

[4] Jean François de Theilmann, lawyer and Belgian statesman. He was one of the most active members of the Liberal party, and was exiled in 1830 together with his friend Potter. Returning to Brussels the following August, he was made Administrator-General of the Interior, member of the Constitutional Commission, Minister of the Interior, and Governor of the Provinces of Antwerp and Liége. He was deputy for Brussels. He was also nominated Councillor of the Court of Appeal for Brabant. He

who, notwithstanding the power afforded them by the large armed force under their authority in Brussels, have not had influence enough to be elected members of the National Congress. It is further added, that the clergy are favourable to the idea of Comte Felix de Mérode, who is said to be very devout; and we must not lose sight of the fact, that the clergy and the religious spirit of catholicism, will for some time to come have an enormous influence in Belgium. We must also not forget that the Belgian clergy blame the French clergy for having joined in the defence of absolute power, and profess loudly that to defend religion effectually, the clergy must show that they defend the liberty of the people.

Under these circumstances therefore it appears, that if it is difficult to flatter ourselves that the Prince of Orange or his son, still a minor, will be chosen, it is no less difficult to procure the choice of a Protestant prince, and the selection must therefore be confined to the small circle of Catholic princes.

There has been some question in Brussels as to the Duc de Leuchtenberg ; and M. de Talleyrand informs us that this suggestion was not even listened to in London. It is very desirable that it should not be so anywhere.

The list of Catholic princes who might be chosen by the Belgians is unfortunately very small. It is thought that they are desirous to ask for one of my sons,[1] but this idea must be put aside, and must not even be discussed, since in the present state of Europe such a discussion would be dangerous, and could have no possible chance of success. The same may be said of the Austrian Archdukes, who must also be eliminated.

There remain therefore only the families of Naples, Saxony, and Bavaria, from which a choice could be made. France would not object to this, and there seems no reason why any of the other Powers should do so either. But we must not conceal from ourselves that the unpopularity of the Neapolitan Royal family, leaves but scant hope that the choice of the Belgians might fall on Prince Charles of Naples,[2] who is nineteen years old, and who is well spoken of. Thus we must realize that there is no other alternative than the choice of Prince John of Saxony,[3] who is thirty years old, of Prince Otto of Bavaria,[4]

retired from public life in 1847, and devoted himself exclusively to magisterial work.   [1] The Duc de Nemours.

[2] Charles Ferdinand, Prince of Capua, born 1811, son of Francis I., King of the two Sicilies.

[3] John of Saxony, born 1801, son of King Anthony, married to the Princess Amelie, daughter of the King of Bavaria. He succeeded to the throne on the death of his brother in 1854, and died in 1873.

[4] Otto Frederick Louis, Prince of Bavaria, born 1815, son of King Louis, was elected King of Greece in 1832, obliged to resign the Crown in 1862, and died in 1867.

who is only ten or eleven years of age, and of Comte Felix de Mérode, either as Regent, or as hereditary Grand Duke.

The result is doubtless not very satisfactory. Let us hope that more favourable opportunities may present themselves, but let us be content with those arrangements which, being more practicable, can alone insure the continuance of European peace. La Fontaine says truly :

> " Les plus accommodants, ce sont les plus habiles.
> On hasarde de perdre en voulant trop gagner."

One cannot but admire in what a very judicious and disinterested way the king in these lines appreciates the various views of the Belgian question, but it is also apparent that he is quite aware of the numerous difficulties which surround its solution. In communicating to him the news that the Belgians had agreed to the armistice, I felt bound to tender him the following remarks : [1]

I have read and re-read the statement of the Belgian question, which is written by so august a hand ; and I was deeply struck by the deep reasoning and profound knowledge of the source from which it is borrowed.

This, as far as the information I have gathered enables me to judge, is the situation of the country and of the different parties.

The Belgian Congress is the real exponent of the national sentiment ; the majority of opinions is incontestably in favour of monarchy.

This is demonstrated by their first proceedings as well as by their choice of a president.[2]

The republican party, and the one desirous of a reunion with France, are represented in about equal numbers.

Were the monarchical party unanimous in their choice of a prince, the advantage would undoubtedly be theirs ; but this question, which is of greater importance than even the royalist principle and form of government to the majority, especially the clergy, will probably cause a division among them. There

---

[1] This fragment is extracted from a letter to Madame Adelaide, dated 1830.

[2] The Congress, which had begun its sittings on the 10th of November, had on the 22nd, by a vote of 174 out of 197, declared in favour of a monarchical form of government, only thirteen members voting for a Republic. On the 11th November, Baron Surlet de Chokier had been elected president. He was one of the chiefs of the monarchist party. He it was who, later on, in the middle of the Congress, brought forward a motion in favour of the election of the Duc de Nemours.

is a fraction of the monarchical party who are even more opposed to the Prince of Orange personally and to the House of Nassau generally, than they would be to the establishment of a republic. That is the quicksand which we have to dread. If the discussion be not preceded by a previous agreement, and by mutual concessions, so that the monarchical party in the Congress may be impressed by an appearance of unanimous action, the opposing factions, strengthened by these divisions, will as surely regain the upper hand. The proclamation of the republic will be their first tentative act ; union with France their second, should the first fail.

Whilst admitting the unity of the royalist party, there would still be another danger to be avoided. Were the Prince of Orange elected, the tactics of his opponents would resolve themselves into attacking the Congress in the integral parts of its constitution, which they would assume to be unpopular ; they would contest its rights, invalidate its decisions, and inflame the country with antagonism against it. But their being in the wrong, they would be more vulnerable.

The portion in the monarchical party in favour of the Prince of Orange, and individually opposed to all the other princes, is the strongest and the most numerous ; it is stronger and even more numerous than the other parties also taken individually.

In saying this, I assume that the choice of the Duc de Nemours, would, as a matter of wisdom, be set entirely aside and put out of the question ; for he would at once turn the scale. The bombardment of Antwerp, and his trip to the Hague, have greatly prejudiced the cause of the Prince of Orange, and it will be difficult to regain the advantage he has lost. It is possible that judicious hints made with the utmost caution by the great Powers, might be productive of some good.

M. de Mérode cannot be regarded as the head of any party, being merely a tool, chiefly of the clerical party. Neither he, nor M. d'Oultremont, nor M. d'Hoogworst,[1] have any real chances.

The Duke of Leuchtenberg would have no following, were it not that his name is connected with recollections of the Empire, and French sympathies generally. Without the support of the great Powers, he is practically of no importance.

The Archduke Charles[2] is supported, in default of M. de Mérode, by the same party.

Left to itself, this subdivision of the Catholic monarchical faction would be completely inert. It might decide the question

[1] Emmanuel Vanderlinden, Baron de Hoogworst, a Belgian General (1781–1866), commanded the National Guard of Brussels in 1830, was made a member of the Provisional Government, and Commander-in-Chief for life of the whole Belgian National Guard.

[2] The son of the Emperor Leopold, and the celebrated adversary of Napoleon.

by strengthening the party of the Prince of Orange, or of one of his sons, a change of religion being the condition of their support in the election of either the above named. On no other terms would they capitulate. As to the princes of Naples, Bavaria or Saxony, their names have not even been suggested to the Belgians. They have no party, but they may become a necessity.

The entire situation is an extremely complicated one, and there is no doubt that the election of the Prince of Orange is the easiest solution of it.

Just at this time, and whilst these questions, in themselves so momentous, were being discussed, another fresh obstacle, as I mentioned before, threatened to delay the proceedings of the conference.

The English ministry, having been defeated in some insignificant matter in the House of Commons, determined to retire. The cause of this action on their part was a discussion as to the desirability of referring the bill relating to the civil list to a special committee ; the Government opposed this step, as contrary to established precedent. A majority of twenty-nine votes in 437 having pronounced against the Government, the Duke of Wellington and his colleagues tendered their resignation, which was accepted by the king. This occurred on the 15th November, the ministers preferring to retire at this first manifestation of the hostility of the Commons, rather than await the discussion of Mr. Brougham's motion. The king thereupon summoned Earl Grey,[1] and entrusted him with the formation of a Cabinet from the moderate Whig party. This event might influence the result of our important negotiations in various ways ; if, personally, I regretted Wellington's withdrawal from office, having had long-standing and reliable relations with him, and he being one of those who enjoyed as did no other man in like degree the confidence of Europe ; on the other hand, the presence of

---

[1] Charles Grey, born in 1764, entered Parliament in 1786, and allied himself closely with Fox. He was head of the Whig party from 1792 till 1802. In 1806 this party having come into power, Mr. Grey was made First Lord of the Admiralty, and after the death of Fox, Minister for Foreign Affairs. He retired in 1807, and succeeded his father the same year, when he entered the House of Lords. In 1830, Earl Grey was requested to form a Cabinet, which, after a short break in 1832, lasted till 1834. He died in 1845.

the Whig party at the head of affairs, being more liberal in its general tendencies, gave rise to the hope that it might offer certain facilities for the progress of the negotiations. This party was in no way responsible for the transactions of 1815 ; and having so frequently deprecated and attacked the same, they would in no way feel themselves bound to uphold them in all their integrity. It is true this advantage was somewhat neutralized by the fear, that the revolutionary party, which was then in such violent agitation on the Continent, might hope to find, and eventually did find, allies in those ministers, who whilst they were in opposition, encouraged, and at times even inflamed their aspirations. Nevertheless, we were forced to accept this change, and to turn the same to the greatest possible advantage to ourselves.

The retiring ministry had announced their intention of retaining the direction of affairs until another administration should be formed. Lord Aberdeen therefore convoked the conference after his resignation had been sent in.

At this sitting our commissioners, who had returned from Brussels, handed in the consent of the provisional government to the proposal of an armistice.[1] This consent had not been granted without some discussion as to the territorial limits which had been fixed by our protocol, but the same objection was raised, and with greater force, by M. Falck, the plenipotentiary of the King of the Netherlands, who protested, in the name of his sovereign, against the proposed limits, as being too prejudicial to Holland. The conference then drew up two protocols, a public and a secret one. In the first, the consent given to the armistice with the Hague and with Brussels was accepted in its integrity ; but in the secret protocol, the commissioners, who were returning to Brussels, were desired to try and obtain the limits demanded by the King of the Netherlands ; should they however encounter too many difficulties in their efforts, they

---

[1] It was on the 10th November that the congress accepted the proposed armistice. The protocol of the 4th November, which enjoined it, gave as the line of demarcation, "the boundaries of Holland, previous to the treaty of Paris of the 30th May, 1814." M. Bresson and Mr. Cartwright, who had brought the news of the acceptance to London, returned to Brussels on the 19th November, and submitted the second protocol of the 17th November to the congress, which was also accepted by the Provisional Government (November 21).

were to keep to the primary basis of the protocol of the 4th November. There was no actual question of a definite demarcation, which was no more prejudiced by the armistice than were all the various other questions to which the events in Belgium had given rise.

Mr. Cartwright and M. Bresson returned to Brussels armed with deeds and full powers from the conference, which, having obtained the suspension of hostilities, could now await with greater security and calmness, the formation of a new ministry in England.

M. Bresson's absence caused me much inconvenience. As I have already observed, my embassy was rather ill assorted ; several young men had been sent to me who had been selected from amongst what was termed the *progressive* party. They were utterly useless for the work of the embassy, in which they were incapable of taking part, and they compromised its dignity by their follies and indiscretions. Thus, one member, assisted at a radical banquet given in honour of Poland, and there proposed a revolutionary toast ; another announced his intention of not drinking the health of King Louis-Philippe until that monarch had abdicated. I had much trouble in ridding the embassy of these awkward and discordant elements. I earnestly implored, that some one might be sent to me who was capable of undertaking the work ; but it was not till the end of November that M. de Bacourt appeared on the scene.

The formation of the new Cabinet was attended by a rather serious complication.

The Duke of Wellington had succumbed to an unexpected and sudden alliance, composed of the Whig party, and a fraction of the extreme Tory party (who had never forgiven the duke for his action in the Catholic Emancipation Bill), [1] and lastly of a few

---

[1] The position of Ireland before the Emancipation Bill is well known. Among her seven million inhabitants, nearly six millions were Roman Catholics, who were ineligible for election, could not enter any of the liberal professions, and had not even the right of owning property. After many vicissitudes, thanks to the efforts and the influence of O'Connell, a strong opposition was formed in 1823, known as the Catholic Association. From that time, the rapidly increasing agitation frightened the Government and hastened its dissolution. Four times already, an Emancipation Bill, passed by the Commons, had been rejected by the Lords, when at last in 1829, it was presented by Wellington and Peel, and was adopted on the 10th of April. The Catholics were admitted to the rights of citizenship.

partisans of Mr. Canning's, who had separated from the Tory party some two or three years previously. Lord Grey represented the Whig party, the Duke of Richmond[1] the extreme Tories, and Lord Palmerston[2] the Canningites. In order to obtain anything like a fusion of these three parties for the formation of a Cabinet, it was of primary necessity to come to an understanding as to the principles which should guide them, and the measures they should propose ; hence the delays and difficulties that arose. Only to cite one amongst many. The fall of Wellington's ministry was evidently due to his too explicit declaration against all parliamentary reform. It was hardly possible that public opinion could be thus directly shaken in this matter without great danger. Some parliamentary reform must necessarily therefore form one of the measures of the new Cabinet.

But one of the fundamental principles of the extreme Tories, and of Canning's administration, had always been a stern opposition to any parliamentary reform. Would they still hold to this doctrine in all its rigour ? If so, they could hardly act in concert with the Whigs ; and if the pressure of circumstances caused them to coalesce, they would only reproduce the precedent of the Duke of Wellington and Mr. Peel on the Catholic Emancipation question. Furthermore, this action would separate them from many of their old and faithful political friends ; and if it brought them new allies, these would by the very act, prove that their fidelity was only conditional. Up to the time I am speaking of, it was very rare for Englishmen to make any compromise in the political principles which they had once professed ; and the desertion of their party would have been an unpardonable and unprecedented offence.

Furthermore, even though public opinion ardently desired some parliamentary reform, the accession to power of the Whig

[1] Charles, Duke of Richmond, born in 1791, entered the House of Lords in 1819, on the death of his father. He was Postmaster-General in 1830 in Earl Grey's Cabinet.

[2] Henry John Temple (Viscount Palmerston), born in 1784, entered the House of Commons in 1807, was Lord of the Admiralty in the Portland Cabinet in 1807, and Secretary of State for War in 1809. He retained this place until 1828. He then became Secretary for Foreign Affairs from 1830 till 1841, and again from 1846 till 1851. Home Secretary from 1852 till 1855, First Lord of the Treasury from 1855 till 1858. and again in 1859 until his death in 1865.

party, inspired public men with a certain amount of dread, and this dread showed itself by a considerable fall in the public funds. For the last century England had become so used to a Tory administration, the intervals of Whig Government had been so short, and I might add so little successful, that the majority of people who were in any way important either by their position or by the interests they represented, did not welcome their return. The *Times*, that newspaper which had been so long the organ of their party, and which was always ready to uphold them, was nevertheless obliged to express the impressions of the " City," where the principal financial and commercial operations of London take place, in the following terms :

" General feeling is not very favourable to a Whig ministry, inasmuch as the Whigs, and the men of this party, do not possess that financial reputation to which public opinion attaches so great an importance; but it is difficult to see what other alternative remains. All practical men are of opinion that a government could hardly be called to take office at a time beset with greater difficulties."

All this, it is very apparent, was the reverse of reassuring. But I did not feel absolutely alarmed thereat, and believed that relations with England would not be materially affected by the recent change. It is true we had been on good terms with the retiring ministry ; and it is not always wise to try to improve a good position. But I thought that the new administration might adopt principles approximate to those of their predecessors in their foreign policy, and that we might thus reap a further advantage : and acting in concert with them, in the same way as we should have done with the late Cabinet, it would probably be viewed with greater popularity in France, consequent on the opinions which were dominant there at the time.

The ministry was formed at last, and was composed as follows:—[1]

Earl Grey, First Lord of the Treasury ; Lord Palmerston,

---

[1] See M. de Talleyrand's views on this new ministry in Appendix, Letter No. 15.

Foreign Secretary; Lord Melbourne,[1] Secretary of State for Home Affairs; Lord Goderich,[2] Secretary of State for War and the Colonies; Lord Althorp,[3] President of the Indian Council; Lord Lansdowne, President of the Council; Lord Durham,[4] son-in-law of Lord Grey, Lord Privy Seal; Mr. Brougham, Chancellor, with the title of Lord Brougham; Lord Holland,[5] Chancellor of the Duchy of Lancaster; Lord Auckland,[6] Secretary of the Board of Trade, without a seat in the council; the Duke of Richmond, Grand Master of the Ordnance.

While this Cabinet was being formed in London, a new modification had taken place in the French ministry, General Sebastiani having become Minister of Marine, in place of Marshall Maison, who had been nominated ambassador to the Court of Vienna.[7] These perpetual changes did not facilitate the progress of affairs; but it must be admitted that a state of semi-revolution was almost general everywhere, and it is

[1] W. Lamb, Viscount Melbourne, born in 1779, entered the House of Commons in 1805, and the House of Lords in 1828 on the death of his father. He was Home Minister in 1830, became First Lord of the Treasury in 1834, and continued at the head of the Government, save for a brief interruption, until 1841. He died in 1848.

[2] Sir Frederick John Robinson (Baron Ripon, and Viscount Goderich), born in 1782, Member of the House of Commons in 1806, Under Secretary of State for the Colonies in the Portland Ministry in 1807, member of the Admiralty Commission in 1810, Chancellor of the Exchequer in 1823, Colonial Secretary in 1827, entered the House of Lords the same year, under the title of Viscount Goderich. In 1827–1828 he was for some months First Lord of the Treasury, than again Colonial Secretary, Lord Privy Seal in 1833, President of the Board of Trade in 1841, and of the India Office in 1843. He retired in 1846, and died 1859.

[3] John Charles Spencer, Viscount Althorp, afterwards Earl Spencer, born in 1782, entered the House of Commons in 1804, Lord of the Treasury in 1806, became Chancellor of the Exchequer in 1830, entered the House of Lords in 1834. On the fall of the Grey Ministry he retired from public affairs, and died in 1845.

[4] John George Lambton, Earl of Durham, born in 1792, entered the House of Commons at a very early age, was created a peer in 1828, and joined Lord Grey's Cabinet as Lord Privy Seal in 1830, was Ambassador at St. Petersburg in 1830, then Governor of the North American Colonies. He died in 1840.

[5] Henry Richard Vassall Fox, Baron Holland, nephew of the celebrated Fox, born in 1773, succeeded his father in the House of Lords, was Lord Privy Seal in 1806–1807. In 1830 he was made Chancellor of the Duchy of Lancaster, which appointment he kept, save for a brief interval in 1835, until his death in 1840.

[6] George Eden, Earl of Auckland (1784–1849), entered the House of Commons in 1810, and in 1814 succeeded his father in the House of Lords. In 1830 he joined the Grey Ministry as President of the Board of Trade and Master of the Mint, and in 1834 he became First Lord of the Admiralty under Lord Melbourne's Ministry. In 1836 he was made Governor-General of India. He retained this until 1842. Then in 1846 he again became First Lord of the Admiralty, and died a few years later (1st January 1849).

[7] On the 17th of November. Marshal Gérard was at the same time replaced as War Minister by Marshal Soult, the Comte d'Argout replaced General Sebastiani as Minister of Marine.

well to know how to deal with any popular phase that may arise.

I had insisted most peremptorily at the last sitting which Lord Aberdeen had attended, that the affairs relating to the armistice between the Dutch and the Belgians should be concluded, and in order to effect this, our sitting had to be prolonged far into the night. I had succeeded in infecting the other members of the conference with my eagerness in this matter.

This eagerness was based on my anxiety, that the matter should assume such proportions as might insure us the co-operation of the new ministers on the same lines we had opened out to them ; my idea being, to ask that, on their first taking office, they would accept all the decisions with reference to Belgium which had been arrived at at the various conferences, as being thoroughly sound and well digested, and that they should themselves declare this conviction on the first occasion that might present itself. I therefore brought as much pressure to bear on the new ministers as I could on this point, being convinced that it must exercise considerable influence over any deliberations that the Belgians might ultimately have on the subject. We were constrained to steer between two opposing currents ; some persons reckoning too much on the Belgians, and others looking most to the King of the Netherlands. I had thus to go charily between these two parties and avoid giving undue umbrage to either. Events, however, turned out as favourably as I could have wished ; and it will be seen later on, that the new Cabinet entered entirely into my views as to the best way of conciliating those interests, in themselves so diverse and complicated, in which not only Belgian questions but also those of European moment, were involved. In order to make my meaning easier of comprehension, it will not perhaps be superfluous to cast a rapid glance on the particular dispositions of the several cabinets existing at the time we are treating of. After which we will briefly sketch those of their representatives in the conference of London, and delineate their general character.

Austria, greatly alarmed by the revolution which had taken place in France and the disturbances that had broken out in

T 2

Brunswick, Saxony and Hesse,[1] continued to stir up discords in Germany, hoping by these measures to oblige the federal army to take active steps, or at any rate to make up its full complement, and tried to find some pretext for engaging her own army on some point of foreign territory. M. de Metternich, far from regretting that he had made no sacrifices to the exigencies of the times, was only vexed not to have further aggravated them, and did not despair of being able to make up for lost time.

The dispositions of Russia were much on the same lines ; she also was preparing considerable armaments. She wished to entrust these to General Diebitch,[2] who had been sent to Berlin, where with the help of the intrigues of Austria, of the Prince Royal, and of M. Ancillon, he sought to destroy the credit of M. de Bernstorf, and to persuade the king into adopting the armed intervention, which the King of the Netherlands so ardently desired.

But happily the King of Prussia, enlightened by his past experiences and his profound knowledge of the state of men's minds in Germany and particularly in Russia, and also one may say from the natural honesty of his character, resisted all the influences and the pressure, which were being brought to bear upon him. Will he however continue to resist them ? The maintenance of peace was hanging on the solution of this question ; and many others also were bound up with it. In the state of affairs I have just described, one was forced to conjecture whether the change which had taken place in the English ministry would make the courts of northern Europe more pliable or more persistent in their demands. Would

---

[1] An insurrection had just broken out in the Duchy of Brunswick. The duke, who had steadily refused to accept the constitution of 1820, was forced to seek refuge in England, and abandoned the Government to his brother William on the 7th September. In Hesse Cassel a similar rising took place, against the Landgrave William. He retired to Hanau, whence he granted his subjects a very liberal charter. Finally in Saxony, both Dresden and Leipzig became the scenes of the most serious insurrectionary movements. King Anton was obliged to dismiss his ministry and promise his people a constitution.

[2] Jean, Comte de Diebitch-Zabalkanski, born in 1785, entered the army in 1797. Went through the campaigns of 1805, 1806, and 1807. In 1812 he was made Major-General, signed the treaty of Reichenbach with England and Prussia in June, 1813, and was made Lieutenant-General after the battle of Leipzig. After the peace he was made head of the Imperial Staff (1820), and Field Marshal in 1829. He commanded the Russian army during the war in Poland in 1831, but died during the campaign on the 9th of June.

they consider themselves capable of entering into contest with a Whig ministry which they could not hope to coerce, or would they think it necessary to make serious preparations for hostilities ? Would they become more suspicious, more irritable ? Finally, would they consider that they had reached a pass, where they ought to hazard everything, in order possibly to win everything ?

It was thus with a mind preoccupied by all these considerations, and the eventualities that might ensue therefrom, that I carefully weighed the language I should use at the forthcoming meeting of the conference, which the new Minister for Foreign Affairs, Lord Palmerston, was about to summon. This conference was composed as follows :

Austria was represented by Prince Paul Esterhazy,[1] who had for fifteen years, held the post of ambassador in London, where he was liked and esteemed by society and the aristocracy of England. Beneath an appearance of great ease, and a temperament which was always gay and of singular amiability, he hid greater perspicacity and greater business qualities, than he has been given credit for. His position as an influential Hungarian magnate endowed him with more liberal views than those held by M. de Metternich, whilst his long residence in England having familiarized him with the usages of constitutional government, had enlarged his ideas, and prepared the way for those concessions which were inevitable under the present state of affairs in Europe. Somewhat later, by Prince Metternich's orders, he was joined by Baron de Wessenberg, the object of this appointment being, either to remove the latter from Vienna where his presence was obstructive, or else to restrain Prince Esterhazy, whose influence M. de Metternich might possibly fear. If this last was his object, he was deceiving himself hugely, as M. de Wessenberg was far more susceptible of being led away than was Prince Esterhazy himself. I had already made the acquaintance of the Baron de Wessenberg at the congress of

---

[1] Paul Antoine, Prince Esterhazy de Galantha, an Austrian diplomat, born in 1786. Began as Secretary to the Embassy at London, then Ambassador at Westphalia in 1810, at Rome in 1814, and at London from 1815 to 1818. He returned to London in 1830, and remained there until 1838. In 1848 he formed one of the Bathyani Ministry. He died in 1866.

Vienna, and I then recognized in him a clever man of business, energetic and hard working, but nothing more. As a statesman, his views are too confined ; thoroughly honest in himself, he believes he has an accurate knowledge of everything, from having for the last forty years been in a position to hear and to remember all the scandal and gossip of Europe.

The Prussian minister, Baron de Bülow,[1] is fully conversant with general affairs; he is a man of ability and humour, of the Prussian type, sometimes pushing adroitness to the verge of cunning. He has married the daughter of William de Humboldt, but has in no way espoused the anti-French mania of the latter, which was so unpleasant to me at the congress of Vienna. M. de Bülow wished to please both the parties which divided the court of Berlin ; that of the king, who was old and cautious, and that of the Prince Royal, who might at any moment succeed to his father's throne and whose leanings were distinctly towards Russia. I had several times to draw him away from these inadmissible sympathies, in order to get him to appreciate clearly the actual course of events.

Russia had two official representatives at the conference in London ; Prince Lieven, and Comte Mantusiewicz. The latter, a Pole by birth, had been educated in France, and was justly proud of having gained the highest prize and honours, in the competition of 1811 at the University of Paris ; his habits, manners and mental faculties, have remained intensely French, and he possesses rare gifts, and a great editorial capacity. He had been sent to London to take part in the negotiations relating to Greece, and he had remained as Russian representative *ad interim*, during Prince Lieven's temporary absence ; I found him filling this post on my arrival in London. He had shown his conciliatory views at the beginning of Belgian affairs, in spite of the antipathy which he knew his sovereign felt towards the new order of things established in France ; but when, a little

---

[1] Henri, Baron de Bülow, born in 1790, entered the army in 1813, went through the campaigns of 1814 and 1815, and was sent to Frankfort after the peace as Minister Plenipotentiary. In 1817 he was attached as Secretary to the London Embassy ; he returned to Berlin and became Privy Councillor and Minister of Foreign Affairs. In 1827 he was appointed Ambassador at London, where he remained till 1840, passed thence to Frankfort (1841), and was made Minister of Foreign Affairs in 184^   He retired in 1844, and died in 1846.

later on, there was a rising in Poland, he showed his great ability in being able to retain his position as Russian plenipotentiary at the conference in London.   It will easily be seen that his equivocal position, as a Pole, did not render him as amenable in our negotiations as he would doubtless otherwise have been. As for Prince Lieven, I owe him the testimony of having helped us greatly by his loyalty, and his resistance to the ill-advised outbursts of anger of the Emperor Nicholas.   M. de Lieven has more ability than is generally supposed ; in this respect however the presence of his wife is detrimental to him, and she moreover effaces him much more than is expedient under the circumstances.

It was generally reported in London that his conciliatory attitude arose chiefly from his desire to retain his appointment as ambassador ; this, however, seemed to me unlikely, and in any case was an unsuccessful attempt on his part, as he ended by being recalled.   But I should be giving an incomplete and defective description of the Russian legation in London, and the important part it was playing there, if I omitted to mention Madame de Lieven.[1]   She would perhaps forgive me less easily than would any one else, were I to pass her name over in silence. Madame de Lieven had been resident in England for nineteen years, having come over in 1812, during the time when Napoleon's foolish enterprise against Russia, had led the Emperor Alexander to seek the friendship of England.   It must be remembered that at this time, not a single legation had been for some years accredited to the court of St. James, with whom every continental cabinet had, either really or only apparently, been forced to sever official relations.   The appearance, therefore, of an embassy from Russia, created an immense sensation.   The Prince Regent, the court, the aristocracy, in fact the whole English nation, received the representative of the

---

[1] Dorothée de Benkendorf, Princess Lieven, born in 1784, married at sixteen to the Prince de Lieven, appointed Lady-in-Waiting in 1828 to the Empress of Russia. When the Prince was recalled to St. Petersburg she remained in Paris.   In 1848 she retired to Brussels.   Again returning to Paris, she remained there until 1854, the date of the Crimean War, when she went back to Brussels, but soon again returned to Paris, where she died in 1857.   Mdme. de Lieven left many *souvenirs* in London and Paris, where she had been on intimate terms with the most prominent political men.   Canning, and later on Lord Grey, were the most constant attendants of her *salon*.

Russian emperor with a warmth amounting almost to enthusiasm. M. de Lieven was welcomed everywhere throughout the country, and Madame de Lieven, who, during her husband's mission in Berlin, had already acquired some celebrity, naturally shared the ovations given to her husband. At the court, in the absence of any queen, the first place became hers by right, and the Prince Regent delighted to attract her to Brighton, where her presence offered some pretext for that of the Marchioness of Coningham, whom few ladies in English society cared to meet. The aristocracy, renowned for their hospitality, received the new ambassadress with open arms, and willingly granted her all those little privileges which are shown to women whose beauty, wit, or fortune, place them at the head of fashionable society; the undoubted empire exercised by Madame de Lieven over English society, dates from this time; and having once gained it, she had the great merit of preserving it for some considerable time; and this was entirely due to her own wit and charm, for it does not appear that she ever had any real beauty. But even when age had tarnished the bloom of youth, she knew how to supply its place by great dignity, an exquisite manner, and a commanding air, which gave her a noble and somewhat haughty appearance, closely resembling the power she wields. Without much education, and stranger still, without having ever read much, she has great natural ability; her style, when writing French, is singularly charming, being varied, original and easy. She writes far better than she speaks, this being no doubt due to the fact, that in her conversation she seeks less to please than to dominate, to interrogate, and to satisfy her own insatiable curiosity; she is therefore more *piquante* by the boldness of her questions, pushed even to provocation, than by the vivacity of her replies; and she gives the impression of rather preferring the satisfaction of embarrassing others, than of wishing to please them by setting them at their ease in her society. She evinced this desire of thus treating her audience, which was rather numerous, at one of our earliest meetings.

"You may say and do what you will," she exclaimed suddenly, "but what has just taken place in France is nothing more or less than a flagrant piece of usurpation."

" You are quite right, Madame," I replied, " but the only thing to be regretted in the matter is, that it did not take place fifteen years ago, when your master, the Emperor Alexander, so ardently desired it."

I am bound to say that since then, she has never provoked me, and that we got on very friendly terms, although she quietly did all in her power to frustrate our negotiations, and this antagonism could hardly fail to be productive of unfavourable results, more especially after the change which had so lately taken place in the English ministry. Madame de Lieven, perhaps in remembrance of her youth, was rather volatile in her political likings; but her ability was chiefly conspicuous, in being able invariably to be even on better terms with the incoming ministers, than with those who were retiring. Thus, after having carefully cultivated the friendship of the Duke of Wellington for a considerable time, she quietly dropped him, in order to gain that of Mr. Canning. On the death of the latter, the duke having again taken up the direction of affairs, Madame de Lieven was not in the same high favour with him, she therefore spared no arts of coquetry to win over Lord Grey as soon as he came into power, and I had many an opportunity of perceiving that in this she had to a certain extent succeeded.

A description of Lord Palmerston, who succeeded Lord Aberdeen in office, will complete this sketch of the members of the conference.

Lord Palmerston is certainly one of, if not quite the ablest of statesmen I have ever met with in all my official career. He possesses all the aptitude and capacity which most contributes to form such a man in England—extensive and varied information, indefatigable activity, an iron constitution, inexhaustible mental resources and great facility of speech in Parliament. Without being what is called a great *debater*, his style of eloquence is biting and satirical, his talent lying more in his power of crushing an adversary under the weight of his irony and sarcasm, than of convincing his auditors; and furthermore, he has great social qualities and highly finished manners. There is one point in his character, however which to my mind, entirely outweighs all these advantages, and would prevent his being considered in the light of a real statesman—he allows his passions to influence him in public affairs, to the extent of sometimes sacrificing the greatest interests to his personal feelings. It may be said, that nearly every political question resolves itself with him into a personal one ; and whilst seeming to defend the interests of his country, it is nearly always those of his hatred or revenge that he his serving. He is very skilful in hiding this secret motive, under what I might call, patriotic appearances ; and it is by this same skill that he nearly always contrives to influence a considerable portion of public opinion, which he leads in whatever direction his own personal passions indicate. I shall often have the opportunity of proving the truth of these remarks, which explains how Lord Palmerston has always retained a certain popularity, even when changing his party, and whilst lending his great talents and abilities in turn, to the Tories, the Whigs, and even at times to the radicals. There are few Englishmen who know as well as he does, how to excite John Bull's patriotic feelings. We worked very amicably together during the first months of the conference, and it is to this accord that the excellent results that were obtained, may be attributed. Having now spoken of the principal men concerned, we may revert to the affairs which occupied them.

Lord Grey, according to my desire, had taken the opportunity of his first speech in Parliament—in which he laid down the lines on which the new ministry proposed to act—to proclaim his peaceful and friendly intentions towards France ; he also said that he considered the governments of the two countries were founded on the same principles. This speech made a great impression on the public. It was essential that our friendly relations with England should be established on a firm foundation, and, this being done, we had to turn it to the greatest advantage.

An incident moreover supervened, which by irritating the Courts of Austria, Prussia, and especially that of Russia, made it still more important that there should be perfect concord between France and England. Before even ratifying an armistice with Holland, which had been obtained through the mediation of the conference, the Belgian congress had quite recently proclaimed the total exclusion of the House of Nassau as candidates for the throne of Belgium. Fortunately for us, this decision had been arrived at, in defiance of vigorous steps taken by the French Government to prevent the same, which clearly demonstrated the good faith it had shown in this matter.[1]

At the first meeting of the conference under the presidency of Lord Palmerston, who informed us, that the Hague and Brussels had definitely accepted our proposals of an armistice, I propounded some views to the assembled plenipotentiaries, which I thought should be transmitted by them to their several governments. I told them :

Gentlemen, we now have the assurance that hostilities will be permanently suspended and that all bloodshed will cease ; the time has therefore arrived for some agreement to be arrived at as to the proper means of settling the very thorny question which has been entrusted to our care. It is very evident that we shall not attain this end, if we do not bring a spirit of conciliation into this council, and if we do not all unite in having one common aim—that of the maintenance of peace, which is such a crying necessity to all parties. It is impossible to ignore the fact, that whatever may have been the motives of the Revolution which has taken place in France, it has more or less shaken nearly every throne in Europe, and has everywhere weakened the fundamental principle of authority.

This I deplore with you, and as much as you do ; but I can see only one remedy for this evil, namely, that we unanimously agree to repair it, by giving each other reciprocal help. There is no doubt that our governments will severally feel increased internal strength, when able to speak in the name of the five greatest Powers of Europe. My own government has recently given you a conclusive proof of the sincerity of its intentions, by trying to prevent the Belgian congress from pronouncing the exclusion of the House of Nassau. I much regret it has not been more successful in this matter, and I shall together with you, loyally seek means of repairing this misfortune, if it be still possible ; but whatever may be the issue of our efforts on this

[1] See page 257 and note. The question *of excluding in perpetuity the members of the House of Nassau from all power in Belgium*, was brought before the congress by M. Rodenbach on the 23rd of November. It was decided by 121 votes against twenty-eight.

point, it is well to be prepared for every eventuality that may occur, and to introduce thorough confidence and firmness (which can alone insure the preservation of peace) into our future deliberations.

These remarks, which I think possessed the merit of being true, had sufficient effect for me to hope, that the maintenance of peace might be attained.

It was agreed during this sitting, that the field should be left open to the endeavours made by the Belgian partisans of the House of Nassau, to restore the Prince of Orange into favour with the congress; and to occupy ourselves meantime with those details which it would be necessary to regulate in any case, *i.e.* those appertaining to the difficulties, which had unsettled the boundaries existing between Holland and Belgium, the understanding which should be established with the Germanic confederation with regard to Luxemburg, the division of the debt, &c . . .[1]

At the time the conference was beginning to discuss these important questions, an emissary arrived in London from the newly constructed French ministry, or at least from several of its members. This was the Comte de Flahaut. His mission was a somewhat complicated one; the pretext given being his former social and amicable relations with some of the members of the new English ministry, Lord Grey and the Marquis of Lansdowne amongst others, and it was supposed that the friendly protection which I had given to M. de Flahaut at the outset of his official career, would make his presence an agreeable adjunct under existing circumstances. M. de Flahaut had also come with the object of preparing the way for his own nomination as ambassador in London, when circumstances should oblige me to resign that post. I quickly extricated these personal particulars from beneath the official covering which had been given to his embassy, for he was the bearer of a despatch and several letters in which General Sebastiani solicited my

---

[1] It is very important to consult the correspondence of M. Bresson and M. de Talleyrand on these various points. We have therefore inserted a few of these letters, which complete what M. de Talleyrand says respecting these negotiations, in the Append⋯ See letters, Nos. 16, 17, 21.

opinion and advice concerning the foreign policy of France ; and he had also been instructed to introduce some hints in his intercourse with me, relating to the manner in which it was thought desirable to conclude the Dutch-Belgian question, after the Belgian congress had passed the vote excluding the House of Nassau. The plan unfolded to me by Comte Flahaut, a plan which had evidently been inspired by M. de Celles and a few other intriguers of the same species, and had, I have reason to believe, been accepted by General Sebastiani, was as follows. It was argued that, as Belgium had rejected the House of Nassau, and the King, Louis-Philippe, had not consented to the election of the Duc de Nemours as sovereign of the newly formed State, there remained only one way of conciliating all parties ; *i.e.* the division of Belgium. By dividing this country in such a way that the neighbouring States should be interested in the division, their consent to the proceeding would easily be obtained. The King of the Netherlands would thus receive a portion, and he would doubtless prefer this arrangement to the total loss of the Belgian States ; Prussia would have her share of territory, and that of France would of course be the largest of all ; but as it would be impossible to prosecute this measure without the consent of England, her claims would have to be remembered, and she would be offered the city and port of Antwerp, and the banks of the Scheld as far as the sea coast. The Comte de Flahaut's mission was to induce me to agree to accept this marvellous conception.

It did not require much reflection on my part, to grasp how utterly senseless and dangerous such a project would be, nor how entirely it was opposed to, and would prevent, the maintenance of a permanent peace ; above all, how adverse it was to the real interests of France, even supposing that it could be accepted by the other Powers. I recalled what it had cost France, and how much bloodshed it had necessitated, to achieve the expulsion of the English from the Continent in past centuries, and I vowed that, for my part, I would rather cut off my right hand, than sign any deed which should be the means of bringing them back there. The extension which it was proposed to offer to Prussia in the direction of our northern frontiers, seemed to me no less objectionable than the proposal to offer England continental territory. I therefore hotly rejected a a scheme so suicidal to international safety, and which bore no other character but that of an intrigue. There was to my mind, only one possible issue to the question which could in any way benefit France ; and that was the creation of a kingdom of Belgium, placed under the sovereignty of some prince who should be too weak to give us any anxiety, and who should not even possess the means of keeping up the garrisons in the belt of fortresses, which were erected and maintained at great expense, in hostility to ourselves.

M. de Flahaut was obliged to be content with this reply from me, and to be the bearer of it, as well as a despatch, to Paris, in which I unfolded my views on French foreign policy, thus replying to the questions that had been put to me by General Sebastiani.

The despatch ran as follows :—[1]

LONDON, *November 27th*, 1830.
" MONSIEUR LE COMTE,
        I am greatly obliged to you for having persuaded M. de Flahaut to come to London ; he is on good terms with the new Ministry, and in this way his presence has been very useful to me ; while his great tact, guided him as to the language which it would be most expedient for him to use.

I hasten to reply to the general questions which have been put to me, as to the foreign policy which France might be induced to follow under present circumstances. France must not dream of forming what are termed alliances. She must be friendly with all parties, and only allow herself special terms of friendship with some Powers ; which friendship she should only express, when political events require it.

Such ties should exist on a different basis from the alliances of former times; the progress of civilization will in future create the ties of our political relationships. We should therefore seek the friendship of those governments who have made the greatest advances in civilization ; and thus establish really friendly embassies. This leads us naturally to look upon England as the Power with whom it is wisest to have close and intimate relations, and I should further remark, that there

---

[1] This is not mentioned in M. Pallain's collection.

are many principles we hold in common with that country, it being the only one with whom we are agreed as regards essentials. If in some points we have the advantage over England, there are, on the other hand, matters in which she is our superior. It would therefore be a mutual benefit to both countries, to be on terms of closer intimacy. All feelings of rivalry are moreover greatly diminished, owing to the severe colonial losses we have sustained.

Europe is certainly at this moment, passing through a great crisis. Well, England is the only Power which, like ourselves, honestly desires to establish peace. The other great Powers still believe in the phantom of some sort of Divine right. France and England alone no longer hold to the belief of this origin. The principle of non-intervention has been adopted by both countries, and I would add, that it is a significant fact, that just now there is a kind of sympathy between the two nations.

It is my opinion that we should make use of all these points of assimilation, in order to obtain that peace for Europe which she so urgently needs. Whatever may be the opinion of some other nations as to the desirability of peace, it is necessary that both France and England should declare that they desire it, and that this declaration, emanating from the two strongest and most civilized countries in Europe, should be made known with all the authority which their power gives them.

Some Ministries, still sailing under the colours of Divine right, have at this present time ancient means of coalition ; they can agree, as they have principles in common ; these principles, it is true, have in some places lost much of their strength, but they nevertheless exist ; and when their Ministries parley with each other, they soon come to some agreement. They support their theory of Divine right by their muskets ; but England and France will henceforth support public opinion by principles ; principles are capable of universal propagation, whilst muskets have only a range which can be calculated and measured to a nicety.

Europe is therefore divided between these two principles of government ; they are those which rule her in the present day. The forces are pretty nearly equally divided between the principle which sets in motion the Austrian and Russian armies, and the principle which, acting by public opinion, commands forces which are nearly if not quite equal. This latter will meet with many allies in the countries which are opposed to it, whereas its antagonists could hardly reckon on any sympathizers, excepting in the Faubourg St. Germain. If there is a doubt, we must weigh down the scale in our favour, and the method of arriving at this, is to induce Prussia to hold views which are less new to her than they would be to the other northern countries. These, it appears to me, are the views which the two Cabinets of London and of Paris should hold. I enlarged upon these ideas at great length, with Lord Palmerston yesterday, and again to-day with Lord Grey ; their opinions coincided with my own, and they will instruct their ministers in Berlin to the same effect. It is very important that our envoys at that court should be men of great observation and powers of persuasion.

You have asked me, M. le Comte, what, in the actual condition of France, should be the political system it would be well for her to adopt. I have endeavoured to answer this question, on which, however, not a single letter but a complete volume might well be written ; the book might be open to objections ; and even this letter may not be wise.

I will now follow the train of thought, and apply those principles, to which I have given vent, during the negotiations in which we are at present engaged. I am convinced that it is with England that France should try to act, and I think that the dispositions of the new English Cabinet will greatly facilitate this move on our part. I was very pleased to see this morning how satisfied the English Ministry were with our measures, in sending M. de Langsdorf to Brussels.[1] The object of this mission has been ably enlarged upon by M. Pozzo, in a letter written by him to M. de Matusiewicz ; he speaks therein with much praise of a conversation he had had with you, and which preceded this mission.

I am inclined to believe that if the Belgians have not completely lost their senses, we shall attain what we desire. It is very difficult to gain any real influence over the people who are directing the movement in Belgium ; for it appears that it is the clergy who are exciting the populace, and silently dominate the deliberations of the Congress. In my private conversations with Lord Grey and with Lord Palmerston, I gathered that if the attempt to reinstate the Prince of Orange was unsuccessful, they might possibly think of the Archduke Charles as a

---

[1] It was M. de Langsdorf who brought the urgent request of the French Government to the Belgian Congress, not to decide on the exclusion of the House of Nassau. As will have been seen, however, this step led to no results. (Note by M. de Bacourt).

Emile, Baron de Langsdorf (1804–1867), was Secretary to the Embassy at Florence in 1828. During the days of July he formed part of the deputation, together with M. de Semonville and M. d'Argout, who went to ask Charles X. to withdraw the proclamations. After his mission to Brussels, he was named successively secretary at Rome, at Turin, at Munich, at Constantinople, at Berlin, and at Vienna ; after that he was made *Chargé d'Affaires* at Rio de Janeiro, at Baden, and at the Hague. He retired in 1848.

candidate. This I regretted, and told them that the presence of a Prince of the House of Austria as ruler of Belgium, would have too much the appearance of a restoration; adding, that it might be well to remember (what I had forgotten), *i.e.* the impressive words uttered by Mr. Fox fifteen years ago, that "the worst of all kinds of revolutions is a restoration."

Up to this time I had not mentioned the name of any candidate, although that of Prince Charles of Bavaria several times occurred to me, he being a Catholic, of forty-eight years of age, and at the same time a man of ability and of courage.[1] This idea has not yet occurred to any one here, and if it were propounded by the French Government, they might have the credit of having done so with the court of Bavaria.

In order to explain to you everything in detail with which I had been charged in this mission, I must not omit to mention the affairs of Greece. As yet the great Powers have not suggested anything on this head, the Belgian affair having absorbed general attention and interest; I do not think that any minister has given the matter a thought, not a single name for Greece having been mentioned at any of our Conferences.[2]

As to Algiers, I have avoided speaking of it, and I should be glad if our newspapers observed the same reticence; it is well that the world at large should get accustomed to our occupation, and silence is the best means to attain this end. I believe that in England public opinion has undergone some change on this subject, and that we shall experience no insurmountable difficulties when we begin to treat of it." [3]

M. de Flahaut returned to Paris with this despatch, and my remarks on the proposed division of Belgium, which project,

---

[1] Prince Charles Theodore of Bavaria, brother of King Louis, was at that time thirty-five, not forty-eight years of age. He was born in 1795, and died in 1876.

[2] The Conference of London had also to settle the affairs of Greece. The treaty of Adrianople (14th September, 1829), between Russia and Turkey, had proclaimed the independence of Greece; it was necessary now to find a sovereign for this new kingdom. The names of the Duc de Nemours, Prince Charles of Bavaria, his brother Prince Otto, the Prince of Hesse Homburg, Prince John of Saxony, Duke Bernard of Saxony, and Prince Leopold of Saxe-Coburg, had all been brought forward. The last named had even gained the suffrage of all the Powers, but he refused the crown (May 21, 1830). It was not till the year 1832 that this question was settled by the advancement to the throne of Prince Otto of Bavaria.

[3] The news of the expedition to Algeria had been received both with anger and anxiety in England, and the English Cabinet had made some very violent and threatening complaints to the government of Charles X. Perhaps it will not be without interest to recall here the proud answer which the English Ambassador one day drew on himself from Charles X. "Monsieur l'Ambassadeur," said the king, "the kindest thing I can do for your government, is not to listen to what I have just heard." The events of July calmed down all this excitement.

however, was again revived, but I succeeded in quashing it completely, as will be seen later on. As regards M. de Flahaut himself, he went shortly afterwards to represent France at the court of Berlin, where, instead of trying to conciliate the Prussian Government towards us, he took up the cause of Poland with such great ardour, that at the end of two or three months he found himself obliged to leave his post, disgusted at not being able to exert any influence on either of the three Courts which had divided Poland between them.

The Russian Ambassador, M. de Lieven, who was on leave when I arrived in England (where however he had left his wife), returned to London towards the end of November, and lost no time in giving assurances of the pacific intentions of his government, both to the English minister and to me. In answer to the question I put to him respecting the arming of Russia which so greatly disquieted Europe, he replied categorically :

"The war preparations we have made, were owing to the original request of our ally the King of the Netherlands, and their only object was to show that troops were in readiness, should circumstances arise requiring them. But I may inform you *authoritatively, for I have the right* [1] *to do so*, that our armies will not and could not act, except with the consent of the four [2] Powers ; I vouch for the truth of this and you can do the same to your government. I have said the same to Lord Grey and Lord Palmerston."

I replied that I knew Lord Grey had pointed out to him, that such a large force naturally would and did cause great disquietude to France, and that the Russian government ought to endeavour to allay this ; while the delay in forwarding the credentials of the Russian Ambassador in Paris, could not but still further augment this anxiety. I added, that he knew Europe too well not to have noticed, that there was now a touchiness among nations, which required careful handling, and that the surest way to accomplish this was to remove all causes for disquietude. To this he replied :

"I am positive the Russian ambassador in Paris will receive

[1] Var. : "le pouvoir" = "the power."
[2] Var. : "les cinq" = "the five."

his credentials at once, if he has not already done so. As for the rest, I am very glad to have had this opportunity of giving you personally the tranquilizing assurance I have just done."

The rising in Poland soon gave us the required opportunity of testing the sincerity of these new feelings on the part of Russia.[1] However I did not hesitate to take in good faith Prince de Lieven's declared assurances, and in transmitting them to Paris, I urged that they should be accepted there in like manner. I pointed out that in the explanations of the Russian ambassador, there had been no question as to the peculiar position of France, and I added:

"We must for the future avoid touching on this subject. France has again taken her place among the great Powers, and she cannot allow the least doubt on this matter to be raised. While maintaining the character[2] with which the events of the month of July have stamped us, we are none the less at liberty to take an equal share with the other Powers in the negotiations of Belgium. It is our duty to uphold the principle of non-intervention; but this principle can be perfectly reconciled with that of the maintenance of frontier treaties. I am glad to be able to submit these remarks to you, for if you adopt them, as I have no doubt you will, it will greatly contribute to strengthen our political position as regards the other states. Our difficulties at present can only come from Belgium. The Belgians, after agreeing to the prescribed boundaries, now raise claims which are not tenable; they are wrong, both as to facts and rights, in their assertions, relative to the line, which before the treaty of May 30th, 1814, separated the possessions of the reigning Prince of the United Provinces, from those which were added to his territory to form the kingdom of the Netherlands. The instructions of Lord Ponsonby were quite in accordance

---

[1] The Polish insurrection broke out at Warsaw on the night of the 29th November. The whole of Poland rushed to arms and assembled under the banner of General Chlopicki, who was proclaimed dictator. After a struggle of ten months, Russia triumphed. Warsaw was taken on the 7th September, 1831. See the impression this insurrection made in Paris in M. de Talleyrand's letter, number 18 in Appendix.

[2] The *political* character.

[3] Lord Ponsonby had been sent to Brussels as Minister of the Conference, to replace Mr. Cartwright, who was obliged to go to his post at Frankfort as English Minister.—(M. de Bacourt).

John, Viscount Ponsonby, was born in 1770, took his seat in the House of Lords

with this opinion,[1] he will maintain the same as we do, that the Belgians have falsified the line, by the manner in which they represent it.

I must tell you that England has quite decided upon the independence of Belgium ; and that Lord Ponsonby, who left this morning, is not to raise any difficulties on this point. He is instructed to renew the assurances of non-intervention, but, like ourselves, his government does not apply this principle to boundary difficulties, which may be violated either by one side or the other."

It will be seen by the extract from this despatch that the English Government had been induced to recognize that Belgium must be irrevocably separated from Holland. This separation being recognized without entailing war, was an immense success for French policy. Provided that a Republican government was not established in Brussels, the choice of the actual sovereign was, according to my view, quite a secondary question ; for I felt sure that whoever the sovereign might be, he would be a near and faithful ally to France. Indeed about this time a certain union was suggested, which offered the best possible solution as to the choice of this sovereign, since it would both please England and satisfy us. This had reference to Prince Leopold of Saxe-Coburg, who, after being elected by the Belgians, and recognized by the Powers, was then to marry one of Louis Philippe's daughters. But this solution will have to pass through many vicissitudes ere arriving at its accomplishment.[2]

Our affairs were therefore going on satisfactorily in London, and if the vexatious delays of the King of the Netherlands, and the ridiculous demands of the Belgians, caused some difficulties at the Conference, the good understanding which existed among the members, gave the assurance that these difficulties would finally be overcome ; besides which, the news of the insurrection

in 1806, and sided with the Whig Party. He entered the diplomatic service, and was accredited to Buenos Ayres, to Rio de Janeiro, to Brussels 1830, and Naples 1832. He was subsequently ambassador at Constantinople, and then at Vienna in 1846. He retired in 1851, and died in 1855.

[1] With what I have the honour of telling you on this subject.

[2] For the preliminary steps of this union, and the first negotiations connected with it, see M. de Talleyrand's letters to Mdme. Adelaide, of the 13th and 14th December, and that of M. Bresson to the Prince on the 25th December in Appendix.

in Poland, which reached us in the beginning of December, acted as an additional and powerful motive for Russia, Prussia and Austria, to show a conciliatory spirit in the arrangement of Belgian affairs. But it was not of a nature to produce a similar effect in Paris, where it greatly excited the populace just at the moment when the trial of Charles X.'s ministers might perhaps provoke dangerous agitations. It was well known that the revolutionary party would employ all their resources to turn this incident to account. Would the government be strong enough to maintain order, and make the course of justice respected? This was a matter of the greatest anxiety in Paris, and this anxiety, as well as its cause, did not render the position of the French ambassador in London any the more comfortable. It is not easy for a negotiator to adopt a high and firm tone, when at any moment he may be asked, "Does your government still exist at this present time?" The sad result of revolutionary times, which must be overcome but which often entails very sorrowful reflections.

Nevertheless I did not permit myself to be discouraged, and I eagerly seized the opening afforded me by the obstinacy of the King of the Netherlands, and the more friendly feelings of the Congress at Brussels, to attain the end I was above all most anxious to secure—the dissolution of the kingdom of the Netherlands. This is what I wrote to M. Sebastiani on the 17th of December :—

M. LE COMTE,
The Ambassador of the Netherlands has written to say he is ill. I believe that he wishes to make use of this indisposition to retard the work of the Conference, and I have just learnt a decision on the part of his sovereign, which confirms me in the opinion, that this Prince is endeavouring to throw all possible obstacles in our way. M. Falck has been informed, that on the receipt of the protocol of our fifth Conference, the King of the Netherlands had selected M. Zuylen de Nyeweldt [1] to proceed to

---

[1] Hugo, Baron de Zuylen de Nyeweldt (1781–1853), a Dutch diplomat, was secretary of the embassy at Paris (1805), and then at Madrid (1807). He retired during the accession of Louis Buonaparte. After 1814 he re-entered the diplomatic career, was made minister at Stockholm, at Constantinople, and plenipotentiary at London. He became Minister of State in 1833, then Minister of Foreign Affairs, and finally Minister of Religion (1842). He retired in 1848.

London as second plenipotentiary, and bringing fresh instructions. It is evident that this nomination is nothing but a measure to gain time, for no one could be better fitted to carry on the king's affairs here than M. de Falck. Besides M. de Falck's reticence lately, and especially just now, only show too plainly that he is embarrassed, and that his government is not keeping faith.

After carefully thinking over this incident, I decided that there was only one way to put an end to our uncertainties, namely, to ask for the immediate declaration of the independence of Belgium. I think I was justified in making this demand, for from the beginning of our negotiations it was agreed that while France was to exert her influence to induce the Belgians to sign an armistice, England would use hers to prevail upon the King of Holland to take the same step. We have been completely successful. The Belgians agree to everything, and we owe them this reward for the willingness they have shown us. The English Cabinet, notwithstanding all its efforts—and they have been quite sincere—has not been able to obtain the positive declaration from the court at the Hague, which we must naturally receive.[1] The character of the King of Holland is an obstacle to everything, but this obstacle must be overcome, and I do not know of any better method to arrive thereat, than to induce the Conference to declare [2] the independence of Belgium. I intend therefore to speak about this to Lord Palmerston before the Conference, and then to lay the proposition formally before the plenipotentiaries of the four Powers. If I obtain this to-morrow, and I hope I shall do so, we shall have made a great step.

It is possible that after my conference with Lord Palmerston, I may get him to make the proposal himself; it would be preferable that it came from him, for it would carry more weight with the King of the Netherlands. As for the rest, I will decide upon what is best after the conference, and will send off the courier you have sent to me. . . . .

As I have given this despatch I cannot do better than continue to give those which followed, and which will explain more clearly than any narrative, how matters were progressing.

LONDON, December 20th, 1830.

M. LE COMTE,

I announced to you in my last despatch the return, on the morrow, of the courier you had sent me; but the amount of business and the length of our conferences, did not allow me to

---

[1] Var. : "attendre" = "expect." [2] Var. : "demain" = "to-morrow."

carry out this intention, and it is only to-day that I am in a position to acquaint you with the important result of our deliberations. The Conference has assembled every day, and one of our sittings lasted over seven hours. You will not be surprised, M. le Comte, at the length of these discussions, when you learn that the English plenipotentiary and I, were alone agreed about the question of the independence of Belgium, and that we had to induce the four other plenipotentiaries to share our opinion. But I attached too great importance to carrying out the king's wishes not to press forward as much as lay in my power, a resolution which it was so important we should pass. I therefore send you the protocol of our Conference, which has this moment been signed ; you will perceive that it embraces all that we could reasonably hope for. I trust the king will be satisfied with it. The signature of the Russian ambassador was most valuable, and difficult to obtain, but you will find it there.[1]

Receive . . . . .

---

[1] The independence of Belgium dated from the signature of this protocol, December 20th, 1830. On account of its importance we here insert it.

" The plenipotentiaries of the five courts having received the formal adhesion of the Belgian Government to the armistice which was proposed to it, and which the King of the Netherlands has also accepted; and the Conference having thus, by arresting the effusion of blood, accomplished the first task it had undertaken, the plenipotentiaries have assembled to discuss the future measures which ought to be taken, in order to remedy the derangements which the troubles that have fallen on Belgium, have wrought on the system established by the treaties of 1814 and 1815.

" In uniting Belgium and Holland by the said treaties, the signatory Powers of these same treaties, and whose plenipotentiaries are at this moment assembled, intended to establish a fair equilibrium in Europe, and to ensure the maintenance of the general peace.

" The events of the last four months have, unfortunately, demonstrated that *this perfect and complete amalgamation, which the Powers desired to effect, between these two kingdoms,* has not been arrived at, that it will in future be impossible to effect it, that thus the very object of the union of Belgium with Holland has been frustrated, and that it will henceforth be indispensable to have recourse to fresh arrangements, in order to fulfil the intentions, for the carrying out of which, this union was to have served as a means.

" Joined to Holland, and forming an integral part of the kingdom of the Netherlands, Belgium had to perform her share of the European duties of this kingdom, as well as the obligations which the treaties had enjoined upon her towards the other Powers. Her separation from Holland will not free her from this part of her duties and obligations.

" The Conference will therefore occupy itself in discussing and arranging the best possible fresh arrangements, which will combine the future independence of Belgium with the stipulations of the treaties, and the interests, and the safety of the other Powers, and at the same time preserve the equilibrium of Europe. To this effect, the Conference, while still continuing these negotiations with the plenipotentiaries of H. M. the King of the Netherlands, will undertake, that the provisional government of Belgium shall, as soon as possible, send commissioners to London, provided with instructions and powers, sufficiently ample, to be consulted and

LONDON, *December 21st*, 1830.

MONSIEUR LE COMTE,

I was rather hurried yesterday by my wish to send off the courier who is bringing you the protocol of our Conference. To-day I can better appreciate the importance of the resolution that has been adopted, and I am already in a position to inform you, that it has produced a powerful impression on the influential people of this country to whom it is known. It is looked upon, if not as an actual guarantee for the maintenance of peace, at least as taking away from the partisans of war a very powerful means of stirring up restless spirits. This view I fully endorse, and I firmly believe that even in the present state of Europe, the recognition of Belgium as an independent State by the five great Powers, must have a very beneficial result for us.

The events that have supervened in Poland, have recalled to me what I, when still young, felt equally with all France, at the time of the division of that kingdom. It is impossible ever to forget the impression it produced in the last century. It destroyed the policy of France, and neither the Duc d'Aiguillon, Minister of Foreign Affairs, nor Cardinal de Rohan, Ambassador at Vienna, ever recovered from the disgrace of having ignored the negotiations which preceded this great act of injustice and spoliation.

Later on, a most favourable opportunity presented itself for re-establishing the kingdom of Poland. In 1807 and in 1812 [1] the Emperor Napoleon could easily have restored its independence (so important to the equilibrium of Europe) to this kingdom ; he would not, however, do so, and I need not recall to your memory, M. le Comte, the grave error which was then committed. In 1814 the chances of war had placed us in the position of being unable to think of anything beyond our mere existence, and we were forced to keep silence, when the subjection of Poland was completed. Now that our voice has regained its weight in the Councils of Europe, it must no longer be the same. I believe that, without disturbing peace, it will be quite possible for you, with the assistance of England, and by choosing a favourable opportunity, to offer our mediation, and to

listened to, on everything that can facilitate the definite adoption of the arrangements of which mention has been made above.

"These arrangements cannot in any way affect the rights which the King of the Netherlands and the German confederation, exercise over the Grand Duchy of Luxemburg.

"ESTERTRAZ, TALLEYRAND, BULORD, LIEVEN,
"WESSEMBERG, PALMERSTON, MATUSIEWICZ."

[1] Suppressed in the text of the archives.

succeed in turning the late events regarding Poland, to the advantage of Europe.

Every one now clearly sees that the kingdom of Poland, strongly constituted, would form the best possible barrier against the menacing invasions of Russia. Many ways present themselves of arriving at this result, and if England would enter frankly into our views, I fancy we should find powerful aids against Russia, in the Grand Duchy of Posen, in Gallicia, in the Polish provinces of Russia, in Finland, perhaps even in Sweden, and also in Turkey. It seems to me that it would be quite possible to attain the end of which I speak without having recourse to war ; the Cabinet of St. Petersburg, properly advised, would perhaps in time, give in to wisely combined measures.

All this would require to be well and carefully thought out. I have only wished to give you some reflections, to which I will add further details if your views coincide with mine on this matter.

Accept . . . . .

While I was obtaining the important declaration of the independence of Belgium from the Conference in London, the French Government in Paris gained a great and glorious victory over the revolutionary party, and on the 22nd of September the trial of the ministers of Charles X. took place before the Court of Peers, without a single capital punishment having been awarded, and without any demonstrations from the mob, obstructing the course of justice. I received the news, I must confess, with immense satisfaction, and the letter in which Madame Adelaide announced it to me, is too honourable to her, and gave me too great pleasure, not to insert it here.

PARIS, *December 23rd*, 1830.

Here we are at last, past the crisis of this terrible trial; this great drama has ended in a manner worthy of our revolution and the king who governs us. Truly, it needed all his strength, his composure and his patience, to arrive at so splendid and happy a climax. He is now doubly rewarded by all the tokens of affection and esteem that are everywhere showered on him. He has just gone out for a ride, amid general acclamations, to make the round of the different wards, in order to express his satisfaction to the brave and excellent

National Guard for their admirable conduct, which was quite beyond all praise.

We have passed through three most anxious days, but we are now more than rewarded for them. I know that General Sebastiani sent a courier to you last night, and that you will already have received the good news when this letter reaches you. It was most necessary that you should be fully informed as to what had really occurred, as no doubt many false and alarming rumours have reached London, for there has evidently been a concerted scheme to spread alarm and terror abroad. Even here, from one quarter and another, we received the most erroneous and vexatious accounts, which, but for the king's calmness and *sangfroid*, might have resulted in the adoption of perfectly wrong measures.

I congratulate you with all my heart on the fortunate result of your Conferences ; it is a grand and most satisfactory success, at which I rejoice doubly, *mon cher prince*, both for you, as well as ourselves. The king is enchanted thereat, and very proud indeed of the success of the Ambassador *of his choice.* He desires me to tell you a thousand charming things. . . .

What now disquiets us is the fate of those poor Poles. I greatly fear for them. . . . .[1]

Our affairs had now taken a turn for the better; the termination of the ministerial trial, greatly relaxed the strain of the situation in Paris, whilst the independence of Belgium, cordially agreed to by the five Powers, assured the maintenance of peace, at least for the time. This was a great gain, but many knotty points had yet to be decided. The Ministry, presided over by M. Lafitte, had neither strength nor credit in France or abroad ; commerce and industries were nearly ruined ; and business generally was bad, the views and the weakness of the Ministry, inspiring the people with but little confidence.

There was also a very serious complication in connection with the proclamation of the independence of Belgium, namely the grand duchy of Luxemburg, which was attached to the Germanic confederation by very special arrangements. The Belgians claimed the right to this province, which in 1814 had been given to the King of the Netherlands, and in which there was a federal fortress, forming part of the general system of

---

[1] See M. de Talleyrand's reply to this letter, No. 22 in Appendix.

defence of the Confederation. It was necessary therefore both to pacify the Confederation, and to satisfy the claims of the King of the Netherlands, as well as those of the Belgians.

This was the subject of very long negotiations which lasted several years, and finally ended in a very suitable arrangement, but which, for a long time, was the cause of endless trouble ; for, in proportion as the political horizon got clearer in Europe, so much more did the German Powers show themselves indisposed to make any concessions.

The protocol of the 20th December, which sanctioned the independence of Belgium, naturally brought forth the most grievous complaints from the Hague. The King of the Netherlands sent a most vehement protest against our decision. It cannot be denied that he had some just grounds for complaint, when it is remembered that the Belgian provinces were ceded to him in 1814 in exchange for the Dutch Colonies, of which England had taken possession. But it was for England to get out of that awkward corner ; as for me, I had only to procure the admission of one point and that was, that the kingdom of the Netherlands having been formed out of hatred to, and as a threat against, France, it was now proved that this piece of work had had its day, and could no longer be allowed to exist. The Conference received the protest of the King of the Netherlands, made no reply to it whatever, and continued its labours for the consolidation of the independence of Belgium, fully determined to carry them through without the concurrence of the King of the Netherlands, should he persist in his opposition.

I believe I have already stated, that before the assembly of the conference of the five Powers to regulate the affairs of Belgium, there was another conference in London, composed of the representatives of France, Great Britain, and Russia, which was occupied in arranging the affairs of Greece. By virtue of the treaty concluded between these three Powers on the 3rd July, 1827,[1] the independence of Greece had been recognised.

---

[1] The treaty of July, 1827, was negotiated and signed in London by the Prince de Polignac, Lord Dudley, and the Prince de Lieven. The three Powers undertook to offer their mediation to both parties, and obtain the adoption of an arrangement on the following bases : the Greeks to be dependent on the Sultan as on a Suzerain Lord ; they will pay him an annual tribute ; they will be governed by Civil authorities, whom

Since the conclusion of this treaty, there had been numerous tedious negotiations in order to obtain, first, the consent of the Ottoman Porte to this dismemberment of its empire; secondly, the recognition by the other Powers of this new state, which for more than a year had been temporarily governed by Count Capo d'Istria. The three protective powers of Greece had at first been zealously occupied in consolidating the independence they had succeeded in procuring; but latterly this zeal had somewhat abated, partly owing to the obstacles introduced into the negotiations by Russia, who now perceived that the independence of Greece did not insure her the advantages she had anticipated, and partly to the events which had lately occurred in France, and which had greatly disturbed all the Cabinets.

It nevertheless became important to put an end to the uncertainty which still existed as to the ultimate fate of Greece ; consequently the three Powers were again called together in conference, and we had our first meeting in the end of December, 1830.

Before speaking of this sitting, it will be well to recall briefly the facts which were to form the subject of our deliberations.

The treaty of the 3rd July, 1827, had arranged the bases of the independence of Greece ; it settled the boundaries of the new state ; its relations with Turkey ; the constitution that would govern it. . . . . . And the three protective Powers, while reserving to themselves the right of nominating the prince who would be called on to govern Greece, had provisionally authorized Count Capo d'Istria (whom the Greeks had asked for) to administer the government of that country. [1]

As soon as the conditions of the treaty became known in Greece, complaints arose as to the boundary lines laid down for the new state. Count Capo d'Istria at once forwarded these complaints ; but Russia, as I have already said, had lost her interest in Greece; England also was not very well disposed

they themselves shall name, but in whose nomination the Porte will also have a voice. An additional article added, that if the Porte persisted in refusing a pacific arrangement, the signatory Powers would afford Greece the support of force.

[1] Capo d'Istria was elected supreme head for seven years by the National Assembly of Trezène (March 31st, 1827). He arrived in Greece in January, 1828, and held this power for nearly four years. He was assassinated on the 6th October, 1831.

towards her ; the Grecian loan had been arranged in London during the War of Independence, and the provisional government of Greece would neither pay the interest nor even guarantee it. This fact, and probably also the surmise, that the neighbourhood of Greece, independent, might prove troublesome to the government of the Ionian Islands,[1] and that the mercantile marine of Greece might occasion a competition injurious to the English mercantile service, all combined to make the cause of Greece very unpopular in England. France alone had remained faithful to her, without any *arrière pensée*. This is a piece of justice with which the government of Charles X. must be credited, and it deserved all the greater praise, for after the catastrophe which overthrew the throne, the poor king only made one reproach against his government, that of having encouraged the revolution by recognizing the independence of Greece.

However that might be, this question of the badly defined boundaries of Greece had, as will be seen, brought on complications of various kinds. After many *pourparlers*, the three courts had offered the crown of Greece to Prince Leopold of Saxe-Coburg, the husband of the late Princess Charlotte of England, who had accepted it. But when the conditions of this acceptance came to be discussed, Prince Leopold declared openly that the three Powers must guarantee him a large loan necessary for the establishment of his government, and, above all, that better boundaries must be obtained for the new state. These propositions were rejected, and Prince Leopold withdrew his acceptance. It therefore became necessary to seek for another prince to replace him, and matters were at this point when the revolution of July broke out in France. The commissioners of the three courts in Greece seconded the entreaties of the Count Capo d'Istria by asking that an end might be put to the precarious state in which the country was placed, almost rent in twain by the various factions and the ambitious views of some of its chiefs.

---

[1] After the treaties of 1815, the Ionian Islands were under the protection of England. They were formed on the lines of a Republic. The executive power was vested in a Senate, the President of which was nominated by England. An English commissioner acted as Minister of Foreign Affairs. This system continued until 1863, when England gave up her protectorate. The islands were then handed over to Greece.

Such was the situation, when Lord Palmerston convoked a
meeting of the Conference on the 28th December, 1830. This
is the account of the sitting that I sent to Paris :

We have this morning had a conference on Greek matters.
Lord Palmerston read aloud the last protocols, which had been
drawn up at the Conferences in which my predecessor had
taken part, and which, owing to the refusal of Prince Leopold,
had led to no results. The enlargement of Greek territory has
been agreed upon between us. This done, I wished to point out,
that as alterations were to be made in the last protocols to
which the Porte had given its acquiescence, it was better to
arrange the proposed boundary line to suit Greece, rather than
make some merely unimportant changes, and that the line
from the Gulf of Volo to that of Arta, seemed to me very
suitable. Lord Palmerston warmly supported this proposal,
giving it weight by bringing forward various powerful reasons
which he had collected from all his different correspondence.

Russia no longer shows the same interest in Greece
since she has re-established her former relations with the
Ottoman Porte,[1] and this makes her plenipotentiaries extremely cautious, and little disposed to do anything on their
own responsibility.

In this state of affairs, we have agreed that England should
empower Mr. Dawkins, *her commissioner in Greece*,[2] to tell Count
Capo d'Istria confidentially, that the Greek frontier would be
improved and to ask him not to divulge these intentions of the
three courts, but to find some plausible pretext, for not carrying
out the evacuation agreed on, of the posts of Arcania and
Etolia, which were then occupied by the Greeks. While this
was being done the Russian plenipotentiaries would ask their
government for authority to sign the Acts, necessary to carry
out the improvements of the boundary line of Greece, by a convention, made to work smoothly by means of a certain sum of
money, this sum to be taken from the loan which will be
guaranteed by the three Powers.

If the Ottoman Porte agrees to these changes, the boundary
commissioners will all have similar duties to carry out. It will
therefore be important that the French commissioner should
proceed there quickly, and take part in all the work that will
be done, so that the Greeks may fully understand that France
defends her interests.

[1] Treaty of peace of Adrianople (14th September, 1829).
[2] Suppressed in the text of the archives.

I pray you to confirm the powers given to my predecessor or to grant me new ones, if you have any other project as to the choice of a sovereign for Greece ; but if you insist, as it seems to me the other Powers are inclined to do, on nominating one of the sons of the King of Bavaria, it would be important, that the administration of the kingdom should be left with Count Capo d'Istria, and even to beg him, as his health is not strong, to suggest a scheme of regency.

You will probably recollect that the government undertook by an Act 3rd May, 1830, to guarantee a loan of sixty millions agreed on by Art. IV. of the Protocol of 20th February, 1830.

I request your commands as to this matter.

Receive . . . .

I wrote again two days later on the same subject :

In my despatch of the day before yesterday, I sent you the result of my last conference on the affairs of Greece with Lord Palmerston and the Prince de Lieven.

The conversations I have since had on this subject with the English ministers, have shown me, that the choice by their government of a sovereign for the new Greek state was fixed on Prince Otto of Bavaria. We must therefore no longer look upon this resolution of the London Cabinet as a project, but as a point which is almost settled ; but my predecessor was authorized to give his adhesion to it. In a correspondence that took place with the King of Bavaria, matters had gone so far as asking what income he was prepared to give his son in order that when he first went to Greece, he should not find himself dependent on the country. . . .

I will return later on to this Greek question when events bring us back to it. At the point at which we had arrived, it seemed less important to think of the prince who should govern Greece, than of him who should be chosen to govern the Belgian provinces ; for on the choice of this latter, depended the pacification of the revolutionary party in Belgium and even in France, and, consequently, the peace of Europe.

It has already been seen that the name of Prince Leopold of Saxe-Coburg has been brought forward. Lord Ponsonby had supported it with the Diplomatic Committee of the Congress of Brussels,[1] which meant that it had been approved of by the English Cabinet, and I was enabled to assure myself of this in conversations with Lord Grey and Lord Palmerston. The President of the Belgian Diplomatic Committee, Mons. Van de Weyer, was then *en route* for Paris and London, where he was commissioned to obtain the consent of Prince Leopold.

This prince had addressed himself to me direct, and I had hastened to assure him, that for my part I should be very well pleased if his candidature was successful.

In truth I knew of no other Prince in Europe who was so well suited as he was, for such a delicate and complicated position.

I had had the opportunity of becoming acquainted with him at the Congress of Vienna, where he had shown great intelligence and loyalty, and had supported the interests of the King of Saxony against Prussia and Russia ; and I remembered the firmness and boldness with which he then resisted the cajoleries, as well as the threats of the Emperor Alexander, though he had served for some years in the Russian army. Prince Leopold as King of Belgium, and married to a French princess, seemed to me the best possible choice that could be made, to solve the difficulties with which we had to contend. Time has proved that in this I was not mistaken.

But this choice completely upset the calculations of some conspirators in Brussels, who wished to unite their personal interests to those of the French Government, and who sought to drag it into their intrigues. They commenced by bruiting abroad the project of choosing Prince Leopold, which had been communicated confidentially (as I have already stated) to the Diplomatic Committee of Brussels. M. de Celles, who was a member of this committee, had hastened to write to his friends in Paris, with the result, that some members of the extreme left of the Chamber of Deputies, at once made use of this project, for the purpose of making an attack on the French Government ; with what effect will be seen by the following letter :

---

[1] The Diplomatic Committee had been appointed by the provisional government on the 20th November to expedite affairs. It was composed of M. Van de Weyer, President Comte de Celles, Comte D'Arschot, and MM. Destriveaux and Nothomb.

GENERAL SEBASTIANI TO THE PRINCE DE TALLEYRAND.

PARIS, *December* 30*th*, 1830.

MON PRINCE,

The discussion which has taken place in the Chamber in consequence of the late disturbances, has just terminated. It has removed the general distrust, which was the real danger of our position. Order has been completely restored, for people's minds have again become tranquil and everything leads us to hope that the labours of the government will no longer be impeded by the vexatious incidents that irritation and disquietude daily brought to light.

Questions of foreign policy were debated in the Chamber during this discussion. They were therefore brought under the influence of the preoccupation and prejudice, which the position of home affairs must inevitably have caused. The Belgian question occupied the greater part of the sitting of yesterday and also of to-day. The king's ministers were very reserved and cautious, but this did not prevent their showing frankly and positively, that their intentions were wholly pacific and far removed from propagandism.

The Prince of Coburg was violently attacked, yesterday by M. Mauguin, and to-day by General Lamarque. This storm which broke out in the Chamber was caused by the newspapers, and, also it must be admitted, by public opinion. The king, who has a sincere friendship for the Prince of Coburg, is the more vexed, as he sees the impossibility of leading the public mind back to this view.

It will therefore be neccessary to look elsewhere for another Prince, who will be acceptable both to Belgium, France, and Europe ; and this is not the least of the difficulties that you have to solve.

The Belgians as a nation would wish either that their country should be re-united to France, or that the Duc de Nemours were called upon to reign over them. In order to obtain this important result, they will willingly consent that Antwerp shall become a free town, and they would perhaps even add Ostend also. In the reunion of Belgium, or in the choice of the Duc de Nemours, France would find a just reparation for the past, and a prospect of peace for the future. This arrangement would, in fact, become a pledge of peace to Europe. Nevertheless we should not wish, in order to arrive at this, to place ourselves in such violent opposition, as would oblige us to make war against the whole of Europe, and overthrow all social order, which is already trembling in the balance. Notwithstanding this, the idea of a political system, which would be so satisfactory to us and the other states, must, with all its greatness and all its truth, recommend itself to your intelligence, mon Prince. If we must abandon it, the sacrifice will be all the more painful, that no thought of ambition has interfered to mar its purity.

We cannot conceal from ourselves that in the exclusion of the House of Nassau, Belgium has included all the other Protestant houses as well as the German dynasties, excepting Bavaria and Saxony. But a Bavarian Prince (when the head of that house possesses Landau, which is a dismembered portion of France), could not be received with any pleasure here. The brother of the King of Naples, a young prince of nineteen years of age, who shows great intelligence and has a fine character, would probably be the one whose elevation would meet with the least opposition in the minds of the French nation. It is to you, mon Prince, that the high mission has been entrusted, of solving so delicate a question in a manner conformable to the dignity and interests of our country. The king awaits your answer with a degree of impatience that you will easily understand. Your experience, your consummate wisdom, will enlighten us as to what it is possible to do to gain the consent of the great Powers. Would England still adhere to the ways of a narrow and jealous policy? Her government, so enlightened as it now is, could it not throw this aside, and only see in this arrangement for Belgium, a combination for the purpose of preventing war for a long term of years, and allowing reason to extend her empire in Europe?

The king has this morning seen M. Gendebien.[1] He spoke to him with a touching frankness, and did not conceal from him that his policy should never be accused of bad faith, and that he would carry out all the engagements he had entered into with the Powers not to turn the revolution in Belgium to his own advantage. He has, therefore, refused the proposal of the re-union, as well as that of the elevation of his son. As for the rest, mon Prince, Europe is more interested than we are in the elimination of this cause of war, which constantly and aggressively crops up. We trust that the issue may be satisfactory.

Accept . . . . .

HORACE SEBASTIANI.

---

[1] Jean François Gendebien, born in 1753, Deputy of Hainault, and President at the Congress of Berlin in 1770. After its union with France, he was elected one of the Five Hundred, and also member of the Legislative Assembly. After 1815 he took his seat in the States-General of the Netherlands. In 1830 he was elected President of the Belgian Congress. Later on he was made President of the Tribunal of Mons, and died in 1838.

Simultaneously with the receipt of this letter, M. Bresson, the French Commissioner of the Conference at Brussels, wrote to me as follows:—

BRUSSELS, *December 31st,* 1830.

MON PRINCE,

My anxieties increase as to the state of this country. The King of Holland, by closing the Scheldt, has upset all the plans of the Conference. Disorder, anarchy, and civil war are at our very door. I do not know what to advise, but it is only a powerful mind and strong measures, that can turn aside the storm which is rapidly growing darker. A French Prince is impossible, he would certainly entail war ; and yet, perhaps, it is only by some concession of this kind that the turbulence of the Belgians will be restrained. What to say !—How to act !—the solution is quite beyond my powers.

Lord Ponsonby maintains that matters are more hopeful than I think. I trust, with all my heart, that he is not mistaken ; but then his country has not so much at stake as we have, and it is therefore natural that our anxiety should be greater.

Pray accept . . . . .

It will be seen that the horizon had become greatly obscured at Brussels, owing to the intrigues of M. de Celles and his friends, who had even succeeded in winning over General Sebastiani to their views. The letter which has already been given, proves that he had entered into their intrigues, and that his judgment, ordinarily sound and clear, had become warped by the false information he had received. In any case, no one but a madman could for a moment imagine, that the great Powers would ever have consented to the re-union of Belgium with France ; or, what comes to the same, the elevation of the Duc de Nemours to the throne of Belgium, without a desperate war, in which France by herself, would have to prove victorious over four other Powers.

I have already several times spoken of M. de Celles without explaining who he was, or how he had been able to acquire a sort of influence both in Belgium and at Paris. The Comte de Celles, descended from a noble Belgian family, was still quite young at the time of the conquest of Belgium by the French Republic, but he had contrived to distinguish himself then

X 2

by the licentiousness of his life and excesses of every kind. He was among the first of the Belgians who rallied round the imperial system of Napoleon, who first appointed him to the State Council, and then made him successively Préfet of Nantes and of Amsterdam.   He won for himself the execration of the Dutch, as much by the excessive rigour with which he carried out the severest measures of the imperial rule, as by the cynicism of his conduct and his habits.   After the fall of the Empire he remained in obscurity for several years ; he was then elected Member of the Chamber of the Netherlands, where he sat with the opposition.   Later on, on his return from a journey to Rome, he approached the King of the Netherlands, who at that time was somewhat troubled in his relations with the Court of Rome.   He succeeded in persuading that Sovereign that no one could so effectually serve him at the Pontifical Court as himself, and boasting that his atheistic and philosophical views prevented his being made a dupe, while his wife through her piety had gained great credit at that court.   The King of the Netherlands thereupon appointed him Ambassador to the Holy See, and, as a fact, a few months later, M. de Celles concluded a *concordat*, which however did not fulfil the king's expectations, and even became the source of all the religious discussions in Belgium, and of the discontent of the Belgian Catholics with the King of the Netherlands.[1]   M. de Celles had again taken his seat in the second Chamber, but he had fallen equally into dis- repute with the Dutch for his past conduct, and with the Belgian Catholcis, who accused him of having tried to betray their interests, for those of the king.   This was M. de Celles' position at the time of the revolution of 1830.   He was one of the first

---

[1] This *concordat* was signed on the 18th of June, 1827, during the Pontificate of Leo XII.   It declared that the *concordat* of 1801, signed by Pius VII. and the first Consul, would remain in force in the southern provinces of the kingdom, and would be also applicable to the northern provinces with the following modifications :—Each diocese shall have its own chapter and seminary.   When a vacancy to an episcopal see has to be filled, the chapter shall present a list of the candidates, who must be approved of by the king.   This approval gained, the chapter can choose any one it likes from this list.   The election shall then be submitted to the Pope for canonical sanction.   The Pope completed these provisions by apostolic letters, in which he reserved to himself the right of appointing the pastors to the Belgian churches.   The bishops might take the oath to the king, but they were to choose their own grand vicars, as well as all the *curés*, and would have full authority over the seminaries. Lastly all the clergy were to receive an endowment from the Crown.

who joined this revolution, and having been elected a member of the National Congress by the Liberal party, he was nominated as Vice-President of the Diplomatic Committee, which had to decide all questions concerning the foreign relations of Belgium.

M. de Celles had married the daughter of General Vallence, who had married a daughter of Mdme. de Genlis. Mdme. de Celles' sister was married to Marshal Gérard, who had been made War Minister after the revolution of July. Mdme. de Genlis' other daughter, the Marquise de Laevestine, married to a Belgian, had left a son, who had distinguished himself as one of the leaders of the Buonapartist party in France.

It will be seen what great influence this relationship gave M. de Celles, through Mdme. de Genlis, with the Palais Royale, and through Marshal Gérard with the government. It was by these means that he intrigued and plotted, to secure the re-union of Belgium with France, or at any rate, the sovereignty to the Duc de Nemours, with the idea, that such a result would give him an influential position in France, and would withdraw him from Belgium, where he felt he had fallen into disrepute.

I have, perhaps, dwelt too long on this very uninteresting person, but this digression was necessary in order to expose the hot-bed of intrigue which impeded the progress of our affairs in England.

It was under these very unfavourable auspices that the year 1830 closed ; a year made memorable by the events which marked its course.

APPENDIX.

IN this Appendix a certain number of letters have been inserted, relating to the events of 1830—1831, taken from the papers of M. de Talleyrand, which, although not included by him in the text of his Memoirs, nevertheless seemed to possess a certain historical and documentary interest. All these letters have been copied literally from the autograph text of the Prince and his correspondents.

In particular, letters will be found from M. de Talleyrand to Madame Adelaide and Madame de Vaudémont. In fact it is well-known that he carried on a close correspondence with the sister of King Louis Philippe, in which he kept her well informed, as to the various phases of the negotiations which were being carried on in London. These letters were then submitted to the King. They were strictly confidential, and entirely distinct from the Ambassador's official correspondence with the Cabinet.

As for the letters to Madame de Vaudémont, a very old and intimate friend of M. de Talleyrand, they were likewise, for the most part, communicated to the Royal family, which renders them all the more important.

No. 1.—THE PRINCE DE TALLEYRAND TO THE PRINCESS DE VAUDÉMONT.

VALENÇAY, *May 20th*, 1830.

I HAVE read the famous proclamation![1] and I see that by it every one's arrangements for the summer have been upset! Up to now, it only strikes me as a *coup d'état* against country house visiting ; perhaps, later on, something more may come of it.

The expedition to Algiers is rather a piece of folly, which may perhaps lead to very grave results. Also, why does not the English Government, which is ready to interfere in the formation of a Brazilian[2] constitution, interfere in the formation of a Ministry at Paris? That would surely be a benefit to all the world. Indeed, under present circumstances, I believe it would be most important ; for then, closely allied with England, we could hold whatever language we pleased, and all small, insignificant opposition

---

[1] The proclamation of May 16th, dissolving the Chamber of Deputies.

[2] This is an allusion to the policy of the Wellington Ministry, which, more or less openly, supported Dom Miguel against his brother Dom Pedro, Emperor of Brazil.

would cease. I know well that it is not pleasant to have to submit to the will of another, but if that other does not know what he wants, then it becomes insupportable.

We must trust that foreign affairs will not become more complicated, but with such a Ministry, can one be sure of anything ? Everything is done in a reckless manner, and the results of this folly may produce serious embarrassment. If this Algerian enterprise is an expedient with the view to facilitate some home matters, *they will find themselves greatly mistaken.* Much simpler means were at hand : the taxes should have been reduced. Since the time of the Emperor's Government, they have increased by more than two hundred millions ; while in England, during the same period, they have diminished by four hundred million francs. But these are the reflections of a veritable rustic ! I will at least not make them lengthy, and will therefore conclude. Adieu.

No. 2.—THE PRINCE DE TALLEYRAND TO THE PRINCESS DE VAUDÉMONT.

VALENÇAY, *June* 11*th*, 1830.

As some one is leaving here for Paris, I take the opportunity of sending you a few lines.

The decisive moment approaches ! I can see neither compass nor pilot, and nothing to prevent a shipwreck : this it is which disquiets every one and people of every class.

The death of the King of England is a momentous event. Everything seems to become more complicated, and we have neither a head to guide, nor scissors to cut the knot. Morally and physically, it is a year of storms : here, during the last week, there have been at least two each day. This however has not prevented the Archbishop and the *Préfet* from taking long and charming drives.

Will England keep her present Ministry ? It will be well if she does not change. When a country like ours is so far from being quiet, it is all the more important that the others should remain firm.

No. 3.—THE COMTE MOLÉ TO THE PRINCE DE TALLEYRAND.

PARIS, *October* 1*st*, 1830.

. . . . IN your letter of the 27th, *mon Prince*, you tell me that you have had your first interview with Lord Aberdeen, and subsequently with the Duke of Wellington. I looked eagerly, I must confess, for the word Belgium, but was surprised not to find it anywhere. The events which are pressing forward in this country, seem to make it imperative that we should be explicit, one with another. I should like much to have heard from you how you found your two interlocutors disposed, with regard to this matter. The following are the views we hold here, with which yours will assuredly accord.

As long as the struggle between the King of the Netherlands and that portion of his subjects continues, we shall keep within the limits of the strictest neutrality ; we shall steadfastly reject all overtures from the Belgians which tend towards their joining us ; but, should they prove the stronger in this struggle, and succeed in making themselves independent, we will not allow any government to be imposed upon them by force of arms. If it is desired that this important question should at once be brought within the scope of the negotiations, we shall be quite willing, and we will honestly endeavour, in concert with the other Cabinets, to find a solution for it, which, while protecting the interests of every one, might be *voluntarily* accepted by Belgium. Think over this carefully, *mon Prince ;* you, better than any one else, will know how to solve this problem, and hit upon some arrangement which will satisfy that principle of national independence, which our existence is interested in making respected, and at the same time insure general peace, instead of destroying it.

Cur Minister, Bertin de Veaux [1] leaves to-morrow for the Hague, with instructions drawn up in this spirit. In order to avoid giving umbrage as much as possible, he will go *viâ* Luxemburg or Ghent, and thus give no occasion for demonstrations, which would certainly have marked his passage through Brussels. Finally, the provisional Government now established in Brussels has sent a Deputy here, chosen by its members. This Deputy arrived yesterday, but I refused to see him.

Notwithstanding the silence preserved in your letter, *mon Prince*, I have no doubt that these serious matters were discussed at your conference with the English Ministers, and that I shall soon receive a despatch from you, informing me fully, how you found them disposed generally.

I may say the same respecting Portugal, concerning which Lord Stuart has made me a very important communication : I will shortly write more fully on this matter, and hope I shall before then have received more particulars from you, as to the line the English Cabinet desires to take.

Accept, *mon Prince*, the renewed assurances of my high esteem and unalterable attachment.

MOLÉ.

No. 4.—The Prince de Talleyrand to Madame Adelaide.

LONDON, *October 2nd*, 1830.

MADEMOISELLE has commanded me to write to her : I obey.

The crossing was very bad, but two hours after I thought no more about it.

At first sight, London struck me as being much handsomer than when I left it ; several parts are entirely new—Mademoiselle would hardly recognize it. The population has increased immensely ; there are now fifteen hundred thousand souls—if one can thus designate the selfish egotists who live here. To my great surprise, I found fairly bright sunshine here on the 24th of September ; the Ministers took advantage of it to leave town and go into the country. I wish ours, and especially the King, might sometimes do the same.

Charles X. is to quit the seaside ; he has accepted the magnificent mansion of Lord Arundel, which is about fifty miles inland. The English Government hinted to him, that by residing so close to the seashore, he gave a pretext to numerous intriguers to make out, by frequent crossings, that they were intrusted with commissions which they had never received. The Duke

---

[1] Louis François Bertin de Veaux, brother of the founder of the *Journal des Debats* (1771-1842). He was elected deputy in 1820, and became peer of France in 1832. In 1830 he accepted a mission to the Hague, but returned soon after to Paris.

of Wellington gave me these few details. The English Government is thoroughly loyal in this matter.

Charles X. has written to Vienna to ask for permission to reside in the hereditary States ; it is not yet known what answer has been sent him.

I think the Duke is now quite convinced that the movement of the French in July was not due to any one person, but that it was entirely caused by the state of general dissatisfaction ; that there was no single intrigue ; that M. le Duc d' Orléans was forced to become Lieut.-General of the Kingdom, and subsequently to accept the crown ; that in so doing he had fulfilled a duty ; and that in fulfilling this duty he has rendered an essential service to the whole of Europe.

The King has many admirers here, and many persons who love him ; his praises are in every one's mouth. . . . .

The desire of all our political partisans is, that the Ministry should remain in, and that the Chambers should not be dissolved. This opinion I have gathered from our warmest friends here. . . . .

I am not kept sufficiently informed respecting news from Belgium. Whatever I learn of this matter, I always hear from the English Cabinet.

No. 5.—The Comte Molé to the Prince de Talleyrand.

Paris, *October 4th*, 1830.

Prince,

You ask me for news by telegraph, and I ask you what is happening in London. Your letter of the 1st of October, which I have this instant received, leaves me still in complete ignorance on this head. The King desires me to tell you that he yesterday heard privately, that England had sent a negative reply to the demand of the King of the Netherlands for assistance.

After your two conferences with the Duke of Wellington and Lord Aberdeen, you would have a right to complain if the English Government has kept this fact hidden from you ; yet the King can hardly believe that the reply can have been communicated to you, since you have said nothing to us about it.

I do not know either, whether the English Cabinet has also left you in ignorance as to its intentions regarding Portugal, but Lord Stuart made a most important communication to me three days ago on this subject, of which I should be much surprised to find you had heard nothing in London.

You will assuredly, *mon Prince*, see the necessity which obliges me to ask you for an entirely different style of correspondence. Hitherto you have kept me in complete ignorance as to the intentions of the London Cabinet, and your communications with it, a state of affairs that cannot but prove injurious to the business and interests with which you and I have been intrusted.

Accept the renewed assurances of my great consideration and attachment.

Molé.

No. 6.—The Prince de Talleyrand to Madame Adelaide.

London, *October 7th*, 1830.

Mademoiselle must, I think, be struck with the improvement in our position, for the news from France seems to me all that one could wish for in home matters, while foreign affairs, regarded from this distance, also appear to me to be proceeding as the King would desire ; they improve each day. His Ambassador enjoys an amount of consideration here never accorded to those of Charles X. Attentions are lavished on the Embassy from all sides. The *on dits,* which circulate so freely in London clubs and drawing-rooms, both on small and great matters, are all of a nature to prove that we have taken the right course, both as regards business and society. The Belgian question is on the road it ought to be, to avoid a war. Each day it progresses further in this direction, but if we were to endeavour to unduly hasten the operations of the English Cabinet, if time were not given to round the sharp angles, we should, I think, not do such good work. In this respect I find foreign affairs rather too hurried.

These are all the observations that time and reflection have enabled me to make. Prussia and Austria have placed themselves under English influence and guidance in all the Belgian complications, and this influence is all in favour of the preservation of peace. I look upon this as a benefit which we owe entirely to time. It was necessary to allow it to take proper effect, to let people recover from their first surprise ; it was necessary to efface some prejudices ; and above all was it necessary to give our Government time to reassure by its acts the foreign Powers, who were quite ready to believe that we were on the verge of anarchy. Not a single step could have been made without endless trouble, if taken in opposition to the excited feeling of the clubs. Now matters are on the footing they ought to be, and I think here we have done what would best suit the French Government, by inducing England to bring forward sensible proposals. It seemed to me that had we taken the initiative, we should not have been such free agents, and I regret that they have thought differently in Paris.

I discerned somewhat of youthful indiscretion in the step taken by M. Molé towards the Duke of Wellington, and which I only heard of from the latter ; he has thereby exposed himself to finding that the determination of which it was the object had already been taken two days ago. However, it is done, and it is no use going over what is past and cannot be undone.

My presentation took place yesterday. I have every reason to be satisfied with it and the address, which Mademoiselle knows has been greatly approved even by the King's immediate surroundings. I trust it will give satisfaction in France. Speaking in the name of our King and of France, I found that I spoke as if in my place in the Constituent Assembly.

Mademoiselle will, I trust, now permit me to leave her for the sunshine, which is so rare here, and which I will go and enjoy for a few moments.

T.

P.S.—I inclose for Mademoiselle's private information a copy of a letter I have to-day sent to M. Molé. It is quite a private letter, written purposely with the object of putting an end to some tendency to irritation, which I always try to avoid.[1]

No. 7.—Madame Adelaide to the Prince de Talleyrand.

Paris, October 8th, 1830.

. . . . The remarks made by the Duke of Wellington as to the inconvenience of Charles X. residing near the coast is quite true. There is no doubt that there *are* constant goings backwards and forwards which can lead to no good. I am very glad that the Duke at last views our grand and

---

[1] See this letter, page 238.

splendid Revolution more fairly, and likewise the noble and loyal conduct of my beloved brother. Here matters are very satisfactory, and become stronger and more consolidated every day. I think there could not be anything more generous and touching than the petition of the wounded, begging the Chamber of Deputies to abolish the punishment of death for political offences. It is doubtful whether this measure will be passed at once, but I hope it will be carried out.

M. de Montesquieu[1] arrived here yesterday at four o'clock from Naples, bringing the recognition and credentials from the King of Naples to Prince de Castelsicala,[2] and those of the Pope to the Nuncio. I am delighted that this latter arrived so quickly ; it will quite smooth away the anxieties and difficulties of the clergy, at least it will no longer leave any excuse. We also expect Athalin every moment. His last letter was dated the 18th of September. He was enchanted with the Emperor, who had been most kind to him. . . . . . . The Belgian affairs have troubled us greatly, but fortunately from what I have heard it seems to me that they are quieting down a little, and that happily (which I hope with all my heart) the general peace will not be disturbed.

You complain that you are not kept sufficiently informed as to news from Belgium. Though I do not wish that my correspondence with you should in any way be a political one, I must tell you in confidence, both in your own interest and in that of the matter which we are so anxious to see progress satisfactorily, that *here* complaints are also made of want of sufficient detail in your despatches, and that you do not keep them here sufficiently *au fait* of what happens in London. This is between you and me, and I ask you to let it remain so. I feel sure that you will do justice to my motive in telling you of it.

No. 8.—The Prince de Talleyrand to Madame Adelaide.

October 15th, 1830.

. . . . The foreign Ministers continue in the same friendly relations with us at the conferences. Whatever the Duke of Wellington proposes or maintains is always adopted by them. I think it is most important for us that he should be kept at the head of affairs as long as possible, at any rate until the fate of Belgium is decided ; for we cannot conceal from ourselves that Russia tries to thwart all our efforts with those Courts over which she has any influence. The language of M. de Matusiewicz has therefore changed somewhat now. M. de Lieven will arrive here in a few days. Madame de Lieven, who has been very distant to the Duke since Mr. Canning has been Minister, now tries to approach him again.

The majority or minority of votes on Mr. Brougham's motion in the coming session is, I think, of very great importance ; you will be informed of it as soon as it is over, but probably Rothschild will already have had his courier. The English Cabinet always obtain their information by him ten or twelve hours before the arrival of Lord Stuart's despatches, and this is not to be wondered at, seeing that the vessels which carry Rothschild's couriers belong to that firm, they take no passengers, and start at all hours. . . . .

---

[1] The Comte de Montesquieu had been commissioned to make the new French Government known to the Courts of Naples and of Rome.

[2] Ambassador to the King of the Two Sicilies in Paris. He had held that post since 1814, having previously been Ambassador in London in 1796, and President of the State Junta, created by the Minister Acton.

No. 9.—THE PRINCE DE TALLEYRAND TO THE PRINCESS DE VAUDÉMONT.

LONDON, *October 15th*, 1830.

I AM sending this to you by M. de la Rochefoucauld,[1] who, to my great regret, is leaving us. He is an excellent young fellow, a fine character, and of good abilities, and I wish him all possible success. It is for this reason that I want him to go to Berlin as First Secretary, for that will advance him in his career ; but if he does not go there, he would like (and so should I) to return to London.

I am perfectly satisfied as to the frankness and loyalty of the English Cabinet here, and particularly so with the Duke of Wellington. One can and one must, be open with him, if one ever hopes to effect anything real and solid. That is what we need ; whether it be popular or not, it is what we require, for it is only in this way that we shall thoroughly establish our new dynasty. I am giving you here my firm conviction ; it is the only possible means, and I earnestly desire that both the King and Mademoiselle may be convinced of it. As for Molé, that is a matter of utter indifference to me : when he once finds that it is to his own interest, he will quickly follow that line. . . . .

I was in the country yesterday, at Lady Jersey's, who has a house you would like immensely ; it is beautiful, decorated in thorough good taste, and full of the rarest and most lovely antiques. The Duke was also there. He was very well, and whatever they may tell you in Paris, he is, and will remain, the master. Adieu.

No. 10.—THE PRINCE DE TALLEYRAND TO THE PRINCESS DE VAUDÉMONT.

LONDON, *October 19th*, 1830.

I HAVE just returned from the country ; I took advantage of the splendid sunshine we have here just now, to go to Lady Jersey's. The Duke also went, and when he is not in London, the presence of the Ambassadors is not *de rigueur*. Matusiewicz was also there.

You have at last obtained the recognition of St. Petersburg. I believe that Pozzo would have liked it to have been the first to reach us, but the delay has not done us any harm.

I presume that in M. Molé's Cabinet, England is not greatly in favour : it was Pozzo who made him Minister. I believe, however, that he will use his influence to strengthen the establishment of our Government. Pozzo is a man of sense, and would have much liked that the conferences which will decide the fate of Belgium should be held in Paris. The Duke of Wellington particularly wishes to have them here, and he is right ; the Ministers here are under his influence, and the Duke's name in Europe is rather different from that of Pozzo and Molé. We shall therefore, I hope, finish this great business in a fortnight, or even less. If it turns out badly it will embroil all Europe ; for we must not conceal from ourselves that it is England which has decided the recognition of St. Petersburg. However, I do not meddle

---

[1] Comte Hyppolyte de la Rochefoucauld, Second Secretary in London, had just been made First Secretary at Berlin.

with it, for it might appear as if I was interested in it, but S—— is there ready to utter plain and unvarnished truths on this matter.

In a word, if the conferences were held in Paris, Pozzo would have had the upper hand ; if they take place here, it will be the Duke of Wellington, who is more interested than any one, in establishing a good order of things in Belgium. Adieu. I pray you to read this letter, and then to burn it. My firm conviction is (and it is this which decides my view) that this great question should be settled here.

No. 11.—The Prince de Talleyrand to the Princess de Vaudémont.

LONDON, *October 22nd,* 1830.

THE Duke of Wellington, dear friend, understands our Revolution as it ought to be understood. For some time past the proceedings of the Government of that unfortunate Charles X. made him foresee a catastrophe ; therefore it did not surprise him. His opinions now are just as far removed from those of the Carlists as they are from those of the Republicans ; and if we do nothing foolish, and do not seek for the impossible, he will do his utmost to establish a dynasty. From this may result either peace or war, for the sentiments of England towards us will decide those of Europe, and we shall commit a grave error by seeking support elsewhere.

No. 12.—The Prince de Talleyrand to Madame Adelaide.

October 29th, 1830.

IT is possible that I have not sufficiently repeated in detail the conversations I may have had with the English Ministry, but I pray Mademoiselle to recall a maxim given me by the Emperor Napoleon, and which I have found infallible during a period of fifteen years. He considered conversational ambassadors (it was thus he described them) as very inferior, because, he said, their conversations were always more or less manufactured, by the wish to please their own Governments, and they were therefore of no value, and taught nothing. He only prized those who transmitted nothing to their Governments but the general impression they had received, and this he believed in, more or less, according to the intelligence possessed by him who wrote.

No. 13.—The Duchesse de Dino to Madame Adelaide.

November 2nd, 1830.

I HAVE this moment returned from the Royal ceremonial. Madame will read the speech, but what I must write to tell you is, that when the carriage of the French Ambassador appeared, the *vivas,* the hurrahs, the "Louis Philippe for ever, no Charles X." commenced and continued all the way from the House of Lords up to Bond Street. There were also a good many "*Viva*

Prince Talleyrand ! " and when I returned, the servants wearing the tricolour cockade, the people shouted " A French lady ! " and I was saluted, and loud cries of *Viva* sounded all the way home.   All the Princes of the Royal family who were present in the hall, came to ask for news of our King, of Mademoiselle, and of the Queen, and to inquire with anxiety (I must say it) if our Ministry had changed.   The King had had a chair prepared for M. de Talleyrand near him, that he might be seated ; but this kindness was not accepted by M. de Talleyrand, who remained standing all the time in the Diplomatic Gallery.

The enthusiasm of the people for the King was very demonstrative ; he must have been well satisfied with his day.   I must beg Madame's pardon for a postscript which is longer than the letter itself, but I thought that the details of this morning might be of some interest.

DUCHESSE DE DINO.

NO. 14.—THE PRINCE DE TALLEYRAND TO MADAME ADELAIDE.

November 10*th*, 1830.

LONDON is pretty quiet just now ; there are still a few people left here and there in town, but the rush and excitement is over.   The Duke attended the King's *levée* this morning, where I met him ; he seemed very ·placid, and replied as I desired, to the request I made him, to continue our conferences, which had been interrupted for a few days.   I believe he will propose that we shall meet to-morrow at two o'clock.

When it became known, the day before yesterday, that there would be no dinner in the City, the Marquis of Wellesley [1] said out loud in the House of Lords, " This is the boldest act of cowardice I ever heard of." Mademoiselle will consider that this is more clever than kind.

Nothing special will be done in Ministerial affairs before December 16th. The Opposition will set all their machinery in motion.   The Duke has perfect confidence in his position ; and thinks he will have a majority against Mr. Brougham's motion.   In six days this great struggle will be decided.   I have not, nor has any one else, an idea as to the result of this sitting, for there are a great many new members whose opinions are not yet known. . . .

NO. 15.—THE PRINCE DE TALLEYRAND TO MADAME ADELAIDE.

November 19*th*, 1830.

THE Ministry will be known to-morrow.   Here are the names of those whom I believe to be certain this evening (here follows the list given on page 248).   The Duke of Wellington has been asked to become Commander-in-Chief, in the place of Lord Hill.[2]   The King has himself carried on this

---

[1] The Marquis of Wellesley (1760-1842), eldest brother of the Duke of Wellington., formerly Governor-General of India and Lord-Lieutenant of Ireland, was one of the most distinguished statesmen of the Whig party.

[2] General Viscount Hill, born in 1772, was an old soldier of the wars of the Revolution and the Empire.   He had fought principally in Egypt and in Spain.   In 1828 he was made Commander-in-Chief of the English army, which appointment he held till his death in 1842.

negotiation. I believe that Lord Grant[1] has received a portfolio, but of this I am not sure. This Government will be strong and favourable to us. I have much friendly intercourse with the principal members who form it. They speak quite frankly of the changes that have taken place, and are still *needed* in France; that is the word they use. They wish that England and France should be in accord in all the dealings they may have with the other Powers; they look upon the prosperity and strength of France as a necessity to the peace of Europe, and all speak of the King with the greatest respect. This is what Frederick Lamb told me this morning. I should like to see him Ambassador at Paris.

All the Ambassadors, having invited the Prince of Orange to dinner, and as he has paid his first visit to the King's Ambassador, I thought I ought to ask him to dine with me. As invitations are sent out here eight or ten days, beforehand, I find that I have invited the chief members of the late Ministry, and important personages connected with the Court, who will probably send in their resignations to-morrow : it is somewhat awkward, but ten days ago no one had any idea of what has now happened.

. . . . Mademoiselle must have said something which has caused the Embassy in London to be no longer neglected by the Ministry as it used to be. During the last eight days I have received more and fuller despatches, than have been sent me during the two preceding months. I thank Mademoiselle for this. . . .

NO. 16.—M. BRESSON TO THE PRINCE DE TALLEYRAND.

BRUSSELS, *November 24th*, 1830.

Private.

MON PRINCE,

M. de Langsdorf arrived here this morning. He brought me orders to urge the provisional Government and the Congress to put an end to the discussion as to the definite exclusion of the House of Nassau.

I have made persistent and fruitless efforts; but 160 votes against 68 carried it. This will greatly complicate matters.

I will return to the question of Luxemburg. The restriction to the declaration presents a somewhat ambiguous meaning. It would seem to infer that Belgium claims the Grand-Duchy, while preserving her connection with the German Confederation. The negotiations relative to the army are progressing; I do not think the present events will injure it. At the conference last night, we settled all the principal points : the respective acceptance of the armistice, the line of demarcation of 1814, &c.; thus the claim to the *whole* left bank of the Scheldt and to the *inclosures*[2] of Limburg have been set aside. The discussions now only have reference to the more or less extended meaning of the Protocol of the 17th, and the return of the prisoners. I trust soon to be able to send you a full account, but (and there is not much cause for surprise at it) we have not yet heard whether Holland on her side has taken steps to carry out the suspension of hostilities. If there is any bad faith or needless delay in that quarter, all our work here will have been in vain. . . . . . .

I lay at the feet of Madame de Dino, and beg to offer you, *mon Prince*, the homage of my respectful attachment, and my most sincere regard.

BRESSON.

[1] Charles Grant. Lord Glenelg, born 1780, had been President of the Board of Trade under the Wellington Ministry. He joined the Cabinet of Lord Grey under the India Board.
[2] These inclosures referred to certain portions of land bordering the Scheldt, and ınclosed in the territory of Limburg.—*Translator.*

No. 17.—M. Bresson to the Prince de Talleyrand.

BRUSSELS, *December 2nd,* 1830, 11 P.M.

Private.

ALTHOUGH my fingers almost refuse to hold the pen, I must communicate to you, *mon Prince,* the most important points of a despatch which I have this evening forwarded to M. Sebastiani, in reply to one he wrote to me on the 28th of November, and which he has, no doubt, made known to you. I send him a duplicate of the one for London to-day, together with the documents accompanying it. It will therefore be unnecessary for you, *mon Prince,* to forward it to him.

"By excluding the House of Nassau for ever from all power in Belgium, the Congress not only annuls all its former rights to the crown, which it might wish to put forward, but also takes from it the possibility of ever being recalled thereto by re-election. This unfortunately is how the resolution taken by the Congress is viewed, and how it has been announced to the nation. Your Excellency will readily perceive how little chance there is, in this phase of the question, of again influencing it in favour of a son of the Prince of Orange, with one exception, which he himself interdicts. I must say, however, that since this *grand coup* has been effected, doubts, regret, and disquietude have, with the greater number of people, replaced the first feelings of anger, and would, if the advice had been given sooner, have taken proper effect, and many complain of having pledged and compromised themselves too soon. It might not be impossible to utilize this return to calmer and more temperate ideas. . . . .

" . . . . . There is one point I find some difficulty in speaking of, which, nevertheless, is a fact ; that is, if the occupation of Luxemburg by the German Confederation might seem natural and right in France, and if it would not cause dangerous conflicts, we should not have much to complain of, for the terror it would inspire here, would immensely facilitate the solution of the Belgian question in the interests of universal peace. But would this peace be possible after the occupation of Luxemburg ? . . . . .

" . . . . . We can count on five or six weeks before the election of the king. This strange fancy for having a native as king, has been almost entirely given up ; of this I can assure your Excellency.

I can also further give you the assurance, that if we must relinquish all hope of making the Belgians see the great advantages and security which the adoption of a member of the House of Nassau would afford them, we can, at least, induce them to renounce the absurd project of balloting for a king, and having first to solicit the assent of the Powers to another choice.

" I am also certain, from *positive knowledge,* that M. Van de Weyer will proceed to Paris in a few days ; that he will then submit to your Excellency a project of such a nature as will conciliate both *French and English* interests (Prince Leopold with a French princess, or some other similar union) ; that, after having obtained your views, he will address himself to the London Conference and ascertain theirs. Only, in order to humour the *amour propre,* always very susceptible in men and nations on their *début,* if you do not agree to the proposal which will be made to you, perhaps you will arrange that that which you substitute for it, instead of appearing here as coming from you, will seem as if it emanated from the country itself. Indeed this is an innocent subterfuge for the sake of securing so such great a gain. . . .

" I shall recommend M. Van de Weyer to go straight to you and M. le

Prince de Talleyrand, so that he should not fall into the hands of those who would ask nothing better than to lead him astray. . . . ."

There, *mon Prince!* These are facts which it is well you should know. I await news from you with the greatest impatience. Would that I were near you! Here I have some cruel moments, and the work is quite beyond my powers.

Accept, *mon Prince*, all my devotion and all my respects. . . . .

BRESSON.

NO. 18.—MADAME ADELAIDE TO THE PRINCE DE TALLEYRAND.

PARIS, *December 9th*, 1830.

. . . . . THE longer your Congress delays in treating with the Belgians and making them a proposal which they would possibly accept, the more the difficulties increase. I always dread, from what we know of their views, and from certain information, that after this declaration, already so vexatious, from its exclusion of the House of Orange, they will make a second one, which will be still more troublesome and more embarrassing to us—that of proclaiming the Duc de Nemours as their king. It is therefore necessary that we, in concert with the other Powers, should hasten to offer them another choice; otherwise this fresh accession of discord will come to us all the sooner, because those unhappy Belgians are so fatally blind as to wish for war, instead of dreading it, and we have some misguided individuals who are of the same opinion.

The *Moniteur* announces the nomination of Marshal Mortier as Ambassador to Russia; until now, the King refused to sanction this publication. after the unpleasant behaviour, to call it nothing worse, of the Emperor of Russia; but he thought that, under present circumstances, he ought to make some small personal sacrifice by giving in to the advice of his Council, who were unanimous on the subject of announcing the nomination in the *Moniteur*. Pozzo is delighted at it; he believes that this will smooth many things especially when joined to the proposal about to be made to the Emperor Nicholas to send to him on a special mission, some one in whom he had, a short time ago at least, great confidence and esteem; you know no doubt to whom I refer.

December 12th.

Madame de Dino having delayed her departure, I have again taken up my letter where I left off, and during this interval how startling is the news of the Revolution at Warsaw! How I long to know what you think of it in London! Those poor Poles, sacrificed for so long a period, interest me greatly, and I very much fear they will be overwhelmed. But the names that are at the head of the movement lead me to hope that it is of some magnitude. As far as we are concerned, this will certainly give us more time.

Ah! if Prussia and Austria would only understand their own interests, how splendid would it be for England and ourselves, if we could obtain a fairer and more tolerable state of things for poor, unhappy Poland! The interest in her is very great and very general here. The Powers are now reaping what the Holy Alliance sowed, and if they do not wish to see and feel, that in order to exist they must change their system, I very much fear that we shall see

Europe in a blaze, for they will be forced into it, and therefore it is better to prevent it ; but how can we hope that they will do this after what we have seen ! Nevertheless, I hope much from England and from you.

It seems, according to the last letters received from Belgium, that they are becoming wiser and more reasonable there, more inclined to enter into *pourparlers*, and to agree to what is possible. . . . .

I will leave off here. Madame de Dino will tell you all I have not written about—that the removal of the Ministers to the Luxemburg passed off very quietly ; that to-day there was a slight attempt made by some hundred young men and others, to disturb the order of the funeral of Benjamin Constant by shouting, when it was leaving the Temple, that he should be conveyed to the Panthéon ; that the National Guard behaved admirably ; that the people did not join in it at all ; and that the whole thing was over at once. They were very soon silenced, and the body was carried to Père la Chaise, without any disorder or riot. This is a good preamble to the trials.

NO. 19.—THE PRINCE DE TALLEYRAND TO MADAME ADELAIDE.

LONDON, *December* 13*th*.

MADEMOISELLE will perhaps have the goodness to tell the King, that Lord Grey and Lord Palmerston have spent a couple of days at Claremont with Prince Leopold of Saxe-Coburg. There is no doubt that during this little trip, which is spoken of as being required for rest, the subject of the future King of Belgium has been discussed. This affair, and the consequences immediately resulting from it, deserve that the King should give them his Royal attention and fatherly forethought. Prince Leopold dines with me on the 17th. If he should say anything to me which means more than ordinary conversation, I will beg him to write direct to Mademoiselle. However, Prince Leopold intends going over to Paris, either the end of this month or the beginning of next. . . . .

. . . . . I would much like if Mademoiselle would have the great goodness to send a portrait of the King to the French Legation in England. Later on I will make the same request for Valençay. But there I could venture to ask for a portrait of Mademoiselle.

NO. 20.—THE PRINCE DE TALLEYRAND TO MADAME ADELAIDE.

TUESDAY, *December* 14*th*, 1830.

I HAVE just had a most interesting conversation with Lord Palmerston.

" There," I said, " is the armistice all but concluded ; it seems to me that the time has arrived to broach the important question of the future King of Belgium."

He seemed very willing, and even quite ready, to enter into this. Many names were suggested, but some, like that of Prince Paul of Würtemberg, were not even discussed.

" Then you would not have the Archduke Charles ? " I told him that we were forced to exclude him, and also the Duc de Leuchtenberg, and that if he liked to press me still further, I would also exclude M. de Mérode. I then felt bound to tell him, " The Belgians think a great deal of M. le Duc de Nemours, but the King wishes to put aside this proposal. I do not know whether he will succeed, but I hope so. He is, in fact, placed in a most singular position, for he is forced to employ all the skill he possesses to refuse that which others use in order to gain what they want."

" It would be difficult to get the other Powers to adopt M. le Duc de Nemours," replied Palmerston, "but let us try and find some one else who, by marriage, might satisfy every one."

" I consider that every one means you and us," I replied.

All this gradually worked up to Prince Leopold, who would marry one of our princesses, and whose name Lord Palmerston himself brought forward. I exhibited some slight astonishment, as if this idea were quite new to me, but my astonishment rather took the form of a pleasant surprise. I had to say that I would at once report the whole of this conversation to Paris, and we could then soon discuss it further.

That is as far as we have got. It is quite evident that Belgium given to Prince Leopold (who would then marry a French princess) would suit the English perfectly. I think, if you approve of this idea, that the proposal should be made at the Conference by Lord Palmerston, and I will undertake to make him do it. If you think otherwise, pray give me your commands ; I believe that whatever you think best will be done.

NO. 21.—M. BRESSON TO THE PRINCE DE TALLEYRAND.

BRUSSELS, *December 25th,* 1830.
Private.   *Midnight.*

MON PRINCE,

M. Van de Weyer was in Paris when the Protocol of the 20th December arrived there. M. le Comte Sebastiani communicated it to him. He took fright at once, and returned here in all haste. He thought everything was lost. If we had spoken of Luxemburg, and he said so in Paris, we had not spoken of nothing. But M. le Comte Sebastiani has authorized him to make known to the Congress, that the independence of Belgium had been recognized in principle by the Congress of London, and he will announce this to-morrow. Then he will immediately depart to bring you full powers. But we shall not appear in this at all ; he must get matters settled by this country itself, *mon Prince ;* from one moment to another, by the very slightest accident, the whole affair may slip through our fingers, and result in some disastrous resolution.

In Paris, M. Van de Weyer has broached the question of a prince. He has asked for the Duc de Nemours ; nothing was said to him about Prince Leopold. They wanted to know if a Neapolitan or Bavarian prince would be acceptable. But nothing has been decided. Whoever it is to be, he ought to be sent here quickly ; there is not a moment to lose. Whenever a fresh difficulty arises, their great argument for getting out of it, is the adoption of the tricolour cockade. The country without Luxemburg would be quite incomplete. It will be necessary to give it to some one it can like, so that it may cling to him, and not be so ready to surrender itself to its neighbour. M. Sebastiani writes to me to-day, in plain language, that if the King of Holland does not raise the blockade with a good grace, France will undertake to make him do so by force. So be it ; but if we go that length, it will be desirable that England should take part in these coercive measures. There would be great danger in our undertaking them alone. I send this evening by courier a ministerial despatch to M. de la Rochefoucauld, requesting him to make known to the Dutch Government, these views of the King's Government. Perhaps King William may have tried to bring matters to this crisis.

After your two letters of the 25th, *mon Prince,* I received the one you did me the honour to write on the 16th.   I resign myself to remaining here, since such is your wish.   But we are still far from the goal, and I shall not see you for a long time. . . . .

Deign to accept, *mon Prince,* the assurance of my most respectful devotion.   BRESSON.

NO. 22.—PRINCE DE TALLEYRAND TO MADAME ADELAIDE.

December 26th, 1830.

THIS memorable week has here been given up entirely to the most terrible anxiety as to the state of Paris [1] especially for me, who have never for one moment had the *Palais Royal,* out of my mind.   I have therefore no news to send Mademoiselle, but I must tell her that never has a heavier, or more painful weight rested near my heart.   The King's sagacity will afford him aid in dealing with the Government.   This crisis will have made known to him who are his true and who are his false friends in the Ministry, and will, in this way, have done him good service.   I have never felt myself more entirely the King's servant than during these two last days, nor more proud of representing him than to-day.   I pray Mademoiselle to ask the King to accept my homage, and also to receive for herself my most tender and respectful compliments, as well as my best wishes for a happy New Year.

[1] The trial of the Ministers commenced on the 15th of December, was not concluded till the 21st, and during this period riots and disturbances had taken place daily in Paris.

END OF VOL. III.

Heroes of the Nations.

EDITED BY

EVELYN ABBOTT M.A., Fellow of Balliol College, Oxford.

A SERIES of biographical studies of the lives and work of a number of representative historical characters about whom have gathered the great traditions of the Nations to which they belonged, and who have been accepted, in many instances, as types of the several National ideals. With the life of each typical character will be presented a picture of the National conditions surrounding him during his career.

The narratives are the work of writers who are recognized authorities on their several subjects, and, while thoroughly trustworthy as history, will present picturesque and dramatic "stories" of the Men and of the events connected with them.

To the Life of each "Hero" will be given one duodecimo volume, handsomely printed in large type, provided with maps and adequately illustrated according to the special requirements of the several subjects. The volumes will be sold separately as follows:

Cloth extra $1 50
Half morocco, uncut edges, gilt top . . . 1 75
Large paper, limited to 250 numbered copies for
    subscribers to the series. These may be ob-
    tained in sheets folded, or in cloth, uncut
    edges 3 50

The first group of the Series will comprise twelve volumes, as follows :

Nelson, and the Naval Supremacy of England. By W. CLARK RUSSELL, author of " The Wreck of the Grosvenor," etc. (Ready April 15, 1890.)

Gustavus Adolphus, and the Struggle of Protestantism for Existence. By C. R. L. FLETCHER, M.A., late Fellow of All Souls College, Oxford.

Pericles, and the Golden Age of Athens. By EVELYN ABBOTT, M.A., Fellow of Balliol College, Oxford.

Alexander the Great, and the Extension of Greek Rule and of Greek Ideas. By Prof. BENJAMIN I. WHEELER, Cornell University.

Theoderic the Goth, the Barbarian Champion of Civilization. By THOMAS HODGKIN, author of " Italy and Her Invaders," etc.

Charlemagne, the Reorganizer of Europe. By Prof. GEORGE L. BURR, Cornell University.

Henry of Navarre, and the Huguenots in France. By P. F. WILLERT M.A., Fellow of Exeter College, Oxford.

William of Orange, the Founder of the Dutch Republic. By RUTH PUTNAM.

Cicero, and the Fall of the Roman Republic. By J. L. STRACHAN DAVIDSON, M.A., Fellow of Balliol College, Oxford.

Louis XIV., and the Zenith of the French Monarchy. By ARTHUR HASSALL, M.A., Senior Student of Christ Church College, Oxford.

Sir Walter Raleigh, and the Adventurers of England. By A. L. SMITH, M.A., Fellow of Balliol College, Oxford.

Bismarck. The New German Empire: How It Arose; What It Replaced; And What It Stands For. By JAMES SIME, author of " A Life of Lessing," etc.

To be followed by :

Hannibal, and the Struggle between Carthage and Rome. By E. A. FREEMAN, D.C.L., LL.D., Regius Prof. of History in the University of Oxford.

Alfred the Great, and the First Kingdom in England. By F. YORK POWELL, M.A., Senior Student of Christ Church College, Oxford.

Charles the Bold, and the Attempt to Found a Middle Kingdom. By R. LODGE, M.A., Fellow of Brasenose College, Oxford.

John Calvin, the Hero of the French Protestants. By OWEN M. EDWARDS, Fellow of Lincoln College, Oxford.

Oliver Cromwell, and the Rule of the Puritans in England. By CHARLES FIRTH, Balliol College, Oxford.

Marlborough, and England as a Military Power. By C. W. C. OMAN, A.M., Fellow of All Souls College, Oxford.

Julius Cæsar, and the Organization of the Roman Empire. By W. WARDE FOWLER, M.A., Fellow of Lincoln College, Oxford.

G. P. PUTNAM'S SONS

NEW YORK   LONDON

27 AND 29 WEST TWENTY-THIRD STREET   27 KING WILLIAM STREET, STRAND

A History of the Thirty Years' War. By ANTON GINDELY, Professor
of German History in the University of Prague. Translated by
ANDREW TEN BROOK, recently Professor of Mental Philosophy in the
University of Michigan. With twenty-eight illustrations and two maps.
With an introductory and a concluding chapter by the Translator.
Two volumes, octavo, pp. xvi. + 456, vi. + 454 . . . $4 00

" Indispensable to the student. For the general reader it is one of the most picturesque in history."—*Hartford Courant.*
" Unquestionably the best history of the Thirty Years' War that has ever been
written."—*Baltimore American.*

A History of American Literature. By MOSES COIT TYLER, Professor
of American History and Literature in Cornell University. Bradstreet
edition. Vols. I. and II., comprising the period 1607–1765. Large
octavo, pp. xx. + 292, xi. + 330, handsomely bound in cloth extra,
gilt tops 6 00
Half calf extra 11 00
Agawam edition, 2 vols. in one, octavo, half bound in leather . 3 00
Half calf 5 00

" It is not only written in a style of exceptional grace, but it is the first of most
thorough research, and consequently it throws light into a great number of corners
that hitherto have been very obscure."—Prest. C. K. ADAMS.

Prose Masterpieces from Modern Essayists. Comprising single
specimen essays (each selection is *unmutilated* and *entire*) from Irving,
Leigh Hunt, Lamb, De Quincey, Landor, Sydney Smith, Thackeray,
Emerson, Arnold, Morley, Helps, Kingsley, Curtis, Lowell, Carlyle,
Macaulay, Froude, Freeman, Gladstone, Newman, Leslie Stephen.
Compiled by G. H. PUTNAM.
Three volumes, 16mo, cloth 3 75
The same, in extra cloth, gilt tops 4 50
The same in flexible imitation seal binding and case, round corners, red
edges 10 00
The same, large-paper edition, octavo, with portraits, cloth extra, gilt
tops, rough edges 7 50

" Three charming little volumes, showing admirable judgment on the part of the
editor."—*Chicago Tribune.*
" A most admirable collection, which presents not only specimens of the best English style, but the methods of thought and characteristic modes of expression of the
several writers."—*Magazine of American History.*

G. P. PUTNAM'S SONS, PUBLISHERS. NEW YORK AND LONDON.

France under Mazarin. By JAMES BRECK PERKINS. With a Sketch
of the Administration of Richelieu. With photogravure portraits
of Mazarin, Richelieu, Louis XIII., and Condé. Two volumes,
octavo $4 00

" It is interesting, it is suggestive, it is trustworthy, and in all essentials it is credit-
able. It can be recommended as a solid, conscientious, thoroughly worked-out book.
. . . Its permanent value is increased by a good index."—*N. Y. Tribune.*

The Peace of Utrecht. By JAMES W. GERARD. An Historical Review
of the Great Treaty of 1713–14, and of the Principal Events of the War
of the Spanish Succession. With Maps. Octavo, cloth, bevelled
boards, gilt tops, uncut edges, pp. xv. + 420 . . . . 3 00

" Mr. Gerard has opened up a mine of historical wealth which will be a revelation
to many who have been accustomed to regard themselves as thoroughly acquainted
with the subject."—*Detroit Free Press.*

English Thought in the Eighteenth Century. By LESLIE STEPHEN,
Author of " Hours in a Library," etc., etc. Second and revised edition. Two volumes, large octavo, pp. xv. + 466, xi. + 469 . 8 00

" A work of research and deliberation, every way worthy of the author's reputation. Conscientious, thoughtful, abounding in ripe reflection, and in judgment tempered and weighed by experience. We feel we have in our hands a book which it is
worth while to read. . . . It is little to say these volumes are the most complete
survey we have of our eighteenth-century literature."—*London Academy.*

The Federalist, a commentary on the Constitution of the United States.
Being a collection of essays written in support of the Constitution
agreed upon September 17, 1787, by the Federal Convention. Re-
printed from the original text of Alexander Hamilton, John Jay, and
James Madison. Edited, with a general Introduction and Notes, by
HENRY CABOT LODGE. Large 12mo, pp. xiv + 586, cloth . 2 00

Among topics discussed are : Foreign Force and Influence, Dissensions
between the States, The Consequences of Hostilities between the States,
The Union as a Safeguard against Domestic Faction and Insurrection, The
Utility of the Union, Objections to the Proposed Constitution, Concerning
the Militia, Concerning the General Power of Taxation, The Influence of
the State and Federal Governments Compared, The Particular Structure of
the New Government, etc., etc., etc.

A History of English Prose Fiction. By BAYARD TUCKERMAN.
From Sir Edward Malory to George Eliot.
Crown octavo, pp. 331 . . . . I 75

" It has the merit of brevity, and gives an intelligible and useful review of the development of English prose fiction."—*Independent.*

G. P. PUTNAM'S SONS, PUBLISHERS,   NEW YORK AND LONDON.

Printed in the United Kingdom
by Lightning Source UK Ltd.
123371UK00002B/30/A